OXFORD STUDIES IN EUROPEAN LAW

Series Editors

PAUL CRAIG
Professor of English Law at St John's College, Oxford

GRÁINNE DE BÚRCA
Professor of Law at New York University School of Law

Secession and European Union Law

OXFORD STUDIES IN EUROPEAN LAW

The aim of this series is to publish important and original research on EU law. The focus is on scholarly monographs, with a particular emphasis on those which are interdisciplinary in nature. Edited collections of essays will also be included where they are appropriate. The series is wide in scope and aims to cover studies of particular areas of substantive and of institutional law, historical works, theoretical studies, and analyses of current debates, as well as questions of perennial interest such as the relationship between national and EU law and the novel forms of governance emerging in and beyond Europe. The fact that many of the works are interdisciplinary will make the series of interest to all those concerned with the governance and operation of the EU.

OTHER TITLES IN THIS SERIES

Fiscal State Aid Law and Harmful Tax Competition in the European Union
Dimitrios Kyriazis

The Abuse of Constitutional Identity in the European Union
Julian Scholtes

Judging European Democracy
The Role and Legitimacy of National Constitutional Courts in the EU
Nik de Boer

EU Values Before the Court of Justice
Foundations, Potential, Risks
Luke Dimitrios Spieker

Postnational Constitutionalism
Europe and the Time of Law
Paul Linden-Retek

The Legislative Priority Rule and the EU Internal Market for Goods
A Constitutional Approach
Eadaoin Ní Chaoimh

The Jurisprudence of Constitutional Conflict in the European Union
Ana Bobić

Reflexive Governance in EU Equality Law
Emma Lantschner

Enhanced Cooperation and European Tax Law
Caroline Heber

Legal Pluralism in European Contract Law
Vanessa Mak

Europe's Passive Virtues
Deference to National Authorities in EU Free Movement Law
Jan Zglinski

Accountability in EU Security and Defence
The Law and Practice of Peacebuilding
Carolyn Moser

Accountability in the Economic and Monetary Union
Foundations, Policy, and Governance
Menelaos Markakis

Secession and European Union Law

The Deferential Attitude

NÚRIA GONZÁLEZ CAMPAÑÁ
Assistant Professor, University of Barcelona

OXFORD
UNIVERSITY PRESS

OXFORD
UNIVERSITY PRESS

Great Clarendon Street, Oxford, OX2 6DP,
United Kingdom

Oxford University Press is a department of the University of Oxford.
It furthers the University's objective of excellence in research, scholarship,
and education by publishing worldwide. Oxford is a registered trade mark of
Oxford University Press in the UK and in certain other countries

Published in the United States of America by Oxford University Press
198 Madison Avenue, New York, NY 10016, United States of America

British Library Cataloguing in Publication Data

Data available

Library of Congress Control Number: 2024930990

ISBN 978–0–19–888259–6

DOI: 10.1093/oso/9780198882596.001.0001

Printed and bound by
CPI Group (UK) Ltd, Croydon, CR0 4YY

For my husband, Josep Maria, and our son, Ignasi
In loving memory of my parents

Series Preface

The issue of secession has been a live and hotly debated one in recent years in the European Union (EU) context, placed on the map by the movements for independence in both Catalonia and Scotland.

For some years, it was generally assumed that questions of the internal political organization of a Member State, and particularly deeply contested national questions concerning regional governance and secession, were in no way a matter for the EU. Lying at the heart of issues of national sovereignty and identity, and lacking any obvious 'inter-state' element, the assumption was that the EU and its institutions would not be involved nor express any view on the outcome of such debates or struggles within a Member State. That viewpoint, however, has changed somewhat in recent years, as issues arising out of the independence movements in both Scotland and Catalonia have pushed themselves into various EU arenas, both legal and political. Further, the question whether the existence of the EU itself as a transnational political community has in some way facilitated or even encouraged secessionist ambitions has been raised, with a variety of different views expressed on the matter.

Núria González Campañá's book tackles aspects of this fascinating subject by exploring 'the normative link between EU law and secession', examining how the EU *should* respond to secessionist moves within the EU, as well as describing some of the responses and developments which have already taken place. She examines the issue of secession in relation to international law as well as in relation to the constitutional law of a range of liberal democratic states, before delving into the question of the EU's approach to secessionist movements within its Member States. In terms of her own normative stance, the author is supportive of the largely deferential approach adopted thus far by the EU, which has treated the question (both within and outside the EU) as one for Member States to resolve within their own political boundaries and constitutional frameworks, and which has tended to support the consensus decision reached within a given state.

The book provides a lucid and helpful analysis of the legal framework for the question of secession from the perspective of at least three different bodies of law—international, comparative constitutional and EU—and a thoughtful account of the ways in which the EU has dealt with secessionist issues as they have arisen.

It is a book which should be of considerable interest to students and scholars of EU law but also scholars of public law and politics, as well as international relations.

Paul Craig
Gráinne de Búrca

Acknowledgements

The origin of this book lies in my doctoral thesis, which I read in Oxford on 9 May 2019. The completion of my DPhil and the resulting monograph has only been possible due to the constant and generous support of my doctoral supervisor, Professor Paul Craig. He has encouraged me at all stages of my work. I owe him a debt that can never be repaid because if it were not for him, I would not be anywhere near where I am today.

Many other scholars have also placed their expertise at my disposal. I want to give special thanks to Professors Carlos Closa, Cathryn Costello, and Dorota Leczykiewicz for reading earlier drafts of this book, and for their input at the DPhil viva and earlier stages. My thanks are also due to Professors César Colino, Asunción de la Iglesia, Tobias Lock, Giuseppe Martinico, Matteo Nicolini, Francesco Palermo, and Xavier Pons, all of whom offered me the opportunity to present my work in different workshops and seminars. I am much obliged to them for their insightful feedback as well. Professors Xavier Arbós, Kalypso Nicolaïdis, Jo Murkens, Johanne Poirier, Helena Torroja, and Daniel Weinstock have also provided me with helpful comments and relevant reading material. Thank you also to the anonymous reviewers who evaluated the manuscript for Oxford University Press and to Ida and Elissa Connor from OUP, for their invaluable support during the publication process.

I extend my thanks to my colleagues at the Constitutional Law Department at the University of Barcelona and to the members of my research group *Grupo de Estudios sobre Democracia y Constitucionalismo* (GEDECO) and the Jean Monnet Chair in European Constitutional Democracy (EUCODEM), especially Professors Enriqueta Expósito, Esther Martín, and Elia Marzal, for their kind and generous support since I joined the University of Barcelona in January 2020. I would also like to mention Professors Julio Añoveros (†) and José María de Areilza, who gave me their unwavering support at the very beginning of my career.

The research that led to this book was funded mainly by the Rafael del Pino Foundation, but also by the British-Spanish Society and the International Council for Canadian Studies. I am very grateful to each of these institutions.

Finally, and most importantly, I would have never found the courage to overcome the difficulties of this project without my friends (both in Oxford and Barcelona) and my family, especially my brother. But, very specifically, my thanks go to my husband, Josep Maria Castellà Andreu, for giving love and understanding (and reading all my work thoroughly). I would also like to mention our dear son, Ignasi, for bringing infinite love and joy into our lives. And I would especially like to remember my parents. I grew up in a family that always encouraged me to believe that I was capable of taking on any project I chose. They are not going to see the book published, but at least they were able to see the start of this intellectual journey. Sadly, I have also lost my dear grandmother. I know that all three are smiling proudly from Above.

Barcelona, 10 August 2023

Contents

Table of Cases

EUROPEAN UNION

EUROPEAN COURT OF HUMAN RIGHTS

INTERNATIONAL COURT OF JUSTICE

AFRICAN COMMISSION ON HUMAN AND PEOPLES' RIGHTS

US

CANADA

UK

SPAIN

OTHER JURISDICTIONS

Table of Other Primary Legal Sources

Abbreviations

BIA	British-Irish Agreement
CET	Common External Tariff
CJEU	Court of Justice of the European Union
EC	European Community
ECHR	European Convention on Human Rights and Fundamental Freedoms
ECtHR	European Court of Human Rights
ECJ	European Court of Justice
EU	European Union
GFA	Good Friday Agreement
ICCPR	International Covenant on Civil and Political Rights
ICJ	International Court of Justice
ICSECR	International Covenant on Social, Economic and Cultural Rights
ILC	International Law Commission
MPA	Multi-Party Agreement
NATO	North Atlantic Treaty Organization
OCT	Overseas Countries and Territories
SNP	Scottish National Party
TEU	Treaty on European Union
TFEU	Treaty on the Functioning of the European Union
TRNC	Turkish Republic of Northern Cyprus
UDHR	Universal Declaration of Human Rights
UN	United Nations
UNMIK	United Nations Interim Administration Mission in Kosovo

1
Introduction

1. General Topic and Background: Relationship between Pro-secession Movements in Europe and the EU

Secession is a live issue in today's Western Europe. Although secession in well-established democracies is something exceptional,[1] in the last decade, we have witnessed the consolidation of pro-independence movements in Scotland and Catalonia. In the near future, we might see their re-emergence or the rise of other pro-secession movements in other European regions. The response of the EU institutions to secession within EU Member States may well be based mainly on political considerations. However, since the EU is a community of law based on the rule of law, it also has to justify its position with normative arguments of principle. This book aims to provide such normative support. The intention is to offer legal reflection that goes beyond a case-specific approach, which could be relevant to any EU Member State. Secession within an EU Member State and the role of the EU are not only hot topics that have been receiving the attention of the media in the last years, but they are also fundamental EU law topics, since they lead to the review and re-think of key features of the EU and the EU legal order. The fact that EU law says nothing about secession within Member States does not mean that EU lawyers can comfortably assume that secession is not really a matter of EU law. It is indeed, as will be shown. This book is based upon two normative premises. First, there is no aim at altering the federal equilibrium between the EU and its Member States, that is to say, there is no intention to advocate in favour of further constitutionalization of the EU. Second, this book is not concerned with the moral legitimacy or political convenience of pro-independence movements in EU Member States. It is assumed as a fact that in some European regions there are strong pro-independence movements challenging the territorial status quo.[2]

[1] Stephane Dion, 'Why Is Secession Difficult in Well-Established Democracies? Lessons from Quebec' (1996) 26(2) British Journal of Political Science 269, 269.

[2] Very often these movements are located in economically advanced regional groups. The classic work of Donald L Horowitz on the logic of secessions gives a good explanation of the phenomenon. Horowitz observes that such advanced regional groups 'are likely to have a regional economic grievance. Advanced regions usually generate more income and contribute more revenue to the treasury of the undivided state than they receive. They believe that they are subsidizing poorer regions.' Donald L Horowitz, *Ethnic Groups in Conflict* (2nd edn, University of California Press 2000) 249–50. In fact, an example Horowitz employs is Catalonia. It should come as no surprise that one of the complaints of the Catalan pro-independence movement is the Catalan taxpayers' 'unreasonable' (according to Catalan nationalists) contribution to Spain's poorest regions. One of the battle cries of the Catalan nationalist

Secession and European Union Law. Núria González Campañá, Oxford University Press. © Núria González Campañá 2024.
DOI: 10.1093/oso/9780198882596.003.0001

The EU has played an important (although clearly unintended) role in these pro-independence trends, since it makes small statehood very appealing: 'it is easier for political groups to mobilise opinion in favour of independence in the European milieu'.[3] Despite some theoretical warnings about the death of the nation State and the need to rethink the classic theory on sovereignty,[4] statehood is still important for pro-independence movements since it 'remains the sole means by which nationalists can be recognized as sovereign equals in the European political system'.[5] Regardless of the transformations of sovereignty, the State itself is still the primary means for some nationalists to achieve their goal: recognition as the legitimate authority over their respective territories. In effect, nationalist parties argue that EU integration has not erased the value of borders and has not undermined the meaning of statehood. On the contrary, statehood still matters, because States remain dominant actors in many policy functions.[6] What is particularly interesting is that without the perspective of the EU umbrella it is difficult to imagine some of these secessionist movements pushing so hard for independence. There has been a 'growing attraction of the concept of "independence in Europe" '.[7] But if, in a globalized world, a country like Singapore can succeed[8] and being a member of

movement is 'Madrid ens roba' (Madrid is stealing from us). Germà Bel, *Anatomia d'un desengany* (Destino 2013) 165. Exacerbated by a context of recession, some narratives stress that Catalonia has disproportionally contributed to central state budgets and receives low public investment in return. Donatella della Porta, Francis O'Connor, and Martín Portos, 'The Framing of Secessionism in the Neo-liberal Crisis' in Carlos Closa, Costanza Margiotta, and Giuseppe Martinico (eds), *Between Democracy and Law. The Amorality of Secession* (Routledge 2020) 163. This claim did not originate with the Catalans, though. The famous slogan 'Roma Ladrona' ('Rome the thief') was popularized in Italy in the 1990s by the *Lega Nord*. It conveyed the idea that the capital takes taxes from the hard-working Northern Italians and wastes it on the lazy South. As seen, the same rationale lies behind the 'Madrid ens roba' complaint. The underlying logic of the Flemish pro-independence demands is very similar, as will be seen in Chapter 3. A good review of the demands of rich regions in Western Europe (although the case of Scotland is slightly different) in Emmanuel Dalle Mulle, *The Nationalism of the Rich: Discourses and Strategies of Separatist Parties in Catalonia, Flanders, Northern Italy and Scotland* (Routledge 2017). Dalle Mulle pictures Catalan nationalism as a 'forerunner of the nationalism of the rich'. ibid 28.

[3] Carlos Closa (ed), 'Troubled Membership: Dealing with secession from a member state and withdrawal from the EU' (2014) 91 EUI Working Papers 4 <http://cadmus.eui.eu/bitstream/handle/1814/32651/RSCAS_2014_91rev.pdf> accessed 30 July 2022.

[4] A recent review of the question to be found at Don Herzog, *Sovereignty, RIP* (Yale UP 2020).

[5] Janet Laible, *Separatism and Sovereignty in the New Europe* (Palgrave MacMillan 2008) 23.

[6] Besides, States are 'still recognized as the primary constitutive elements of legitimate political order in the EU and in the world system more generally'. ibid 205. And, in fact, secession does not challenge the very notions of statehood and sovereignty. Costanza Margiotta, 'An Update on Secession as the "Ultimate Right" ' in Carlos Closa, Costanza Margiotta, and Giuseppe Martinico (eds), *Between Democracy and Law. The Amorality of Secession* (Routledge 2020) 9.

[7] Kathryn Crameri, 'Do Catalans Have the Right to Decide? Secession, Legitimacy and Democracy in Twenty-First Century Europe' [2015] Global Discourse: An Interdisciplinary Journal of Current Affairs and Applied Contemporary Thought 1, 3.

[8] As Alesina and Spolaore explain, the economically viable size of countries depends on the trade regime: '[w]hile small countries may not be viable in a world of trade barriers, they may be prosperous in a world of free trade and global markets'. Alberto Alesina and Enrico Spolaore, *The Size of Nations* (MIT Press 2003) 82. Donald Wittman shares this opinion about feasibility of small States in an open economy and considers that '[a]n international regime of free trade among nations allows for smaller scale political units because economic production is not limited by the demand and supply of domestic markets'.

the North Atlantic Treaty Organization (NATO) guarantees your territorial integrity, why is it that, according to the polls, remaining within the EU is so important for those supporting pro-independence movements across Europe?

One could argue that small States enjoy a relatively good status within the EU[9] and that the EU has not been able to build a sophisticated Europe of the regions.[10] In effect, small States in Europe have seen that their relative standing on the international scene has been strengthened as a result of EU membership and its amplifying effects for a member's voice. The strengthening of their voice is also due to 'the formal equality of small and big Member States, including the lack of a European equivalent to the UN Security Council', which ensures a unique voice opportunity for everyone in the decision-making process, particularly because in the EU most of the decisions are reached through consensus.[11] As for regions within the EU, and despite the initial optimism in the 1980s, Maastricht reforms (eg the creation of the Committee of the Regions, the introduction of the principle of subsidiarity, and the legal possibility for regional ministers to join or lead national delegations at the Council of Ministers) gave only a limited recognition to regions.[12]

Donald Wittman, 'The Wealth and Size of Nations' (2000) 44(6) The Journal of Conflict Resolution 868, 870. In their concluding remarks Alesina and Spolaore go further and argue that thanks to free trade, 'Catalonia is a region that may not "need" Spain if it were to become a member of the European Union. To put it differently, once a region is a member of a large common market, including even a common currency area, and can enjoy free trade, the incentives for the region to seek independence or autonomy increases. The national government is much less important for the economy of the region ... the cost of being politically small is decreasing with economic integration. In Europe, we see that many regions can afford to be independent if they enjoy the benefits of the European common market.' Alesina and Spolaore (n 8) 213–14. Keating and Harvey share a similar opinion when they remind us that '[t]he European Union, the European Economic Area and partnership agreements with non-EU States have secured large domestic markets and provided external economies of scale through cooperation'. Michael Keating and Malcolm Harvey, 'The Political Economy of Small European States: And Lessons for Scotland' (2014) 227(1) National Institute Economic Review 54, 55.

9 Bearing in mind that no organization can turn the world's power relations upside down, small States understand that 'within the EU they can exert more influence and achieve more than they would outside it'. Esko Antola, 'The Future of Small States in the EU' in Mary Farrell and others (eds), *European Integration in the 21st Century* (SAGE 2002) 74. According to Wivel, '[s]mall state influence is protected by formal EU institutions making traditional power capabilities less important and by codifying what is deemed acceptable behaviour within the EU'. Anders Wivel, 'From Small State to Smart State: Devising a Strategy for Influence in the European Union' in Robert Steinmetz and Anders Wivel (eds), *Small States in Europe* (Ashgate 2010) 23.

10 In the 1980s, it became popular to envision a 'Europe of the regions'. Keating even thought that 'a role for regions within the EU might be a useful mechanism for accommodating nationalities', a way to counter-act pro-independence movements turning their demands into obsolete pretensions. Michael Keating, 'European Integration and the Nationalities Question' (2004) 32(3) Politics & Society 367, 375.

11 Anders Wivel, 'The Security Challenge of Small EU Member States: Interests, Identity and the Development of the EU as a Security Actor' (2005) 43(2) Journal of Common Market Studies 393, 399.

12 Charlie Jeffery, 'Regions and the European Union: Letting Them in, and Leaving Them Alone' in Stephen Weatherill and Ulf Bernitz (eds), *The Role of Regions and Sub-national Entities in Europe* (Hart Publishing 2005) 35. According to nationalist voices within European regions, the EU has made very limited steps to accommodate the participatory demands of certain sub-national entities. 'European strategies tend to underestimate the importance of regional governments in delivering on key strategic goals.' Noreen Burrows, 'Scotland's European Strategy' in Roger Scully and Richard Wyn Jones (eds), *Europe, Regions and Regionalism* (Palgrave MacMillan 2010) 122.

The EU, one could argue, bolsters the significance of statehood by limiting full participation in its institutions to Member States, despite the Treaty of Lisbon efforts,[13] and by doing that it has given supporters of independence an additional reason (or excuse) to claim that only statehood guarantees full political participation in Europe.[14]

However, there might be a simpler argument beyond the privileged position of small States within the EU and the lack of attention towards regions at the EU decision-making level: pro-secession movements desire independence from their EU Member States, but their supporters do not know what it would be like outside the EU. If at least EU membership is assured, uncertainties are reduced. As noted earlier, the EU umbrella permits the carrying on of a risky and uncertain process like independence with a lifeboat (ie the EU). This is what Michael Keating seems to be highlighting when he argues that 'independence within Europe may represent an attenuated and less risky form of independence, since many of the externalities are catered for'.[15] Piris concludes, '[t]he EU is thus objectively one of the causes, albeit indirect and unintended, of the recent resurgence of separatist movements in some of its Member States'.[16] In this book, however, I will show that not any type of independence process can receive the supporting umbrella of the EU legal order.

[13] It is true that the Treaty of Lisbon granted regions new tools for participating in EU decision-making, directly or through national parliaments and governments, but these regional powers have not been fully exploited. Cristina Fasone, 'Secession and the Ambiguous Place of Regions Under EU Law' in Carlos Closa (ed), *Secession from a Member State and Withdrawal from the European Union* (CUP 2017) 56–59.

[14] Christopher K Connolly, 'Independence in Europe: Secession, Sovereignty and the European Union' (2013) 24 Duke Journal of Comparative & International Law 51, 54. Fasone follows a similar reasoning and concludes that 'the EU can be seen as a destabilising force on relationships between Member States and their internal components'. Fasone (n 13) 54.

[15] Keating, 'European Integration and the Nationalities Question' (n 10) 369. Duerr also believes this to be the case: 'Membership in the EU is seen by many citizens (but certainly not all) as integral for the economic success of any region within Europe. It also provides smaller states with a sense of protection in the event of economic undulations caused by a recession.' Glenn Duerr, *Secessionism and the European Union: The Future of Flanders, Scotland and Catalonia* (Lexington Books 2015) 150. Besides, Duerr argues that since 'secessionist political parties of Flanders, Scotland and Catalonia tend to be some of the most Europhile parties on the continent ... [i]t would be almost unthinkable for any pro-independence party to seek independence without membership in the EU'. ibid 151. Finally, she considers that 'what is certain is that the EU remains a major influencer of voters and citizens in Flanders, Scotland and Catalonia. Ongoing membership in the EU is a non-negotiable component of support for independence. Voters who have sympathy for independence, but may not be sold on the issue of de jure sovereignty, need reassurances. However, nationalist leaders have been unable to provide ironclad assurances.' ibid 172–73.

[16] Jean-Claude Piris, 'Political and Legal Aspects of Recent Regional Secessionist Trends in Some EU Member States (I)' in Carlos Closa (ed), *Secession from a Member State and Withdrawal from the European Union* (CUP 2017) 76. He argues that 'the EU is partly "responsible" for this resurgence of separatist trends, because it is seen as able to carry out tasks which cannot be accomplished as well by small entities. These entities can envisage independence more securely, if they were certain of remaining under the protection of the EU umbrella.' ibid 77. A lengthy argumentation following this line to be found at Núria González Campañá, 'Small States and the EU: Does the EU Promote Secession Within EU Member States?' (2020) 190 Revista de Estudios Políticos 43.

The normative link between EU law and secession is an unexplored field: first, because economic and political science have until now dominated the field concerning secession and the European Union. And second, because lawyers have usually viewed secession only through the lens of international law and more recently of constitutional law. The study of secession with an EU approach is, therefore, not a common angle. This is precisely the focus of this book: secession and EU law. It will not cover economic, political science, or political philosophy dimensions. As stated above, the book has its origins in a political situation, the rise of pro-independence movements across Europe, but it aims to offer a legal analysis. Thus far, some authors have written about EU law and secession.[17] There are, however, only a few monographs on this topic.[18] This book aims to fill such a niche in EU legal scholarship.

2. Research Questions and Hypotheses

The main focus of this book is the following: how should EU law respond to secessionist attempts within EU Member States? Should the EU approach towards secession be generous, restrictive, or neutral? As will be shown, my argument is that the EU should have a deferential understanding of, and therefore be sensitive to, national constitutional legal orders. Thus, the central claim of the book, based on article 4(2) of the Treaty on European Union (TEU), is that the EU duty to respect national identity generates obligations in the context of secession to respect Member States' constitutional orders, provided that the values enshrined in article 2 TEU are not violated by the Member State affected. This book is therefore an

[17] Among others, Carlos Closa, 'Secession from a Member State and EU Membership: The View from the Union' (2016) 12(2) European Constitutional Law Review 240; Javier Tajadura, 'Los procesos secesionistas y el derecho europeo' (2016) 37 Teoría y Realidad Constitucional 347; Dimitry Kochenov and Martijn Van den Brink, 'Secessions from EU Member States: The Imperative of Union's Neutrality' University of Edinburgh School of Law Research Paper Series No 2016/06 1; Merijn Chamon and Guillaume Van der Loo, 'The Temporal Paradox of Regions in the EU Seeking Independence: Contraction and Fragmentation versus Widening and Deepening?' (2014) 20(5) European Law Journal 613; Phoebus Athanassiou and Stéphanie Laulhé Shaelou, 'EU Accession from Within? An Introduction' (2014) 33(1) Yearbook of European Law 335; Daniel Kenealy and Stuart MacLennan, 'Sincere Cooperation, Respect for Democracy and EU Citizenship: Sufficient to Guarantee Scotland's Future in the European Union?' (2014) 20(5) European Law Journal 591; Josu de Miguel, 'La cuestión de la secesión en la Unión Europea: una visión constitucional' (2014) 165 Revista de Estudios Políticos 211; Alan Boyle and James Crawford, *Annex A Opinion: Referendum on the Independence of Scotland—International Law Aspects* (UK Government 2013) <https://assets.publishing.service.gov.uk/government/uploads/system/uploads/attachment_data/file/79408/Annex_A.pdf> accessed 30 July 2022; David Edward, 'EU law and the Separation of Member States' (2013) 36(5) Fordham International Law Journal 1151; Araceli Mangas, 'La secesión de territorios en un Estado Miembro: efectos en el derecho de la Unión Europea' (2013) 25 Revista de Derecho de la Unión Europea 47.

[18] Carlos Closa (ed), *Secession from a Member State and Withdrawal from the European Union* (CUP 2017); Pau Bossacoma, *Secessió i integració a la Unió Europea. Catalunya nou Estat de la Unió?* (Institut d'Estudis de l'Autogovern 2016); Manuel Medina Ortega, *El Derecho de Secesión en la Unión Europea* (Marcial Pons 2014).

inquiry as to how the EU should respond to any type of secessionist project. As will be shown, the features of the secession determine the different possible types of EU responses: that is, if domestic law considers that secession is unlawful (based on the legal criteria established by each EU Member State's constitutional legal order), EU law should respect that position by not recognizing the statehood of the secessionist entity. If, on the contrary, the domestic legal order has authorized the secessionist attempt, EU law should respect that outcome by recognizing the new entity as a sovereign State and by entering negotiations in good faith. Thus, I believe that EU law does not (and should not) have an autonomous position towards secession, but a deferential one.

3. Overview and Chapter Summary

3.1 Chapter 2: Main Legal Terms

The aim of Chapter 2 is to establish the necessary legal framework of the book by clarifying and exploring some of the concepts and legal relations that permeate and sustain the book. Secession within an EU Member State is an issue that touches upon three different legal orders that interact in a certain territory, namely the EU's territory: international law, national constitutional orders, and EU law. First, the chapter explains the extent to which EU law is compelled by international law. A legal discussion as to how EU law accommodates international law is central since Chapter 3 explores the EU legal obligations that derive from international law when it comes to self-determination, a concept closely linked to secession (as will be explained in Chapter 3), and Chapter 7 will analyse the international legal framework of succession of States in case of secession and the restrictions on citizenship law derived from international law. In this sense, it is particularly relevant to establish the binding character of international norms vis a vis EU law. Second, the chapter addresses the question of how should EU law relate to national constitutional provisions. The central claim of the book is that the EU duty to respect national identity generates obligations in the context of secession to respect Member States constitutional orders. Thus, it is necessary to explain why EU law should show a certain deference to national legal orders. It is particularly relevant to reflect on the relationship between EU law and national constitutional provisions. Third, this chapter explores the legal concept of secession, both from an international and constitutional law perspective, and the different types of secession, consensual vs non-consensual, and lawful vs unlawful. A clear distinction between these types will be required later in the book, since it will be argued that the EU response will depend on the concrete circumstances of secession and the lawfulness criteria used by each constitutional legal order.

3.2 Chapter 3: Secession and International Law

This chapter explores the regulation of secession by international law. Is it prohibited? Should, then, EU law oppose any type of secession? Or is there a right to secede under international law? Under what circumstances? As explained in Chapter 2, EU law is constrained by international law and will have to take into account its approach when drafting its legal response to secessions. As for the prohibition of secession, the International Court of Justice (ICJ) stated in 2010 that there is no general prohibition against unilateral declarations of independence, even if they occurred against the will of the parent State.[19]

As for the right to secede under international law, apart from the right to self-determination of colonies or territories subject to alien domination and exploitation, there is no positive entitlement to secession. Scholars discuss whether, under extreme circumstances, a region can be entitled to a similar right, the so-called 'remedial secession'. Some international courts have admitted the existence of such a right if gross violations of human rights take place.[20] However, the ICJ stated that there is not enough consensus around this topic.[21] In any case, sub-national entities within Member States cannot qualify for a right to secede under international law, since European regions cannot be regarded as colonial or occupied territories. If there was ever a situation of systematic and gross human rights violations in a certain EU region, we would need to revert to article 7 TEU, a mechanism to guarantee the protection of EU core values, with an early warning system in case of a risk of breaches, and a sanctions mechanism in the event of a serious and persistent breach by a Member State. Save for this unlikely situation, there is no right under international law for EU regions to secede.

3.3 Chapter 4: Secession and Constitutional Law

If international law does not play a prominent role when assessing secession within constitutional democracies (where, by definition, there is no situation of gross human rights violations that could trigger a discussion about remedial secession), the way forward in the legal analysis is constitutional law.[22] This is the

[19] *Accordance with International Law of the Unilateral Declaration of Independence in Respect of Kosovo*, Advisory Opinion, ICJ Reports 2010, 403, para 81.

[20] See *Katangese Peoples' Congress v Zaire, African Commission on Human and Peoples' Rights*, Comm No 75/92 (1995) para 6 and *Kevin Mgwanga Gunme et al / Cameroon, African Commission on Human and Peoples' Rights*, Comm No 266/03 (2009) para 194.

[21] *Accordance with International Law of the Unilateral Declaration of Independence in Respect of Kosovo* (n 19) para 82.

[22] Jure Vidmar, 'Catalonia: The Way Forward Is Comparative Constitutional Rather than International Legal Argument' (*Blog of the European Journal of International Law*, 24 October 2017) <https://www.ejiltalk.org/catalonia-the-way-forward-is-comparative-constitutional-rather-than-international-legal-argument/> accessed 30 July 2022.

aim of Chapter 4, which examines the different responses offered by constitutional democracies that have faced secessionist challenges, and the organization of referendums on independence, or at least the attempt to organize such plebiscites (referendums as one tool of carrying out an independence process): mainly the US (as the classic paradigm), Canada (the new paradigm), UK, Spain, and briefly, Italy, Germany, and Belgium. It will be seen that there are some common trends. Such trends enable us to talk about lawful and unlawful secessions according to constitutional legal precepts. These criteria (or common trends of constitutionalism) will become key when assessing the EU implicit responses to secession (Chapter 6). For instance, none of them recognizes a unilateral right, or a procedure, to secede. Thus, if secession is carried out unilaterally it is considered unlawful by most constitutional legal orders, since it denies the fundamental basis of a constitutional pact.[23] At most, we find acceptance of consensual secession, as in the cases of Canada and the UK. This acceptance might appear due to a judicial process, like in the case of Canada, or as the result of political negotiation, as in the UK (arguably also in the case of Belgium). In any case, the prominent position of central or national authorities is uncontested. At the same time, it will be shown that the strict Spanish response, which does not allow for a referendum on secession (unless there is a constitutional amendment), is not unique. Although the circumstances vary, since none of them faces the same type of secessionist challenge, the US, Italian, and German constitutional legal orders have similar strict responses to secession.

3.4 Chapter 5: EU Approach to Secessionist Challenges. Precedents, Statements, and Reactions

There is no clear and explicit EU law provision regarding secession within EU Member States. There has never been a proper secession within a Member State either. But there are some precedents of territorial changes within EU Member States and secession crises in neighbouring territories that might provide some guidance. Additionally, we have official statements and reactions to the Scottish independence referendum in 2014, and the 2017 Catalan crisis. The initial focus will be on those situations concerning territorial changes that occurred within EU Member States: the independence of Algeria (within the decolonization paradigm, not properly a case of secession), the withdrawal of Greenland, and the reunification of Germany. Second, the case of the Turkish Republic of Northern Cyprus and the EU

[23] David Haljan, *Constitutionalizing Secession* (Hart Publishing 2014) 345.

attitude towards it since its declaration of independence will be considered. This is an extraordinary example of how pivotal a role a Member State can play in EU policy formation if its national interest is at stake. Next, the chapter examines the experiences of the countries born right after, or immediately before, the crumbling of the Soviet Union. These are all examples of national fragmentation in the post-communist world and cannot be considered genuine secessionist challenges comparable to those posed in constitutional and liberal democracies. However, some lessons drawn from these experiences might tell us something relevant about EU and secession. Furthermore, in recent decades, EU officials have been asked about hypothetical scenarios in case of secession within an EU Member State. Their responses will be analysed, despite not constituting a fully articulated policy. Lastly, given political events in certain Member States (particularly Spain in 2017), EU institutions have been forced to react.

3.5 Chapter 6: EU Law Approach to a Secessionist Challenge: Implicit Responses Within EU Provisions?

This chapter reviews the scholarly debate in the field, from those who consider that any secessionist movement is against the ethos of the European integration, to those who believe that welcoming new States emerging out of democratic secessionist processes is the duty of the EU institutions. The argument advanced in this book lies, however, in between those positions. I am in alignment with those authors who make a distinction between lawful and unlawful secessions. Lawfulness and unlawfulness will be based on the legal criteria established by each EU Member State's constitutional legal order, as explained in Chapter 4. The key provision to justify and base this deferential or neutral EU law response to secession is to be found in the principle of respect for fundamental constitutional structures (art 4(2) TEU). Drawing on this provision, which is an example of constitutional tolerance to be found within the EU, as established in Chapter 2, it will be explained that EU law should respect domestic constitutional orders, with the consequence that if domestic law considers that secession is unlawful, EU law should respect that position by not recognizing the statehood of the secessionist entity. If, to the contrary, the domestic legal order has accepted the secessionist attempt, EU law should respect that outcome by recognizing the new entity as a sovereign State and enter into good faith negotiations. The limits of this EU deferential attitude are to be found within the very same EU legal order. In this regard, article 2 TEU points to those limits: Member States affected will enjoy the benefits of constitutional tolerance as long as they do not violate the values enshrined in article 2 TEU.

3.6 Chapter 7: EU Law in Relation to States Emerging out of Secession

This chapter will explore the legal situation that arises when a new State has emerged and has been recognized by the EU and EU Member States following the recognition policy explained in earlier chapters (ie lawful and consensual secession). The chapter will first address the debate about State continuity and succession: will the rump Member State be the continuing State and, therefore, retain its EU membership, while the seceding territory would become a new, successor State that would have to ask for membership? Or, following internal enlargement theory, will both States maintain EU membership? As will be shown, in the event that the new State is interested in EU accession, it will be argued that the rump State will continue with its EU membership, while the seceded new State will have to ask for EU membership. A further important issue concerns the route towards EU membership, thereby requiring discussion of article 49 TEU and article 48 TEU. Thus, should the new independent State follow the ordinary path of article 49 TEU or is there any possibility to treat this accession as an amendment to the treaties and, therefore, invoke article 48 TEU? I will argue that discussion about accession routes is of limited relevance, since regardless of the chosen legal route, both require a high degree of political consensus, this being unanimity and a ratification process by all EU Member States. In any event, it will be argued that, from a legal standpoint, the most suitable approach is recourse to article 49 TEU. The chapter will also take into consideration the debate around EU citizenship, nationality, and secession. It will be considered how far nationality law, which is in principle mainly governed by internal law, is constrained by international and, above all, EU law. In other words, would the withdrawal of national citizenship rights and consequently EU citizenship rights, as a possible result of secession negotiations, violate EU law? Could EU citizenship have any effect at all in the EU approach towards secessionism? It will be argued that EU Member States still hold an important degree of autonomy when it comes to defining nationality and, therefore, the EU citizenship can have only limited impact. Finally, the chapter will address the hypothetical scenarios of an independent Scotland and the possibility of Irish reunification and the EU position towards both situations.

4. Methodology

As noted above, this book's field of inquiry, secession and EU law, is situated at the crossroads of European Union constitutionalism, international law, and constitutional law. The subject of the book is secession within EU Member States. This can be studied through different lenses and methodologies: political science, history, and economics. This work is limited to the study of secession within EU Member

States through a legal methodology: the theoretical-doctrinal analysis of concepts and institutions following an abstraction process based on concrete rules, taking into account evolving reality and case law. The legal approach has three dimensions, given the three different legal orders that interact at the EU level (namely, international law, EU law, and national constitutional law).

In this book, I draw on a variety of primary and secondary sources. Primary sources include international treaties, applicable legislation, and case law. Beyond the analysis of textual sources of law, I have sought to incorporate other materials such as scholarly work, government documentation, reports of EU institutions and other international organizations, and media sources to shed some light on the 'law in action'. Most of the book is based on legal doctrinal research,[24] since there is no extensive regulation or case law on the issue. When undertaking the legal scholarship, there will be reasoning and analysis of the law so that it can be interpreted, critiqued, and validated, with constant references to the internal logic of the legal system and the need for coherence.

My aim is to avoid a merely descriptive or expository argumentation, a purely mechanical application of rules. On the contrary, through interpretation, doctrinal research enables not only the systematic analysis of existing rules, but also the evaluation of existing or proposed rules.[25] Doctrinal work is prescriptive, in the sense that it aims at influencing law's development and, along with it, decisions by public decision-makers.[26] Law is a practical discipline which helps us to understand social problems and provides us with tools to resolve problems. This book offers decision-makers recommendations on how the law (and their political decisions) should develop in the event of pro-independence movements within Member States. Prescription is a distinguishing feature of 'true scholarship'.[27] Law can both reflect the civic and political values of a community, and also play a creative role in determining social and normative categories.[28] Law does not merely express constitutional identity, it also helps to constitute or influence it.[29] The EU legal-political response advanced in this book will, it is hoped, contribute to legally frame the social and political phenomenon of secession.

Since the object of the book is secession within EU Member States, EU legal scholarship deserves special attention. EU law has been emancipated, methodologically speaking, from both international and national constitutional law. While

[24] Considered by some as synonymous with the academic study of law. WT Murphy and Simon Roberts, 'Introduction' (1987) 50(6) Modern Law Review 677.

[25] Douglas W Vick, 'Interdisciplinarity and the Discipline of Law' (2004) 31(2) Journal of Law and Society 163, 179.

[26] Edward L Rubin, 'Law and the Methodology of Law' (1997) 3 Wisconsin Law Review 521, 529.

[27] ibid 523.

[28] Roger Cotterrell, 'Why Must Legal Ideas Be Interpreted Sociologically? (1998) 25(2) Journal of Law and Society 171, 176.

[29] Vicki C Jackson, 'Comparative Constitutional Law: Methodologies' in Michael Rosenfeld and András Sajó (eds), *The Oxford Handbook of Comparative Constitutional Law* (OUP 2013) 60, 71.

it shares certain general modes of interpretation, it also has some specificities.[30] For instance, European Court of Justice (ECJ) case law and teleological interpretation play a very prominent role in the systematic interpretation of EU constitutional law.[31] Moreover, EU constitutional law operates with terms and concepts that are often derived from national constitutional law. There is a risk of misinterpretation and of inadequately strict application: 'it seems incumbent on European constitutional scholarship to break the current state-monopoly on legal concepts and to resurvey their concrete content and meaning in a Union context'.[32]

Another important methodological feature is comparative constitutional law. Chapter 4, as explained, examines different responses offered by constitutional democracies that have faced secessionist challenges: 'the comparative legal approach suggests that while each case is different, problems are similar and, often, so are the instruments with which to tackle them'.[33] While identifying common challenges in the US, Canada, the UK, Spain, Italy, Germany, and Belgium, their varied legal responses are tested. Comparative analysis aims to provide illustrative common features. In conducting this comparative inquiry, it is important to choose the appropriate jurisdictions and systems to examine.[34] Since the book deals with EU law and secession, it is only focused on pro-independence attempts within consolidated liberal democracies. Thus, the focus of Chapter 4 is responses by liberal democratic regimes to secession. Hence, what makes all these countries (the US, Canada, the UK, Spain, Italy, Germany, and Belgium) fitting subjects for the study of comparative constitutional law is not only the existence of pro-independence attempts, but their commitment to liberal constitutional democracy.

Due to colonial ties, Canada, the US, and UK have shared foundations in their political and legal systems. But, interestingly, there are important differences between these countries in their approach towards secession. In fact, the UK and the US represent the two contrasting models when dealing with secession: the right to constitutionalize secession and constitutional prohibition respectively. When conducting a comparative analysis, research must also incorporate the historical context and evolution.[35] Federal bargains 'are always historically contingent',[36] as exemplified by the approach to secession. It is interesting to inquire to what extent the fact of belonging to the same supranational institution, the EU, has permeated

[30] Philipp Dann, 'Thoughts on a Methodology of European Constitutional Law' (2005) 6(11) German Law Journal 1453, 1462.

[31] ibid.

[32] ibid 1469.

[33] Francesco Palermo and Karl Kössler, *Comparative Federalism. Constitutional Arrangements and Case Law* (Hart Publishing 2017) 5.

[34] Konrad Zweigert and Hein Kötz, *An Introduction to Comparative Law* (3rd edn, OUP 1998) 34

[35] Nick Barber, *The Constitutional State* (OUP 2010) 2.

[36] Jackson (n 29) 71. See also Lucio Pegoraro and Angelo Rinella (eds), *Derecho Constitucional Comparado 2. Sistemas constitucionales* (vol A, Giappichelli Editore 2018) 36.

the position of its Member States vis a vis their approach to secession. We will see that it has not.

Comparative analysis will show that, despite the differences, there are nonetheless common features. What is also noteworthy is that comparative analysis discloses the migration of constitutional ideas.[37] Identifying such migration permits the discovery, through comparative study, of 'principles of justice and political obligation that transcend the cultural bound opinions and conventions of a particular political community'.[38] As Vicki Jackson explains, this universalist approach is

> motivated by a search, implicit or explicit, for transcendent principles—of good, or the just—in constitutional theory, institutions, and doctrine . . . not with a view to understanding their comparative setting, but rather with a view towards constructing a general theory, using various legal sources as examples to help to refine, and to clarify, the analytics of a general problem in democratic or political theory.[39]

This is the aim of Chapter 4. The purpose goes beyond the solely comparative setting or an exercise in self-reflection. The chapter aims to reveal common features that can be identified as general or transcendent[40] principles, 'to develop an understanding of normatively preferable "best practices"'[41] to which the EU, grounded in reasons developed in Chapter 6, should have to commit,[42] namely: (1) there is no right to secede within a constitutional democracy; (2) the process must be subject to the law; and (3) the central authorities of the affected State will have to play a critical role in it. It is precisely in these two chapters (4 and 6) that the book reveals its normative character: there is a clear support for what EU law should stand for: deference to national constitutionalism.

Another important methodological feature is interdisciplinarity. The subdivision of knowledge into disciplines is unavoidable, for without the semblance of order social phenomena would seem incomprehensible.[43] The boundaries, however, are social constructions, that include the risk of certain arbitrary exclusions.

[37] Sujit Choudhry (ed), *The Migration of Constitutional Ideas* (CUP 2007) 13.

[38] Donald P Kommers, 'The Value of Comparative Constitutional Law' (1976) 9(3) John Marshall Journal of Practice and Procedure 685, 692.

[39] Jackson (n 29) 60.

[40] Note the difference between universal and transcendent pointed out by Choudhry: whereas a universal principle is to be found in all legal systems, a transcendent principle is simply to be found in more than one legal system. Sujit Choudhry, 'Globalization in Search of Justification: Toward a Theory of Comparative Constitutional Interpretation' (1999) 74(3) Indiana Law Journal 819, 844.

[41] Jackson (n 29) 70.

[42] In this regard, the work of the Venice Commission becomes a helpful tool. As Professor Craig points out, the Venice Commission plays an important transnational role in the dispersion of legal norms concerning democracy, human rights, and the rule of law. Paul Craig, 'Transnational Constitution-Making: The Contribution of the Venice Commission on Law and Democracy' (2017) 2 UC Irvine Journal of International, Transnational, and Comparative Law 57, 70.

[43] Vick (n 25) 166.

An overly strict attachment to the boundaries might lead to an unsuccessful or superficial comprehension of the phenomena on which one is trying to shed light:

> Interdisciplinarity broadens legal discourse, both in terms of the additional information it can provide and in terms of the conceptual framework within which information can be evaluated. It allows problems to be addressed in a wider context, and it allows the researcher to engage problems whose solutions can only be found through combinations of disciplinary approaches and perspectives.[44]

In some cases, it can even provide hard evidence concerning a specific research question. This is the aim of Chapter 5, which focuses on history and international relations. The only way to test whether the legal reasoning developed throughout the book (mainly in Chapter 6) is feasible beyond 'the law in the books' or legal scholarship is to explore, politically and historically, EU behaviour. Has it been in conformity, or at least not at odds, with the legal arguments suggested in the book? The research in this book is embedded in a widely shared line of reasoning that claims that law can only be justified if it has beneficial social effects, it expresses public values or it serves the public interest.[45] Law cannot be imposed from legal doctrine alone, or from legal scholarship blind to political realities. Legal reasoning may reflect certain social values, but cannot explain or justify those values alone. General philosophical values and historical traditions inform legal systems.[46] This is the rationale for the interdisciplinary Chapter 5. The thesis advanced should not only be normatively acceptable, but also politically feasible.

[44] ibid 181.

[45] George L Priest, 'The Growth of Interdisciplinary Research and the Industrial Structure of the Production of Ideas: A Reply to Judge Edwards' (1993) 91(8) Michigan Law Review 1929, 1931.

[46] Kommers (n 38) 689.

2
Main Terms and Legal Framework of the Book

1. Introduction

As explained in Chapter 1, the main research question of this book is the following: how should European Union (EU) law respond to secessionist attempts within EU Member States? The central claim of the book, based on article 4(2) of the Treaty on European Union (TEU), is that the EU duty to respect national identity generates obligations in the context of secession to respect Member States' constitutional orders, provided that the values enshrined in article 2 TEU are not violated by the Member State affected. The aim of this chapter is to establish the necessary legal framework of the book by clarifying and exploring some of the concepts and legal relations that are used throughout.

First, this chapter will deal with the EU law interaction with public international law and national constitutional order having very much in mind the question at hand, that is, secession. In particular, Section 2.1 will address the following question: to what extent is EU law compelled by international law? A legal discussion as to how the EU accommodates international law is central to this book, since Chapter 3 explores the EU legal obligations that derive from international law when it comes to self-determination,[1] a concept closely linked to secession (as will be explained in Chapter 3); and Chapter 7 will analyse the international legal framework of succession of States in case of secession and the restrictions on citizenship law derived from international law. In this sense, it is particularly relevant to establish beforehand the binding character of international norms vis a vis EU

[1] For instance, as an example of the relevance of these obligations, note the decision of the Court of Justice of the European Union (CJEU) on the validity of the EU-Morocco Fisheries Partnership Agreement and its application to the territory of Western Sahara, a non-self-governing territory to be decolonized in accordance with the international legal principle of self-determination. The Court's exclusion of Western Sahara ensures the compatibility of the Agreement with international law. Case C-266/16 *Western Sahara Campaign UK* [2018] ECLI 118, paras 63–64: '[i]f the territory of Western Sahara were to be included within the scope of the Association Agreement, that would be contrary to certain rules of general international law that are applicable in relations between the European Union and Kingdom of Morocco, namely the principle of self-determination, stated in Article 1 of the Charter of the United Nations, and the principle of the relative effect of treaties, of which Article 34 of the Vienna Convention is a specific expression ... That being the case, the territory of Western Sahara is not covered by the concept of "territory of Morocco" within the meaning of Article 11 of the Fisheries Partnership Agreement.'

Secession and European Union Law. Núria González Campañá, Oxford University Press. © Núria González Campañá 2024.
DOI: 10.1093/oso/9780198882596.003.0002

law. Section 2.2 will address the question of how EU law should relate to national constitutional provisions. It should be borne in mind that the central claim of the book is that the EU duty to respect national identity generates obligations in the context of secession to respect Member States' constitutional orders. To what extent is the classic notion of 'primacy' of EU law undermined by this assumption? Why should EU law show deference to national legal orders? In this sense, it is particularly relevant to reflect on the relationship between EU law and national constitutional provisions.

Section 3 will explore the concept of secession. How is secession understood from a legal point of view? Leaving aside legitimacy considerations, we will focus on the legal debate around secession, both from international and constitutional law points of view. In addition, we will also explore different types of secession. In this sense, how can consensual or non-consensual secession be defined? And how can lawful or unlawful secession be described? A clear distinction between these concepts will be necessary in the further development of the book (particularly in Chapter 6). To what extent should EU law take into account the different types of secession? We will also address the relationship between self-government and secession, since the EU is obliged to respect regional and local self-government within EU Member States. Is there any possibility to justify secession based on regional self-government?

2. Interaction between EU Law, Public International Law, and National Constitutional Orders

This book, when dealing with secession within an EU Member State, is at the same time touching upon three different legal orders that interact in a certain territory, namely the EU's territory: international law, national constitutional orders, and EU law. How do they relate to each other? This is the question that we will address in Section 2, with one section (Section 2.1) devoted to international law and another (Section 2.2) focused mainly on national constitutional legal orders.

2.1 EU Law and International Law

Although the EU is, in many ways, a creature of public international law (in the sense that the Community legal order is created by an instrument of international law, ie international treaties, which are governed by international law), from the very beginning the Court of Justice of the EU (CJEU) famously stated the autonomy of the EU legal order in the *Van Gend & Loos* decision.[2] Thus, although

[2] '[T]he Community's "operating system" is no longer governed by general principles of public international law, but by a specified interstate governmental structure defined by a constitutional charter

the European treaties are subject to the fundamental rules of the law of the treaties, '[t]hat does not mean that the European legal order as a whole is subject to the basic principles and mechanisms of international law'.[3] How then does the EU relate to international law? EU treaties remain virtually silent on the role, impact, and effect of international law on EU law. But the ECJ, in its extensive case law, has offered some guidance. Advocate General Poiares Maduro recalled the basic foundations, noting that the EU has traditionally played an important role as an active and constructive member of the international community when it comes to the development and consolidation of international law. Therefore, '[t]he application and interpretation of Community law is accordingly guided by the presumption that the Community wants to honour its international commitments'.[4] This is in fact the essence of the current article 347 of the Treaty on the Functioning of the European Union (TFEU):

> Member States shall consult each other with a view to taking together the steps needed to prevent the functioning of the internal market being affected by measures which a Member State may be called upon to take in the event of serious internal disturbances affecting the maintenance of law and order, in the event of war, serious international tension constituting a threat of war, or in order to carry out obligations it has accepted for the purpose of maintaining peace and international security.[5]

But the ECJ has also stated that the EU, when determining the effect of international obligations within its own legal order, should also take into account the conditions set by EU law itself. Thus, even when the EU is obliged by international law, it seeks, first and foremost, to preserve the constitutional framework created by the treaties:

> Thus, it would be wrong to conclude that, once the Community is bound by a rule of international law, the Community Courts must bow to that rule with complete acquiescence and apply it unconditionally in the Community legal order. The relationship between international law and the Community legal order is governed

and constitutional principles.' Joseph HH Weiler, 'The Transformation of Europe' (1991) 100 Yale Law Journal 2403, 2407.

3 Jean d'Aspremont and Frédéric Dopagne, 'Kadi: The ECJ's Reminder of the Elementary Divide between Legal Orders' (2008) 5 International Organizations Law Review 371, 374.

4 Opinion of the Advocate General Poiares Maduro, 16 January 2008, Case C-402/05 P *Yassin Abdullah Kadi v Council and Commission* [2008] ECR I-06351, para 22.

5 De Burca refers to the 'traditional self-presentation of the EU as a virtuous international actor in contradiction to the exceptionalism of the United States' and 'Europe's distinctive fidelity to international law'. Grainne de Burca, 'The EU, the European Court of Justice and the International Legal Order after Kadi' (2009) 1(51) Harvard International Law Journal 1, 3, 6.

> by the Community legal order itself, and international law can permeate that legal order only under the conditions set by the constitutional principles of the Community.[6]

Note that the reference explicitly says 'once the Community is bound by a rule of international law', which means that not any rule of international law is binding or compulsory. Thus, the question remains: when is international law compelling? When is EU law subject to international law? How can we be sure that EU law is bound by the right to self-determination (that might lead to secession), assumed by international courts as a customary norm of international law? First, we have to distinguish between international agreements and customary international law. And among international agreements, we will have to distinguish between treaties signed by the EU and treaties signed solely by EU Member States.

As for international treaties signed by the EU, in general, it should be noted that, while the EU has accepted the primacy of international treaties over secondary EU legislation, it continues to place international treaty norms below EU primary law, that is, the EU constitutional framework. Consider article 218(11) TFEU that sets forth the following:

> A Member State, the European Parliament, the Council or the Commission may obtain the opinion of the Court of Justice as to whether an agreement envisaged is compatible with the Treaties. Where the opinion of the Court is adverse, the agreement envisaged may not enter into force unless it is amended or the Treaties are revised.

In short, this article foresees that international treaties will have to comply with EU treaties. If they do not, they will have to be amended. Otherwise, primary law will have to be revised. In the event of conflict, EU treaties prevail. According to the ECJ, international treaties signed by the EU (and compatible with the EU legal order) form an integral part of the EU legal system and are, therefore, directly applicable in the EU legal order.[7] And even when lacking direct effect, EU secondary legislation must, so far as possible, be interpreted in a manner that is consistent with the agreement.[8] In sum, international treaties signed by the EU prevail over secondary legislation, but will have to comply with EU primary law.

[6] Opinion of the Advocate General Poiares Maduro (n 4) para 24. This line of reasoning was later accepted by the ECJ.

[7] Case C-181/73 *R & V Haegemann v Belgium* [1974] ECR 449, para 5: 'The provisions of the Agreement, from the coming into force thereof, form an integral part of Community law.'

[8] Case C-61/94 *Commission v Germany* [1996] ECR 3989, para 52: 'the primacy of international agreements concluded by the Community over provisions of secondary Community legislation means that such provisions must, so far as it is possible, be interpreted in a manner that is consistent with those agreements.'

As for the international treaties to which the EU is not a party, the question about the relationship with the EU legal order will only arise when all the EU Member States are parties. If this is the case, the ECJ assumed, in the famous *International Fruit Company* decision, the so-called 'succession doctrine': if the EU has assumed certain policies (in this particular case, tariff and trade policy) formerly implemented by EU Member States through international treaties, Member States are showing their wish to bind the EU by the obligations entered into under the international agreements.[9] Therefore, says the ECJ, the EU is equally bound by the treaties that are signed and ratified by all Member States.

Finally, as for customary international law, the ECJ has also made clear that it 'must respect international law in the exercise of its powers', including customary international law.[10] In effect, the ECJ has confirmed that since the EU must respect international law in the exercise of its powers, '[i]t is therefore required to comply with the rules of customary international law when adopting a regulation ... It follows that the rules of customary international law ... are binding upon the Community institutions and form part of the Community legal order.'[11] There are, however, some doubts as to the question of direct effect and hierarchical rank that customary international law enjoys within the EU legal order.[12] It seems clear that customary international law should prevail over secondary legislation, but it is less clear whether it should prevail over the primary treaties. This is still a controversial question.

In short, as has been explained, international treaties signed by the EU, those ratified by all Member States, and customary international law are binding upon the EU, without the need for any formal act of incorporation[13] and (at least) as long

[9] Joined Cases 21 to 24/74 *International Fruit Company and others NV v Produktschap voor Groenten en Fruit* [1974] ECR 1219, paras 14–15.

[10] Case C-286/90 *Anklagemyndigheden v Peter Michael Poulsen and Diva Navigation Corp* [1992] ECR I-6048, paras 9–10: 'As a preliminary point, it must be observed, first, that the European Community must respect international law in the exercise of its powers and that, consequently, Article 6 abovementioned must be interpreted, and its scope limited, in the light of the relevant rules of the international law of the sea.... In this connexion, account must be taken of ..., in so far as they codify general rules recognized by international custom ... It has not entered into force, but many of its provisions are considered to express the current state of customary international maritime law.' Bear in mind also the reference to customary international law made in *Van Duyn*: 'it is a principle of [customary] international law, which the Treaty cannot be assumed to disregard in the relations between Member States, that a State is precluded from refusing its own nationals the right of entry or residence'. Case C-41/74 *Van Duyn v Home Office* [1974] ECR 1337, para 22. Anne Peters also considers that there exists an unwritten norm that foresees the incorporation of customary international law into the EU legal order. Anne Peters, 'The Position of International Law Within the European Legal Order' (1997) 40 German Yearbook of International Law 9, 21.

[11] Case C-162/96 *A Racke GmbH & Co v Hauptzollamt Mainz* [1998] ECR I-3655, para 46.

[12] Robert Schütze, 'On "Middle Ground". The European Community and Public International Law' (2007) 13 EUI Law Working Papers 12 <https://cadmus.eui.eu/bitstream/handle/1814/6817/LAW-2007-13.pdf;sequence=3> accessed 2 August 2022.

[13] The EU legal order has traditionally proven very monist in that it has not subjected the introduction of treaty law and customary international law to any formal requirement. D'Aspremont and Dopagne (n 3) 377.

as they do not conflict with the constitutional framework of the EU. This final condition, underlined in the abovementioned quotation of Advocate General Maduro, is particularly relevant for this book, because it underlines one of the key aspects of the relationship between the three legal orders in the European milieu: the need for accommodation. This issue warrants further analysis. This condition of subordination to the main constitutional principles of the EU became particularly noteworthy after *Kadi*.[14] Yassin Abdullah Kadi was a Saudi Arabian national who was listed in the annex of an EU (then EC) Regulation as a person suspected of supporting terrorism. The EU Regulation was adopted to implement Security Council Resolutions approved under Chapter VII of the UN Charter. The effect of the EU Regulation was that all his funds and financial assets in the EU would be frozen. As a result, he brought an action for annulment before the then Court of First Instance insofar as the EU Regulation affected him. The General Court (at that time, the Court of First Instance) reached the conclusion that it had no jurisdiction to review the legality of the contested regulations regarding fundamental rights protected by EU law, following an examination of the relationship between the UN Charter obligations and the EU treaties obligations upon Member States:

> From the standpoint of international law, the obligations of the Member States of the United Nations under the Charter of the United Nations clearly prevail over every other obligation of domestic law or of international treaty law including, for instance, for those of them that are members of the Council of Europe, their obligations under the ECHR and, for those that are also members of the Community, their obligations under the EC Treaty.... It also follows from the foregoing that, pursuant both to the rules of general international law and to the specific provisions of the Treaty, Member States may, and indeed must, leave unapplied any provision of Community law, whether a provision of primary law or a general principle of that law, that raises any impediment to the proper performance of their obligations under the Charter of the United Nations.... Following that reasoning, it must be held, first, that the Community may not infringe the obligations imposed on its Member States by the Charter of the United Nations or impede their performance and, second, that in the exercise of its powers it is bound, by the very Treaty by which it was established, to adopt all the measures necessary to enable its Member States to fulfil those obligations.[15]

[14] Santos Vara has indicated that the line of reasoning followed by the ECJ in *Kadi* 'is more consistent with the previous case-law on the relationship between European and international [law] and on the protection of fundamental rights than the General Courts rulings'. Juan Santos Vara, 'The Consequences of *Kadi*: Where the Divergence of Opinion between EU and International Lawyers Lies?' (2011) 17(2) European Law Journal 252, 256.

[15] Case T-315/01 *Kadi v Council and Commission* [2005] ECR II-3649, paras 181, 190, 204.

This ruling was widely criticized.[16] Eeckhout, for instance, argues that the individual is increasingly a subject of international law, and must thus be guaranteed effective judicial protection. If international law is not able to offer it, municipal courts have to step into the breach by applying domestic constitutional standards of protection of fundamental rights. He understands that this approach is not ideal, 'but it would be consistent with the now firmly established European Solange tradition. As long as the international legal order does not provide the individual listed in a UN Security Council Resolution with an effective remedy, Community law, as a kind of municipal legal system, cannot dispense with review on the basis of its own constitutional standards.'[17]

This is, precisely, what the General Court failed to do, but what the ECJ did in the appeal. In effect, when the ruling was appealed, the ECJ adopted a 'robustly pluralist approach to international law and governance, emphasizing the separateness, autonomy, and constitutional priority of the EC legal order over international law'.[18] The ECJ affirmed firstly that the EU is based on the rule of law and cannot avoid reviewing the legality of acts of the EU institutions. That is why the ECJ was obliged to control the legality of the EU Regulation invoked. Secondly, according to settled case law, fundamental rights form an integral part of the EU general principles of law. The ECJ recalled here the importance of the constitutional traditions common to the Member States and also the guidelines supplied by international instruments for the protection of human rights on which the Member States have collaborated or to which they are signatories. Moreover, according to settled case law, respect for human rights is a condition of the lawfulness of EU acts:

> It follows from all those considerations that the obligations imposed by an international agreement cannot have the effect of prejudicing the constitutional principles of the EC Treaty, which include the principle that all Community acts must respect fundamental rights, that respect constituting a condition of their lawfulness which it is for the Court to review in the framework of the complete system of legal remedies established by the Treaty. In this regard, it must be emphasised that, in circumstances such as those of these cases, the review of lawfulness thus to be ensured by the Community judicature applies to the Community act intended to give effect to the international agreement at issue, and not to the latter as such.[19]

[16] See, among others, Christine Eckes, 'Judicial Review of European Anti-Terrorism Measures—The Yusuf and Kadi Judgments of the Court of First Instance' (2008) 14 European Law Journal 74. She refers to 'radical legal constructs' and 'various errors of law'. ibid 91–92.

[17] Piet Eeckhout, 'Community Terrorism Listings, Fundamental Rights, and UN Security Council Resolutions. In Search of the Right Fit' (2007) 3 European Constitutional Law Review 183, 205.

[18] De Burca (n 5) 7.

[19] Case C-402/05 P *Yassin Abdullah Kadi v Council and Commission* [2008] ECR I-06351, paras 285–86.

In short, the ECJ held that the EU is subject to the rule of law and that respect for fundamental rights is part of its constitutional legal framework and, therefore, it cannot accept the lawfulness of an EU act that violates the referred rights, even if such act has been passed in compliance with the UN Security Council Resolutions. This means that EU law, as an autonomous legal order, decides for itself, like any other municipal legal order, whether or not to incorporate rules laid down in another legal order, that is, international law. For de Burca, this strongly pluralist decision has meant a departure from the classical approach of the ECJ,[20] while for Klabbers it has fenced off EU law against intrusion from international law.[21] Hinojosa criticized the ECJ for calling into question the hierarchy of norms in the international legal order by applying the European standards of protecting fundamental rights and, therefore, annulling the Council Regulation derived from Security Council Resolutions:[22]

> Paragraph 282 of the Kadi judgment places the EC Treaty above the UN Charter as the source of validity in European law. By doing so, it goes well beyond the traditional reference to the 'constitutional' character of the constituent Treaties, meaning that they contain a complex political structure and a system for the protection of fundamental rights, and it places these Treaties at the level of the *Grundnorm* of a Sovereign, the Constitution of a State.[23]

In any event, the message from the ECJ seems clear: where the Member States use EU legislation to fulfil their obligations arising under the United Nations, they have to comply with the constitutional principles of the EU legal order.[24] This position is very similar to that conducted by the national constitutional courts when applying the Solange doctrine.[25] As Santos Vara states:

> The constitutional courts of the Member States have expressed their willingness not to review Community acts on the basis of domestic constitutional law as long as an adequate level of protection is guaranteed at EC level (Solange). If the ECJ have decided not to review the contested regulations in the light of the fundamental rights protected by the EC law, some constitutional courts may try to ensure the protection of human rights, and such a judicial intervention will negatively affect the primacy of Community law over internal law.[26]

[20] De Burca (n 5) 49.

[21] Jan Klabbers, 'Straddling the Fence: The EU and International Law' in Anthony Arnull and Damian Chalmers (eds), *The Oxford Handbook of European Union Law* (OUP 2015) 68.

[22] Luis M Hinojosa Martínez, 'Bad Law for Good Reasons: The Contradictions of the Kadi Judgment' (2008) 5 International Organizations Law Review 339, 346.

[23] ibid 343.

[24] Schütze (n 12) 17.

[25] See also d'Aspremont and Dopagne (n 3) 378.

[26] Santos Vara (n 14) 274.

The issue remains however controversial, since some scholars have also criticized the ECJ's decision and prefer the General Court approach.[27] The General Court, as has been mentioned before, took a different path when confronted with the same question in the *Yusuf* case and decided that the EU 'may not infringe the obligations imposed on its Member States by the Charter of the United Nations or impede their performance',[28] even if that meant leaving aside the standard of human rights protection required by the EU. While the General Court showed the greatest respect for international law, the ECJ's position rests essentially on EU-based arguments.[29]

Doubts concerning the hierarchical position of international law within the EU legal order are particularly relevant if and when there is a conflict between the two normative orders. As we will see throughout the book, in the case at hand (ie secession within an EU Member State), there is no such conflict. First, Chapter 3 will show that the right to self-determination (that might lead eventually to secession) cannot be applied to regions within EU Member States. Second, international law will be incorporated when there is an EU vacuum or lack of regulation, as in the case of succession of States (Chapter 7); by definition, if there is no EU law, there cannot be a conflict between laws. It is for that reason that there is no need to define further the relationship between the EU and international legal orders.

2.2 EU Law and National Constitutional Orders

As for the relationship between EU law and national legal orders,[30] 'one of the more remarkable features of EU law and its relations with Member States' law is the near universal agreement among EU and Member State institutions that EU law has priority over Member States' law'.[31] Labelled by Kumm as 'European monism', this embodies the proposition that European law is supreme and that the ECJ alone has the power to review and annul Community measures on any grounds and the

[27] De Burca, for instance, argues that 'instead of adopting a strongly pluralist approach to international law, the ECJ could and should have followed the soft-constitutionalist approach which it and other European courts have used on different occasions to mediate the relationship between the norms of the different legal orders'. De Burca (n 5) 4. She also regrets the potential implications of *Kadi* 'for the image the EU has long cultivated of itself as an actor which is committed to "effective multilateralism", professing a distinctive allegiance to international law and institutions'. De Burca (n 5) 49. Hinojosa refers to 'extreme assertion of autonomy' that is 'not sound law' and appears as 'legal contradictions'. Hinojosa (n 22) 343, 356.

[28] Case T-306/01 *Ahmed Ali Yusuf and Al Barakaat International Foundation v Council and Commission* [2005] ECR II-3533, para 254.

[29] Santos Vara (n 14) 263.

[30] In *Internationale Handelsgesellschaft* the ECJ rejected, based on EU law autonomy, the referral to national rules in order to assess the validity of norms adopted by the EU institutions. Case C-11/70 *Internationale Handelsgesellschaft* [1970] ECR 1125, para 3.

[31] Keith Culver and Michael Giudice, 'Not a System but an Order' in Julie Dickson and Pavlos Eleftheriadis (eds), *Philosophical Foundation of European Union Law* (OUP 2012) 55.

Member States may not invoke their Constitutions to justify not applying EU law in their territory.[32] As explained by the ECJ in its seminal decisions, supremacy of EU law is required in order to ensure the uniform application of the Community's law, necessary to establish a coherent legal order.[33] However, this claim must be examined more closely. National constitutional courts (mainly the German one) have contended that they have the final say in determining whether EU law violates basic rights. While this review will be undertaken in cooperation with the ECJ, if the latter performs its tasks unsatisfactorily, national courts will resume their role.[34] Thus, practice shows that the acceptance by Member States of EU law primacy is based on the national courts' own constitutional terms, not by virtue of the inherent nature of EU law, as the ECJ argues.[35] In other words, constitutional courts have tried to prevent unwarranted intrusion by EU law in defence of basic rights and democratic self-government invoking a traditional conception of the sovereign nation State.[36] At the same time, constitutional courts also find themselves in the sometimes conflictual position of being enforcers of EU law and guardians of national constitutions.[37] We will come back to this debate in Chapter 6 when assessing article 4(2) TEU.

When examining EU law and national law (particularly constitutional national law), we must accept that we are faced with competing legal orders with potential normative conflicts, which can only be resolved through cooperation and respect. This is the rationale for the development in the legal literature of a pluralist reading of the relation between EU law and national law.[38] As MacCormick advised, we should not be wedded to notions like hierarchy in thinking about the relations

[32] Mattias Kumm, 'Who Is the Final Arbiter of Constitutionality in Europe?: Three Conceptions of the Relationship between the German Federal Constitutional Court and the European Court of Justice' (1999) 36 Common Market Law Review 351, 354.

[33] Case C-26/62 *Van Gend en Loos v Netherlands* [1963] ECR 11; Case C-6/64 *Costa v Enel* [1964] ECR 585; Case C-11/70 [1970] *Internationale Handelsgesellschaft* ECR 1125.

[34] The famous Maastricht Judgment of the German Constitutional Court brought to the fore the risks of conflicts between EU law and national constitutional legal orders. The decision had been preceded by the well-known Solange cases of 1974 and 1986. Other constitutional courts across Europe had been contributing to the same debate and were strengthened by the decision of the German Court. As Baquero Cruz explains, '[t]he German Court ha[d] acted as a sort of Pied Piper of Hamlin, attracting some national courts with the charming song of the defence of State-based constitutional democracy, leading them out of the walls of the European city, into the river of national constitutional dogmatics'. Julio Baquero Cruz, 'The Legacy of the Maastricht—Urteil and the Pluralist Movement' (2007) 13 EUI Working Paper <https://cadmus.eui.eu/handle/1814/6760> accessed 2 August 2022.

[35] Bruno de Witte, 'The Nature of the Legal Order' in Paul Craig and Grainne de Búrca (eds), *The Evolution of EU Law* (OUP 2011) 352.

[36] Kumm, 'Who Is the Final Arbiter of Constitutionality in Europe?' (n 32) 374.

[37] Marta Cartabia, 'The Italian Constitutional Court and the Relationship Between the Italian Legal System and the European Community' (1990) 12(1) Michigan Journal of International Law 173, 175.

[38] Among the leading contributions, see Neil Walker, 'Late Sovereignty in the European Union' in Neil Walker (ed), *Sovereignty in Transition* (Hart Publishing 2003) 3; Miguel Poiares Maduro, 'Contrapunctual Law: Europe's Constitutional Pluralism in Action' in Neil Walker (ed), *Sovereignty in Transition* (Hart Publishing 2003) 501; Mattias Kumm, 'The Jurisprudence of Constitutional Conflict: Constitutional Supremacy in Europe before and after the Constitutional Treaty' (2005) 11 European Law Journal 262.

between EU law and national legal systems.[39] In effect, the relationship between EU law and national legal orders seems to have created a pluralistic legal system or a multilevel constitutional system where hierarchical relationships of validity do not accord properly to the current legal reality. In 1995 MacCormick became the first one to introduce the concept of 'constitutional pluralism' affirming that:

> [T]he most appropriate analysis of the relations of legal systems is pluralistic rather than monistic, and interactive rather than hierarchical. The legal system of Member States and their common legal system of EC law are distinct but interacting systems of law and hierarchical relationships of validity within criteria of validity proper to distinct systems do not add up to any sort of all-purpose superiority of one system over another.[40]

That is why Kumm considers that 'within a pluralist framework, it does not make sense to speak of a final arbiter of constitutionality in Europe'.[41] No one should pretend to be able to give the definitive or final word on legal sovereignty. Basically, the emerging idea of hierarchy between national constitutional law and EU law appeared 'inherently unstable, or unresolved, and destined to remain so. The idea of a potential stability in instability was conceived'.[42] In the same vein, Von Bogdandy argues that 'European legal unity is not to be perceived as unitary and hierarchical, but as pluralistic and dialogical'.[43] In fact, he argues that there is a mutual dependence that leads to a concept of 'complementary constitutions'.[44] He explains his position:

> The concept of legal pluralism does not imply a strict separation between legal regimes. Rather, it promotes the insight that there is an interaction among the different legal orders. This concept has far-reaching consequences for the understanding of constitutional law: any given constitution does not set up normative *universum* anymore but is, rather, an element in a normative *pluriversum*.[45]

[39] Neil MacCormick, *Questioning Sovereignty* (OUP 1999) 117–18.

[40] Neil MacCormick, 'The Maastricht Urteil: Sovereignty Now' (1995) 1 European Law Journal 259, 265.

[41] Kumm, 'Who Is the Final Arbiter of Constitutionality in Europe?' (n 32) 384. In fact, it has been stated that the theory of constitutional pluralism emerges as a response to the decisions of national constitutional courts. Baquero Cruz (n 34).

[42] Leonardo Pierdominici, 'The Theory of EU Constitutionalism Pluralism: A Crisis in a Crisis?' (2017) 9(2) Perspectives on Federalism 119, 124.

[43] Armin von Bogdandy, 'Neither an International Organization nor a Nation State: The EU as a Supranational Federation' in Erik Jones, Anand Menon, and Stephen Weatherhill (eds), *The Oxford Handbook of the European Union* (OUP 2012) 765.

[44] ibid 769.

[45] Armin von Bogdandy, 'Pluralism, Direct Effect, and the Ultimate Say: On the Relationship between International and Domestic Constitutional Law' (2008) 6 International Journal of Constitutional Law 397, 401.

The emergence of the ideas of legal pluralism to explain the relationship between EU law and national law has nuanced the original notion of primacy. As Maduro explains, constitutional pluralism propagated the idea that both the EU and national legal orders could co-exist and could be conceived of as constitutional systems, even if it was impossible to reconcile competing claims of authority.[46] In fact, he argues, not only does the final authority question remain open, it should remain so.[47] Or, as MacCormick contends, within a constitutionally plural territory like the EU, it is possible that each constitutional legal order acknowledges 'the legitimacy of every other within its own sphere, while none asserts or acknowledges the constitutional superiority over another'.[48] In essence, constitutional pluralism has emerged as a theory to better understand the nature of a complex polity like the EU. In fact, as Kennedy admits, 'legal pluralism is not a fact about the world. It is a professional experience: the experience that things don't add up, that coherence fails, that incommensurability must be acknowledged.'[49] In effect, as Walker admits, 'the advent of multilevel constitutionalism is a product first and foremost of objective changes in the socio-political world rather than of innovation in the world of ideas'.[50] However, this does not deprive these concepts of their relevance and influence. Indeed, 'multilevel constitutionalism', a concept coined by Pernice, has contributed to the understanding of the constitutional structure of the European juridical space as a complex and inclusive unity,[51] and the main argument advanced in this book is good proof of that. EU law and domestic legal orders have been defined 'as two interdependent, interwoven and reciprocally influential parts of one unit'.[52] Maduro has argued that one aim of Europe's constitutional pluralism is to prevent constitutional conflicts: to adjust to each other.[53] Thus, Member States and EU both claim sovereignty, but try to avoid direct conflicts through making concessions to each other. In a related vein of argument, Barber has pointed out that the European pluralist legal system arms national and EU law with weapons that may help to ensure mutual respect and restraint.[54] As Craig points out, at present, the resolution of the possible clashes between the

[46] Miguel Poiares Maduro, 'The Three Claims of Constitutional Pluralism' in Matej Avbelj and Jan Komarek (eds), *Constitutional Pluralism in the European Union and Beyond* (Hart Publishing 2012) 67–68.

[47] ibid 75.

[48] MacCormick, *Questioning Sovereignty* (n 39) 102.

[49] David Kennedy, 'One, Two, Three, Many Legal Orders: Legal Pluralism and the Cosmopolitan View' (2007) 31 New York University Review of Law and Social Change 641, 641.

[50] Neil Walker, 'Multi-level Constitutionalism: Looking Beyond the German Debate' (2009) 8 LEQS Paper <http://eprints.lse.ac.uk/53361/1/__Libfile_repository_Content_European%20Institute_LEQS%20Discussion%20Papera_LEQSPaper8Walker.pdf> accessed 2 August 2022.

[51] ibid.

[52] Ingolf Pernice, 'The Treaty of Lisbon: Multi-level Constitutionalism in Action' (2009) 2 WHI 26.

[53] Maduro, 'Contrapunctual Law' (n 38) 531.

[54] Nick Barber, *The Constitutional State* (OUP 2010) 171.

norms is done through the ECJ's jurisprudence, in constant and tolerant dialogue with national courts, 'an intricate process':

> It entails a complex discourse in which the national courts have been able to structure their reaction to the European Court of Justice's jurisprudence in a way that is acceptable to them. It allows for points of difference to exist. It enables national courts, if they so wish, to qualify acceptance of Community law supremacy in certain respects by hypothesising situations in which they would not give unequivocal support to Community law supremacy.[55]

This also entails the admission that 'constitutionalization of the process of European integration will be difficult without the involvement of the national constitutional courts'.[56]

Weiler explains very nicely the ultimate reason behind this choice in favour of constitutional tolerance, which he regards as one of Europe's most important constitutional innovations: the attachment of Europeans to their own national constitutional orders:

[55] Paul Craig, 'Constitutions, Constitutionalism and the European Union' (2001) 7(2) European Law Journal 125, 144. This idea of an intricate process and the dialogical nature of the relationship is constantly tested. In recent years, one of the most-high profile encounters has been the *Weiss* case. On 5 May 2020, within the framework of a preliminary procedure on the European Central Bank bond-buying powers, the German Constitutional Court (GCC) explicitly defied EU's legal order by rejecting the *Weiss* decision (Case C-493/17 *Weiss and others* [2018] ECLI 1000). The GCC dismissed the ECJ's ruling as incomprehensible and ultra vires and urged EU institutions, particularly the European Central Bank, to provide more explanation. See Miguel Poiares Maduro, 'Some Preliminary Remarks on the PSPP Decision of the German Constitutional Court' (*Verfassungsblog*, 6 May 2020) <https://verfassungsblog.de/some-preliminary-remarks-on-the-pspp-decision-of-the-german-constitutional-court/> accessed 2 August 2022. It has been argued that by doing so, the GCC declared itself the ultimate arbiter of EU law in Germany. Immediately after, on 8 May 2020, the ECJ issued a press release whereby it recalled that a judgment in which the Court gives a preliminary ruling is binding on the national court for the purposes of the decision to be given in the main proceedings and that national courts are required to ensure that EU law takes full effect. However, despite this apparent clash, EU institutions took note of the disagreement. In June 2020, in the first meeting after the GCC decision, the European Central Bank addressed the German concerns by offering more explanations and justifications of the proportionality of its monetary instruments, which were accepted by the German government as being sufficient to meet the GCC requirements. Phedon Nicolaides, 'The ECB is Responding to the Federal Constitutional Court of Germany: A Comparison of Monetary Policy Accounts' (*EULawLive*, 29 June 2020) <https://eulawlive.com/op-ed-the-ecb-is-responding-to-the-federal-constitutional-court-of-germany-a-comparison-of-monetary-policy-accounts-by-phedon-nicolaides/> accessed 2 August 2022. This conflict has been described as a 'constructive misunderstanding'. Mattias Wendel, 'Constructive Misunderstandings—How the PSPP Conflict Was Eventually Settled and How it Reflects Constitutional Pluralism' in Matej Avbelj (ed), *The Future of EU Constitutionalism* (Hart Publishing 2023) 53–70. Another relevant example of dialogue between courts, although with a much more conciliatory approach, is to be found in the *Taricco* case, where the Italian Constitutional Court asked the Court of Justice to interpret *Taricco II* (Case C-42/17 *M.A.S. and M.B.* [2017] ECLI 936, para 61) in a way that is compatible with the Italian constitutional legal order and the ECJ, despite the opinion of the Advocate General, decided to strike a balance between a constitutional right and the primacy of EU law. Giovanni Zaccaroni, 'The Good, the Bad and the Ugly: National Constitutional Judges and the EU Constitutional Identity' (2018) 10 Italian Journal of Public Law 421, 443.

[56] Zaccaroni (n 55) 424.

> Our national constitutions are perceived by us as doing more than simply structuring the respective powers of government and the relationships between public authority and individuals or between the state and other agents. Our constitutions are said to encapsulate fundamental values of the polity and this, in turn, is said to be a reflection of our collective identity as a people, as a nation, as a state, as a community or as a union.[57]

According to Weiler, this is why national courts have become even aggressive in their own constitutional orders' defence. If it wants to last, the EU legal order cannot become a threat to national constitutions. As will be argued in Chapter 6, article 4(2) TEU and the way the ECJ is approaching the concept of national identity are an expression of this pluralistic and tolerant standpoint.[58] Legal pluralism, as opposed to the constitutionalist approach which assumes a single integrated legal system, emphasizes the separateness and distinctiveness of legal orders. It values the diversity and difference among different (international and national) normative systems and underlines the undesirability and implausibility of constitutional approaches which seek hierarchy between these systems.[59] And it encourages tolerance and mutual accommodation. In sum, it promotes a deferential attitude. This is probably the approach that best defines the current competing claims and judicial dialogue between the highest courts of the different legal orders within the EU territory. This is also the main hypothesis underlying this book: deference should be the guiding principle when approaching EU response to secessionism within EU Member States.

Needless to say, constitutional pluralism has also been called into question. Although it became an orthodox paradigm in the study of EU law, some have not accepted the constitutional narrative of the EU, which is the basis of EU constitutionalism.[60] Criticism became particularly acute after the Euro-crisis and the

[57] Joseph HH Weiler, 'On the Power of the Word: Europe's Constitutional Iconography' (2005) 3 (2–3) International Journal of Constitutional Law 173, 184. Weiler argues further that this option in favour of constitutional tolerance embraces a civilizing strategy of dealing with the other: 'We acknowledge and respect difference and what is special and unique about us all as individuals and groups and also bridge differences in recognition of our essential humanity. The significant elements in this strategy are the maintenance, on the one hand, of the identity of the alien, who is not invited to be saved by becoming one of us, and the acceptance of the alien in his alienship, according him human dignity while preserving the boundaries between "I" and "the alien"'. ibid 187.

[58] Armin von Bogdandy and Stephan Schill, 'Overcoming Absolute Primacy: Respect for National Identity under the Lisbon Treaty' (2011) 48(5) Common Market Law Review 1417, 1452.

[59] De Burca (n 5) 32.

[60] The ideas of constitutionalism beyond the State or multilevel constitutionalism have attracted some criticism from those who hold an essentialist conception of constitutionalism. Thus, there are authors who contest that the category of constitution is necessarily restricted to and deeply embedded in the nation State concept. For instance, Dieter Grimm argues that constitutionalism is bound to the State in the sense that its comprehensive validity claim was territorially limited from the beginning: 'Although the idea of constitutionalism claimed universal validity, it was realized in the particular, in different states, from the start'. Therefore, '[t]he decline of statehood places not individual constitutions but constitutionalism as such in question'. For him, however, the more important question is whether constitutionalism can be transferred to the international level: 'the question is whether the constitution, as a

austerity measures triggered by EU institutions, and the emergence of legal and political conflicts with Central and Eastern European Member States, where some of these countries are finding it hard to implement certain EU law provisions. However, all in all, and despite the flaws and the controversies, it is difficult to deny that constitutional pluralism is the theory that is best able to describe the current state of affairs of EU constitutionalism. It retains, therefore, its strong empirical claim. It depicts the European phenomenon of a plurality of constitutional sources and claims of ultimate authority, and the inherent potential constitutional conflicts that are not hierarchically regulated.[61]

When referring to European constitutionalism we are implicitly admitting that it is the society, not the State, whose order is secured by a constitution. In this sense, constitutionalism is not only about an original constituent power of a people—something, needless to say, that is missing at the EU level—but also about limiting the power and securing rights of peoples within different political authorities. The very existence of the EU (and also other elements of the current 'postnational constellation'[62]) calls into question the Westphalian model of constitutional statehood and requires a notion of constitutionalism beyond the State or multilevel constitutionalism. Again, constitutional pluralism is not so much about what it should be, but about describing and reflecting accurately the problems of authority and community within the EU territory.

3. Definition of Secession

In this section, the notion of secession will be considered. How can it be legally understood? What are the different types of secession? A clear understanding of these notions will clarify the further discussion throughout the book.

form of the juridification that originally referred to the state, can be detached from it and transferred to non-state political entities that exercise public power'. According to Grimm, the EU experience lacks one essential element that prevents constitutionalism within the EU: its democratic origin, since the public power the EU exercises emanates not from the people, but from the Member States. Dieter Grimm, 'The Constitution in the Process of Denationalization' (2005) 12 Constellations 447, 453–59. Loughlin, eg, underlines the alleged legal inconsistencies of constitutional pluralism: 'Constitutional pluralism fails both to provide evidence for its claims about the nature of existing relations between member states and the EU and to offer a coherent account of a sustainable future state. Its so-called empirical claims amount to a catalogue of unsubstantiated assertions about the "autonomous" nature of EU institutional arrangements and a conflation of the concepts of legal with constitutional ordering. Its normative claims lead either to a radical claim of openness that undermines the basis of its own authority or to a modified "pluralism under international law" that turns out to be monist rather than pluralist in nature.' Martin Loughlin, 'Constitutional Pluralism: An Oxymoron?' (2014) 3(1) Global Constitutionalism 9, 29.

61 Pierdominici (n 42).

62 Jürgen Habermas, *The Postnational Constellation* (MIT Press 2001).

3.1 Secession in International Law

There is no officially recognized definition of secession, but there is an extensive scholarly debate. One conclusion of such debate is that there is little consensus among scholars on a precise definition.[63] What is clear, though, also from its Latin linguistic roots, is that secession is associated with leaving or withdrawing from a place.[64] From an international law approach, secession is the ultimate challenge to State sovereignty, since it involves the creation of a State by the dismemberment in whole or in part of an existing State. This explains the limited scope of the right to self-determination under international law, as we will see in Chapter 3. Secession is a process, it 'is not an instant fact. It always implies a complex series of claims and decisions, negotiations and/or struggle, which may—or may not—lead to the creation of a new State.'[65]

Some scholars consider that secession requires the use or threat of force and the lack of consent of the former sovereign.[66] In this regard, Crawford has offered a definition that has become classic and reads as follows: secession is 'the creation of a State by the use or threat of force without the consent of the former sovereign'.[67] In fact, this has been usually the case in history: secession has occurred against the will of the parent State and very often through violent means. Others prefer to omit the references to the use of force and define secession as 'the unilateral attempt of one section of the polity to dissociate itself from the rest'.[68] In both cases, however, 'unilaterality' is a key characteristic. Other authors, on the other hand, believe that secession can also encompass those processes whereby consent of the former parent State is granted, the so-called 'consensual secession' or consensual dissolution of the polity.[69] Thus, Radan prefers a 'definition of secession [that] extends secession beyond unilateral secession. It includes the creation of new states out of existing states by consent of the existing states.'[70] Finally, some authors believe that decolonization cases fall within the definition of secession, while others exclude all such cases of State creation from their definitions of secession.[71]

[63] Peter Radan, 'Secession: A Word in Search of a Meaning' in Aleksandar Pavkovic and Peter Radan (eds), *On the Way to Statehood, Secession and Globalization* (Ashgate 2008) 17.

[64] ibid 18.

[65] Marcelo G Kohen, 'Introduction' in Marcelo G Kohen (ed), *Secession: International Law Perspectives* (CUP 2012) 19.

[66] James Crawford, *The Creation of States in International Law* (2nd edn, OUP 2006) 375.

[67] ibid.

[68] David Haljan, *Constitutionalising Secession* (Hart Publishing 2014) 14. Also, John Dugard, 'A Legal Basis for Secession—Relevant Principles and Rules' in Julie Dahlitz (ed), *Secession and International Law* (T.M.C. Asser Press 2003) 89.

[69] Peter Radan, 'Secessionist Referenda in International and Domestic Law' in Matt Qvortrup (ed), *Nationalism, Referendums and Democracy. Voting on Ethic Issues and Independence* (Routledge 2014) 10.

[70] ibid.

[71] For instance, Radan accepts decolonization cases as secession cases. Radan, 'Secession: A Word in Search of a Meaning' (n 63) 23.

In order to encompass a broad range of scenarios, but accepting the most common and broad meaning, let us assume for now that secession involves the creation of a State by the dismemberment in whole or in part of an existing State. Although we will explore the international legal debate around secession in depth in the next chapter, including the relationship between the right to self-determination and secession, I should already make clear that secession is not prohibited or promoted by international law, except for very particular cases. Thus, secession is prohibited by international law where independence has been gained through the violation of basic principles of international law. And, second, international law promotes or grants a right to secede to very concrete political communities. Beyond these particular cases, analysed in depth in the next chapter, the main legal discussion around secession is to be found in constitutional law.

3.2 Secession in Constitutional Law

From a constitutional law standpoint, secession implies much more. From the nation State perspective, 'a secession crisis is quintessentially a situation of constitutional disorder'.[72] Disorder is constitutionally an appropriate word to define secession for the following reasons. Many countries, some of them well-functioning democracies, declare in their written constitutions the indivisibility of the country. This is so, for example, in the US, France, Italy, Australia, and Spain. The ultimate reason on which such indivisibility is based is the bond that unites the citizens and regions within a country, namely solidarity within a secular political community.[73] All citizens owe to each other a certain amount of solidarity (mutual help, assistance) as fellow countrymen. The basis of modern communities, their essential nature as polity, is precisely the cooperative effort of the intertwining of

[72] Haljan (n 68) 9. Following a similar reasoning, Bengoetxea argues that '[s]ecession is always a critical and tragic constitutional process of rupture: the state of things, relations between a people and the polity within which it is embedded, the matrix or parent, state have to get to a very difficult and critical point for secession to be envisaged'. Joxerramon Bengoetxea, 'Secession v forceful Union. A Provisional Enquiry into the Right to Decide to Secede and the Obligation to Belong' in Carlos Closa, Costanza Margiotta, and Giuseppe Martinico (eds), *Between Democracy and Law. The Amorality of Secession* (Routledge 2020) 33. In effect, secession is tragic, as the consequences 'affect a large number of persons and people, some who did, and some who did not take part in the process or in the deliberations, some who wanted secession, and some who did not, and if the proportions are even, extreme care is necessary to preserve societal cohesion'. ibid 35.

[73] Stephane Dion justifies his opposition to secession within a well-functioning democracy invoking a similar idea: 'The democratic ideal encourages all the citizens of a country to be loyal to each other, regardless of language, race, religion or regional considerations. Secession asks the opposite of citizens, asking them to break the solidarity that unites them, and to do so, almost always, based on considerations related to specific affiliations, such as language or ethnic origin. Secession is that rare and unusual exercise, in a democracy, whereby a choice is made as to which ones of our fellow citizens we want to keep and which ones we wish to transform into foreigners.' Stephane Dion, 'Secession and Democracy: A Canadian Perspective' (*Real Instituto Elcano*, 9 April 2013) <https://www.realinstitutoelcano.org/en/analyses/secession-and-democracy-a-canadian-perspective/> accessed 2 August 2022.

commitments, benefits, and burdens. Or as Haljan puts it, what binds us to the State is the fairness principle:

> Insofar as an individual enjoys benefits arising out of a political association [eg physical protection and minimal care], that individual is also morally bound to assume the burdens consequent upon such an association, the chief of which is to obey the laws of the association [eg redistribution of wealth].[74]

But what if a group of citizens reject unilaterally, for whatever reason,[75] such bonds?

> A secession crisis arises when a section of the polity purports to reject the established constitutional order and to substitute itself as sole political and legal authority over a defined territory.[76]

Secession challenges some of the most basic values and assumptions of liberal theory related to autonomy, consent, and democracy.[77] As Buchanan argues, '[i]f democracy is popular sovereignty, government by the people, then secession might be seen simply as the effort of various peoples to govern themselves, to be politically self-determining in the most literal sense, by forming their own states'.[78] There is an extensive philosophical debate on the morality of secession, but leaving aside legitimacy and justice considerations that go beyond the limits of this book, from a legal standpoint what seems clear is that it constitutes a constitutional crisis, a moment of constitutional disorder. This is something that we will have to bear in

[74] Haljan (n 68) 95.

[75] There are different reasons given by the various pro-independence movements across EU Member States to justify their secessionist aspirations. Very often economic reasons or the rejection of solidarity bonds are the basis of the movements (that is why the majority of strong pro-independence movement are to be found within advanced regions), as has been briefly noted in Chapter 1. However, economic reasons tend not to be enough to mobilize a political community against a well-functioning democracy. There are usually other reasons linked to self-recognition and national identity of minorities. In a State with a significant minority, that minority might ask itself if it is seriously taken into account by the majority, if the majority cares about them. Is the majority able to recognize legally and symbolically certain characteristics of the minority that make it different from the rest? If such recognition is not perceived by the minority, it feels marginalized and ignored. See Charles Taylor, *Acercar las soledades* (Tercera Prensa-Hirugarren Prentsa 1999) 301. Taylor also explains why such recognition is so important for minorities. According to the communitarian philosophy, man is not an isolated atom in society, but a 'self' inserted into the community. Personality is made through permanent dialogue with the others. From Taylor's point of view, human identity is forged by the interactions with the others, the 'significant others'. Charles Taylor, *La ética de la autenticidad* (Paidós 1994) 68. A healthy identity requires recognition on the significant other's part. Thus, the social and political community plays a constitutive role in defining humans' identity. The recognition, or lack thereof, will determine if such identity can be lived naturally or in a conflictive way. Taylor argues that the lack of recognition may distort or oppress, which can ultimately promote the emergence of pro-secession movements. ibid 84.

[76] ibid.

[77] Wayne Norman, 'The Ethics of Secession as the Regulation of Secessionist Politics' in Margaret Moore (ed), *National Self-Determination and Secession* (OUP 1998) 34.

[78] Allen Buchanan, 'Democracy and Secession' in Margaret Moore (ed), *National Self-Determination and Secession* (OUP 1998) 15.

mind constantly when exploring and finally justifying the EU deferential approach to national constitutional legal orders facing pro-secession attempts.

The connection between the American Civil War and secession resulted in a political demonization of secession, and its configuration as being incompatible with constitutionalism.[79] In recent decades, however, the emergence of peaceful pro-secession movements within well-functioning democracies and the 1998 Supreme Court Canadian opinion, which will be explained in more detail in Chapter 4, resulted in a change of constitutional paradigm,[80] by admitting the possibility of constitutionalizing secession.[81] Other European constitutional courts, in turn, still hold valid the classic US paradigm, as we will see. In any event, as Haljan explains, constitutionalizing secession is not so much about establishing a unilateral procedure or a right that offers a route for secession to a particular group,[82] but about opening a national debate, a process of deliberation and negotiation that at the end might imply rejection, modification or acceptance of secessionist claims.[83] In sum, each national legal order will decide by itself the lawfulness of secession (Chapter 4).

3.2.1 Relationship between secession and self-government

After this literature review concerning the definition of secession, the focus shifts to whether there is any relationship between self-government and secession. This is relevant because although EU law does not refer to secession, it does establish the EU obligation to respect the regional and local self-government structures of Member States (art 4(2) TEU). The concept of regional and local self-government within EU Member States is different in constitutional terms from secession, since self-government refers to different tiers of government—central, regional, and local—over a defined territory,[84] while secession, on the contrary, as has been explained, is aimed at the sole sovereign power in a given territory and polity.

First, one should recall, as the Committee of the Regions has stated, that 'the EU Member States are under no obligation to choose a particular model for their institutional structure or for the devolution, transfer or sharing of powers between

[79] Susanna Mancini, 'Secession and Self-determination' in Michael Rosenfeld and András Sajó (eds), *The Oxford Handbook of Comparative Constitutional Law* (OUP 2012) 494.

[80] Alberto López Basaguren, 'Estado democrático y secesión de territorios. Un análisis comparado sobre el tratamiento democrático de las reclamaciones secesionistas' in Joseba Arregi Aranburu (ed), *La Secesión de España* (Tecnos 2014) 51. In the same vein, Giuseppe Martinico, *Il diritto costituzionale come speranza. Secessione, democrazia e populismo alla luce della Reference Re Secession of Quebec* (G. Giappichelli Editore 2019) 47–48.

[81] *Reference re Secession of Quebec* [1998] 2 SCC 217, para 88.

[82] This thesis of including a right to secede in national constitutions has been advocated by some legal scholars, as will be explained in Chapter 4.

[83] Haljan (n 68) 249.

[84] This distinction is related to the federal principle, classically described as 'the method of dividing powers so that the general and regional governments are each within a sphere co-ordinate and independent'. Kenneth C Wheare, *Federal Government* (4th edn, OUP 1963) 11.

the different models of governance, but points out at the same time that the EU also respects regional and/or local self-government, as highlighted, in particular, in Article 4(2) TEU'.[85] Therefore, the unitary, regional, or federal character of the Member State is a decision to be taken by the Member State concerned, without the EU promoting any particular trend.

Second, if regional self-government is recognized by a Member State, what are the limits of such self-government? Is secession permitted? Should, therefore, the EU promote it or at least protect it? In this regard, it is noteworthy to invoke the 2001 Opinion of the Committee of the Regions concerning a European Charter of Regional Self-Government, where it is established that '[t]he definition of regional self-government recognises the existence of an intermediate tier between central government and local authorities. The task of determining the division of decision-making powers between national, regional and local authorities is a matter for national authorities.'[86] Therefore, one could argue that national legal orders establish the limits of regional self-government, whose scope and characteristics are constrained by the law and, particularly, by the Constitution. As will be explained in depth in Chapter 4, there is no EU Member State constitutional legal order entitling regional entities to unilaterally secede. Thus, there is no EU obligation to protect a provision, a hypothetical secession clause, which has not been included by EU Member States.

3.2.2 Consensus (and lack of) and lawfulness (and lack of) related to secession

As has been already stated, the main claim of the book (developed in Chapter 6) is that EU law, based on article 4(2) TEU, should defer to national constitutional law, as long as the national legal order complies with the values enshrined in article 2 TEU. It will be argued that if domestic law considers that secession is unlawful and non-consensual, EU law should respect that position by not recognizing the statehood of the secessionist entity. As will be explained in Chapter 5, this is exactly what occurred in October 2017 when the regional Catalan government unilaterally declared its independence. My argument is that the EU response was in accordance with EU law. If, on the contrary, the domestic legal order has authorized the secessionist attempt (consensual and lawful secession), EU law should respect that outcome by recognizing the new entity as a sovereign State and by entering into good faith negotiations. In order to facilitate the discussion, it is necessary to address some basic legal precepts such as consensual and non-consensual secession, and lawful and unlawful secession. Note also that this book is solely focused on the

[85] Committee of the Regions, 'Devolution in the European Union and the place for local and regional self-government in EU policy making and delivery' 2013/C 139/08.

[86] Committee of the Regions, 'Recommendation of the Congress of Local and Regional Authorities of Europe on a European Charter of Regional Self-Government' 2001/C 144/02.

response to secession within the EU. Therefore, we will be approaching secession assuming that it occurs within an EU Member State, where (at least so far) the high thresholds to active remedial secession (as explained in the following chapter) are not met. If an EU Member State grossly violates values enshrined in article 2 TEU, we would be facing a different and far-fetched scenario.

The key here is, firstly, to distinguish between the concepts of consensus and lawfulness. They both refer to two different levels of analysis. Constitutional consensus touches upon the values and goods reified through deliberative process into institutions and legal concepts included in the constitutional order.[87] Consensus is related to the formation of the democratic will, the commitment and pact of a plural polity.[88] Except in the UK, in constitutional liberal democracies this pact tends to crystallize in a written constitution, interpreted by a constitutional court or a Supreme Court. In modern constitutional terms, consensus tends to equate with the principle of democracy. Yet, the democratic will, the principle of democracy, as the Canadian Supreme Court stated in 1998, 'cannot exist without the rule of law',[89] which means that consensus requires lawfulness. The will has to be subject to the legal procedure: '[i]t is the law that creates the framework within which the "sovereign will" is to be ascertained and implemented' held the Canadian Court.[90] 'Democratic institutions must rest, ultimately, on a legal foundation.'[91] In constitutional democracies, the democratic will, the agreement, the consensus will not be legitimate outside the law, but equally, 'a system of government cannot survive through adherence to the law alone.... The system must be capable of reflecting the aspirations of the people.... A functioning democracy requires a continuous process of discussion',[92] in order to achieve a conciliatory interaction between the democratic consensual will and the law. Lawfulness, or to be more precise, lawfulness in a democratic State also requires consensus. In sum, in a constitutional democracy, consensus and lawfulness should go hand by hand.

As for secession, (1) a consensual secession can be defined as a secession agreed upon between the parent State and the regional seceding government. The agreement can be reached during the process or afterwards (for instance, in the case of supervening political recognition); (2) non-consensual secession refers to the lack of agreement between the parent State and the regional seceding government; (3) lawful secession refers to the scenario where secession is conducted following a certain legal procedure. Subject to limited exceptions (explored in Chapter 4), national legal orders do not foresee any procedure or right for secession. However,

87 Haljan (n 68) 46.

88 Miguel Herrero de Miñón, 'La Constitución como pacto' (1998) 44 Revista de Derecho Político 17, 19.

89 *Reference re Secession of Quebec* (n 80) para 67.

90 ibid.

91 ibid.

92 ibid.

several Supreme and constitutional courts have argued that in the event of a political agreement to accept secession, there is a need to amend the constitution in order to include a formal procedure and subject the secessionist bid to the law. In EU Member States, where reform of the constitution tends to require wide consensus,[93] lawful secession will imply consensual secession; (4) unlawful secession is one conducted against the national legal order, and probably also against the will of the parent State, of the national legal order, that is, revolutionary or unilateral secession. Usually, unlawful secession implies non-consensual secession. As will be seen, when referring to lawfulness, we are adopting the constitutional law point of view, since international law barely refers to secession beyond the extraordinary scenarios that will be explained in Chapter 3.

In practice, consensual secession tends to be lawful and non-consensual secession tends to be unlawful. The Catalan secessionist movement (see Chapter 4) is an example of non-consensual and unlawful secession (prohibited by Spanish legal order). Montenegro (see Chapter 5) was an example of consensual and lawful secession (permitted by the State Union of Serbia and Montenegro legal order), as the European Council expressly admitted. Scotland (see Chapter 4) would have been an example of consensual and lawful secession (permitted by the British legal order). However, it is necessary to explore the possibility of other scenarios to facilitate the discussion in Chapter 6, where the principal claim of the book is tested. The present chapter is not the appropriate place to discuss the EU response to the different scenarios, which will be further explored in Chapter 6, but to clearly elaborate different hypotheses, even if they look like far-fetched scenarios. Thus, only a brief reference to the contours of the scenarios will be given here.

Consensual but unlawful secession

A consensual but unlawful secession connotes the idea that the legal framework requires a certain procedure or plainly outlaws secession,[94] but the central government nonetheless reaches a political deal with the secessionist entity. This could generate a constitutional crisis in that Member State,[95] since, by definition,

[93] As the Venice Commission stated '[i]t is a fundamental feature of all written constitutions (unlike ordinary statutes) that they contain provisions for amending themselves. In almost all constitutions such change is more difficult than with ordinary legislation, and typically requires either a qualified parliamentary majority, multiple decisions, special time delays or a combination of such factors. Sometimes ratification by popular referendum is required, and in federal systems sometimes ratification by the entities.' Venice Commission, 'Report on Constitutional Amendment', CDL-AD (2010) 001, para 6.

[94] To what extent outlawing secession is effective is of course another debate. Often, this doctrine serves more as a threat than a reality. See Rivka Weill, 'Secession and the Prevalence of Both Militant Democracy and Eternity Clauses Worldwide' (2018) 40 Cardozo Law Review 905, 960.

[95] Although this is, in principle, a difficult scenario to imagine, in fact it resembles the situation which occurred with the dissolution of Czechoslovakia, as explained in Chapter 5. In this hypothetical scenario, the constitutional legal order of the country concerned has failed to fulfil its function of comprehensively juridifying public power, since the Constitution has lost acceptance. Grimm (n 60) 453.

the constitutional identity of the country is in the making, and there is a profound mismatch between the legal order and the political legitimacy that has to back it: a transitional constitutional moment. The fact that constitutional change, or mutation, can occur outside the formal amendment process is not an alien idea for constitutional scholars,[96] nor for EU lawyers.[97] Based on his theory of dualist democracy, Ackerman famously argued that major constitutional shifts can occur outside the amendment process, 'when political movements generated mobilized popular consent to new constitutional solutions'.[98] The Venice Commission also points out that '[f]ormal amendment is not the only form of constitutional change, and in some systems not even the most important. Leaving aside revolutionary or unlawful acts, the two most important alternative ways of legitimate constitutional change are through judicial interpretation and through the evolvement of unwritten political conventions supplementing or contradicting the written text'.[99] In this scenario of constitutional transformation, there are basically two options: (1) either no one challenges the situation and there is no High/Supreme/Constitutional Court denouncing, for the time being, the unlawful situation, or (2) the deal and/or its consequences are challenged before a court.

In the first scenario, we are faced with evolution of the constitutional order. The constitutional order cannot be explained solely by the letter of the Constitution or the case law of the highest courts, but also by the laws and regulations that apply and interpret it. And, mainly, by the political consensus upon which the constitutional order is built. As the Canadian Supreme Court stated:

> The Constitution should not be viewed as a mere collection of discrete textual provisions. It has an architecture, a basic structure. By extension, amendments to the Constitution are not confined to textual changes. They include changes to the Constitution's architecture, that modify the meaning of the constitutional text.[100]

[96] We refer to the tacit understanding of law and politics held by the government and accepted by the governed when there is a new constitutional meaning but without new constitutional writing. See Richard Albert, 'How Unwritten Constitutional Norms Change Written Constitutions' (2015) 38(2) Dublin University Law Journal 387, 393.

[97] Agustín José Menéndez, for instance, reminded us that '[t]he ongoing European constitutional transformation is the cumulative result of decisions, which have not been adopted through "standard" supranational Treaty amendment processes or national constitutional reform processes, but taken off the beaten constitutional track through ordinary law-making procedures, through peculiar intergovernmental negotiations and last but not least, through the toleration of new institutional practices'. He insisted that '[i]t could well be argued that unconventional constitutional reform is as European as stopping the clock in the meetings of the Council of Ministers or European Councils ending in the small hours'. Agustín José Menéndez, 'Editorial: A European Union in Constitutional Mutation?' (2014) 20(2) European Law Journal 127, 127.

[98] Bruce Ackerman, *We the People. Foundations* (Harvard UP 1991) 31.

[99] See Venice Commission, 'Report on constitutional amendment' (n 93).

[100] *Reference re Senate Reform* [2014] 32 SCC 704, 706.

Once the deal is consolidated (either ultimately through a formal amendment or without it), the constitutional identity of the country has evolved.

In the second scenario, if the court confirms the unlawfulness of the deal, the political players will be forced to undertake the constitutional foreseen amendment procedures. The court has also another option. Under the common-law doctrine of 'effectiveness' a court can exercise a supra-constitutional jurisdiction in determining whether a revolutionary act (secession against the law might be considered a revolution) ought to be given legal recognition. In this regard, it would be important to explore the question of popular support for the new constitutional framework and whether a majority of the people are behaving, by and large, in conformity with the new reality.[101] In both cases there is constitutional identity in transition.

Non-consensual but lawful secession

A non-consensual but lawful secession is an even more difficult scenario to imagine, since within the EU there was only one country, namely the UK before its withdrawal, where there is a partial recognition of a right to secede, that is, a route to secession legally foreseen. As will be further explained in Chapter 4, we are referring to the legal obligation contained in article 1 of the British-Irish Agreement (BIA) of 10 April 1998 as to the right to self-determination in Northern Ireland. If the conditions established in the Agreement reached in the Multi-Party Talks (a political agreement annexed to the BIA and, therefore, part of the text of the BIA) are met (those conditions will be explained in Chapter 4), but the British government refuses to authorize the organization of the referendum, we might end up facing a situation where the British constitutional legal order is entitling a collective right whose fulfilment is denied by the central government due to a lack of political will or consensus. In such a scenario, there would be a violation of the constitutional order by the Member State concerned. If there is ever an EU Member State admitting a legal path to secession, the EU will have to distinguish the type and extent of the unlawfulness and act accordingly.

Non-consensual, unlawful secession but widely supported secession move

A non-consensual, unlawful secession, but one which is widely supported, is another hypothesis that should be tested. What kind of situation are we referring to? We have in mind a situation where a large part of a national polity, usually concentrated in one region, rejects by some significant margin[102] the current constitutional legal order and advocates secession. In other words, a situation where, over

[101] George Williams, 'The Case that Stopped a Coup? The Rule of Law and Constitutionalism in Fiji' [2001] Oxford University Commonwealth Law Journal 73, 85–86.

[102] Following the Canadian clarity doctrine, explained in Chapter 4, this will imply more than just 50 per cent of the population concerned.

time, there is a repeated and sustained support for independence in regional elections, where pro-independence parties obtain more than 50 per cent of popular support, but the Constitution rejects independence and the central government refuses to negotiate any accommodation formula.[103] In Europe, this is an unknown scenario. In Catalonia, for instance, as will be explained in Chapter 4, pro-independence parties have never obtained more than 50 per cent of popular support. However, we should not dismiss this scenario in the future.

4. Conclusion

This chapter has established the necessary legal framework by clarifying some of the concepts that underpin the book. Throughout this work, we will be invoking international law provisions that might affect the behaviour of EU institutions and Member States. We will also be referring constantly to internal legal orders. It was therefore necessary to explore the relationship between these orders. Additionally, since the response of national constitutional legal orders (and, therefore, EU law) depends on the type of secession, it was also necessary to explore the different kinds of secession possible (namely, consensual, non-consensual, lawful, and unlawful).

[103] Josep Maria Castellà, 'Sobre el encaje constitucional del pretendido referéndum de secesión en Cataluña' in Eva Sáenz and Carlos Garrido (eds), *La Funcionalidad del Referéndum en la Democracia Representativa* (Tirant Lo Blanch 2017) 152.

3

Secession and International Law

1. Introduction

The aim of this chapter is to analyse to what extent the European Union (EU) has any international law obligation when it comes to secession. It will be shown that the classic position of international law concerning secession is that of neutrality and that, therefore, the EU has no obligation towards secession derived from international law. However, it must be explained that since the second half of the twentieth century, with the emergence of the right to self-determination, international law includes a right to independence under certain circumstances (which can be viewed as an 'improper'[1] right to secession). In particular, this right refers to non-self-governing units in the context of decolonization, alien subjugation, and, presumably, apartheid. Today there is considerable scholarly debate surrounding the evolution of this right, specifically as to whether and to what extent it has evolved. This debate now includes other types of sub-national units beyond the colonial paradigm. In effect, the revival of secessionist movements in many parts of the world raises the question of whether there exists a right to secede under international law.[2] That is the main inquiry of this chapter. Does the evolution of the right to self-determination include any right to separation (or secession) for regions within EU Member States that the EU should be aware of?

As Sterio points out, 'it is unclear what the contours of the right to self-determination may be outside of the decolonization paradigm'.[3] As we will see, despite an important academic debate, no international treaty recognizes such a right, there is not enough practice, and there is no consensus among States. Professor Shaw summarizes this position as follows: 'Self-determination as a concept is

[1] 'Improper' in the sense that usually colonial movements are excluded from the term 'secession': 'Decolonisation, the most important means of creation of new States during the second half of the twentieth century, was not viewed by the international legal order as a case of secession.' Marcelo G Kohen, 'Introduction' in Marcelo G Kohen (ed), *Secession: International Law Perspectives* (CUP 2012) 1. However, some authors believe that a broad definition of secession can also encompass colonial movements, as was explained in Chapter 2. For instance, Peter Radan, 'Secession: A Word in Search of a Meaning' in Aleksandar Pavkovic and Peter Radan (eds), *On the Way to Statehood, Secession and Globalization* (Ashgate 2008) 23. See also Glen Anderson, 'Unilateral Non-Colonial Secession and Internal Self-Determination: A Right of Newly Seceded Peoples to Democracy' (2017) 34(1) Arizona Journal of International and Comparative Law 1, 11.

[2] Photini Pazartzis, 'Secession and International Law: The European Dimension' in Marcelo G Kohen (ed), *Secession: International Law Perspectives* (CUP 2012) 355.

[3] Milena Sterio, *Secession in International Law* (Edward Elgar 2018) 18.

Secession and European Union Law. Núria González Campañá, Oxford University Press. © Núria González Campañá 2024.
DOI: 10.1093/oso/9780198882596.003.0003

capable of developing further so as to include the right to secession from existing states, but that has not yet convincingly happened.'[4] Therefore, it cannot be said that international law has extended a right to separate from the parent State beyond the colonial scenario. This chapter describes the current legal framework of secession in a discipline closely connected to EU law before analysing the position of EU law vis a vis secession. It does not try to present a comprehensive theory on secession, but rather to explore the extent to which EU law is subject to international legal obligations for the treatment of secession within the EU. Is EU law constrained by international law in its approach to secession?

2. International Law and Secession

As noted in the previous chapter, Crawford offered a classic definition of secession in international law by virtue of which secession could be considered as 'the creation of a State by the use or threat of force without the consent of the former sovereign'.[5] However, other scholars prefer to omit the references to the use of force[6] and some even argue that secession can also encompass those processes whereby consent of the former parent State is granted, the so-called 'consensual secession' or consensual dissolution of the polity.[7] In order to encompass a broad range of scenarios and for the sake of permitting a dialogue with a large number of scholars, I will assume, as noted in Chapter 2, that secession involves the creation of a State by the division in whole or in part of an existing State, with or without the consent of the parent State.[8]

[4] Malcolm Shaw, *International Law* (8th edn, CUP 2017) 203.

[5] James Crawford, *The Creation of States in International Law* (2nd edn, OUP 2006) 375.

[6] David Haljan, *Constitutionalising Secession* (Hart Publishing 2014) 14. See also Dugard: 'I prefer to see secession as the unilateral withdrawal of part of an existing State from that State without the consent of the government of that State. Secession by agreement is better described as dissolution of a State.' John Dugard, 'A Legal Basis for Secession—Relevant Principles and Rules' in Julie Dahlitz (ed), *Secession and International Law* (T.M.C. Asser Press 2003) 89. Torroja Mateu also defends a rigorous interpretation of secession as a non-consensual process and in violation of internal constitutional legal norms. Helena Torroja Mateu, *La libre determinación de los pueblos, ¿un derecho a la independencia para cualquier pueblo ?* (Thomson Reuters Aranzadi 2022) 54. In fact, she argues that when the State gives its consent, we are then faced with separation of territories, not secession. ibid 49. López Martín and Perea Unceta agree with the approach of secession as being an eminently non-consensual process and they uphold a very strict notion of secession: 'By State creation through secession we mean the effective separation of one part of the territory—and its population—from what we call a "parent State", and which persists as such, without the consent of the latter, but always outside the context of decolonization and in order to constitute a new State, not to join one that already exists.' Ana Gema López Martín and José Antonio Perea Unceta, *Secession and Statehood* (Routledge 2022) 13.

[7] Peter Radan, 'Secessionist Referenda in International and Domestic Law' in Matt Qvortrup (ed), *Nationalism, Referendums and Democracy. Voting on Ethic Issues and Independence* (Routledge 2014) 10.

[8] This broad definition can be found in Sterio, *Secession in International Law* (n 3) 29.

3. Secession as a Legally Neutral Act in Public International Law

The orthodox position is that secession, broadly considered, is a matter of fact where international law should remain neutral. Lauterpacht says that '[i]nternational law does not condemn rebellion or secession aiming at the acquisition of independence'.[9] According to Crawford '[t]he position is that secession is neither legal nor illegal in international law, but a legally neutral act the consequences of which are regulated internationally'.[10] Cassese agrees and argues that

> international law does not ban secessionism: the breaking away of a nation or ethnic group is neither authorized nor prohibited by legal rules; it is simply regarded as a fact of life, outside the realm of law, and to which law can attach the legal consequences depending on the circumstances of the case.[11]

The League of Nations clearly stated the position of international law in the 1920s, that is, international law has nothing to say when it comes to separation claims:

> Positive International Law does not recognize the right of national groups, as such, to separate themselves from the State of which they form part by the simple expression of a wish, any more than it recognizes the right of other States to claim such separation. Generally speaking, the grant or refusal of the right to a portion of its population of determining its own political fate by plebiscite or by some other method, is exclusively an attribute of the sovereignty of every State which is definitely constituted. A dispute between two States concerning such a question, under normal conditions therefore, bears upon a question which International Law leaves entirely to the domestic jurisdiction of one of the States concerned. Any other solution would amount to an infringement of [the] sovereign rights of a State and would involve the risk of creating difficulties and a lack of stability which would not only be contrary to the very idea embodied in the term 'State', but would also endanger the interests of the international community.[12]

[9] Hersch Lauterpacht, *Recognition in International Law* (CUP 1947) 8.

[10] Crawford (n 5) 390. Crawford explains that in effect classic international law followed a non-legal approach, but an efficacy principle: 'nineteenth-century practice . . . established that a seceding territory could properly be recognized as a State if it governed its territory effectively and with sufficient stability, such that there was no real likelihood of the previous sovereign . . . reasserting its position'. ibid 382.

[11] Antonio Cassese, *Self-determination of Peoples. A Legal Reappraisal* (CUP 1995) 340.

[12] 'Report of the International Committee of Jurists Entrusted by the Council of the League of Nations with the Task of Giving an Advisory Opinion upon the Legal Aspects of the Aaland Islands Question' (1920) Official Journal of the League of Nations (3) 5. Cassese explains why the Aaland Islands dispute did fall within the jurisdiction of the League of Nations: 'This was not because of any alleged "right" to self-determination which outweighed issues of State sovereignty but because Finland, only recently liberated from Russian control, in the International Committee of Jurists' Opinion, "had

Musgrave summarizes this traditional position as follows:

> Secession is a domestic matter, and therefore a legally neutral act in international law.... Although secession produces consequences in international law when a new state is formed, the act of secession itself is essentially political rather than legal in nature. As a political act, secession cannot be characterized by legal formulations.[13]

Some would allege that international law is predicated upon the idea of the nation State[14] and that the principle of territorial integrity is one of the most fundamental and well-established principles of international law. In this sense, 'secession is the antithesis of territorial integrity',[15] which includes an implicit prohibition of secession. Therefore, international law should not remain neutral, but should prohibit secession. This was the argument advanced by Russia and Serbia before the International Court of Justice (ICJ) when the ICJ was deciding upon the 2010 Kosovo Advisory Opinion. However, the ICJ responded that such a principle is only opposable to third States, not to political units within the State, following the reasoning submitted in the US written statement, among others. In effect, the Court established that the principle of territorial integrity does not apply to groups within a State: 'the scope of the principle of territorial integrity is confined to the sphere of relations between States'.[16] Thus, it could be understood that 'international law does not protect states from disaggregation from within. Action which would be prohibited if committed by other states is left unregulated by international law when committed by non-state actors.'[17] Interestingly, the ICJ reformulated the question asked by the General Assembly: from 'is the Declaration of independence in accordance with international law?' to 'does the Declaration violate international law?'[18] As the Court noted:

not yet acquired the character of a definitively constituted State" and was not an independent member of the international community.' Cassese, *Self-determination of Peoples. A Legal Reappraisal* (n 11) 29.

[13] Thomas D Musgrave, *Self-Determination and National Minorities* (OUP 1997) 210. Sterio also notes that 'international law is mostly neutral on the issue of secession'. Sterio, *Secession in International Law* (n 3) 40.

[14] Rosalyn Higgins, 'Self-determination and Secession' in Julie Dahlitz (ed), *Secession and International Law* (T.M.C. Asser Press 2003) 23.

[15] Musgrave (n 13) 181. In fact, it is by reason of territorial integrity that the international community does not recognize a general right of secession. Antonio Cassese, *International Law* (OUP 2003) 113.

[16] *Accordance with International Law of the Unilateral Declaration of Independence in Respect of Kosovo, Advisory Opinion, I.C.J. Reports 2010* 403, para 80. Before this 2010 Opinion, scholars used to discuss the internal application of the principle. Marc Weller, 'The International Response to the Dissolution of the Socialist Federal Republic of Yugoslavia' (1992) 86(3) The American Journal of International Law 569, 572. For a critical view on the neutrality interpretation of the ICJ, see Torroja Mateu (n 6) 144 ff.

[17] Christian Walter, 'The Kosovo Advisory Opinion. What It Says and What It Does Not Say' in Christian Walter, Antje von Ungern-Sternberg, and Kavus Abushov (eds), *Self-Determination and Secession in International Law* (OUP 2014) 22.

[18] ibid 24.

> The Court is not required by the question it has been asked to take a position on whether international law conferred a positive entitlement on Kosovo unilaterally to declare its independence or, a fortiori, on whether international law generally confers an entitlement on entities situated within a State unilaterally to break away from it. Indeed, it is entirely possible for a particular act—such as a unilateral declaration of independence—not to be in violation of international law without necessarily constituting the exercise of a right conferred by it. The Court has been asked for an opinion on the first point, not the second.[19]

The formula chosen by the General Assembly ('in accordance with') seemed to presuppose that the issue is regulated by law: it must be either allowed or prohibited. The ICJ's formula ('not in violation of') does not presuppose such regulation. The reformulation merely reflects the approach taken by the Court: since the international legal principle of territorial integrity is not applicable to non-State actors, and since no other international legal norms are applicable to the case, international law is silent. A positive ruling holding the declaration in question to be 'in conformity with' international law is therefore excluded.[20] That is why some authors have considered that the ICJ Advisory Opinion was read to mean that the judgment of whether a political entity is a sovereign State was not a genuinely normative judgment.[21] In effect, if one takes a look at the following paragraph, it seems that the success of a declaration of independence had little to do with the normative support behind it:

> During the eighteenth, nineteenth and early twentieth centuries, there were numerous instances of declarations of independence, often strenuously opposed by the State from which independence was being declared. Sometimes a declaration resulted in the creation of a new State, at others it did not. State practice during this period [eighteenth, nineteenth, and early twentieth centuries] points clearly to the conclusion that international law contained no prohibition of declarations of independence.[22]

It is true, however, that in some cases (eg Katanga, Southern Rhodesia, the Turkish Republic of Northern Cyprus) the UN Security Council has characterized secession as illegal.[23] However,

[19] *Accordance with International Law of the Unilateral Declaration of Independence in Respect of Kosovo* (n 16) para 56.

[20] Walter (n 17) 25.

[21] Stefan Oeter, 'The Role of Recognition and Non-Recognition with Regard to Secession' in Christian Walter, Antje von Ungern-Sternberg, and Kavus Abushov (eds), *Self-Determination and Secession in International Law* (OUP 2014) 49.

[22] *Accordance with International Law of the Unilateral Declaration of Independence in Respect of Kosovo* (n 16) para 79.

[23] In effect, the UN Security Council referred to secessions of Katanga and Southern Rhodesia as illegal. For instance: UN Security Council Resolution 169 (1961), of 21 February, '[s]trongly deprecates

> [i]n all of those instances the Security Council was making a determination as regards the concrete situation existing at the time that those declarations of independence were made; the illegality attached to the declarations of independence thus stemmed not from the unilateral character of these declarations as such, but from the fact they were, or would have been connected with the unlawful use of force or other egregious violations of norms of general international law.[24]

In conclusion, with the 2010 ICJ Advisory Opinion on Kosovo the classic position is reaffirmed and it is clear that, even without the consent of the parent State, secession is not prohibited by general international law. However, is there any right to secession under international law? Is there any legal obligation that the EU should be aware of?

4. Right to 'Secede' or Become Independent Recognized in Certain Circumstances

International law remains neutral when it comes to secession. But, under certain circumstances, international law recognizes a right to become a sovereign, independent State. This became evident since the end of the Second World War with the appearance of the right to self-determination that created a limited right to independence. In effect, as will be shown, the right to self-determination enables non-self-governing entities subject to colonial rule or alien subjugation to become independent from the metropolitan State. This right to become independent could be seen as a right to secede, if we assume a broad and improper meaning of secession.

the secessionist activities illegally carried out by the provincial administration of Katanga, with the aid of external resources ... '; UN Security Council Resolution 216 (1965), of 12 November, '[d]ecides to condemn the unilateral declaration of independence made by a racist minority in Southern Rhodesia; 2. Decides to call upon all States not to recognize this illegal racist minority regime in Southern Rhodesia and to refrain from rendering any assistance to this illegal regime'.

[24] *Accordance with International Law of the Unilateral Declaration of Independence in Respect of Kosovo* (n 16) para 81. Crawford had already explained that after reviewing the debates of the cited resolutions, 'there is little or no reliance on legal rules prohibiting secession; rather, reference is made to the internal law of the metropolitan State. Any international concerns associated with secession movements relates to the existence of foreign intervention (as in Katanga) or the existence of a threat to international peace and security (as in Rhodesia).' Crawford (n 5) 390. See also UN Security Council Resolution 541 (1983), of 18 November, concerning northern Cyprus and UN Security Council Resolution 787 (1992), of 16 November, concerning the Republika Srpska.

4.1 From the Principle to the Right to Self-determination

This right emerged after the Second World War, but appeared in the international arena much earlier as a political principle. In fact, the philosophical principles behind the concept of self-determination can be traced back to the combined emergence of liberalism in the eighteenth century and of nationalism in the nineteenth century.[25] The principle of self-determination itself appeared on the international scene with the advent of the First World War and the Bolshevik Revolution. For US President Woodrow Wilson, it was a key principle to build a lasting peace in Europe.[26] 'It was recognized that lasting, peaceful arrangements could be achieved only by clearing the way for the establishment of comprehensive national states and by recognizing the rights of occasional minorities within such States.'[27] Although the meaning remained vague and imprecise, it was understood as the proposition that every people (understood as any cultural nation) should freely determine its own political status and its economic, social, and cultural development.[28] The principle began to emerge in the wake of the plebiscites held in Europe after the First World War.[29] However, it was applied inconsistently. 'Self-determination in 1919 had little to do with the demands of the peoples concerned, unless those

[25] Cassese, *Self-determination of Peoples. A Legal Reappraisal* (n 11) 11; Hurst Hannum, *Autonomy, Sovereignty, and Self-Determination. The Accommodation of Conflicting Rights* (revisited edn, University of Pennsylvania Press 1996) 27; Simone F van Driest, *Remedial Secession. A Right to External Self-Determination as a Remedy to Serious Injustices?* (Intersentia 2013) 35.

[26] Cassese, *Self-determination of Peoples. A Legal Reappraisal* (n 11) 13. Not everyone in the US government was satisfied with the appearance of the concept. Robert Lansing, the US Secretary of State who negotiated the 1919 Paris Peace Agreement, explained in his memoirs the reluctance he always had towards the expression: 'The more I think about the President's declaration as to the right of self-determination, the more convinced I am of the danger of putting such ideas into the minds of certain races. It is bound to be the basis of impossible demands on the Peace Congress and create trouble in many lands ... The phrase is simply loaded with dynamite. It will raise hopes that can never be realised. It will, I fear, cost thousands of lives.' Robert Lansing, *The Peace Negotiations. A Personal Narrative* (Constable and Company Ltd 1921) 87.

[27] Markku Suksi, *Bringing in the People: A Comparison of Constitutional Forms and Practices of the Referendum* (Martinus Nijhoff 1993) 241.

[28] John P Humphrey, 'Political and Related Rights' in Theodor Meron (ed), *Human Rights in International Law: Legal and Policy Issues* (1st vol, OUP 1984) 193. Still today, self-determination remains a diffused and inspirational concept, with undoubted power and resonance in world politics, but without a conclusive agreement about its precise meaning. Alexander M Johnston, 'Self-Determination in Comparative Perspective: Northern Ireland and South Africa' (1990) 17(2) Politikon: South African Journal of Political Studies 5, 7. See also Xabier Arzoz and Markku Suksi, 'Comparing Constitutional Adjudication of Self-determination Claims' (2018) 25(4) Maastricht Journal of European and Comparative Law 452, 453: 'the content of the right to self-determination remains insufficiently determinate, at best alleged'.

[29] Radan, 'Secessionist Referenda in International and Domestic Law' (n 7) 11. Markku Suksi explains previous historical examples of referendums linked to self-determination: 'One of the first instances where the population's right of self-determination ... might have had any practical implications was the annexation of Toul, Metz, and Verdun to France in 1552. It was probably the first time in such a context that a procedure was used which could be referred to as a referendum. During the seventeenth century, natural-law theorists, such as Grotius and Pufendorf, expressed the opinion that transfer of territory from one state to another required the consent of the people living on the territory in question.' Suksi (n 27) 238.

demands were consistent with the geopolitical and strategic interests of the Great Powers.'[30] In fact, a great number of areas affected by the First World War were subject to change of sovereignty without any consultations with the people concerned being carried out.[31] Although the principle was well known in those years, it was not included in the Versailles Treaty. Self-determination as political principle only entered the realm of international law in 1945,[32] when it was proclaimed in articles 1(2) and 55 of the United Nations (UN) Charter. But even then, no clear legal obligation was imposed on States.[33] In effect, after the First World War 'self-determination evolved from a mere political principle into a legal entitlement. But the precise status remained ambiguous.'[34]

UN General Assembly Resolutions 1514 (1960), 1541 (1960), and 2625 (1970), adopted unanimously, defined the scope and meaning of the right. The right to self-determination was reserved for the so-called 'non-self-governing territories': territories geographically separated from the metropolitan State, ethnically distinct and politically subordinated to the referred State. These territories qualified to decide freely their destiny, either through integration within the colonial power, through a free association agreement or through independence, this latter being the mechanism chosen by the majority of the old colonies and the one mostly promoted by the UN.[35] The distinction between self-determination and secession seems clear: while self-determination is a process of decision or expression of the will of the people (that might, but would not necessarily, lead to a change of status), secession (at least successful secession) always involves a change of status.[36]

In 1966, the legislative process culminated in the adoption of the two international covenants on human rights, the International Covenant on Civil and Political Rights (ICCPR) and the International Covenant on Social, Economic and Cultural Rights (ICSECR), whose common article 1 proclaimed the right 'of all peoples to self-determination'. At first glance, it might seem that the wording of the article was highly inclusive. However, how was that right to be understood and applied? Even well-known proponents of human rights like Eleanor Roosevelt warned about the risk of instability attached to such a right: 'Does self-determination mean the right of secession? Does self-determination constitute a right of fragmentation or a justification for the fragmentation of nations? ... Obviously not.... Just as the

[30] Hannum (n 25) 28.
[31] Suksi (n 27) 243.
[32] Cassese, *Self-determination of Peoples. A Legal Reappraisal* (n 11) 65.
[33] ibid.
[34] Van Driest (n 25) 36.
[35] Hanum explains the UN's clear preference for independence: 'The clear preference for independence as the normal result of exercise of the right to self-determination is evidenced by detailed requirements for the free and informed consent of the peoples concerned if either free association or integration is chosen.' Hannum (n 25) 40.
[36] Joxerramon Bengoetxea, 'Secession v Forceful Union. A Provisional Enquiry into the Right to Decide to Secede and the Obligation to Belong' in Carlos Closa, Costanza Margiotta, and Giuseppe Martinico (eds), *Between Democracy and Law. The Amorality of Secession* (Routledge 2020) 32.

concept of human liberty carried to its logical extreme would mean anarchy, so the principle of self-determination given unrestricted application could result in chaos.'[37] The content of the right is analysed below.

4.2 Content of the Right to Self-determination

Buchheit affirms that it would be a mistake to assume that article 1 of both the ICCPR and the ICSECR meant the general acceptance of secession. On the contrary:

> Article 1 of the covenants appears in spite of its possible secessionist interpretation, rather than as a confirmation of that interpretation. The felt need for a strong, sweeping statement of the right to self-determination as a weapon against colonialism overcame the implorations of the Western powers for cautious draftsmanship.[38]

The *travaux préparatoires* show that the right was merely invoked for the liberation of colonial territories, not construed as implying a general new right of creation of States.[39] Thus, self-determination was a vehicle for decolonization, not an authorization of secession.[40] As Margaret Moore explains:

> Whereas self-determination in the Wilsonian period was conceived of as the political independence of ethnic or national communities—a conception that still has force today—the principle has been elaborated in international law in the post-Second World War period to make clear that the 'peoples' in question are not ethnic or national groups, but, rather, multi-ethnic people under colonial rule.[41]

[37] Eleanor Roosevelt, 'The Universal Validity of Man's Right to Self-determination' (1952) XXVII(702) Department of State Bulletin 919. <https://babel.hathitrust.org/cgi/pt?id=msu.31293008121307;view=1up;seq=395> accessed 2 August 2022.

[38] Lee C Buchheit, *Secession: The Legitimacy of Self-determination* (Yale UP 1978) 84.

[39] ibid 84. Note the reservation included by India: 'With reference to Article 1 . . . , the Government of the Republic of India declares that the word "the right to self-determination" appearing in those articles apply only to the peoples under foreign domination and that these words do not apply to sovereign independent States or to a section of a people or nation—which is the essence of national integrity.' <https://indicators.ohchr.org> accessed 2 August 2022. Hannum explains that such reservation 'represents in direct terms the view of many countries which support a restricted interpretation of self-determination' and that only three States filed objections to the Indian reservation. Hannum (n 25) 42.

[40] Buchheit (n 38) 87.

[41] Margaret Moore, 'Introduction' in Margaret Moore (ed), *National Self-determination and Secession* (OUP 1998) 3.

In this regard, note the comments made by UN Secretary General U Thant at a press conference in Dakar on 9 January 1970 regarding the conflict between Biafra and Nigeria:

> You will recall that the United Nations spent over 500$ million in the Congo primarily to prevent the secession of Katanga from the Congo. So, as far as the question of secession of a particular section of a Member State is concerned, the United Nations' attitude is unequivocable [sic]. As an international organization, the United Nations has never accepted and does not accept and I do not believe it will ever accept the principle of secession of a part of its Member State.[42]

As Musgrave explains, this conflict illustrates the problems surrounding the proper meaning of self-determination:

> Nigeria maintained that the right of self-determination was simply that of decolonization in a non-self-governing territory, and that once this had occurred the territorial integrity of the emergent independent state was inviolable. Biafra, on the other hand, asserted that the right of self-determination was available to any people with a grievance, and that it included the right to secede.[43]

The UN did not accept the position of Biafra. Thus, despite the references of 'all' peoples in the UN General Assembly (UNGA) Resolutions and in the two International Covenants, in practice the right of self-determination has been limited to peoples under colonial or alien domination. No State has accepted the right of 'all' peoples to self-determination. In fact, it is the principle of national unity that has been almost universally followed by the international community, which, after all, is composed of States whose interest is to protect their own boundaries. 'State practice and the overwhelming view of States remain opposed to secession. Indeed, it seems that this is one of the few areas on which full agreement exists among all States.'[44] In effect, it became evident that the definition of peoples 'was that of non-European inhabitants of former colonies, without further regard for ethnicity, language, religion, or other objective characteristics of such colonized peoples (apart from the fact of colonization itself)'.[45] Cassese reminds us that States have consistently opposed an understanding of the right to self-determination that goes beyond three areas: as an anti-colonialist standard, as a ban on foreign military occupation, and as a standard requiring that those racial groups be given full access to government.[46] These two latter fields refer, basically, to the cases of

[42] (1970) VII (2) UN Monthly Chronicle 36.
[43] Musgrave (n 13) 197.
[44] Cassese, *Self-determination of Peoples. A Legal Reappraisal* (n 11) 123–24.
[45] Hannum (n 25) 36.
[46] Cassese, *Self-determination of Peoples. A Legal Reappraisal* (n 11) 319.

Namibia when it was subject to military occupation and to the apartheid regime of South Africa. Apart from these two examples, 'a brief look into the historical evolution of the right of self-determination tells us that there is only one clear core area where the bearer of the right is beyond dispute: the case of decolonization'.[47] And decolonization referred to the whole territory under colonial rule. An example of this shared approach can be found in the view expressed by the British Foreign Minister in 1983 in Westminster when replying to a question about the problem of self-determination for Somalis in Ethiopia:

> Our position is one of support for the Organisation of African Unity policy of accepting the colonial boundaries inherited by the newly-independent African states: indeed, it has been widely accepted at the United Nations that the right of self-determination does not give every distinct group or territorial sub-division within a State the right to secede from it and thereby dismember the territorial integrity or political unity of sovereign independent States.[48]

African States, who were among the leaders in developing the post-1945 right in the context of decolonization, have been the ones adopting an extraordinarily narrow interpretation. Because of the extreme ethnic heterogeneity of most African States and the resulting difficulties in developing a sense of statehood in the immediate post-independence period, the principles of territorial integrity and unity have been determined to be more fundamental than that of self-determination. As Pomerance says, the UN 'has opted for the *territorial* over the ethnic criterion'.[49] Clearly, the international community did abandon the Wilsonian approach. In effect, the 1964 Cairo Declaration of the Organisation of African Unity established as a principle the intangibility of borders inherited from colonization (*uti possidetis juiris* principle). Thus, the idea of ethnic self-determination, or the creation of new nations out of the existing States, was rejected categorically by recently independent African States.[50] The fear was that the same right that had enabled their freedom would end up carving up their territory.[51] The conclusion is very simple: ethnic groups within States, indigenous populations or minorities have never been recognized as holders of a right to self-determination involving secession,[52] but only

[47] Oeter (n 21) 53.

[48] [1983] British Yearbook of International Law 409.

[49] Michla Pomerance, *Self-Determination in Law and Practice. The New Doctrine in the United Nations* (Martinus Nijhoff 1982) 18.

[50] For instance, the 1963 Constitution of Senegal prohibited 'any act of racial, ethnic or religious discrimination and any regionalist propaganda prejudicial to the internal security of the State or to the integrity of the territory of the Republic'. This provision is still in force and can be found in art 5 of the current Constitution of Senegal, proclaimed in 2001.

[51] 'It is precisely those States which benefited from the principle of self-determination when they liberated themselves from colonial rule, which now rank among the staunchest supporters of a strict interpretation of self-determination.' Cassese, *Self-determination of Peoples. A Legal Reappraisal* (n 11) 318.

[52] Christian Tomuschat, 'Secession and Self-determination' in Marcelo G Kohen (ed), *Secession: International Law Perspectives* (CUP 2012) 34–37.

the colonial people as a whole.[53] Self-determination is a child of the UNGA and in the eye of the GA, as Tomuschat explains, 'external self-determination as a right to establish an independent State does not exist for ethnic communities which constitute integral elements of a sovereign State'.[54] Koskenniemi, for instance, admits (although in his view this is somehow arbitrary) the 'domestication' of national self-determination since it is limited to decolonization, and Weller has pointed out that 'the immense power of the doctrine of colonial self-determination is however balanced by its restrictive field of application in the colonial context'.[55]

Recent cases of independence like the ones from East Timor and South Sudan, that have received the endorsement of the UN, do not reflect changes in public international law. Needless to say, these countries became independent because they received at some point, and for different reasons, the support of some powerful States. But their independence processes also had some normative support. It could be argued that both situations, considered by many as examples of secession, enjoyed a normative backing since both are, arguably, cases of delayed decolonization, and therefore cases that could fall within the scope of the UN right to self-determination.[56]

[53] Cassese, *Self-determination of Peoples. A Legal Reappraisal* (n 11) 331. In this sense, Margiotta points out that in the event 'the international community decides to recognize a right to secede, there should be no reference to self-determination, as the latter has never provided the delineation of borders'. Costanza Margiotta, 'An Update on Secession as the "Ultimate Right"' in Carlos Closa, Costanza Margiotta, and Giuseppe Martinico (eds), *Between Democracy and Law. The Amorality of Secession* (Routledge 2020) 16.

[54] Tomuschat (n 52) 37.

[55] Martti Koskenniemi, 'National Self-determination Today: Problems of Legal Theory and Practice' (1994) 43 International and Comparative Law Quarterly 241, 242; Marc Weller, 'Secession and Self-determination in Western Europe: The Case of Catalonia' (*Blog of the European Journal of International Law*, 18 October 2017) <https://www.ejiltalk.org/secession-and-self-determination-in-western-europe-the-case-of-catalonia/> accessed 2 August 2022. See also Fabry: 'there is continuing general agreement that self-determination cannot be made into a universal positive right'. Mikulas Fabry, *Recognizing States. International Society and the Establishment of New States Since 1776* (OUP 2010) 220. As Margiotta underlines, 'the international community deplores secession'. Outside the colonial context, 'the strenuous defence of the prerogatives of external sovereignty, [which] requires the absence of a right of secession in the international legal system'. Margiotta (n 53) 14.

[56] The case of East Timor seems very clear. The UN Security Council had already in the 1970s admitted the 'inalienable right of the people of East Timor to self-determination and independence in accordance with the principles of the Charter of the United Nations and the Declaration on the Granting of Independence to Colonial Countries and Peoples'. UN Security Council Resolution 384 (1975), of 22 December. See also UN Security Council Resolution 389 (1976), of 22 April. The ICJ also confirmed the view that East Timor fitted in within the decolonization paradigm when, in 1995, in a case between Portugal and Australia concerning maritime resources, it affirmed, after concluding its lack of jurisdiction, that '[t]he Court recalls in any event that it has taken note in the present Judgment (paragraph 31) that, for the two Parties, the Territory of East Timor remains a non-self-governing territory and its people has the right to self-determination'. *East Timor (Portugal v Australia)*, Judgment, ICJ Reports 1995 90, para 37. Thus, clearly, the 1999 independence of East Timor cannot be considered a departure from the traditional UN doctrine on self-determination, but a reassurance, although delayed. As for South Sudan, its independence and its quick incorporation into the international community as a sovereign and independent State cannot be confused with a broad acceptance of secession in international law. First, the independence process was a consensual one. South Sudan counted on the backing of North Sudan. Secondly, as in the case of East Timor where the territory was clearly considered a non-self-governing unit, it could also be argued that South Sudan was a case of delayed colonialism. 'It is possible to argue that the South Sudan's exercise of self-determination is a case of

4.3 How Was Self-determination Viewed in Europe, Outside the Colonial Context?

The European Convention on Human Rights and Fundamental Freedoms (ECHR, 1950) contains no provision regarding self-determination. Later, both the 1975 Helsinki Final Act[57] and the 1990 Charter of Paris[58] refer to the right to self-determination, since it had already crystallized as a key principle of international law. However, both documents emphasized the need to implement it in conformity with the UN Charter and with the relevant norms of international law, including those relating to the territorial integrity of States. How then to reconcile self-determination and territorial integrity? Europe turned its eyes to the concept of internal self-determination by promoting pluralistic democratic societies where minority rights are protected and promoted.[59] In effect, international organizations across Europe have promoted 'the development of *internal* self-determination, namely, the guaranteeing of democratic, representative government for all groups residing in the State'.[60] The Council of Europe, either through the European Court of Human Rights (ECtHR) or the Venice Commission,[61] has never recognized a right to secede to minorities.[62] This reluctance 'reflects the

delayed decolonization: that South Sudan should have been granted independence at decolonization and should not have been incorporated into the larger state of Sudan.' Milena Sterio, *The Right to Self-determination under International Law. 'Selfistans', Secession, and the Rule of the Great Power* (Routledge 2013) 167. Having said that, although South Sudan independence might not have altered the state of the law, the political impact of the process in the region should not be ignored. 'The quest for secession in South Sudan, which is generally regarded as a case of a failed attempt at equal participation and socio-economic opportunities among people of different identities, may become a reference point for other excluded or marginalised groups and communities in other African countries. The South Sudanese experience may thus inspire such groups and communities to explore secession as a means to address their perceived political exclusion and socio-economic marginalisation sustainably.' Mupenda Wakengela and Sadiki Koko, 'The Referendum for Self-determination in South Sudan and its Implication for the Post-Colonial State in Africa' (2001) 3 Conflict Trends 20, 26.

57 1975 Helsinki Final Act, Principle VIII: 'The participating States will respect the equal rights of peoples and their right to self-determination, acting at all times in conformity with the purposes and principles of the Charter of the United Nations and with the relevant norms of international law, including those relating to territorial integrity of States.'

58 1990 Charter of Paris: 'We reaffirm the equal rights of peoples and their right to self-determination in conformity with the Charter of the United Nations and with the relevant norms of international law, including those relating to territorial integrity of States.'

59 Dinah Shelton, 'Self-determination and Secession: The Jurisprudence of International Human Rights Tribunals' in Julie Dahlitz (ed), *Secession and International Law* (T.M.C. Asser Press 2003) 55.

60 Pazartzis (n 2) 359–60.

61 In 2000, the Venice Commission stated that '[t]he principle of territorial integrity commands very widespread recognition—whether express or tacit—in constitutional law. On the other hand, constitutional law just as comprehensively rules out secession or the redrawing of borders. This should come as no surprise since that branch of law is the very foundation of the state, which might be deprived of one of its constituent parts if such possibilities were provided for.' Venice Commission, 'A general legal reference framework to facilitate the settlement of ethno-political conflicts in Europe', CDL-INF (2000) 16, 3.

62 Pazartzis (n 2) 361.

state of the law'.[63] Neither has the Badinter Commission, an international arbitration commission set up by the then European Community to legally deal with the Yugoslav crisis, dared to recognize any right to secede, despite the fact that the preamble of the 1974 Constitution of Yugoslavia recognized the right to secede to the nations of Yugoslavia.[64] In fact, as Pazartzis explains:

> [T]he legal justification given to the events by the Arbitration Commission, namely the treatment of the disintegration as an instance of dissolution rather than as an exercise of self-determination, served as the legal basis to international recognition, and thus the international response in this case is not seen as creating a precedent in favour of a right of secession.[65]

It is true, however, that the rhetoric of self-determination had an impact in legitimizing the separation of the Yugoslav republics.[66] '[S]elf-determination has operated at the level of *political rhetoric*, as a *set of political principles* legitimizing the secession of national States from central, oppressive States structures.'[67] Cassese argues that despite the fact that demands for secession by minorities do not find any basis in legal norms, 'national and ethnic groups do find support in, and indeed vociferously rely upon, the tenets of political philosophy underpinning the international legal standards (or, alternatively, they invoke what the ordinary man in the street erroneously considers to be self-determination).'[68] Self-determination started to be used by politicians, journalists, and laypersons in general as 'a reference point for undermining the territorial integrity of multi-ethnic States'.[69]

To sum up, outside the colonial context:

> The international community has been extremely reluctant to accept unilateral secession of parts of independent States if the secession is opposed by the government of that State. In such cases the principle of territorial integrity has been a significant limitation. Since 1945 no State which has been created by unilateral secession has been admitted to the United Nations against the declared wishes of the government of the predecessor State. By contrast there are many examples of

[63] Shelton (n 59) 67.

[64] As Karl Lowenstein explained, the content of the Constitution of a communist country cannot be considered normative, but rather it is semantic. Instead of the fundamental norm of a country, communist constitutions tend to be propaganda, being the commands of the ruling communist party, the real source of law. Karl Loewenstein, *Political Power and the Governmental Process* (University of Chicago Press 1957).

[65] Pazartzis (n 2) 372.

[66] Shelton (n 59) 62.

[67] Cassese, *Self-determination of Peoples. A Legal Reappraisal* (n 11) 273.

[68] ibid 339–40.

[69] Rein Müllerson, 'Sovereignty and Secession: Then and Now, Here and There' in Julie Dahlitz (ed), *Secession and International Law* (T.M.C. Asser Press 2003) 141.

failed attempts at unilateral secession, including cases where the seceding entity maintained *de facto* independence for some time.[70]

This is exemplified by the fact that in October 2015, bearing in mind the Catalan pro-independence movement, the former UN Secretary General Ban Ki Mun admitted in an interview to a Catalan newspaper that although the UN has accepted the right to self-determination under certain circumstances, 'Catalonia does not fit within the category of territories entitled to self-determination'.[71] He made clear that those territories enjoying self-government (internal self-determination) within a well-established State do not benefit from the right to external self-determination.

5. Unilateral Secession Rejected Almost Unequivocally: Kosovo as a Unique Case

The end of the Cold War has not modified the previously established practice.[72] '[P]ractice has continued to inhibit secession without consent of the sovereign government in question as a legitimate way of acquiring statehood'.[73] The secessionist movements in Nagorno-Karabakh (Azerbaijan), Abkhazia and South Ossetia (Georgia), and Transnitria (Moldova) have all been met with general foreign non-recognition, except for Russia.[74] In addition, the 2014 crisis in Crimea is an example of the traditional reluctance of the international community to accept unilateral declarations of independence. This latter case is aggravated by the fact that the referendum process was backed by foreign troops. However, it is true that the major Western powers recognized the unilateral independence of Kosovo in

[70] Crawford (n 5) 390. Pazartzis reaches the same conclusion: 'State practice with regard to secessionist movements witnessed in Europe does not support the existence of a right of secession as an aspect of self-determination. The strongly prevailing view of the international community is that, beyond the right of peoples under colonial or other comparable alien domination, self-determination support will not be given to secession from an existing State against the will of the government of that State.' Pazartzis (n 2) 371.

[71] Fernando García, 'Ban Ki Mun: "Cataluña no está en la categoría e territorios con derecho a la autodeterminación"' *La Vanguardia* (Barcelona, 30 October 2015) <https://www.lavanguardia.com/politica/20151030/54438498099/ban-ki-moon-catalunya-derecho-autodeterminacion.html> accessed 24 November 2018.

[72] Oeter (n 21) 59.

[73] Fabry (n 55) 179.

[74] These cases will not be reviewed in this book, given the limited EU involvement. Nicu Popescu, *EU Foreign Policy and Post-Soviet Conflicts. Stealth Intervention* (Routledge 2011) 20. Scholars note that 'the EU remains an observer, rather than a policy shaper'. Bohdana Dimitrovova, 'Imperial Re-bordering of Europe: The Case of the European Neighbourhood Policy' (2012) 25(2) Cambridge Review of International Affairs 249, 253. The main reason for this low involvement and observer status is that the EU does not want to undermine its relationship with Russia. Stephen Keukeleire and Tom Delreux, *The Foreign Policy of the European Union* (2nd edn, Palgrave 2014) 261.

2008,[75] although they 'went to extraordinary lengths to justify their move as a special, non-precedent-creating exception to, rather than as a qualification or abandonment of, the post-decolonization norm of territorial integrity'.[76] Recall that in the Kosovo Opinion the ICJ did not address a general question about the right to secede in a post-colonial scenario. It assumed that this was not covered by the narrow and specific General Assembly question. The Court limited the scope of its Opinion to the question of whether Kosovo's declaration as such violated international law. In an exercise of self-restraint, the ICJ avoided treating the case as a leading Opinion that could settle a contested issue. The Court might have feared that sanctioning the unilateral Declaration of Independence as lawful might open Pandora's Box, and that is why it avoided any pronouncement on the legality of secession, admitting only that such a declaration did not violate international law.[77] The US and the rest of the recognizing States tried to avoid labelling the case as a legal situation. 'There simply did not exist any normative argument that could override Serbia's legitimate interest in territorial integrity'.[78] Instead, they preferred to insist on the uniqueness of Kosovo: the NATO intervention, it was argued, was motivated by human rights concerns.[79]

Explicit in this message was that Kosovo could never be a model for any other separatist movement, and that Kosovo was not about remedial secession or external self-determination. Rather, Kosovo was simply unique—because the great powers had decided so. Kosovo illustrates the great powers' rule at its best, as well as the evisceration of legal rules on self-determination in favour of political determination and strategic factors.[80]

In any case, the recognition of Kosovo has met strong resistance and 'the international community remains divided over whether such recognition makes sense (or is even legally feasible)'.[81] As a proof of such division, note that Kosovo is not

[75] In fact, in 2014 Kosovo was used by Russia, as the latter had done in the past with the 2008 Georgian conflict, as the precedent that justified Crimean annexation. See in this regard the discussion between Nico Krisch, Christian Marxsen, and Anne Peters at the Blog of the European Journal of International Law. Anne Peters, 'Crimea: Does the West Now Pay the Price for Kosovo?' (*Blog of the European Journal of International Law*, 22 April 2014 <https://www.ejiltalk.org/crimea-does-the-west-now-pay-the-price-for-kosovo/> accessed 2 August 2022.

[76] Fabry (n 55) 180. This position has been consistently held in the following years. For instance, this was the opinion of the UK in the 2010 Security Council meeting that discussed the ICJ Advisory Opinion: 'Kosovo is a unique case. Its independence is contingent on its particular facts. It does not provide a template for secession elsewhere.' See UN doc S/PV.6367 3 August 2010 <http://www.un.org/ga/search/view_doc.asp?symbol=S/PV.6367&Lang=E> accessed 2 August 2022.

[77] Walter (n 17) 25.

[78] Oeter (n 21) 66.

[79] Stephen Tierney, 'The Long Intervention in Kosovo: A Self-Determination Imperative?' in James Summers (ed), *Kosovo: A Precedent? The Declaration of Independence, the Advisory Opinion and Implications for Statehood, Self-determination and Minority Rights* (Martinus Nijhoff 2011) 249. See the Statement Issued at the Extraordinary Ministerial Meeting of the North Atlantic Council held at NATO Headquarters, Brussels, on 12 April 1999, declaring that the 'massive humanitarian catastrophe' justifies the military action <https://www.nato.int/docu/pr/1999/p99-051e.htm> accessed 2 August 2022.

[80] Sterio, *The Right to Self-determination under International Law* (n 56) 125.

[81] Oeter (n 21) 45.

yet a member of the UN or the Council of Europe. Tierney asks whether Kosovo is an example of the international community adopting a wider approach to self-determination.[82] Clearly, for recognizing States, Kosovo was not meant to be a precedent, but it remains to be seen to what extent it has an impact on future self-determination struggles and on the perception of individual States on this.[83]

6. Current Theories of the Right to Self-determination

Some claim that the current conception of self-determination fails to pay regard to the aspirations of nations and minorities.[84] However, others argue that international law offers a last resort option for entities outside the colonial context, the so-called safeguard clause of paragraph 7 of the principle of self-determination of (1970) UNGA 2625 Resolution:

> Nothing in the foregoing paragraphs shall be construed as authorizing or encouraging any action which would dismember or impair, totally or in part, the territorial integrity or political unity of sovereign and independent States conducting themselves in compliance with the principle of equal rights and self-determination of peoples as described above and thus possessed of a government representing the whole people belonging to the territory without distinction as to race, creed or colour.

It has been said that paragraph 7 seems to recognize the legitimacy of secession under certain circumstances outside the colonial context.[85] What are these circumstances? *A contrario*, a government not representing the whole people belonging to the territory without distinction as to race, creed, or colour.

[82] Tierney, 'The Long Intervention in Kosovo: A Self-determination Imperative?' (n 79) 276.

[83] Snezana Trifunovska, 'The Impact of the Kosovo Precedent on Self-determination Struggles' in James Summers (ed), *Kosovo: A Precedent? The Declaration of Independence, the Advisory Opinion and Implications for Statehood, Self-Determination and Minority Rights* (Martinus Nijhoff 2011) 375. In fact, not everyone agrees that Kosovo is not setting a dangerous precedent: 'To accept otherwise, to allow any ethnic, linguistic or religious group to declare independence and break away from the territory of the State of which it forms part, outside the context of decolonization, creates a very dangerous precedent. Indeed, it amounts to nothing less than announcing to any and all dissident groups around the world that they are free to circumvent international law simply by acting in a certain way and crafting a unilateral declaration of independence, using certain terms.' Dissenting Opinion of Judge Koroma to be found in *Accordance with International Law of the Unilateral Declaration of Independence in Respect of Kosovo* (n 16).

[84] Cassese, *Self-determination of Peoples. A Legal Reappraisal* (n 11) 325. Sterio, for instance, argues that 'international law is manifestly outmoded, because it does not address secession outside the context of decolonization or foreign occupation. Most secessions in the modern-day occur outside of these two paradigms, and it would be preferable to develop an international law framework to apply to such secessions, instead of letting politics dominate and determine secessionist outcomes.' Sterio, *Secession in International Law* (n 3) 162.

[85] Buchheit (n 38) 92, 93.

> [I]f a government does not represent the whole people it is illegitimate and thus in violation of the principle of self-determination, and this illegitimate character serves in turn to legitimate 'action which would dismember or impair, totally or in part, the territorial integrity or political unity' of the sovereign and independent State.[86]

Based on these stipulations in the (1970) UNGA 2625 Resolution, many scholars and commentators have argued that there exists a so-called 'remedial' right of secession.[87]

6.1 What Is Remedial Secession?

There is no international document, apart from UNGA Resolution 2625, that clarifies the meaning and scope of remedial secession. In fact, there is considerable legal debate.[88] Some commentators maintain that it is narrowly worded so as to provide very little real basis for secession. Pomerance, for example, notes that the racial context of the period might have influenced the wording of the paragraph and that one possible interpretation could be to deduce that paragraph 7 restricts this right to racist regimes.[89] Other commentators have interpreted paragraph 7 much more broadly. For them, 'paragraph 7 represents only one aspect of a wider rationale for secession. Therefore, even if the criteria of paragraph 7 are not strictly satisfied, secession will still be legitimate if there have been other serious violations of fundamental human rights.'[90] Thus, 'the parameters of oppression ... extend far beyond

[86] ibid.

[87] Radan, 'Secessionist Referenda in International and Domestic Law' (n 7) 11. It is probably in the field of political philosophy where this theory has found most support. In 1991 Allen Buchanan launched the contemporary moral debate about secession with *Secession: the Morality of Political Divorce from Fort Sumter to Lithuania and Quebec*. In this work, he advanced the idea of remedial secession. Wayne Norman has also become a well-known defendant of this theory. See, for instance, Wayne Norman, 'The Ethics of Secession as the Regulation of Secessionist Politics' in Margaret Moore (ed), *National Self-determination and Secession* (OUP 1998).

[88] Not everyone accepts that a qualified right to secession can be deduced from the safeguard clause. See <REF:BKCH>Daniel Thürer and Thomas Burri, 'Secession' in *Max Planck Encyclopedia of Public International Law* (OUP 2009) para 17. See also James Summers, *Peoples and International Law: How Nationalism and Self-determination Shape a Contemporary Law of Nations* (Martinus Nijhoff 2007). Torroja Mateu believes that those defending the existence of the so-called 'remedial secession' commit an error of isolated misinterpretation. Torroja Mateu (n 6) 154. López Martín and Perea Unceta also reject the idea that there is a conventional norm that recognizes a right of secession in favour of peoples integrated in States and after analysing international practice, they also conclude that 'it can be stated that there is no international custom that justifies extending the right of self-determination of peoples and/or establishes a right to secede as a last resort due to the serious and discriminatory violation of a minority population within a State. Its existence has not been claimed by the majority of States or international organisations, neither in most of the successful cases nor in rejecting those that have been thwarted or that survive without general recognition.' López Martín and Perea Unceta (n 6) 107.

[89] Pomerance (n 49) 39.

[90] Musgrave (n 13) 188.

the strict confines of paragraph 7 of Resolution 2625 (XXV)'.[91] For Tomuschat, the threshold must be high:

> A mere lack of representativeness of a government would not suffice to bring about a right to secession as a form of a right of resistance. The phrase employed rightly conveys the idea that exceptional circumstances are capable of sustaining a claim for secession—circumstances which may roughly be summarized as a grave and massive violation of the human rights of a specific group in a discriminatory fashion.[92]

In the same vein, Oeter believes as follows:

> Only if the fundamental right to survival of such distinct groups are put in danger, by forms of genocide, massive 'ethnic cleansing', gross and consistent patterns of violations of fundamental human rights that threaten to destroy the group, may a legal claim directed towards separate statehood makes sense. Separate statehood is 'remedial' in these cases since it cures a proven impossibility to live together in one state.[93]

And Hannum considers that 'international law should recognize a right to secession only in the rare circumstance when the physical existence of a territorially concentrated group is threatened by gross violations of fundamental human rights'.[94]

Thus, remedial secession becomes a tool for genuine cases of extreme emergency.[95] At the same time, these authors admit that State practice is extremely reluctant to accept such reasoning[96] or at least it does not show sufficient and compelling support.[97] In conclusion, even if we side with those authors accepting the existence of a right to remedial secession, we must concede that there is not enough consistent international practice, as was made clear by the 2010 Kosovo Advisory Opinion. The ICJ was presented with the opportunity to clarify the law on this issue. Nevertheless, as has been noted, the Opinion avoided dealing with the substantive question of whether a right to remedial secession exists. The Court considered that there is no consensus 'regarding whether international law provides

[91] ibid 191.

[92] Tomuschat (n 52) 35. Tomuschat argues that the Kosovo case meets those requirements, coming 'within the purview of remedial secession'. ibid 42.

[93] Oeter (n 21) 57. Anderson also argues that customary law requires human rights abuses *in extremis*, despite his belief that a lower threshold should suffice. Anderson (n 1) 17.

[94] Hurst Hannum, 'Rethinking Self-Determination' (1993) 34(1) Vienna Journal of International Law 1, 47.

[95] Oeter (n 21) 60.

[96] ibid 58–59.

[97] Van Driest (n 25) 187.

for a right of "remedial secession" and, if so, in what circumstances'.[98] Moreover, the Court realized that it was not necessary to resolve this question in order to deliver an Opinion in the case at hand.[99] Thus, in an exercise of judicial minimalism[100] and self-restraint, the Court decided to leave open the issue of remedial secession. This case, with hugely diverse written statements, is the best illustration of the fact that States have not yet reached a consensus around this issue.[101]

6.2 International Bodies and Remedial Secession

To date, no court has granted the right to remedial secession. However, there are different cases where international bodies have admitted the existence of such a right, although the circumstances at hand did not convince them of the suitability of its application. In 1995 after a request to recognize the independence of Katanga, the African Commission on Human and People's Rights considered the following:

> In the absence of concrete evidence of violations of human rights to the point that the territorial integrity of Zaire should be called into question and in the absence of evidence that the people of Katanga are denied the right to

[98] *Accordance with International Law of the Unilateral Declaration of Independence in Respect of Kosovo* (n 16) para 82.

[99] ibid para 83. However, in two separate Opinions, Judge Yusuf and Cancado-Trincade endorsed the view that a remedial right of secession did exist in international law, while Judge Koroma came to the opposite conclusion.

[100] Walter (n 17) 19. The ICJ Opinion has been criticized for being 'undoubtedly frustrating—for not taking the opportunity to resolve the scholarly dispute—and extremely cowardly, as its purely advisory nature means that it could have been extended to other matters deemed to be connected to the literal question, as the validity and conditions of a possible international law of secession clearly are.' López Martín and Perea Unceta (n 6) 114. It is true that the Court did not address many of the questions that underpinned the request: the need for Serbian consent following the spirit of the UNSC 1244 Resolution; Kosovo's positive entitlement to statehood in accordance with self-determination theory; the consequences of the declaration of independence and the issue of the validity of recognition by third States. This was probably due to the narrowly framed question submitted by the General Assembly. Marc Weller, 'Modesty Can Be a Virtue: Judicial Economy in the ICJ Kosovo Opinion?' (2011) 24(1) Leiden Journal of International Law 127, 132.

[101] 'While the claim that there is a "right of secession of last resort" has been supported by some writers and by *a contrario* reasoning . . . , it is without support in State practice. It has not emerged as a rule of customary law. It is not found in any treaty. And it has no support from the practice of the UN.' Written Statement of the Republic of Cyprus, 3 April 2009, para 143. Similar claims are to be found in the written statements of Argentina, China, Brazil, Serbia, Chile, Spain, Romania, Iran, and Venezuela. On the other hand, Germany concluded that while the right to self-determination should, as a rule, be exercised internally, the same right 'may exceptionally legitimize secession if this can be shown to be the only remedy against a prolonged and rigorous refusal of internal self-determination'. Written Statement of Germany, 15 April 2009, para VI.2. Similar arguments to be found in the written statements of the UK, Russia (although it held that it was not applicable to the case of Kosovo), Albania, Estonia, Finland, Ireland, the Netherlands, Poland, Slovenia, Switzerland, Jordan, Japan, Latvia, and the Czech Republic. Remaining States did not declare themselves in favour of accepting remedial secession, like the US. The lack of unanimous *opinio iuris* shows how legally unconvincing this supposedly legal concept is. López Martín and Perea Unceta (n 6) 115.

> participate in government as guaranteed by Article 13(1) of the African Charter, the Commission holds the view that Katanga is obliged to exercise a variant of self-determination that is compatible with the sovereignty and territorial integrity of Zaire.[102]

Reasoning *a contrario*, arguably, it could be inferred that the African Commission admitted the possibility of remedial secession if there was (1) evidence of violations of human rights and/or (2) denial of people's right to participate in government. However, in the case at hand it did not consider that those circumstances were present. In 2009, the African Commission reasserted this view when referring to the right of self-determination of the population of Southern Cameroon. It noted that the test set out in the Katanga case (ie violations of human rights and/or denial of people's right to participate in government) had to be met in order to have a basis for the exercise of an external self-determination (ie secession).[103] Although the ECtHR has never addressed this issue explicitly or directly, in the 1996 landmark case of *Loizidou v Turkey*, Judge Wildhaber, joined by Judge Ryssdal, admitted in their concurring Opinion as follows:

> Until recently in international practice the right to self-determination was in practical terms identical to, and indeed restricted to, a right to decolonisation. In recent years a consensus has seemed to emerge that peoples may also exercise a right to [external] self-determination if their human rights are consistently and flagrantly violated or if they are without representation at all or are massively under-represented in an undemocratic and discriminatory way.[104]

The reference to remedial secession was only to be found in a separate Opinion. Yet, it shows how this theory has been gaining support among international judges. For instance, the Spanish Constitutional Court, in its 17 October 2017 judgment annulling Catalan Law 19/2017, of 6 September, on the Self-determination Referendum, which will be addressed in the next chapter, admitted the existence of remedial secession: 'The alleged right of separation is only possible in cases of colonial domination, peoples annexed by conquest, foreign domination or occupation, and peoples oppressed by massive and flagrant violation of their rights' (author's own translation).[105] However, needless to say, the Court did not consider it to be applicable to the case at hand.

[102] *Katangese Peoples' Congress v Zaire*, African Commission on Human and Peoples' Rights, Comm No 75/92 (1995) para 6.

[103] *Kevin Mgwanga Gunme et al / Cameroon*, African Commission on Human and Peoples' Rights, Comm No 266/03 (2009) para 194.

[104] *Loizidou v Turkey* App no 15318/89 (ECtHR, 18 December 1996).

[105] STC 114/2017, 17 October, para I.1 G.

In any event, to date, no judicial body has accepted a (qualified) right to unilateral secession as an entitlement of a particular people in a specific case.[106]

6.3 Right to Remedial Secession for Sub-national Entities

Even if we accept the existence of the right to remedial secession, 'what seems to be required is a denial of political freedom and/or human rights as a *sine qua non*'.[107] Would Quebecers, Welsh, Scots, Catalans, or Flemish qualify for such a right? Should the EU admit and honour a right provided by international law to regional entities within EU Member States wishing to secede? As Buchheit admits:

> Their respective States are under no obligation imposed by international law to recognize their demands beyond providing protection for human rights, a representative government that does not discriminate on the basis of race, creed, or colour, and the other requirements set forth in the declaration.[108]

It is difficult to imagine that in 'prosperous and fairly stable and just multinational states' like Canada, Spain, UK, and Belgium,[109] any sub-national entity could qualify for such a right. As stated in the well-known 1998 Supreme Court of Canada Opinion on Quebec:

> The population of Quebec cannot plausibly be said to be denied access to government. Quebecers occupy prominent positions within the government of Canada. Residents of the province freely make political choices and pursue economic, social and cultural development within Quebec, across Canada, and throughout the world. The population of Quebec is equitably represented in legislative, executive and judicial institutions.[110]

Fasone states forcefully that '[n]o region within the EU Member States is definitely in the exceptional situation of oppression, violation of human rights, or colonisation which could allow a seceding territory to struggle for its self-determination'.[111]

Further, more importantly, '[t]he continuing failure to reach agreement on amendments to the Constitution, while a matter of concern, does not amount to

[106] Van Driest (n 25) 186.
[107] Buchheit (n 38) 94.
[108] ibid.
[109] Daniel Weinstock, 'Constitutionalizing the Right to Secede' (2001) 9(2) Journal of Political Philosophy 182, 200.
[110] *Reference re Secession of Quebec* [1998] 2 SCC 217, para 136.
[111] Cristina Fasone, 'Secession and the Ambiguous Place of Regions Under EU Law' in Carlos Closa (ed), *Secession from a Member State and Withdrawal from the European Union* (CUP 2017) 65.

a denial of self-determination'.[112] In this sense, Weller argued that Catalonia could be tempted to invoke the doctrine of remedial secession following the suspension of autonomy in 2017,[113] but he admits firstly that remedial secession is a contested doctrine and secondly that it is unclear whether the amount of 'repression' suffered in Catalonia is sufficient to trigger the referred doctrine:

> According to that still contested doctrine, repression of a population, or its exclusion from representation in the state, generates a self-determination entitlement in the sense of secession. However, it is not clear that the gravity of repression or exclusion is sufficiently well established as yet to trigger the application of the doctrine.[114]

In any event, if we ever face a situation of gross violation of human rights or significant denial of internal self-determination within an EU Member State that can qualify for remedial secession, there would be a need to trigger article 7 TEU without any hesitation. Otherwise the whole European project would be put at risk.

7. Primary Right Theories

Primary right theories conceive of the right to secede as a general right. These theories have been conceived as the modern, non-colonial version of the right to self-determination.[115] Nationalist theory of secession claims that 'nations have a right to self-determination, including a right to a state in which the members of the nation form a majority'.[116] The choice theory of secession, a more radical approach, simply states that if the majority in a region express a desire to secede, such withdrawal of consent serves as a sufficient and effective ground for separation. Unlike in the previous nationalist theory, there is no need to prove that the group is a nation, culturally or ethnically distinct. In both cases, there is no need to prove any injustice or wrongdoing from the central government. Both theories anchor the legitimacy of secession in the value of democracy and of individual autonomy.[117]

112 *Reference re Secession of Quebec* (n 110) para 137.

113 A suspension that lasted from 27 October 2017 to 2 June 2018, when, following Catalan regional elections held on 21 December 2017, all members of the new pro-independence but law-abiding Catalan government took office and the suspension was automatically lifted.

114 Weller, 'Secession and Self-determination in Western Europe: The Case of Catalonia' (n 55). Bossacoma, who believes that liberty, equality, democracy, and self-determination upheld by political liberalism tilt the balance towards tolerating and in certain cases protecting secession, seems to argue that violations of intra-State autonomy agreements, failure to negotiate in good faith, or failed attempts to negotiate should give rise to a right to secede. Bossacoma Pau, *Morality and Legality of Secession. A Theory of National Self-determination* (Palgrave 2020) 180. The problem with this argument, though, is the lack of clarity to decide when such a situation exists and who should decide that this is so.

115 Bengoetxea (n 36) 40.

116 Norman (n 87) 35.

117 Daniel Philpott, 'In Defense of Self-determination' (1995) 105(2) Ethics 352, 367.

What generates this right is simply the same feature that generates all States and political groupings, namely freedom of association. The critical element to political obligation is consent or the continued will to belong. Secession occurs by virtue of the withdrawal of consent to be bound to a particular political body. It is a no-fault divorce.[118] Following that, a majority voting in a referendum or its functional equivalent (democratic elections) could be enough to trigger an independence process. As Nielsen explains:

> The right of secession should be treated like the right to a no-fault divorce.... No prior or imminent injustice need be shown in either case. If the parties want to split in either case, they have the right to split provided certain harms (not all harms) do not accrue to the other party.[119]

However, the very same authors who defend this position acknowledge that '[t]he mainstream international law position holds that the right of peoples to self-determination does not accord a right to statehood, even when there is a democratic vote for independence or its functional equivalent'.[120] Although these theories have some defenders within the field of political philosophy, few lawyers make these arguments. In fact, no international treaty, Resolution, document, or international court has ever defended this possibility. The reason is straightforward: territorial integrity is a key principle governing international relations and States only accept that it is trumped if there are strong justifications. If it were otherwise, order and stability would be put seriously at risk.

These primary right theories have found particularly strong advocates in the Catalan pro-independence movement. The Catalan government, in its attempt to legitimize its unilateral strategy, has been pushing to introduce into the legal agenda the concept of 'the right to decide', which is closely connected with the choice right theory. It is a legal-political term different from the classic notion

118 Allen Buchanan, *Secession: The Morality of Political Divorce from Fort Sumter to Lithuania and Quebec* (Westview 1991)134. Buchanan, unlike those philosophers who argue in favour of primary right theories, holds that secession is only legitimate if there is a just cause. In fact, for him, not all forms of oppression justify secession: only a few are sufficient and necessary. ibid 108–10.

119 Kai Nielsen, 'Secession: The Case of Quebec' (1993) 10 Journal of Applied Philosophy 29, 35.

120 Steven Wheatley, 'Modelling Democratic Secession in International Law' in Stephen Tierney (ed), *Nationalism and Globalization* (Hart Publishing 2015) 133. Wheatley admits 'no serious academic' argues that Crimea has a right to determine unilaterally its own status, as it did in 2014. However, he is in favour of applying a constitutional model that recognizes a general right of democratic secession, provided that the authorities and the populations engage in reasoned, democratic deliberations concerning the allocation of political authority. ibid 154. This argument, marginal in terms of international support, should not be confused with the growing international requirement of due process, ie that the seceding entity needs to adopt some kind of due process (eg negotiating in good faith, no use of force, granting minority rights to its own minorities) before it declares independence. This is a requirement that finds some support in practice and in scholarly circles. Antonello Tancredi, 'A Normative "Due Process" in the Creation of States through Secession' in Marcelo G Kohen (ed), *Secession: International Law Perspectives* (CUP 2012) 194.

of self-determination created, precisely, due to the difficulties of including the Catalan case in the classic doctrine of the right to self-determination under international law.[121] As explained in a report published originally by the Foreign Affairs Department of the Catalan government and authored by international scholars, the democratic 'right to decide' would justify the Catalan popular demand for a referendum on political independence. According to the authors of this report, the so-called democratic 'right to decide' 'has evolved from the more traditional and long-standing legal framework to the "national right to self-determination". In other words, demands for political independence have been legitimized by a democratic principle invested in the Catalan people.'[122] Again, the problem with this concept is, as Gaudreault-DesBiens explains, that 'no general and absolute legal right to decide exists under international law'. However, certain sectors among the Catalan pro-independence movement constantly affirm its existence because it 'represents a politically efficient discursive strategy'.[123] To speak constantly of a 'right' might have a performative effect, it can convince those who hear about it that their desire is in accordance with the law. However, as noted, this right can be characterized as a moral one at best:

> It may very well be that an international legal regime governing the conditions of exercise of the right to external self-determination by sub-states nations incorporated in democratic states is warranted.... But it does not exist yet, and affirming the contrary, based on an overstretched interpretation of the ICJ's Kosovo opinion, is at best misleading.[124]

8. Conclusions

Since the ICJ 2010 Advisory Opinion on Kosovo, it is clear that international law does not prohibit secession. But a lack of prohibition is not the same as a right. Thus, when it comes to recognizing a unilateral right to external self-determination, or a right to secede, 'States continue to be the prime actors, demarcating their own playing field and the applicable rules of play',[125] among them the principle of territorial integrity. And that is why, outside the colonial context and the emergent

[121] Xavier Pons Ràfols, *Cataluña: Derecho a decidir y derecho internacional* (Reus 2015) 306.

[122] Nicolas Levrat and others, *Catalonia's Legitimate Right to Decide. Paths to Self-determination* (2017) 138 <https://www.unige.ch/gsi/files/9315/0461/7440/CATALONIAS_LEGITIMATE_RIGHT_DECIDE.pdf> accessed 13 February 2024.

[123] Jean-François Gaudreault-DesBiens, 'The Law and Politics of Secession: From the Political Contingency of Secession to a "Right to Decide"? Can Lessons Be Learned from the Quebec Case?' in Giacomo Delledonne and Giuseppe Martinico (eds), *The Canadian Contribution to a Comparative Law of Secession* (Palgrave 2019) 58.

[124] ibid 62. The constant reference to a right probably 'seeks to assuage the fears of citizens who could otherwise have doubts'. ibid 59.

[125] Van Driest (n 25) 319.

theory of remedial secession, 'there is no recognition of a unilateral right to secede based merely on a majority vote of the population of a given sub-division or territory'.[126] In effect, at present there are no international mechanisms or specific norms of international law (either treaty or customary law) which could be used to determine whether a given people has the right to secession, or which would regulate the relationship between a secessionist movement, a State, and third parties.[127] Recently, some authors have tried to advance the idea of a primary right to democratic secession. However, there is no practice, nor international documents nor case law supporting this trend. Nor is the position sustained by a large number of scholars.

To conclude: (1) unilateral declarations of independence by sub-national units (even within well-functioning democracies) could be considered not in violation of international law, but (2) it cannot be argued that such entities qualify for a right to self-determination, since they do not fall within the well-established categories of non-self-governing territories nor within the emerging category of remedial secession. That is why, where there is no massive abuse of human rights, public international law yields the site to national constitutional law. This international law analysis leads to the conclusion that, in terms of EU law's approach towards secession, EU institutions are not constrained by any binding international norm of relevance, provided no situation of gross human rights violations emerges.

[126] Crawford (n 5) 417.
[127] Stanislav V Chernichenko and Vladimir S Kotliar, 'Ongoing Global Legal Debate on Self-determination and Secession: Main Trends' in Julie Dahlitz (ed), *Secession and International Law* (T.M.C. Asser Press 2003) 78, 79.

4
Secession and Constitutional Law

1. Introduction

The aim of this chapter is to analyse constitutional law as it relates to secession. If, as is claimed (and further developed in Chapter 6), the European Union (EU) duty to respect constitutional identity (art 4(2) of the Treaty on European Union (TEU)) generates obligations in the context of secession to respect Member States' constitutional orders, we will have to examine closely EU Member States' constitutional regulations on secession.

Usually, constitutional law is silent when it comes to secession, but certain European States (also the US and Canada) have been obliged to develop a legal approach to secession, since they have faced, or are currently facing, secessionist challenges and the organization, or attempted organization, of referendums on independence, namely the UK and Spain (but also Italy). However, as indicated in Chapter 1, the intention is to offer legal reflection that goes beyond a case-specific approach, which could be of relevance to any EU Member State in the future. Therefore, the chapter offers a broader analysis of constitutionalism (not limited to EU Member States' constitutional legal orders) and secession that might be useful in different scenarios.

First, we will review theoretically the link between constitutionalism and secession. Then, we will analyse those constitutional orders that have emerged as the two main paradigms in this debate: on the one hand, the US (the classic paradigm and the one followed by Spain, Italy, and Germany). On the other hand, the Canadian legal order (the new paradigm[1] and the one followed to a certain extent by the UK and arguably by Belgium). After reviewing the British and Spanish orders, we will also, though briefly, take into account the Italian and German legal orders' position towards secession, since they are the only other EU Member States' legal orders that have expressed a position on this issue. Belgium will also be analysed, because of the importance of the Flemish pro-independence movement, despite there being no clear constitutional framework regarding secession. As will be shown,

[1] The Supreme Court of Canada's 1998 *Reference Re Secession of Quebec* became a turning point in the comparative constitutional law on secession. 'Until then, the overwhelming prevailing constitutional thought assumed that constitutions are based on an inherent principle of self-preservation.' Francesco Palermo, 'Towards a Comparative Constitutional Law of Secession?' in Giacomo Delledonne and Giuseppe Martinico (eds), *The Canadian Contribution to a Comparative Law of Secession* (Palgrave 2019) 265.

Secession and European Union Law. Núria González Campañá, Oxford University Press. © Núria González Campañá 2024.
DOI: 10.1093/oso/9780198882596.003.0004

the common trend of all these constitutional legal orders is that none recognize a unilateral right, or a procedure to secede. At maximum, we find the acceptance of consensual secession, as in the cases of Canada and the UK. This acceptance might be due to a judicial process, as in the case of Canada, or the result of a political negotiation, as in the case of the UK. However, in both cases the prominent position of the central or national authorities is uncontested. At the same time, it will be shown that the strict Spanish response, following the classic US paradigm of not allowing for a referendum on secession, is not unique in the EU. Although the circumstances vary, since neither of them faces the same type of secessionist challenge, Italian and German constitutional legal orders take similar strict or classic responses to secession.

2. Constitutional Law and Secession

It used to be assumed that constitutional law had nothing interesting to say on the subject of secession. However, constitutional literature is increasingly dealing with the topic.[2] When dealing with constitutional law, unlike in the previous chapter devoted to international law, it must be borne in mind that there is no single or global constitutional legal order regulating secession. As a consequence, we will find different responses depending on the concrete constitutional legality that we review. However, as will be shown, there are many common trends in the way liberal constitutional orders have faced secessionist challenges. In the past only a few constitutions from communist countries formally included a right to secede (eg the Union of Soviet Socialist Republics, Burma).[3] However, as in any right included in the constitution of a communist State, their inclusion cannot be considered normative, but rather, semantic,[4] since the ultimate source of legal authority is not the Constitution, but the Communist Party. That is why framing these rights in legal terms is pointless.[5] At present, examples of a right or a procedure to secede are very limited: Uzbekistan,[6] Ethiopia,[7] Liechtenstein,[8] and St Kitts and

[2] Rivka Weill, 'Secession and the Prevalence of Both Militant Democracy and Eternity Clauses Worldwide' (2018) 40 Cardozo Law Review 905, 908. Ginsburg and Versteeg note the same. However, they argue that legal scholars still take a narrow approach, since they have almost exclusively been concerned with theoretical questions about whether or not a constitution should grant a right to secession. Tom Ginsburg and Mila Versteeg, 'From Catalonia to California: Secession in Constitutional Law' (2019) 70 Alabama Law Review 923, 928.

[3] See, for instance, the 1948 Constitution of the Union of Burma, Chapter X; or the 1977 Constitution of the Union of Soviet Socialist Republics, art 72.

[4] Karl Loewenstein, *Political Power and the Governmental Process* (University of Chicago Press 1957).

[5] In Chapter 5, when explaining the independence process of the Baltic States, we will see that despite the inclusion of a secession clause in the 1977 USSR Constitution, Moscow did not allow the Baltic States to separate from the USSR.

[6] See the Uzbekistan Constitution, art 74.

[7] See the Ethiopian Constitution, art 39(4) c).

[8] See the Constitution of the Principality of Liechtenstein, art 4(2).

Nevis.[9] This should come as no surprise. As mentioned in Chapter 2, secession challenges some of basic foundations of the constitutional pact. Indeed, for many years secession was understood as a sort of 'constitutional taboo'.[10] At first glance, a constitution does not seem like a good place to include secessionist clauses. In fact, 'it is far more common for constitutions to explicitly ban secession, proclaim the indivisibility of the nation, or provide that the country's territorial integrity may not be compromised'.[11]

The debate about the suitability of dealing with secession on a constitutional level is far from new. Back in the 1990s, Sunstein made a clear statement, upon which he insisted years later: regardless of the grounds that might justify secession, a right to secede should not be placed in a founding document, since that would increase partisan politics and reduce the prospects for compromise. According to Sunstein, such a clause would degrade day-to-day politics and, more dangerously, it would create a risk of blackmail endangering the prospects for long-term commitments.[12] His approach seems highly pragmatic: a constitution should be committed to the success of the social enterprise of our common life together:

> The right to secede is different from other potential vetoes on national legislative action precisely because it raises fundamental and often emotional issues having to do with the claims of ethnicity, territory, and history to separation and self-determination. These issues have a peculiar tendency to inflame both subunits and those who want them to remain part of the nation. They tend to raise emotional stakes in such a way as to make the ordinary work of politics—not to mention day-to-day interactions in other spheres—extremely hard to undertake.[13]

[9] See the St Kitts and Nevis Constitution, art 113(2) b). In 1998 Nevis attempted to secede, but it failed to meet the constitutional requirements: 'only' 61.7% of the voters supported independence, whereas the Constitution requires at least two-thirds of all the votes cast at the referendum. All these rare examples are unhelpful precedents as they belong to underdeveloped democratic systems (note that the war in the Ethiopian region of Tigray shows the weakness of the Ethiopian constitutional clauses on self-determination and secession) or with little political significance in the international community. Manuel Arias Maldonado, 'Sobre la legitimidad de la secesión territorial dentro del marco liberal-democrático' in Pere Almeda (ed), *Cataluña-Espanya. Del conflicto al diálogo* (Catarata 2021) 350. It is also true that the Act on Greenland Self-Government, art 21 recognizes the possibility of Greenland's accession to independence. However, the almost colonial situation of Greenland represents a very particular situation.

[10] Susanna Mancini, 'Secession and Self-determination' in Michael Rosenfeld and András Sajó (eds), *The Oxford Handbook of Comparative Constitutional Law* (OUP 2012) 494.

[11] Ginsburg and Versteeg (n 2) 939.

[12] The risks of blackmail are examined by Andrew Shorten. He considers that although secession rights facilitate exit threats, cynical threats are almost impossible to execute and other threats can be prevented by a well-designed secession clause. Andrew Shorten, 'Constitutional Secession Rights, Exit Threats, and Multinational Democracy' (2014) 62(1) Political Studies 99.

[13] Cass R Sunstein, 'Constitutionalism and Secession' (1991) 58 University of Chicago Law Review 633, 650–51.

Buchanan shares this view. For him, democratic values tell against a majoritarian right to secede: '[r]ecognition of such a right would tend to undermine the conditions for a flourishing democracy, by stimulating destructive behaviour and by weakening the incentives citizens have for principled political participation'.[14] According to Buchanan, following Sunstein's view, if such a right is recognized, a territorially concentrated minority could use the threat of secession as a strategic bargaining tool. Besides, a unilateral right to secede would mean the rejection of a deliberative process where all constituent parties (not only a sub-unit) could take part. It would mean the abandonment of the idea of having the entire population working in the formation of the democratic will.[15]

Other authors, such as Weinstock, Norman, and Mancini, have expressed disagreement with this view, since a constitutional secession clause would force secessionists to make a cold and lucid cost/benefit analysis. Besides, such a right, as Weinstock reminds us, would allow secessionists to engage in the kind of debate they want to be part of, one that refers to their own destiny. Understanding that symbols matter, Weinstock believes that the right to secede would take away one of the main sources of dissatisfaction national minorities have with the State to which they belong, which is, basically, that they are not allowed to decide whether they want to stay or go.[16] And, above all, by constitutionalizing the right to secede 'one can attempt to control a process which would otherwise go uncontrolled'. Since 'secessionist politics will occur anyway, regardless of legal silences and prohibitions, and that its occurring in a legal vacuum will be more harmful than were it to occur within well thought out legal and procedural parameters'.[17] In a similar vein, Susana Mancini writes:

> [T]o proceduralize secession, making it democratic, and surrounding it with guarantees—that is, to make secession a legal and not just a political issue—can actually help to protect all of the groups involved, and not just the secessionist

[14] Allen Buchanan, 'Democracy and Secession' in Margaret Moore (ed), *National Self-Determination and Secession* (OUP 1998) 21. However, Buchanan also admits that under certain special circumstances a heavily proceduralized constitutional right, with special exit costs, waiting periods, and supermajority requirements, may be appropriate. ibid 31.

[15] David Haljan, *Constitutionalising Secession* (Hart Publishing 2014) ch 7. In a similar vein, Horowitz states that '[t]he very existence of a right to secede, moreover, is likely to dampen efforts at coexistence in the undivided state, including the adoption of federalism or regional autonomy, which might alleviate some of the grievances of putatively secessionist minorities'. Donald L Horowitz, 'The Cracked Foundations of the Right to Secede' (2003) 14(2) Journal of Democracy 5, 6.

[16] Daniel Weinstock, 'Constitutionalizing the Right to Secede' (2001) 9(2) Journal of Political Philosophy 182, 201–02. Similarly, Barber, for he considers that '[t]he principal benefit of a secession right is its capacity to encourage the larger part of the state to consider the interests and wishes of a smaller region'. He thinks that such a clause is 'a reminder of the constitutional significance of the region'. Nick Barber, 'The Constitutional Regulation of Scottish Secession' (2015) 38 Oxford Legal Studies Research Paper 1, 15.

[17] Weinstock (n 16) 196. Ginsburg and Versteeg seem to agree with this: 'when a right to secession is constitutionalized, secessionist disputes are less likely to be violent'. Ginsburg and Versteeg (n 2) 951. They believe that constitutions can make a difference by changing the incentives to mobilize.

majority. It is clear that this will apply to ultimate choices, made in contexts in which the wish for separation is such as to make secession a genuine possibility.[18]

Norman, for instance, believes that 'a secession clause in a constitution would serve a similar function to rules for elections or amending the constitution. It would regulate a form of politics by specifying clear criteria for success and failure.'[19] In his view, a reasonable secession clause would take the following form: it would specify which sorts of regions or groups would have access to the procedure; the question or strict guidelines to the question; the entity that has authority to negotiate the terms of secession; and the voting procedure that should be applicable in such instances.[20] Mancini, when discussing the secession clause, urges the introduction of a 'cooling-off' period that might be a useful tool to avoid the risk of secession resulting predominantly from emotional situations.[21]

In any event, this discussion is mainly circumscribed to scholarly or political debates. As has been noted, only a few constitutions allow for secession to take place, but this does not mean that the other constitutional legal orders exclude the possibility of secession. In fact, there are some judicial opinions, as in Canada, or political experiences, as in the UK, from which it could be inferred that secession can be governed and subjected to constitutional principles. Radan, for instance, sees the Canadian 1998 Advisory Opinion on Quebec as the recognition of an implicit right of secession.[22]

As explained in the introduction of this chapter, we shall review different responses of liberal constitutional legal orders to secessionist challenges below. Since almost no constitutional text addresses the issue, we will focus mainly on case law.

[18] Susana Mancini, 'Rethinking the Boundaries of Democratic Secession: Liberalism, Nationalism, and the Right of Minorities to Self-determination' (2008) 6(3–4) International Journal of Constitutional Law 553, 578. See also Bossacoma: '[c]onstitutionalizing a qualified right to secede can be a more rational and just public choice than submitting secession to negotiation under no abstract constitutional provisions'. Pau Bossacoma, *Morality and Legality of Secession. A Theory of National Self-determination* (Palgrave 2020) 221 ff.

[19] Wayne Norman, 'The Ethics of Secession as the Regulation of Secessionist Politics' in Margaret Moore (ed), *National Self-determination and Secession* (OUP 1998) 48.

[20] ibid 53–54. Norman also admits that it is unlikely that States will include such a clause. If they are not currently experiencing a regional pro-independence movement, 'they are not going to tempt fate by opening up a national debate about fair terms for secession; and if a secessionist movement is under way, it would be difficult to get the secessionists' agreement to legitimize a clause based on anything but a choice or nationalist theory'. ibid 55.

[21] Mancini, 'Rethinking the Boundaries of Democratic Secession' (n 18) 580. Barber does not refer to cooling-off periods, but to the frequency of referendums, which should be limited, since referendums should be rare occurrences occurring once in a political generation. In his view a period of 20 or 30 years between referendums would be a good option. Nonetheless, he also believes that there needs to be a device whereby the regional authority can override the time limit on secession referendums and call a referendum before this period has elapsed as long as the vital interests of the region were at stake. Barber (n 16) 14–15.

[22] Peter Radan, 'Secessionist Referenda in International and Domestic Law' in Matt Qvortrup (ed), *Nationalism, Referendums and Democracy. Voting on Ethic Issues and Independence* (Routledge 2014) 16.

However, secessionist attempts rarely arise in case law. 'When it has, it has been in the context of federal states where a sub-unit of such a state has attempted to secede.'[23] We only find judicial decisions specifically addressing an attempt to secede in the US, Canada, Spain, Italy, and Germany. The British case is also an essential case study that enriches the analysis, notwithstanding the fact that there is no relevant case law and despite the fact that British constitutionalism (without a rigid and supreme constitution) departs from the common trends of liberal constitutionalism and therefore its suitability in comparative terms is limited. However, the British case is an interesting constitutional model, since it offers two slightly different responses to pro-secession attempts within the same territory, Northern Ireland and Scotland, which underlines the idea that secession clauses are not just the product of abstract legal theories, but institutions rooted in the history and the concrete circumstances of each country. And Belgium, as noted, is relevant and worthy of mention for the importance of the Flemish nationalist movement and its centrality in Europe.

3. The Classic and the New Paradigms: The US and Canada

3.1 The US

Secession as a contested issue in US constitutionalism was at its height in the mid-nineteenth century, when the discussion around slavery became a hot political issue. In the decades leading up to the Civil War the question as to whether the Constitution permitted a State to secede was subject to a lively debate.[24] It was the American statesman and political thinker John C Calhoun, from South Carolina, who made popular the idea that the Federation was still, like the Confederation, composed and legitimized by States, not by citizens. As Bassani explains, the linchpin of Calhoun's political theory was the defence of the Southern States and their position in the American Union. For him, the Constitution was not some higher law open to evolving with the spirit of the times, majority will, or the preferences of the Supreme Court (as it has occurred), but a compact between sovereign States, renegotiable only through amendments, that require the ratification of

[23] Aleksander Pavkovic and Peter Radan, *Creating New States* (Ashgate 2007) 221. The reference here to 'federal states' has to be understood in a broad meaning, as decentralized States. Neither Spain, nor the UK or Italy can be technically considered (constitutionally speaking) 'federal' States.

[24] David A Strauss, 'The Irrelevance of Constitutional Amendments' (2001) 114(5) Harvard Law Review 1457, 1486. The westward expansion of the US sparked the debate on whether or not to allow the practice of slavery. In order to preserve the Union, the so-called 'Missouri Compromise Statute' was adopted, which established a demarcation line between slave and free States. The Compromise was, however, quickly repealed. Erin Ryan, 'Secession and Federalism in the Unites States: Tools for Managing Regional Conflict in a Pluralist Society' (2017) 96 Oregon Law Review 123, 143–45.

three-quarters of them.[25] Calhoun insisted that the Southern States would never have ratified the Constitution if it had not protected slavery. Therefore, the attempts to abolish it were attacks on the constitutional agreement forged in Philadelphia.[26]

Calhoun's views were shared by other Southerner politicians, who considered that if the Union was a pact between parties with equal rights and duties (ie States), each State could unilaterally decide whether the rest had violated some of the clauses of the pact, and, therefore, after attempts to redress the conflict had failed, unilaterally withdraw from the pact.[27] In other words, if the States were independent sovereigns prior to ratifying the Constitution, they should therefore be able to reclaim their political independence. The new system created by the Constitution was a compact between States, not a Constitution over them. The right to secession would be similar to the ancient right of resistance against unjust authority.[28] '[T]here was a widespread acceptance across the American political spectrum of the right of unilateral secession and secession was often threatened by various states over a variety of issues.'[29] And, in fact, in 1860 and 1861 territorial referendums were organized in Texas, Tennessee, Virginia, and Arkansas, each declaring victory for secession. 'The balloting in each state suffered from problems

[25] Marco Bassani, 'John C. Calhoun: Nullification, Secession, Constitution' (*Abbevilleinstitute*, 8 August 2014) <https://www.abbevilleinstitute.org/john-c-calhoun-nullification-secession-constitution/> accessed 4 August 2023.

[26] Alan Tarr, 'Introducció' in John C Calhoun, *Discurs sobre la Constitució i el govern dels Estats Units i alters textos* (Institut d'Estudis Autonòmics 2009) 13.

[27] Judah P Benjamin, 'The Right of Secession (December 31, 1860)' in Jon L Wakelyn (ed) *Southern Pamphlets on Secession. November 1860–April 1861* (University of North Carolina Press 1996) 107–08. See also Stephen C Neff, 'Secession and Breach of a Compact: The Law of Nature Meets the United States Constitution' (2012) 45(2) Akron Law Review 405, 412.

[28] Ginsburg and Versteeg (n 2) 936. In August 1832 Calhoun wrote a very long letter to James Hamilton, the governor of South Carolina, where he developed fully his view on (in Calhoun's words) 'the right of a State to defend her reserved powers against the encroachment of the General Government'. In the first place, Calhoun was not a secessionist but he wanted to make sure that Southern interests were protected. Beyond the attempts to abolish slavery, he also protested against the protectionist policies promoted by US Congress to protect the emergent Northern industries that, at the same time, were undermining the Southern economy. In order to keep the union, he argued that States should be free to nullify federal laws, ie the right of States to block the enforcement of a federal law if they deemed it unconstitutional. But if the attempts to resolve the conflict failed, then secession was clearly an option. For Calhoun, 'the object of secession is to free the withdrawing member from the obligation of the association or union, and is applicable to cases where the object of the association or union has failed, either by an abuse of power on the part of its members, or other causes'. John C Calhoun Letter to James Hamilton. <http://onlinebooks.library.upenn.edu/webbin/book/lookupname?key=Calhoun%2C%20John%20C%2E%20%28John%20Caldwell%29%2C%201782%2D1850> accessed 4 August 2023. It seems that secession could only be resorted to if there was a just cause and after all constitutional attempts to overcome the conflict had failed. Martinico has explained that Calhoun considered secession to be a last resort, both a legal right and remedy. Giuseppe Martinico, *Il diritto costituzionale come speranza. Secessione, democrazia e populismo alla luce della Reference Re Secession of Quebec* (G. Giappichelli Editore 2019) 49, 64.

[29] Peter Radan, 'An Indestructible Union ... of Indestructible States: The Supreme Court of the United States and Secession' (2006) 10 Legal History 187, 196. In fact, although usually secessionism has been considered a purely Southern phenomenon, New England had previously flirted with secession as well. Craig S Lerner, 'Saving the Constitution: Lincoln, Secession, and the Price of Union' (2004) 102(6) Michigan Law Review 1263, 1267.

of fraud and intimidation that call into question the legitimacy of their results, but they still may have reflected a majority view among the voting population.'[30] The American Civil War radically changed the political atmosphere and settled the issue.[31] In effect, the Union's triumph provided the final settlement of the legality of State secession from the Union.

Shortly after the Civil War, in 1869 the US Supreme Court dealt with the legality of the attempted secession of Texas in *Texas v White*. Texas had just joined the Union in 1845 and attempted to secede in February 1861. The key argument underpinning the ruling was that Texas became part of an 'indestructible Union, composed of indestructible States'.[32] The Supreme Court recalled that Article XIII of the Articles of Confederation and Perpetual Union of 1777 declared that the US union was to be perpetual, while the preamble to the US Constitution of 1787 established that such Constitution was proclaimed 'to form a more perfect union'. As the Supreme Court observed, 'it is difficult to convey the idea of indissoluble unity more clearly than by these words. What can be indissoluble if a perpetual Union, made more perfect, is not?'[33] The issue about the legality of secession in the US has been settled since then[34] and as Sunstein admits, 'no serious scholar or politician now argues that a right to secede exists under American constitutional law'.[35] The response offered by the US Supreme Court was highly influenced by the political thinking of the winning side of the Civil War, the Northern States and their leader, Abraham Lincoln, who advanced the idea of federal sovereignty instead of a State-sovereignty approach. When reviewing the First Inaugural Address, one can see how Lincoln argued that a constitutional order is not an agreement from which the parties could unilaterally withdraw. A democratic government is based on the will of a majority limited by the rules that the people has given itself, the Constitution. For him secession was to be ruled out in order to prevent anarchy:

[30] Ryan (n 24) 144. For Margiotta, the fact that between 1790 and 1861 at least three amendments were proposed to make secession unconstitutional means that they were trying to limit a power that existed. Costanza Margiotta, *L'ultimo diritto. Profili storici e teorici della secession* (Il Mulino 2005) 67.

[31] 'The law is made—its interpretations settled—by great events, not law review articles; by wars, not words; by presidents, not professors. The Constitution we have today is in substantial measure the result of the single most decisive legal interpretative event of American history: the Civil War. The outcome of *Grant v Lee* resolved the most important issue of antebellum constitutional dispute—the nature of the Union—in favour of the nationalist view of sovereignty and against the South's state-sovereignty view.' Michael Stokes Paulsen, 'The Civil War as Constitutional Interpretation' (2004) 71 University of Chicago Law Review 691, 691. Along the same lines, '[t]he person on the street would say that the Civil War settled it, and that person would be right. The Civil War settled it, even though no formal amendment was added to the Constitution.' Strauss (n 24) 1486. In effect, '[t]he American Civil War was fought over the protection of the Union no less than the abolition of slavery'. Weill (n 2) 954.

[32] *Texas v White* 74 US 700 (1869) 725.

[33] ibid.

[34] Subsequent decisions of the Supreme Court followed the same approach: *White v Hart* 80 US 646 (1871) 651; *Taylor v Thomas* 89 US 479 (1874) 491; *Daniels v Tearney* 102 US 415 (1880) 418.

[35] Sunstein (n 14) 633.

> Plainly the central idea of secession is the essence of anarchy. A majority held in restraint by constitutional checks and limitations, and always changing easily with deliberate changes of popular opinions and sentiments, is the only true sovereign of a free people. Whoever rejects it does of necessity fly to anarchy or to despotism. Unanimity is impossible. The rule of a minority, as a permanent arrangement, is wholly inadmissible; so that, rejecting the majority principle, anarchy or despotism in some form is all that is left.[36]

In *Texas v White*, however, the Supreme Court recognized that a State could secede from the Union through revolution or through the consent of the States: '[t]he union between Texas and the other States was as complete, as perpetual, and as indissoluble as the union between the original States. There was no place for reconsideration, or revocation, except through revolution, or through consent of the States.'[37]

3.1.1 Secession through revolution

The idea of revolution was obviously not alien to US constitutionalism, since the very foundation of the country lay in a revolutionary war against the colonial power. What is key in the event of a revolution is the ultimate success of the enterprise. In 1877 in *Williams v Bruffy*, when discussing the validity of acts in the event of secession, the Supreme Court ruled as follows:

> The validity of its acts, both against the parent State and its citizens or subjects, depends entirely upon its ultimate success. If it fail to establish itself permanently, all such acts perish with it. If it succeed, and become recognized, its acts from the commencement of its existence are upheld as those of an independent nation.[38]

The Court is not admitting here any right: a revolution is a question of fact, not law. As the Canadian Supreme Court also admitted, in the context of secession, what matters is the efficacy principle: 'the viability of a would-be state in the international community depends, as a practical matter, upon recognition by other states'.[39]

3.1.2 Secession through consent of the States

When the Supreme Court referred to 'consent', what did it mean? Unanimous consent of all the States of the US? Some consider that 'consent' means unanimous agreement of all the States of the US. Other authors believe that '[t]he consent of

[36] Roy P Basler and others (eds), *Collected Works of Abraham Lincoln* (vol 4, Rutgers UP 1954) 256–57.

[37] *Texas v White* (n 32) 726.

[38] *Williams v Bruffy* 96 US 176 (1877) 186.

[39] *Reference re Secession of Quebec* [1998] 2 SCC 217, para 142.

the States requirements could, however, be taken to mean their consent to a constitutional amendment approved by three-quarters of the states as set in Article V of the US Constitution'.[40] Article V stipulates that a constitutional amendment needs to be proposed by a resolution passed by a two-thirds majority of both Houses of Congress or by the legislatures of two-thirds of the number of States. This is 'an almost impossible political hurdle for any state wishing to secede'.[41] Thus, according to some interpretations, '[t]he decision in Texas v. White only renders unilateral secession illegal and leaves it open for constitutionally legal secession to take place'.[42] Others, however, consider that amending the Constitution to provide a clause for secession is also against the spirit of the US Constitution. Thus, an amendment process cannot include the right to secede, since the amendment capacity is a limited power within the Constitution itself and secession is a revolutionary process linked with the dissolution of the people that sustains the Constitution.[43]

Secession is no longer an issue in US constitutionalism ('[h]istory is written by the victors, and the idea of secession has been dead since Appomattox'[44]). There is no strong independence movement within the US and there is an overall rejection of secession.[45] There are some regional parties or movements in certain States (such as California, Texas, Vermont, Alaska, New Hampshire, and Hawaii) advocating for secession, yet their popular support is low. However, the debate about sovereignty goes on and the issue remains unsettled, even today.[46] The orthodox position of US Courts and law professors is, and it is called the classic paradigm of secession, that the US Constitution does not provide for a unilateral right to secede.[47] And even if we accept that the US Constitution would permit a

[40] Pavkovic and Radan (n 23) 223.

[41] Radan, 'An Indestructible Union . . . of Indestructible States' (n 29) 195.

[42] Radan, 'Secessionist Referenda in International and Domestic Law' (n 22) 19. See also Radan, 'An Indestructible Union . . . of Indestructible States' (n 29) 191.

[43] Daniel Farber, *Lincoln's Constitution* (University of Chicago Press 2003) chs 2 and 4.

[44] ibid 81. This is the dominant position among authors. However, there are some exceptions. See Sanford Levinson, 'Is Secession the Achilles Heel of "Strong" Federalism?' in Jörg Fedtke and Basil S Markesinis (eds), *Patterns of Regionalism and Federalism* (Hart Publishing 2006) 207–28; Mark E Brandon, 'Secession, Constitutionalism and American Experience' in Stephen Macedo and Allen Buchanan (eds), *Secession and Self-determination* (NYU Press 2003) 272–314.

[45] As Craig Lerner points out, '[i]t is difficult for Americans today to take seriously the legal claims in favour of a right of secession. The cause of secession in 1860 became commingled with a defence of slavery, and our repugnance for that institution carries over into our rejection of secession. Furthermore, there is a sense among many Americans that our country has, on balance, had a salutary influence on global affairs. Any suggestion that we might have been better off as separate nations prompts a lecture on the United States' role in the twentieth century as an agent of freedom and the inevitable lament that, had America not been united, Germany would have won World War II.' Lerner (n 29) 1264.

[46] William G Gale and Darell M West, 'How seriously should we take talk of US state secession?' (*Brookings*, 13 December 2021) <https://www.brookings.edu/blog/fixgov/2021/12/13/how-seriously-should-we-take-talk-of-us-state-secession/> accessed 3 August 2022. The authors warn that according to polls, nearly 40% of likely voters (from different political spectrum) would support State secession if their candidate loses. They argue that the shocking breadth of support for secession is one troubling sign of the deteriorating civic mood in the US.

[47] A much modern case in Alaska confirms this view. In 2006, the Supreme Court of Alaska rejected the organization of a popular referendum on secession, since under Alaskan law a popular referendum cannot take place if it proposes something unconstitutional. The concrete question that was intended

constitutional amendment to include a secession clause, one must admit that such a process is, from a political point of view, a hugely difficult task.

3.2 Canada

In order to understand the position of Canadian constitutionalism towards the secessionist attempts of the French-speaking province of Quebec, which has been called a 'new paradigm',[48] or a 'major departure from the practice of liberal-democratic states',[49] it is necessary to become acquainted with Canadian history.

To start with, it must be pointed out that '[t]he French community in what is now the Canadian Federation predates all but the aboriginal settlement'.[50] In effect, in the second half of the eighteenth century the British began to rule over a territory that had been mainly settled by inhabitants with French origins since the early 1600s. Very rapidly the British realized the need to secure the loyalty of French settlers and accepted the survival of Catholicism and French civil law. Even in 1840 when the divided territories of Upper Canada (majority of English-speaking settlers) and Lower Canada (majority of French-speaking settlers) were united, '[f]ar from submerging the French-Canadian identity, the Act of Union and its aftermath reaffirmed the central position of French-Canadian law, language and leaders in the Canadian constitutional system'.[51] This dualism, and the self-perception of the Quebecers as founding people, justify the central position of the principle of federalism in Canadian constitutionalism. At least since the British North America Act of 1867, Canada can be described as a federal system[52] where, apart from the formal constitutional arrangements, many conventions guarantee the role of the provinces and the special status of Quebec.[53]

to be posed to the public was the following: 'Shall the State of Alaska obtain independence from the United States of America, and become an independent nation, if such independence is legally possible, and if such independence is not legally possible under present law, shall the State of Alaska seek changes in existing law and Constitutional provisions to authorize such independence, and then obtain independence?' According to the Court, the proposed referendum was *ultra vires*. The decision was based on *Texas v White* and the idea that secession is against the US Constitution. *Kohlhaas v State, Office of Lieutenant Governor (Kohlhaas I)*, 147 P.3d 714 (Alaska 2006).

[48] Alberto López Basaguren, 'Estado democrático y secesión de territorios. Un análisis comparado sobre el tratamiento democrático de las reclamaciones secesionistas' in Joseba Arregi Aranburu (ed), *La Secesión de España* (Tecnos 2014) 51.

[49] Zoran Oklopcic, 'Independence Referendums and Democratic Theory in Quebec and Montenegro' in Matt Qvortrup (ed), *Nationalism, Referendums and Democracy. Voting on Ethic Issues and Independence* (Routledge 2014) 28.

[50] Peter Oliver, 'Canada's Two Solitudes' in Stephen Tierney (ed), *Accommodating National Identity. New Approaches in International and Domestic Law* (Kluwer Law International 2000) 65.

[51] ibid 71–73.

[52] According to the Canadian Supreme Court, '[f]ederalism was the political mechanism by which diversity could be reconciled with unity'. *Reference re Secession of Quebec* (n 39) para 43.

[53] For instance, according to the 1985 Supreme Court Act, art 6, '[a]t least three of the [nine] judges shall be appointed from among the judges of the Court of Appeal or of the Superior Court of the

Quebec separatism began in the late 1950s[54] when, after years of political conservatism, Quebec elected a liberal government committed to change: the Quiet Revolution that pretended to promote further the special treatment of French language and culture. The francophone fear concerning their minority situation within the Canadian federation was, and remains, mainly cultural and linguistic ('feelings of attachment'), but in the past at least it also embodied economic demands.[55] As Gaudreault-DesBiens explains, Quebec nationalism

> emerged in a context where the province's French-speaking majority was marginalized both in Canada as a whole and in the province's economic sphere. This precarious situation combined with the unique linguistic and religious characteristics of that group, led to the development of a nationalism that revolved around the defence of the majority's cultural, political and economic interests.[56]

Quebec organized sovereignty referendums in 1980 and 1995.[57] It should be noted that those plebiscites were organized according to the Quebec competences, and, therefore, without the opposition of the central government. In Canadian constitutional law, though, referendums had no legal effect, which flows from the principle of parliamentary supremacy, inherited from the UK.[58] The questions posed to the public in those referendums were not clearly asking about the independence of Quebec,[59] but it was read this way throughout the country and

Province of Quebec or from among the advocates of that Province'. The reason that justifies this special treatment is that Quebec is the only province using civil law, while the rest of the country follows common law.

[54] Quebec's secessionist movement is one of the oldest of the sort in any democratic country. Jean-François Gaudreault-DesBiens, 'The Law and Politics of Secession: From the Political Contingency of Secession to a "Right to Decide"? Can Lessons Be Learned from the Quebec Case?' in Giacomo Delledonne and Giuseppe Martinico (eds), *The Canadian Contribution to a Comparative Law of Secession* (Palgrave 2019) 33.

[55] André Blais and Richard Nadeau, 'To Be or Not to Be Sovereignist: Quebeckers' Perennial Dilemma' (1992) XVIII(1) Canadian Public Policy/Analyse de politiques 89, 96. See also Stephane Dion, 'Why Is Secession Difficult in Well-Established Democracies? Lessons from Quebec' (1996) 26(2) British Journal of Political Science 269, 279.

[56] Gaudreault-DesBiens (n 54) 48.

[57] After the 1980 referendum, the Canadian government negotiated and attempted to recognize Quebec's distinctiveness within the body of the Constitution. In the 1987 Lake Meech accord, it offered a 'distinct society' clause. But this offer was rejected by some provinces. The 1992 Charlottetown Accord was rejected both by Quebec and by other provinces. No accommodation attempt was successful. See, among many others, Peter W Hogg, *Meech Lake Constitutional Accord Annotated* (Carswell1988) and Alan C Cairns, 'The Charlottetown Accord: Multinational Canada vs. Federalism' in Douglas E Williams (ed), *Reconfigurations: Canadian Citizenship and Constitutional Change—Selected Essays by Alan C. Cairns* (McClelland and Stewart 1995).

[58] Gaudreault-DesBiens (n 54) 35.

[59] The question in the 1980 referendum was the following: 'The Government of Quebec has made public its proposal to negotiate a new agreement with the rest of Canada, based on the equality of nations; this agreement would enable Quebec to acquire the exclusive power to make its laws, levy its taxes and establish relations abroad—in other words, sovereignty—and at the same time to maintain with Canada an economic association including a common currency; any change in political status resulting

abroad.[60] After the tight results of 1995 the Canadian government sent a reference case to the Supreme Court (SC), in order to obtain an advisory opinion in the form of a judgment on the legality of the Quebec government's secession plans.

3.2.1 1998 Supreme Court Opinion on Quebec

The reference became known as one of the most important cases in Canadian history and it has also exercised an enormous influence in comparative law.[61] As Martinico points out, it was a crucial decision, because the Court dealt frontally with secession, 'going beyond a formalist reading of its constitutional text(s), ie rejecting the argument according to which secession was banned since no written provision provided for that'.[62] In effect, after carefully reviewing Canadian history, the SC, in a unanimous decision, admitted that there was no constitutional provision addressing secession, and rejected the right of Quebec to secede unilaterally under both the Canadian Constitution and international law, but established that the secession of a province from Canada was permitted following a constitutional amendment.[63] However, the Court said something else. It identified four implicit constitutional principles that underpin Canadian constitutionalism: federalism; democracy; constitutionalism and the rule of law; and respect for minorities.[64]. These led the Court to admit that:

> [t]he clear repudiation by the people of Quebec of the existing constitutional order would confer legitimacy on demands for secession, and place an obligation on the other provinces and the federal government to acknowledge and respect that expression of democratic will by entering into negotiations.[65]

from these negotiations will only be implemented with popular approval through another referendum; on these terms, do you give the Government of Quebec the mandate to negotiate the proposed agreement between Quebec and Canada?' The results were 40.44% Yes and 59.56% No. The question in the 1995 referendum was the following: 'Do you agree that Quebec should become sovereign after having made a formal offer to Canada for a new economic and political partnership within the scope of the bill respecting the future of Quebec and of the agreement signed on June 12, 1995?' The results were 49.42% Yes and 50.58% No.

[60] For instance, US officials supported Canadian unity through several declarations: US Secretary of State Warren Christopher suggested than an independent Quebec might not enjoy the same economic relationship with the US that it enjoyed as part of Canada. Peter Morici, 'A Sovereign Quebec and US National Interests' (1997) 27(1) The American Review of Canadian Studies 143, 147-148.

[61] As for its influence in the 2006 Montenegro referendum on independence, Oklopcic (n 49) 28.

[62] Giuseppe Martinico, '"A Message of Hope": A Legal Perspective on the Reference' in Giacomo Delledonne and Giuseppe Martinico (eds), *The Canadian Contribution to a Comparative Law of Secession* (Palgrave 2019) 249.

[63] *Reference re Secession of Quebec* (n 39) para 84.

[64] 'These defining principles function in symbiosis. No single principle can be defined in isolation from the others, nor does any principle trump or exclude the operation of any other.' ibid para 49.

[65] ibid para 88.

A clear repudiation meant, in the Court's view, a referendum 'free of ambiguity both in terms of the question asked and in terms of the support it achieves'.[66] With this warning, the Court might have implicitly suggested that the 1980 and 1995 referendums did not meet that standard.[67] The requirement of more than a simple majority ('clear repudiation') is 'justifiable in terms of establishing procedural barriers against a too easy right to exit that may undermine the very basis of democratic politics'.[68] The Court holds a complex notion of democracy that cannot be reduced to the majority rule. Constitutional democracies should honour a strong counter-majoritarian nature. There is a need to understand democracy 'as a mosaic where the will of majority cannot be treated as a trump card against other constitutional values'.[69] The SC might have opted for a straightforward prohibition of secession, probably the expected response of the Canadian government. Or, as Tierney puts it, the Court delivered a 'complex opinion that was far from the unequivocal statement sought by the federal government'.[70] Instead, the SC opted for encouraging discussions and negotiations to sort out a political conflict. In fact, according to the Court, all constitutional participants have a binding, constitutional duty to negotiate. The Court emphasized that 'a functioning democracy requires a continuous process of discussion'.[71] As Hogg points out, the obligation to negotiate was a new idea in Canadian constitutionalism and the Court 'found it to be a corollary of the fundamental, but unwritten, constitutional principles of democracy and federalism'.[72] One of the difficulties of the decision lies in determining whether the Court 'is referring to legal or political rights and obligations, and whether even legal rights and obligations always produce clear legal consequences'.[73] In effect, in an exercise of self-restraint, and being aware that this type of conflict could only be resolved by politics and not by courts, the concrete content of the obligation to negotiate was not specified. Specifically, the Court admitted the following:

66 ibid para 87.

67 Pavkovic and Radan (n 23) 228. See also Gaudreault-DesBiens (n 54) 40. In effect, 'the first two referendums questions were not unambiguous, as both referred, directly or indirectly, to the possibility of a renewed partnership between Quebec and Canada. The reason they were formulated as such by avowedly secessionist governments is simple: they knew very well that Quebecers overwhelmingly preferred renewed federalism or a EU-like agreement over outright separation from Canada.' ibid 47.

68 Margaret Moore, 'The Ethics of Secession and a Normative Theory of Nationalism' (2000) 13 Canadian Journal of Law & Jurisprudence 225, 247. As Romero Caro explains very well, this is one of the most obscure concepts, because it was not defined by either the Supreme Court or the 2000 Clarity Act. The 'clear repudiation' concept contains the desire to ensure that a complex issue such as secession is not decided by a floating majority that could change within a short period of time. The clear majority must represent broad and stable support for secession. Francisco Javier Romero Caro, 'La cuestión catalana a la luz de la experiencia de Quebec y Escocia' in Laura Baamonde, Ana Espinosa, and Daniel López (eds), *Reflexiones constitucionales sobre la participación política directa* (CEPC 2021) 506.

69 Martinico, '"A Message of Hope": A Legal Perspective on the Reference' (n 62) 256.

70 Stephen Tierney, *Constitutional Referendums: The Theory and Practice of Republican Deliberation* (OUP 2012) 143.

71 *Reference re Secession of Quebec* (n 39) para 68.

72 Peter W Hogg, *Constitutional Law of Canada* (5th edn, Carswell 2015) 5–36.

73 Oliver (n 50) 80.

> The workings of the political process are complex and can only be resolved by means of political judgments and evaluations. The Court has no supervisory role over the political aspects of constitutional negotiations. Equally, the initial impetus for negotiation, namely a clear majority on a clear question in favour of secession, is subject only to political evaluation, and properly so.[74]

It seems that the obligations inferred from the constitutional principles by the Court are indeed legal, but its details and enforcement are to be left entirely to the political sphere.[75] For instance, the unwillingness to negotiate following a clearly expressed will to secede would undermine the default party's legitimacy in the eyes of the international community.[76] Haljan has warned against a common misreading of the Opinion:

> That a clear majority approving secession on a clear question entails that Parliament and the other provinces must negotiate the terms of secession without room to reject the proposal, or without the ability to call for amendments to vary it in any degree. That is, the Supreme Court has recognised a 'right to secede'.[77]

Thus, 'a proposal for change is just that: a suggestion. It is accordingly by definition mutable, variable and open to acceptance or rejection.'[78] Haljan is correct in his approach, since the Court highlighted the following:

> No negotiations could be effective if their ultimate outcome, secession, is cast as an absolute legal entitlement based upon an obligation to give effect to that act of secession in the Constitution. Such a foregone conclusion would actually undermine the obligation to negotiate.[79]

Therefore, a right to negotiate does not imply automatically a right to secede. Thus, the SC 'did not recognise a proper right to secession; rather it treated secession as an option that may be tolerated only in the presence of some important safeguards'.[80] The Court refrained from advising on failed negotiations, probably because this was beyond its judicial duty. The legal title granted by the Court was simply a right to negotiate in good faith. The concrete results of the negotiations have to be sorted out by the diverse political actors. But one should also bear in

[74] *Reference re Secession of Quebec* (n 39) para 100.
[75] Oliver (n 50) 80.
[76] *Reference re Secession of Quebec* (n 39) para 103: 'Thus, a failure of the duty to undertake negotiations and pursue them according to constitutional principles may undermine that government's claim to legitimacy which is generally a precondition for recognition by the international community.'
[77] Haljan (n 15) 343.
[78] ibid 341.
[79] *Reference re Secession of Quebec* (n 39) para 91.
[80] Martinico, '"A Message of Hope": A Legal Perspective on the Reference' (n 62) 251.

mind the following: while the democratic principle provided the foundation for the duty to negotiate, it cannot obscure another important obligation, which is the need to respect the rule of law. Accordingly, 'if negotiations were to fail and a unilateral declaration of independence ensued, that declaration would be illegal under domestic law'.[81] The decision of the Court not only garnered a huge amount of attention among Canadians, but has also been considered a 'landmark decision for worldwide constitutionalism'.[82] As part of a larger constitutional moment, the decision developed a constitutional doctrine to accommodate a political tension.[83] The Court 'produced a compromise which gave half a loaf to each side'.[84] It became a turning point and since then the debate has been about how to constitutionalize secession 'and how to tame something which had been considered for a long time as a sort of "beast" that is hard to domesticate'.[85] Later on, the Canadian government attempted to encapsulate the SC doctrine in the 2000 Clarity Act. This Act accepted the constitutional duty to negotiate but established strict requirements to trigger such an obligation.[86] In sum, Canadian provinces are free to organize referendums on independence, and, provided that the question submitted is free of ambiguity and there is a clear majority in favour of independence, there is a constitutional duty to negotiate for both sides.

4. The Constitutional Responses of EU Member States (including the UK before Brexit) to Secession

4.1 The UK

4.1.1 Scotland

On 18 September 2014 Scotland organized what is, so far, the latest referendum on independence in the Western world, at least, a legal one that is accepted by all the members of the political community. The results are well-known: contrary to what the polls suggested, the 'no' side prevailed, by a margin of 55.3 to 44.7 per cent,

81 Gaudreault-DesBiens (n 54) 54.

82 Peter H Russell, *Constitutional Odyssey: Can Canadians Become a Sovereign People?* (3rd edn, University of Toronto Press 2004) 244.

83 Jonathon W Penney, 'Deciding in the Heat of the Constitutional Moment' (2005) 28 Dalhousie Law Journal 217, 221.

84 Russell (n 82) 245.

85 Martinico, '"A Message of Hope": A Legal Perspective on the Reference' (n 62) 250.

86 Article 1 establishes that the Canadian House of Commons shall consider the question featured in the referendum and shall set out (unilaterally) its determination on whether the question is clear. Likewise, article 2 provides that the Canadian House of Commons shall consider whether there has been a clear expression of a will by a clear majority of the population of that province. Thus, the decision on whether there is a clear will to secede is left entirely in the hands of the Canadian House of Commons.

with an enthusiastic turnout of 84.6 per cent.[87] However, the issue is far from being settled, since the Brexit turmoil led the Scottish First Minister to urge for a second referendum.

Yet, beyond political uncertainties, our focus here is to review the flexible response offered by British constitutionalism. In effect, in the eyes of foreign observers, what was probably most astonishing was how the flexibility of British constitutionalism enabled a solution: the referendum was agreed upon between the Scottish and the British governments in October 2012.[88] Since the Union between Scotland and England took place, in 1707, all power residing in the Scottish Parliament was transferred to the UK Parliament at Westminster. Even legislation that only pertained to Scotland was enacted by Westminster.[89] However, there has been wide acceptance about a Scottish right to decide their own destiny 'implicit in the concept of union'.[90] The Union was formally an international treaty[91] between the Scottish and the English parliaments and this legal reality underpins the Scottish understanding that an international treaty can always be renegotiated.[92] The general perception is that the UK is a nation composed of four historic nations.[93] This is so even when it is hard to talk about a sovereign, independent, and national Scotland before the Union treaty, since those terms are difficult to apply to European units of the Middle Ages when the nation State model was not yet consolidated. In any event, what cannot be denied is that Scotland has a long history of statehood elements and a Scottish sense of common identity.[94] It is hard to tell whether Scottish history, centuries of almost uninterrupted British parliamentary tradition, pragmatic economic reasons, or all those together are behind the tolerant and flexible way British politics faces Scottish secession.[95] In any event, even

[87] Results available at <http://www.bbc.com/news/events/scotland-decides/results> accessed 3 August 2022.

[88] The UK Prime Minister and the Scottish First Minister signed an agreement on a referendum for Scotland on 15 October 2012. The referendum legislation had to decide: (1) the date of the referendum; (2) the franchise; (3) the wording of the question: (4) the rules on campaign financing; and (5) other rules for the conduct of the referendum. Although the agreement insisted on holding a legal and fair referendum 'producing a decisive and respected outcome', no reference was made to the required majority to secede. As Palermo explains, 'the very concept of entrenched majorities is alien to the political nature of the British constitution and it was never really considered as an option.' Palermo (n 1) 270.

[89] Matt Qvortrup, 'The Referendum Challenge to Constitutional Sovereignty: The Case of Scotland' (*Jus Politicum*, 2013) <http://juspoliticum.com/uploads/pdf/JP9-Qvortrup.pdf> accessed 3 August 2022.

[90] Michael Keating, *The Independence of Scotland. Self-government and the Shifting Politics of Union* (OUP 2009) 81.

[91] Mullen notes that strictly speaking there was no treaty in the modern sense, but the England Act passed by the Scottish Parliament and the Scotland Act passed by the English Parliament. Tom Mullen, 'The Scottish Independence Referendum 2014' (2014) 41(4) Journal of Law and Society 627, 628.

[92] Keating (n 90) 18.

[93] Colin R Munro, 'Scottish Devolution: Accommodating a Restless Nation' in Stephen Tierney (ed), *Accommodating National Identity. New Approaches in International and Domestic Law* (Kluwer Law International 2000) 134

[94] ibid 135.

[95] 'Most English people [think] that Scottish independence would make no difference to England's prosperity.' Keating (n 90) 45. Keating admits that this is a remarkable thing, since in other comparable

opponents of Scottish devolution accept the right of Scotland to decide its own destiny. The very same Margaret Thatcher, who showed no interest in promoting a second referendum on Scottish devolution,[96] admitted that:

> As a nation, they [the Scots] have an undoubted right to national self-determination; thus far they have exercised that right by joining and remaining in the Union. Should they determine on independence no English party or politician would stand in their way, however much we might regret their departure.[97]

Thus, given that the Westminster parties agree that a Scottish desire for independence should be respected,[98] the only decision to be made refers to the concrete constitutional procedure. Any discussion about British constitutionalism starts with the famous (and contested) doctrine of parliamentary sovereignty.[99] In the case of *R (Miller) v. Secretary of State for Exiting the European Union* [2016] EWHC 2768 (Admin),[100] the Divisional Court reminded us that '[t]he United Kingdom does not have a Constitution to be found entirely in a written document. This does not mean there is an absence of a constitution or constitutional law. On the contrary, the United Kingdom has its own form of constitutional law.'[101] Some of it is written and some of it is reflected in fundamental rules of law recognized by both

liberal democracies like Canada or Spain, the idea of secession 'stirs powerful passions on the sides of both minority nations and the state majority, who see secession as an existential threat to their political identity and being.' ibid 46.

[96] In 1979, under a Labour government, the first attempt to devolve powers to Scotland by re-establishing the Scottish Parliament failed because the threshold requirement of 40% was not met. Only in 1997, with another Labour government, was a second referendum organized and this time, despite the lack of popular enthusiasm, the Scotland Act was passed. The powers devolved followed broadly the outlines of administrative devolution which had been operating for decades. Mullen (n 91) 630.

[97] Margaret Thatcher, *The Downing Street Years* (HarperCollins 1995) 624.

[98] In January 2012, the UK government presented to the Parliament a statement entitled 'Scotland's constitutional future'. Michael Moore, then Secretary of State for Scotland, announced that '[t]he Scottish National Party entered the May 2011 election with a manifesto pledge for a referendum on independence. They have campaigned consistently for independence, and while the UK Government does not believe this is in the interests of Scotland, or the rest of the United Kingdom, we will not stand in the way of a referendum on independence: the future of Scotland's place within the United Kingdom is for people in Scotland to vote on.' <https://www.gov.uk/government/uploads/system/uploads/attachment_data/file/39248/Scotlands_Constitutional_Future.pdf> accessed 3 August 2022. The debate that followed in the House of Commons is remarkable in the sense that it only lasted approximately one hour (from 5.09pm to 6.22pm) and no member of the Parliament (57 took the floor) opposed the organization of such a referendum. The concerns raised related to the fairness of the referendum, the instability that the interim situation would create, and the concrete legal procedure. Hansard, 10 January 2012, Cols 51–72. <http://www.publications.parliament.uk/pa/cm201212/cmhansrd/cm120110/debtext/120110-0002.htm#12011056000001> accessed 3 August 2022.

[99] There was a lively debate among British constitutional lawyers about the role of Parliament in the Brexit process that culminated in the 24 January 2017 decision of the UK Supreme Court. *R (Miller) v Secretary of State for Exiting the European Union* [2017] UKSC 5.

[100] *R (Miller) v Secretary of State for Exiting the European Union* [2016] EWHC 2768 (Admin).

[101] ibid para 18.

Parliament and the courts, says the Court. The Court then identified the meaning of parliamentary sovereignty:

> It is common ground that the most fundamental rule of UK constitutional law is that Crown in Parliament is sovereign and that legislation enacted by the Crown with the consent of both Houses of Parliament is supreme .... Parliament can, by enactment of primary legislation, change the law of the land in any way it chooses. There is no superior form of law than primary legislation, save only where Parliament has itself made provision to allow that to happen.[102]

Parliamentary sovereignty, thus, is opposed to the Western widespread idea of democracies governed by a supreme and rigid constitution. This is a powerful tool that provides the system with an enormous amount of constitutional flexibility, unlike in many other legal orders. A second important characteristic of British constitutionalism that has to be taken into account when reviewing Scotland's secessionist attempt is the distribution of competences between Westminster and Holyrood. '[T]he scheme is not federal, and the Scottish Parliament is merely a devolved institution. There is no reason, legally, why the Scottish Parliament could not be abolished by a later Act of the Parliament at Westminster.'[103] Unlike in federal systems or other regional orders (like Spain[104]), the unilateral abolition of Scottish autonomy by Westminster would be legally possible.[105] But the key issue here is not so much the legal subordination of the Scottish Parliament, but the limits of its powers, with certain competences 'reserved' to Westminster. According to section 29(2)(a) of the Scotland Act, the Scottish Parliament cannot enact laws on reserved matters. Reserved matters are listed in Schedule 5 of the Act and include among other issues (eg defence, foreign affairs, monetary policy, etc) the Union and the Constitution. This restriction is significant, since, arguably, Scotland therefore has no competence to legislate for independence, or even to hold a referendum on independence.[106] This was the position of the UK government, as established in the

[102] ibid para 20.

[103] Munro (n 93) 147.

[104] This prerogative should not be confused with the possibility of enforcing coercive measures against a Spanish region acting against the Constitution. See Section 4.2 on Spanish constitutionalism and Catalonia.

[105] Page seems to disagree with that, for he considers that the Scottish Parliament and government form part of the British constitutional order and they will continue to be so for as long as Scotland remains within the Union. Alan Page, 'El referéndum de independencia escocés' (2016) 37 Teoría y Realidad Constitucional 437, 446.

[106] Adam Tomkins was one of the most notable defenders of this view, arguing that the Scottish Parliament lacked the capacity to call a referendum. Adam Tomkins, 'Scotland's Choice, Britain's Future' (2014) 130 Law Quarterly Review 215, 224–30. See also Qvortrup (n 89). Others, however, disagreed. Neil MacCormick had argued in the past that an advisory referendum on independence would have no direct legal effect and that the Scottish government was constitutionally allowed to organize it. Neil MacCormick, 'Is There a Constitutional Path to Scottish Independence?' (2000) 53 Parliamentary Affairs 721, 725–26. Nick Barber also argued that 'the Scottish Parliament can hold a referendum on independence. But it would only be an advisory referendum: it would be open to the United Kingdom

2012 statement 'Scotland's constitutional future'.[107] After reaching an agreement on holding the referendum in October 2012, the debate turned on the procedure. There were basically two procedural options to organize a legal referendum, outlined in the January 2012 statement: (1) either legislate to give the Scottish Parliament the power to deliver a referendum (amending the Scotland Act); or (2) legislate directly in the UK Parliament for a referendum on Scottish independence. The UK government opted for option (1), formalized by the Scotland Act 1998 (Modification of Schedule 5) Order 2013, which devolved to the Scottish Parliament the competence to legislate for a referendum on independence which had to be held no later than 31 December 2014.[108] This temporal detail is not a trivial issue. The Order in Council was an ad hoc, temporary devolution, only valid to hold the 2014 referendum, but not a general, unspecific, and unlimited modification that would allow Scotland from then on to organize referendums on independence. In October 2016, the Scottish government published a 'Consultation on a Draft Referendum Bill', where it implicitly admitted that Westminster approval is necessary if a second referendum is to be held: 'it would be expected that a section 30 order would be sought and agreed, as in 2014'.[109] However, as noted, because of Brexit the then Scottish First Minister, Nicola Sturgeon insisted on a new referendum[110] and, until

Parliament to ignore the vote.' Nick Barber, 'Scottish Independence and the Role of the United Kingdom' (*UK Constitutional Law Association Blog*, 11 January 2012) <https://ukconstitutionallaw.org/2012/01/11/nick-barber-scottish-independence-and-the-role-of-the-united-kingdom/> accessed 3 August 2022. Again, Nick Barber, 'The Constitutional Regulation of Scottish Secession' (2015) 38 Oxford Legal Studies Research Paper 1, 7. The November 2023 UKSC decision, addressed in the following pages, has settled this issue.

107 '[I]t is the UK Government's view that any Bill introduced in the Scottish Parliament providing for a referendum on independence would be outside the powers of the Scottish Parliament and, if challenged, would be struck down by the courts.' UK Government, 'Scotland's constitutional future' (n 98) 11. This view was supported by the House of Lords Constitution Committee, which established that although an authoritative determination of the legal issues could be given only by the courts, 'we are of the clear view that the legal analysis offered by the UK Government is correct. Without amendment, the Scotland Act 1998 confers no legislative power on the Scottish Parliament to pass an Act purporting to authorise a referendum about independence.' House of Lords Constitution Committee, 'Referendum on Scottish Independence' (2012) 24th Report <https://publications.parliament.uk/pa/ld201012/ldselect/ldconst/263/26304.htm#a7> accessed 30 July 2022.

108 Besides, with that ad hoc devolution the UK government also addressed and settled some other main concerns such as (1) the question of the referendum had to be clear and direct about independence ('the ballot paper must give the voter a choice between only two responses'), despite the desire of the then Scottish First Minister, Alex Salmond, to organize a multiple-choice referendum; and (2) the British general electoral rules (ie the 2000 Political Parties, Elections and Referendum Act) were to be applied.

109 'Consultation on a Draft Referendum Bill' (Scottish Government 2016) 6 <https://consult.scotland.gov.uk/elections-and-constitutional-development-division/draft-referendum-bill/supporting_documents/j456862.pdf> accessed 3 August 2022.

110 The second referendum petition brings to mind the sage comments made by Neil Walker, when he affirmed in 2013, before Brexit was a realistic option, that 'we cannot assume that the decisive referendum will produce a decisive result'. Neil Walker, 'The Receding Tape' (*UK Constitutional Law Association Blog*, 22 September 2013) <https://ukconstitutionallaw.org/2013/09/22/neil-walker-the-receding-tape/> accessed 30 July 2022.

now, the UK government has refused to agree to this. On 29 June 2022 Sturgeon declared that a new independent referendum would take place on 19 October 2023 and that the Lord Advocate (the principal legal adviser to the Scottish government) had made a reference to the UK Supreme Court, under paragraph 34 of Schedule 6 to the Scotland Act 1998, on whether a Bill for consultative referendum on Scottish independence would fall within the Scottish Parliament's legislative competence.[111] Beyond some procedural discussions,[112] the Scottish government was hoping that, since the Bill had made clear in clause 1 that the purpose of the Act 'is to make provision for ascertaining the views of the people of Scotland on whether Scotland should be an independent country',[113] the Supreme Court might consider that the referendum is not about breaking up Britain unilaterally, but about getting a view from the public. The Bill was stressing that the intended effect of the referendum was advisory only. So, the Scottish argument was that a consultative referendum (ie not self-executing) does not relate to the reserved matters of the Union.[114] But this argument is not convincing enough. And that is precisely what the UK Supreme Court declared in November 2023: whilst the referendum might not be binding in law, it might be seen as binding in practice, or politically. A secession vote would be hard to ignore. A vote to leave cannot be regarded as a sort of opinion poll. The judgment was handed down by the UK Supreme Court on 23 November 2022. The Court devoted the first few pages to examining issues of admissibility. As noted, there had been some controversy about whether the legal basis for this consultation was section 33 or 34 of the Scotland Act, the latter provision being the one favoured by the Supreme Court. Section 34 can be understood as a residual clause that allows referring to any other matter related to 'returned powers' or to the territorial Parliament. In addition, the Court decided not to use

[111] Scottish Government, 'Independence Referendum: First Minister's statement' 28 June 2022 <https://www.gov.scot/publications/ministerial-statement-independence-referendum/> accessed 30 July 2022.

[112] A discussion on preliminary issues to be found at Kenneth A Armstrong, 'A Matter for Another Day? Will the Supreme Court Accept the Lord Advocate's Independence Referendum Reference?' (*UK Constitutional Law Association Blog*, 29 June 2022) <https://ukconstitutionallaw.org/2022/06/29/kenneth-a-armstrong-a-matter-for-another-day-will-the-supreme-court-accept-the-lord-advocates-independence-referendum-reference/> accessed 30 July 2022. See also Alison L Young, 'Will Scotland hold an independence referendum in October 2023?' (*Constitutional Law Matters*, 29 June 2022) <https://constitutionallawmatters.org/2022/06/will-scotland-hold-an-independence-referendum-in-october-2023/> accessed 30 July 2022. One of the main problems detected in the referred analysis is that, arguably, the Lord Advocate could not refer a Bill to the Supreme Court until it had been passed by the Scottish Parliament. This was in fact the UK government view, that published a statement on 12 July 2022, considering the examination to be premature. On the substantive question, the UK government held its traditional position, ie that a Bill legislating for a referendum on independence would be outside the legislative competence of the Scottish Parliament. <https://www.gov.uk/government/news/statement-on-supreme-court> accessed 30 July 2022.

[113] Scottish Government, 'Draft Independence Referendum Bill' 28 June 2022 <https://www.gov.scot/publications/scottish-independence-referendum-bill/> accessed 30 July 2022.

[114] Aileen McHarg, 'Securing Scotland's independence: moving beyond process?' (*The Constitution Society*, 12 July 2022) <https://consoc.org.uk/securing-scotlands-independence/> accessed 30 July 2022.

its discretionary powers to reject the consultation, as requested by the British government and as it had done on other occasions, considering that it was a legal question of the utmost practical importance and that it was in the public interest that the Court assumed the task of giving a legal response. 'The answer to the question will have practical consequences: it will determine whether the proposed Bill is introduced into the Scottish Parliament or not. The question is therefore not hypothetical, academic or premature.'[115]

Next, the Court briefly analysed the merits of the matter: what was to be determined was whether an independence referendum proposed by the Scottish government Bill referred to ('relates to') matters reserved to the British Parliament of the mentioned in the Scotland Act of 1998. Because if that was the case, as has already been indicated, the organization of the referendum would be outside the competence of Scotland. The Court had already stated on previous occasions that the objective of paragraph 1 of Schedule 5 is that those matters in which the Union has an interest should continue to be the responsibility of the British Parliament (eg in *Imperial Tobacco* [2012] UKSC 61, para 29). In order to decide whether a consultative independence referendum 'refers' to reserved matters, there must be some kind of connection, but not necessarily a direct and legal effect between the norm and the reserved matters, the Court warned. The objectives and effects of the aforementioned standard have to be examined. In relation to the objectives, they were made explicit in the Bill: to organize a legal referendum on independence, which, 'obviously', observed the Court, is related both to the Union and to the sovereignty of the British Parliament (para 77). And, regarding the effects, the Court rejected the notion that only the direct effects prescribed in said rule should be considered. The practical consequences must also be taken into account. Thus, although the referendum is not self-executing, it cannot be equated to a mere public consultation exercise:[116]

> The effect of the Bill, however, will not be confined to the holding of a referendum. Even if it is not self-executing, and can in that sense be described as advisory, a lawfully held referendum is not merely an exercise in public consultation or a survey of public opinion. It is a democratic process held in accordance with the law which results in an expression of the view of the electorate on a specific issue of public policy on a particular occasion. (para. 78)

Here the Court agreed with the arguments of the Italian Constitutional Court developed in Judgment 118/2015 (addressed later in this chapter, see Section 4.3),

[115] *Reference by the Lord Advocate of devolution issues under paragraph 34 of Schedule 6 to the Scotland Act 1998* [2022] UKSC 31, para 53.

[116] Echoing here Stephen Tierney's view on referenda: 'the very act of staging a constitutional referendum is itself both a declaration that a people exists and a definition of that people' Tierney (n 70) 374–75.

although it did not mention it, on the unconstitutionality of an independence referendum in the Veneto region. The political importance of the referendum cannot be underestimated, as the history of UK referendums has shown and as has also been admitted by the Court in the past (para 79). Thus, a legal referendum, even if it does not generate any specific obligation for the UK government, would constitute an expression of democracy and would strengthen or undermine the democratic legitimacy of the Union, depending on the response, and would support or diminish the democratic credentials of the independence movement. In other words, the Court took into account the purpose sought by the Scottish government (ie the independence of Scotland) and manifested in documents of a political or programmatic nature. In short, for the UK Supreme Court it is clear that the organization of such a referendum refers to matters reserved to the British Parliament and is, therefore, excluded from the competences of Scotland. The Court's conclusion rests on political or practical effects (the impact a referendum might have on the legitimacy of the Union).[117]

Finally, the Court also examined an argument raised by the Scottish National Party (SNP) regarding the right to self-determination. The High Court rejected the argument that this right of public international law has any application in this case and brought up the well-known 1998 Opinion of the Supreme Court of Canada on the secession of Quebec. The Court held that the arguments then applied to Quebec are equally relevant in the case of Scotland: 'In our view these observations apply with equal force to the position of Scotland and the people of Scotland within the United Kingdom' (para 89). Following the Canadian reasoning, the UK Supreme Court assumed that the right to external self-determination (which could lead to secession)[118] applies only in situations of former colonies or oppressed peoples, a situation that does not apply to Scotland, endowed with institutions of self-government. Consequently, if the Scottish government wants to legally organize a new referendum on independence, it will have to reach an agreement with the British government, as has been done in the past (ie Agreement of 15 October 2012).

The Court's answer was no surprise for some commentators like Douglas-Scott who, being aware of legal precedents taking a narrow approach to devolution, had already anticipated the Court's approach: '[a]ll of this tends to imply

[117] Pravar Petkar, 'A Second Scottish Independence Referendum and Schrodinger's Sub-State Constituent Power' (*IACL-AIDC*, 29 November 2022) <https://blog-iacl-aidc.org/new-blog-3/2022/11/29/a-second-scottish-independence-referendum-and-schrodingers-sub-state-constituent-power> accessed 6 August 2023.

[118] It is important to highlight an aspect that often leads to confusion, even among lawyers. Denying that the right to self-determination of peoples developed by and within the United Nations (UN) is applicable to regions such as Scotland or Quebec, does not mean that the constitutional law of a given State does not grant an autonomous right to decide (or if one prefers to continue using the term, a right to self-determination). But then, references to the 'widely recognized right of self-determination' should be avoided for the sake of academic accuracy.

that the Supreme Court is unlikely to find a referendum Bill within the Scottish Parliament's powers'.[119]

The UK Supreme Court's negative answer provoked immediate reactions on both sides. While the UK Prime Minister welcomed 'the clear and definitive ruling', the then Scottish First Minister, despite her disappointment, stated that she would respect it. But, at the same time, she indicated her intention to use the next UK general election as a 'de facto' referendum on the single question of Scottish independence. This would represent 'a partial return to pre-2000 SNP policy that a winning majority of seats (rather than votes) at a devolved or UK election in Scotland would constitute a "mandate" to begin independence negotiations'.[120] However, at the moment, such an approach remains unclear, particularly after Sturgeon's resignation in February 2023.

Alternatively, an agreement with the UK government could pave the way for a second referendum with a sound legal basis. Again, although that might seem highly unlikely today, political circumstances can change very quickly and no one can exclude the possibility of such an agreement if there is a change of leadership in the UK government.

In any event, for our purposes, what should be underlined is that even a flexible constitution like Britain's has made sure that Scotland cannot exercise a unilateral and uncontrolled right to secede.

4.1.2 Northern Ireland

The Northern Ireland case is another example to test the British approach to self-determination and secession. In this case, however, self-determination is not so much linked to secession and independence, but to the attempt of joining another country: Ireland. Following Irish independence in 1922, the Northern part of the island (with a Protestant majority) remained part of the UK. The Protestant majority in Northern Ireland had traditionally tried to keep the union with Britain, while the significant Catholic minority, which considers itself distinctly Irish, had consistently sought to promote greater integration and potential union with

[119] Sionaidh Douglas-Scott, 'A Second Scottish Independence Referendum in the UK Supreme Court' (Verfassungsblog, 14 October 2022) https://verfassungsblog.de/a-second-scottish-independence-referendum-in-the-uk-supreme-court/ accessed 6 August 2023. However, anticipation of the argument should not be confused with support for it. Douglas-Scott believes that the UK constitutional situation is very different from, for instance, Spain or the US, where either the Constitution (in the former case) or the Supreme Court (in the latter one) establishes the indissolubility of both countries. In her view, '[s]ince 1707, Scotland has maintained its own separate civic institutions, legal system and cultural heritage- all factors which point to the Union as a continuing agreement between two independent nations. This in turn, suggests that, should Scotland no longer wish to continue the Union, there is the right to terminate this agreement.' In fact, she even considers that if the UK government continues to reject any negotiation, Scotland status is reduced to 'a colony or a region with no history of independent statehood.' ibid.

[120] David Torrance, 'Scottish Independence Referendum: Legal Issues' (2022) House of Commons Library 1, 93.

Ireland.[121] Unlike in the Scottish case, where the possibility to secede depends on the political will of the parties involved (ie the Scottish and British governments), in Northern Ireland the British government is constitutionally obliged to permit such a right under certain conditions. In effect, on 10 April 1998 the Belfast Agreement, a peace agreement also known as the Good Friday Agreement (GFA), was reached between the British and Irish governments and most of the political parties in Northern Ireland. This agreement is made up of two inter-related documents. First, there is the 'Agreement reached in the multi-party negotiations', also known as the Multi-Party Agreement (MPA), to which is annexed the British-Irish Agreement (BIA). Second, there is the BIA, which also includes the MPA as Annex 1. While the BIA is legally a treaty, or international agreement, made between two contracting States, and signed by the UK and Irish governments, the MPA is a political or moral agreement between the political parties. The two States are legal parties, but only through Annex 1, and only to the extent that the content of the MPA contains obligations binding on the States parties in international law. In effect, the BIA contains an annex (the political agreement) that is also legally binding under international law, as established by article 2 BIA.[122] Article 1 BIA permits the people in Northern Ireland to exercise the right of external self-determination—by seceding from the UK and joining with the Republic of Ireland upon a majority vote of the population.[123] Importantly, and before examining this question in depth, the constitutional relevance of the Belfast Agreement must be underlined: 'it cannot be changed piecemeal or unilaterally. It is constitutional in its provision for a complex institutional unity with multiple checks and balances that are difficult to undo.'[124] In effect, the current devolved political system of Northern Ireland, the 1998 Northern Ireland Act, which includes the right to self-determination, is based on the 1998 Belfast Agreement. After decades of a long and bloody conflict and attempts to solve the *Troubles*[125] between the two communities in the region, peace process negotiators[126] were able to produce a strongly consociational agreement.[127] Such agreement (in particular the MPA) provides for,

[121] Paul R Williams and Sabrineh Ardalan, 'The Northern Ireland Peace Agreement: Evolving the Principle of Self-determination' (1999) 12 Leiden Journal of International Law 155, 156.

[122] A detailed legal analysis of the Belfast Agreement to be found at Austen Morgan, *The Belfast Agreement: A Practical Legal Analysis* (The Belfast Press 2000).

[123] ibid 164.

[124] Bill Kissane, *New Beginnings: Constitutionalism and Democracy in Modern Ireland* (University College Dublin Press 2011) xii–xiii. Furthermore, in a landmark case (*Robinson v Sec'y of State for Northern Ireland and others*, 2002) the GFA was accepted as the necessary framework for understanding and interpreting the Northern Ireland Act (1998). Kieran McEvoy and John Morison, 'Beyond the "Constitutional Moment?: Law, Transition, and Peace-making in Northern Ireland' (2002) 26(4) Fordham International Law Journal 961, 967.

[125] Williams and Ardalan (n 121) 157.

[126] The agreement, however, is not so much the product of a negotiation, but the product of a planning process. Donald Horowitz, 'Explaining the Northern Ireland Agreement: The Sources of an Unlikely Constitutional Consensus' (2002) 32 British Journal of Political Science 193, 199.

[127] 'The peace process is based on the conviction that a system of shared autonomous government offers the best framework for resolving the conflict.' Rogelio Alonso, 'Pathways Out of Terrorism in

a grand coalition, power sharing by proportional inclusion of parties in the executive, a certain amount of cultural autonomy (particularly in education and language), and group vetoes to assure Protestant and Catholic communities that important decisions will only be made with the broad consent of representatives of the relevant community.[128]

The need for a wide consensus is one of the key relevant characteristics of the devolved political system, but as stated above, our focus here is on the right to secede conceded to Northern Ireland. The Belfast Agreement (both art 1 BIA and Annex A of the Constitutional Issues of the MPA) affirms the right to national self-determination for the Irish people and redefines it so that it must be exercised by agreement between the two parts of the island:

1. The participants endorse the commitment made by the British and Irish Governments that, in a new British-Irish Agreement replacing the Anglo-Irish Agreement, they will:
   (i) recognise the legitimacy of whatever choice is freely exercised by a majority of the people of Northern Ireland with regard to its status, whether they prefer to continue to support the Union with Great Britain or a sovereign united Ireland;
   (ii) recognise that it is for the people of the island of Ireland alone, by agreement between the two parts respectively and without external impediment, to exercise their right of self-determination on the basis of consent, freely and concurrently given, North and South, to bring about a united Ireland, if that is their wish, accepting that this right must be achieved and exercised with and subject to the agreement and consent of a majority of the people of Northern Ireland;[129]

Annex A of the Constitutional Issues of the MPA (incorporated in the 1998 Northern Ireland Act, s 1 and, therefore, constitutionally binding as part of the UK constitutional legal order) further states the following:

(1) Northern Ireland in its entirety remains part of the United Kingdom and shall not cease to be so without the consent of a majority of the people of Northern

Northern Ireland and the Basque Country: The Misrepresentation of the Irish Model' (2004) 16(4) Terrorism and Political Violence 695, 706.

[128] Horowitz (n 126) 194.
[129] Jennifer Todd, 'Contested Constitutionalism? Northern Ireland and the British-Irish Relationship since 2010' (2017) 70 Parliamentary Affairs 301, 303.

Ireland voting in a poll held for the purposes of this section in accordance with Schedule 1.

(2) But if the wish expressed by a majority in such a poll is that Northern Ireland should cease to be part of the United Kingdom and form part of a united Ireland, the Secretary of State shall lay before Parliament such proposals to give effect to that wish as may be agreed between Her Majesty's Government in the United Kingdom and the Government of Ireland.

Schedule 1 provides that 'the Secretary of State [member of the British government] may by order direct the holding of a poll for the purposes of section 1 on a date specified in the order'. Such a poll is known in as a 'border poll'. Interestingly, Schedule 1 also establishes that the Secretary of State shall call a border poll if 'it appears likely to him that a majority of those voting would express a wish that Northern Ireland should cease to be part of the United Kingdom and form part of a united Ireland'.[130] That is, the poll will only be called if it is highly likely that the majority will choose to leave the UK and join the Republic of Ireland. Thus, the referendum proceeds when the attitude of the electorate is already sufficiently clear in favour of the option of leaving. The poll would not be the starting point of a process, but would confirm a state of mind that is already majoritarian among voters.

There are two additional issues that should also be highlighted: the question about the demos, and the presumed unilateral character of the right. Or, put another way, the discretionary power of the Secretary of State to call a border poll.

First, these provisions address the difficult question about the demos, which has been a matter of contestation in Northern Ireland, 'the question at the very heart of disputes about sovereignty and self-determination, a question known locally as the "constitutional question"'.[131] In short, is there one single demos in the whole island, as Irish republicanism has always argued,[132] or two separate demoi: an Irish demos and a Northern Ireland demos? The Belfast Agreement resolves the question in the latter sense, by declaring that Northern Ireland itself is entitled to decide. This approach is known as the 'principle of consent'. It assumes that a united Ireland can only come about with the consent of a majority of the population in Northern Ireland.[133] It acknowledges the traditional Ulster Protestant approach: 'Ulster Protestants seek recognition of what to them is an inescapable historical fact, that Ireland has two peoples having the right to self-determination, not one.'[134]

[130] Such provisions are to be found both in the 1998 Belfast Agreement and in the 1998 Northern Ireland Act.

[131] Arthur Aughey, 'Northern Ireland Narratives of British Democracy (2012) 33(2) Policy Studies 145, 147.

[132] Throughout their history, the IRA and Sinn Fein had rejected the possibility of providing Northern Ireland alone with a right to self-determination. Alonso (n 127) 700.

[133] ibid.

[134] Alexander M Johnston, 'Self-determination in Comparative Perspective: Northern Ireland and South Africa' (1990) 17(2) Politikon: South African Journal of Political Studies 5, 8.

Second, the right to withdraw from the UK and join the Republic of Ireland is not a unilateral right, in the sense that it can be decided by the Northern Ireland government at any time. As has been noted, there is an '[i]mplicit distinction between the ground of sovereignty in self-determination, and the exercise of sovereignty (presently by the British state)'.[135] It is the Secretary of State (belonging to the British government) who is entitled to decide if there is a majority within Northern Ireland wishing to break its ties with the UK and, therefore, the one allowing for the organization of a border poll.[136] In addition, the discretion enjoyed by the Secretary of State is quite broad, as the High Court of Justice in Northern Ireland recalled in 2018. In *Re Raymond McCord*, the High Court discussed whether the Secretary of State was bound as a matter of law to formulate and publish a policy which sets out the circumstances in which they will order the holding of a border poll. The Court recalled that the Secretary of State: (1) is given a discretionary power to order a border poll for a number of reasons and in different circumstances (eg they could call a poll in order to give quietus to the controversial question of a united Ireland for a period of time if they think a majority would vote in favour of remaining in the UK); and (2) is given a duty to call a border only (as previously stated) if it appears to the Secretary of State that a majority would be likely to vote in favour of leaving the UK. The Court pointed out that the precise circumstances and the political context of such a decision are 'variable' and 'highly political' and that the Northern Ireland Act 'does not specify the matters which must be taken into account or left out of account in deciding whether a border poll is or is not appropriate'.[137] As regards the duty to call a border poll, the Court concluded by stating that 'the Secretary of State must honestly reflect on the evidence available to her to see whether it leads her to the conclusion that the majority would be likely to vote in favour of a united Ireland', but at the same time concedes that the 'overall evidential context on how it should be analysed and viewed is a matter for the Secretary of State'.[138]

In sum, Northern Ireland has constitutional recognition of a right to change its status quo (also an internationally binding provision, since it was first established in an international agreement). However, such a right will be monitored by the British government: it cannot be exercised unilaterally.

[135] Todd (n 129) 306.

[136] As Qvortrup points out, 'one of the most persistent and controversial questions regarding national self-determination and the referendums, is who is allowed to initiate a vote'. Qvortrup (n 89). The British Secretary of State has a similar role to that held by the Canadian House of Commons when having to verify (although in this case *a posteriori*) the existence of a majority, notes Martinico. Martinico, '"A Message of Hope": A Legal Perspective on the Reference' (n 62) 257. In this regard, Murray and O'Donoghue note that when required to interpret the Good Friday Agreement, 'judges have frequently blanched at its "intensely political" nature and the multiple readings that its terms support'. Colin RG Murray and Aoife O'Donoghue, 'Life after Brexit: Operationalising the Belfast/Good Friday Agreement's Principle of Consent' (2018) 42(1) Dublin University Law Journal 147, 149.

[137] *Re Raymond McCord* [2018] NIBQ 106, para 18.

[138] ibid para 20.

4.2 Spain

At this moment, Spain is the European country that is facing the most serious secessionist crisis.[139] The 2017 secession attempt of the Catalan government and the reactions thereto across the rest of Spain, at both the judicial and the political levels, created an atmosphere of tension that was still intense in 2023. After the July 2023 inconclusive general elections, in November, Spain's socialist Prime Minister Pedro Sánchez reached a controversial deal to win the backing from pro-independence parties and secure another term in office. This agreement includes an Amnesty Law for pro-independence leaders and supporters. It remains to be seen whether this will bring harmony to the country. For now, the rhetoric used in the political agreement has angered many Spaniards because, among other things, it attacks the judiciary by mentioning 'lawfare' when referring to court decisions applied to the 2017 Catalan pro-independence crisis.

Since 2012 the government of Catalonia has attempted to organize a referendum or consultation on independence, but the Spanish government has challenged these attempts before the Spanish Constitutional Court (SCC), which has declared them contrary to the Spanish Constitution. This section will review the different Resolutions, which show that Spanish constitutionalism concerning secession follows the classic paradigm initiated by the US in the nineteenth century. Before doing so, the law should be placed in context.

Unlike in the case of Canada, where Quebec has already organized two referendums without the opposition of the central government and unlike in the British scenario, where the British and the Scottish governments agreed on the organization of one referendum in the recent past, in Spain the lack of political will, along with rigid constitutional impediments, have prevented holding such a referendum. As previously stated, 'the very act of staging a constitutional referendum is itself both a declaration that a people exists and a definition of that people'[140] and that constitutional referendums in general, and independence referendums in particular, can have a 'vital nation-building role'.[141] In Spain, accepting the organization of such a referendum would mean admitting the national and sovereign character of Catalonia. Many feel that this would threaten the national sovereignty of the Spanish people as a whole. This is one of the main reasons underpinning

[139] Apart from Catalonia, there is another Spanish region with a noted pro-independence movement, namely, the Basque country. In recent years, however, the Basque government has not shown any interest in following a pro-independence path, although it is currently negotiating extending the Basque self-government but in an agreed manner and within the legal limits. Ironically, the approaches of both nationalist movements seem to have interchanged. Thus, during the second half of the nineteenth century, the Basque nationalist leader Sabino Arana 'publicly denounced what he termed the "Catalanist error" of seeking autonomy and co-operation within the Spanish framework, insisting that the Basque movement demanded total separation'. Stanley Payne, 'Nationalism, Regionalism and Micronationalism in Spain' (1991) 26(3/4) Journal of Contemporary History 479, 485.

[140] Tierney (n 70) 374–75.

[141] ibid 366.

the Spanish government's opposition (from the current and the previous ones) to the organization of such a referendum. The current legislative decentralization of Spain, which is a quasi-federal polity,[142] was only recently established with the democratic restoration in 1978. Yet, decentralization is not totally alien to Spanish history.

It is true that since 1714 Spain was a highly centralized State. However, decentralization dates back to the very origins of Spain as a political unit. Throughout the Middle Ages, Hispania was just a factitious unity to a complex of Crowns and kingdoms—Castile and León, Navarre, Aragon (that included the kingdoms of Aragon, Valencia, and Mallorca, and the Principality of Catalonia), Portugal, and the Moorish Kingdom of Granada, each having its own institutions. But this fragmentation changed in 1469. 'The marriage of Ferdinand and Isabella in 1469 and their joint rule over Castile and Aragon from 1479 signalized to the world at large the emergence of a new European nation, the birth of Spain.'[143] The Spanish monarchy established then a confederal structure called *Unión Real*, where Catalonia and other territories enjoyed a certain level of self-government and autonomy within the Spanish Crown. After the Spanish Succession War (1702–1715) the new King, Philiph V,[144] grandson of French King Louis XIV, abolished public local laws and institutions of the territories of the Crown of Aragón (in Catalonia, Mallorca, and Aragon local private law was maintained, while in Valencia both local public and private law was abolished), and introduced French centralist patterns in Spain in his attempts to rationalize the bureaucracy and to limit local freedoms.[145] During the period of the second Spanish Republic (1931–1936) there was an initial attempt to decentralize Spain,[146] but the Franco dictatorship (1939–1975) that followed the Civil War (1936–1939) brought an end to that attempt and the continuation of a highly centralized State.

As for Catalonia, Elliot admits that in the Middle Ages 'Catalonia was a distinctive national community, whose inhabitants were united by ties of language, culture and history'.[147] But he has also criticized the misuse of modern words such as 'nation' or 'sovereignty' to medieval or early modern entities.[148] Catalanism, or

[142] Víctor Ferreres Comella, *The Constitution of Spain. A Contextual Analysis* (Hart Publishing 2013) 161–99. See also Eliseo Aja, *Estado Autonómico y Reforma Federal* (Alianza Editorial 2014).

[143] John H Elliot, *The Revolt of the Catalans. A Study in the Decline of Spain (1598–1640)* (CUP 1963) 2.

[144] The Bourbon Philiph V came to power after winning the Spanish Succession War in which Catalans fought against him in support of the Habsburg Dynasty. Barcelona was finally defeated after a 14-month siege on 11 September 1714.

[145] David D Laitin, 'Linguistic Revival: Politics and Culture in Catalonia' (1989) 31(2) Comparative Studies in Society and History 297, 305.

[146] Payne, 'Nationalism, Regionalism and Micronationalism in Spain' (n 139) 484.

[147] Elliot, *The Revolt of the Catalans* (n 143) 43. In any event, the argument that there are 'ethnic' differences between Catalans and other Spaniards, as suggested by Ginsburg and Versteeg, is dubious, to say the least. Ginsburg and Versteeg (n 2) 946.

[148] John H Elliot, *History in the Making* (Yale UP 2012) 60.

the political movement that demanded Catalan self-government within Spain, only originated in the second half of the nineteenth century.[149]

In any event, and despite the decentralized origins of Spain as a country in the fifteenth century, the current Spanish constitutional legal order does not admit that the inhabitants of a self-autonomous community can decide by themselves the division of the country. Spanish constitutionalism has been tested with a severe secession attempt carried out by Catalan institutions.[150] In order to simplify the picture, one could highlight two Resolutions and two laws of the Catalan Parliament that have been challenged by the Spanish government before the SCC. The review of the subsequent judicial decisions will shed light on the Spanish legal order.[151]

4.2.1 Judgment 42/2014

The SCC rendered this judgment on a Resolution that had been passed by the Catalan Parliament on 23 January 2013. Basically, this Resolution proclaimed that the Catalan people are sovereign and that therefore they have the 'right to decide' their own future. The SCC held that considering the Catalan people as sovereign is contrary to articles 1.2 and 2 of the Spanish Constitution. Article 1.2 of the Spanish Constitution establishes that '[n]ational sovereignty belongs to the Spanish people, from whom all State powers emanate'. Thus, national sovereignty cannot be divided.[152] Article 2 proclaims that '[t]he Constitution is based on the indissoluble unity of the Spanish Nation, the common and indivisible homeland

[149] Catalanism was born due to four major influences: the rebirth of Catalan vernacular literature in a period of cultural effervescence known as *Renaixença*; concerns of the Catalan bourgeoisie because of the Spanish economic decline (especially after the disaster of 1898); the influence of federalist and progressive ideals; and the anti-Bourbon traditionalism (residues of Catalan Carlism). This is the widely accepted thesis about the origins of Catalanism. It was developed for the first time by a Jesús Pabón, who became the biographer of one of the most important Catalan politicians of the twentieth century, Francesc Cambó. Jesús Pabón, *Cambó. 1876–1947* (Alpha 1999) 71–127. His thesis is accepted by Payne, who considers Pabón's work to be the best Spanish biography of the century. Stanley Payne, 'Catalan and Basque Nationalism' (1971) 6(1) Journal of Contemporary History 15, 20.

[150] There are hundreds of books and articles dealing with the current Catalan pro-independence movement. While some scholars tend to accept the reasoning advanced by many pro-independence supporters that the current crisis has its main origins in a lack of political accommodation (see Karlo Basta, 'The State between Minority and Majority Nationalism: Decentralization, Symbolic Recognition, and Secessionist Crises in Spain and Canada' (2017) 48(1) Publius: The Journal of Federalism 51, 63), others also point out the impact of the significant economic crisis suffered in Spain in 2010–2012 and how it enabled the pro-independence movement to present secession as a way out of the situation. See, for instance, Kathryn Crameri, 'Do Catalans Have 'the Right to Decide'? Secession, Legitimacy and Democracy in Twenty-first Century Europe' [2015] Global Discourse 1, 7. See, for a similar approach, Angel Rodríguez-Vergara, 'Moving Towards Independence—Breaching the Law: Self-determination and Secession in Catalonia' (2019) XVII Rassegna di diritto pubblico europeo 343, 346.

[151] In the past, the Spanish Constitutional Court had already dealt with self-determination demands from the Basque Government: Constitutional Court Judgments 76/1994, 14 March and 103/2008, 11 September.

[152] In fact, in 1978 during the drafting of the Constitution a Basque Member of the Spanish Parliament, Francisco Letamendía, proposed including the right to self-determination. However, even members of the main Catalan nationalist party rejected the proposal. Diario de Sesiones de las Cortes Generales. Congreso de los Diputados, 91, 16 June 1978, 3427–3435 <http://www.congreso.es/public_oficiales/L0/CONG/DS/C_1978_091.PDF> accessed 3 August 2022.

of all Spaniards'. The Court held[153] that an autonomous community cannot unilaterally call a referendum of self-determination to decide on its integration in Spain, because sovereignty is only reserved to the Spanish nation. Thus, territorial integrity is at the core of the Spanish foundational pact, and should not be at the disposal of a majoritarian vote.[154] The Court accepted that the so-called 'right to decide' is a legitimate political aspiration. However, this aspiration, since it is precluded in the current constitutional framework, should be channelled through the appropriate procedure: constitutional amendment. The Court nonetheless accepted that, unlike in Germany with its model of militant democracy, in Spain there are no constitutional principles excluded from the constitutional amendment procedure. The Court also considered, using imprecise and vague wording, that some preparatory measures towards secession are possible before the amendment of the Constitution. The Court did not explain further what type of measure would be legally acceptable. It only ruled out the possibility of a proper referendum on secession. It could be argued that the Court might accept some other type of consultation.[155] In this decision the SCC referred explicitly to the 1998 Opinion of the Canadian Supreme Court and asked the involved authorities to start a political dialogue ('there is a cry here for the political branches to assume the burden of negotiating a political solution to a deep constitutional crisis'[156]), but also reminded the political actors about the constitutional framework within which political decisions must ultimately be made. The Court, following the Canadian example, was eager to speak to the actors by examining the constitutionality of the parliamentary resolution, even if it could easily have avoided the case.[157]

4.2.2 Judgment 259/2015

In this decision the Court essentially followed the reasoning of the previous judgment. The Court was, again, asked about the constitutionality of another Resolution passed by the Catalan Parliament on 9 November 2015. The referred Resolution, with strong rhetoric, proclaimed the beginning of a democratic disconnection from Spanish institutions to move toward independence from Spain. To that end, Catalan institutions would no longer be bound by the central government's edicts or the decisions of the SCC:

[153] The main reasoning of the Court is to be found in *Fundamentos Jurídicos*, 3 and 4.

[154] Rodríguez-Vergara (n 150) 367.

[155] Josep Maria Castellà Andreu, 'Tribunal Constitucional y proceso secesionista catalán: respuestas jurídico-constitucionales a un conflicto político-constitucional' (2016) 37 Teoría y Realidad Constitucional 561, 575.

[156] Víctor Ferreres Comella, 'The Spanish Constitutional Court Confronts Catalonia's "Right to Decide"' (Comment on the Judgment 42/2014)' (2014) European Constitutional Law Review 571, 585.

[157] 'According to its case law, parliamentary acts can only be challenged before the Constitutional Court if they generate legal effects. It is hard to specify what exactly are the legal effects that the Declaration of sovereignty produces. It rather looks like a purely political act, to be understood as part of the political game, which does not give rise to any legal effects on the institutions or on citizens. The Court, however, concluded that the resolution could be reviewed against the Constitution.' ibid 579.

> The Parliament of Catalonia, as the depositary of sovereignty and the expression of the constituent power, reiterates that this Chamber and the process of democratic uncoupling from the Spanish State shall not be subject to the decisions of the institutions of the Spanish State, in particular the Constitutional Court, which it considers devoid of legitimacy and jurisdiction following its Judgment of June 2010 on the Statute of Autonomy of Catalonia, previously voted on by the people in a referendum, among other Rulings.[158]

In the Court's opinion, this Resolution was contrary to the Spanish Constitution, since it represented a foundational act of the creation of a Catalan independent State. Referring to its own consolidated case law, the Court noted that the unity of sovereignty is the foundation of the Spanish Constitution. Moreover, the Court reminded us of the supremacy of the Constitution in the Spanish constitutional legal order and considered that the democratic principle was subordinated to the constitutional text: there is no democracy outside the rule of law.

These two judgments are the main decisions that express the Spanish constitutionalist position regarding attempts at secession.[159] The Court's position was very clear: (1) self-autonomous communities do not have the right to organize unilaterally a referendum on independence; and (2) the organization of such a referendum requires amendment of the Constitution. This position is based on the fact that Spain is a constitutional democracy, where ordinary laws have to be subject to a supreme norm, the Constitution. This line of reasoning has been largely accepted by Spanish legal scholarship.[160] However, some authors have even rejected the possibility of including a secession clause in a future constitutional reform, since the unity of the country is an (implicit) immanent limit to such reform,[161] following the approach adopted by the Italian Constitutional Court, which is considered in Section 4.3.

Despite the clarity and severity of the Constitutional Court's position,[162] in September 2017 the pro-independence majority in the Catalan

[158] Catalan Parliament, Resolution 1/XI of 9 November 2015. As Carmen Plaza has suggested, the process 'was conceived not as an attempt to modify the Spanish Constitution, but as a unilateral act to break free from its jurisdiction'. Carmen Plaza, 'Catalonia's Secession Process at the Constitutional Court: A Never-Ending Story' (2018) 24(3) European Public Law 373, 385.

[159] There are also other decisions issued by the SCC regarding public consultations or secessionist activities carried out by the Catalan government. For instance, Constitutional Court Judgments 31/2015 and 32/2015, 25 February and 138/2015, 11 June. And more recently, Constitutional Court Judgment 114/2017, 17 October, which deemed unconstitutional, by unanimity, the Catalan Law 19/2017, of 6 September, on the Self-Determination Referendum, that will be discussed further in this chapter.

[160] Josep Maria Castellà Andreu, 'Constitution and Referendum on Secession in Catalonia' in Alberto López Basaguren and Leire Escajedo (eds), *Claims for Secession and Federalism* (Springer 2019) 405 ff.

[161] Javier Ruipérez Alamillo, 'La nueva revindicación de la secesión de Cataluña en el contexto normativo de la Constitución española de 1978 y el Tratado de Lisboa' (2013) 31 Teoría y Realidad Constitucional 89, 131.

[162] Here I would disagree with Ginsburg and Versteeg when they refer to the constitutional ambiguity of Spanish legal framework regarding secession. Ginsburg and Versteeg (n 2) 975. At least until now, the SCC has been very clear and the Spanish constitutional legal order cannot be described as ambiguous

Parliament[163] passed two laws: 19/2017, on a referendum on self-determination and 20/2017, on the foundation of the Republic. Both laws, ordinary Catalan laws, established that they prevailed over the Catalan Statute of Autonomy and over the Spanish Constitution. Note here that according to article 222.1.b) of the Catalan Statute of Autonomy, the approval of its reform requires the favourable vote of two-thirds of the members of Parliament, namely 90 MPs (out of 135). Since the Catalan Statute is considered a fundamental law of the Catalan community, a qualified majority is required in order to amend it. It should be borne in mind that these laws that challenged the fundamental order of Catalonia (and Spain) were passed by 'only' 72 MPs. Thus, from a procedural standpoint they were considered ordinary, while their scope and impact clearly exceeded the limits of the Catalan autonomy. Besides, the extraordinary parliamentary procedure used to approve those norms reduced the period for discussion and amendment to less than a day for each Bill. The Catalan Legal Advisory Council itself unanimously rejected the move.

Both laws were immediately challenged before the SCC, which suspended the laws and their effects, based on the preceding doctrine of the Court that has been already analysed (particularly, SCC Judgment 114/2027, 17 October). However, the referendum took place on 1 October 2017, although without procedural guarantees. The voting led to harsh confrontation and some violent clashes with police, who were trying to prevent its occurrence, pursuant to Court orders. According to the Catalan government, 43 per cent of the population went to the polls to vote in favour of independence.[164] The former Catalan President Carles Puigdemont

when it comes to secession. Yet, it is true that following the political negotiations that led to the re-election of Pedro Sánchez in November 2023 it is not entirely unthinkable that some type of consultation or referendum will be agreed upon. In fact, the Catalan government in September 2023 presented a 'Clarity Agreement', drafted by a group of scholars, that outlines options for holding a referendum. Those options have already been rejected by most constitutional law scholars in Spain and the SCC in previous rulings, as explained above, but the possibility of a change of jurisprudence in the future cannot be ruled out completely, particularly after the composition of the Court changed significantly in December 2022.

[163] It should be noted that, although in September 2017, pro-independence political forces enjoyed an absolute majority position in the Catalan Parliament (72 out of 135 seats, following the 2015 elections), they did not enjoy the same type of popular support (47.8% following the 2015 elections). The reason for this mismatch is that, like in many other electoral systems, rural areas have an overrepresentation in terms of seats in the Catalan Parliament and it is precisely in these areas, unlike in Barcelona and surrounding areas, where support for independence is higher. The picture after the 2017 and 2021 Catalan elections is very similar. Catalonia is a deeply divided society. According to the latest Omnibus poll from Catalonia's public polling agency (conducted in June and July 2022), 41% of Catalans want Catalonia to become an independent State. On the other hand, those Catalans who oppose independence exceed half the population: 52%. When more options are available, complexity is added to the picture: 34% favour independence, 30% prefer being an autonomous community within Spain, 22% choose a federal solution, and 8% would prefer less self-government <https://ceo.gencat.cat/ca/barometre/detall/index.html?id=8428> accessed 28 July 2022.

[164] Detailed results to be found at <https://govern.cat/salapremsa/notes-premsa/303541/govern-trasllada-resultats-definitius-referendum-1l-doctubre-parlament-catalunya> accessed 3 August 2022. The low turnout indicates that it was not perceived by a significant part of the community as an official referendum, since 'the average turnout in the 40 independence referendums held since 1980, has been 86%'. Matt Qvortrup, 'Independence Referendums. History, Legal Status and Voting Behaviour'

declared unilaterally the independence of Catalonia on 27 October. In response, the Spanish Senate enacted coercive measures in Catalonia like the imposition of the direct rule by the Spanish government (art 155 of the Spanish Constitution): the dissolution of the Catalan Parliament and the Catalan Cabinet and the call for early elections on 21 December. Surprisingly, and despite initial concerns and hesitation in Madrid, direct rule was accepted peacefully by the Catalan parties and society, with no resistance or opposition. Probably, since independence has never been embraced by a truly large majority of the Catalan voters, the pro-independence parties lacked the internal support to further continue the game. Meanwhile, Supreme Court judges initiated criminal actions against the main Catalan authorities with the preventive imprisonment of some of them. Others, like former President Puigdemont, left Catalonia to escape judicial charges. Although all of the imprisoned politicians were finally convicted and given long sentences in October 2019,[165] at the beginning of 2020 they were already partially released from prison and in June 2021 all were pardoned. Today, there is certain normalization, but as noted before, it is still too soon to assess the impact of the new political agreement between the Socialist Party and Catalan pro-independence parties reached in November 2023.

As we have seen, the Spanish approach follows (at least until now) the classic paradigm (represented by the US) and diverges from the Canadian and British perspectives in the sense of not even permitting a referendum on independence. However, both in Canada (as in Italy and Germany) and in Spain, respect for institutions and authorities of the rule of law and the Constitution are considered key principles of the Constitution:

> In all these legal orders, the final decision on secession necessarily implies a constitutional reform. Thus, unilateral secession is excluded, for the sovereignty power is the Spanish people as a whole and not the territorial entities that constitute Spain.[166]

4.3 Italy

Italy has not yet faced a serious and persistent secessionist challenge like Spain, but has a long tradition of pro-independence movements in the North of the country. However, the issue of secession has not given rise to public discussions and has

in Carlos Closa, Costanza Margiotta, and Giuseppe Martinico (eds), *Between Democracy and Law. The Amorality of Secession* (Routledge 2020) 136.

[165] Criminal Judgment 459/2019 of the Supreme Court, Criminal Chamber, Section 1, Rec 20907/2017, of 14 October.

[166] Castellà Andreu, 'Constitution and Referendum on Secession in Catalonia' (n 160).

remained completely out of the national political debate[167] except among certain constitutional scholars. Yet, it is interesting to take a brief look at the position of the Italian Constitutional Court, since it is very similar to the Spanish position. In June 2014, the regional council of the Veneto, a rich Northern-Eastern Italian region, passed two laws (15/2014 and 16/2014) regarding consultative referendums on (1) improving the autonomy of Veneto and (2) the independence of Veneto. Both laws were immediately challenged before the Italian Constitutional Court by the central government. In April 2015, the Italian Constitutional Court rendered its decision in a joint case.[168] The reasoning of the Court regarding the Veneto Regional Law no 16 of 19 June 2014 (calling of the consultative referendum on independence for Veneto),[169] which was declared unconstitutional, is particularly interesting. First, the Court noted that 'it is legally mistaken to assert that a consultative referendum is equivalent to any other spontaneous exercise of freedom of expression by citizens in a coordinated manner' (para 5). This was because even in the case of consultative referendums without immediate legal effects, the Court argued the following:

> A referendum performs the function of activating, initiating or opposing public decision making processes, which largely have legislative status. For this reason, popular referenda on national or regional level, including consultative referenda, are typified institutions and must be conducted in the manner and subject to the limits laid down by the Constitution or stipulated on the basis of the Constitution. (para 5)

In sum, a referendum is not a qualified poll, it implies much more. The Court also rejected the argument that the constitutional principles of pluralism and autonomy justify 'initiatives involving the consultation of the electorate—albeit only for consultative purposes—concerning prospective secession with a view to the creation of a new sovereign body' (para 7.2). Furthermore, the Court continues, a consultative referendum on independence concerns fundamental choices on the constitutional level,

> which are as such precluded from the scope of regional referendums according to the case law of the Constitutional Court cited above, but seeks to subvert the

[167] Cristina Fasone, '"Italian-style" secession and the semi-indifference of national politics' (*Verfassungsblog*, 21 April 2015) <https://verfassungsblog.de/italian-style-secession-and-the-semi-indifference-of-national-politics/> accessed 3 August 2022.

[168] Italian Constitutional Court Judgment 118/2015, 29 April. The conclusions of the decision are available in English <http://www.cortecostituzionale.it/documenti/download/doc/recent_judgments/S118_2015_en.pdf> accessed 3 August 2022.

[169] That law provided for the calling of a consultative referendum in order to establish the wishes of the voters of Veneto concerning the following question: 'Do you want Veneto to become an independent and sovereign Republic? Yes or No?'.

> institutions in a manner that is inherently incompatible with the founding principles of the unity and indivisibility of the Republic laid down in Article 5 of the Constitution. *The unity of the Republic is an aspect of constitutional law that is so essential as to be protected even against the power of constitutional amendment* (see Judgment no 1146 of 1988) (para 7.2) [emphasis added].

The Court here implicitly reminds us of the distinction between autonomy (granted to regions) and sovereignty[170] (granted to the Italian people as a whole). It is also pointing out that a referendum on secession is revolutionary in the sense that it challenges State sovereignty.[171] Besides, unlike in Spain, the Italian Constitutional Court considers that there are implicit limits to the constitutional amendment process. One of these limits is the unity of the Republic, the territorial integrity of the Italian State. Therefore, the Court excludes secession even from a future constitutional amendment, or as Martinico underlines, excludes secession in such a manner in the name of the principles of unity and indivisibility that, from this perspective, he argues, the Italian Constitutional Court seems to be more radical than the Spanish Constitutional Court.[172] This restrictiveness, although with the exceptions we will mention, is also to be found in the German constitutional legal order.

4.4 Germany

Secessionist movements are almost non-existent in Germany.[173] Yet, there has been a case that shows the legal reaction of the German constitutional order to a

[170] Xabier Arzoz and Markku Suksi, 'Comparing Constitutional Adjudication of Self-determination Claims' (2018) 25(4) Maastricht Journal of European and Comparative Law 452, 457.

[171] It has been labelled a 'direct attack against the unity and indivisibility of the Italian Republic'. Fasone (n 167). As Fasone points out, 'the question posed is not limited to reaching a condition of strengthened autonomy, but it aims to secede'. Furthermore, in execution of the contested Law, the regional government of the Veneto promptly adopted a series of provisions dealing with the propaganda, the voting procedures in the referendum, and the steps to be taken for the official proclamation of the results and those concerning the economic and financial aspects of the referendum.

[172] Giuseppe Martinico, 'Identity Conflicts and Secession before Courts: Three Case Studies' (2017) 21 Revista de Derecho Público Comparado 1, 27. It should also be mentioned that the Italian Constitutional Court had already faced similar cases in the past, although they were not as subversive of the constitutional order as the Veneto Laws nos 15 and 16/2014. In those decisions (decision nos 470/1992 and 496/2000) the Court had already established some of the main principles that were recalled in 2015. For instance, in the decision no 496/2000 the Court stated that 'when dealing with great questions of general interest, in the relationships with state institutions, it is the [national] electoral body as a whole that is called to express its will, at the same time. It is not admissible to acknowledge to a regional consultative referendum, given the participation of the only regional population, the same value as a national consultative referendum.' Fasone (n 157).

[173] Bavarian independence is not currently a political issue in Germany, but it is true that historically it has been an uneasy region for the consolidation of the German unity. -Klaus Jürgen Nagel, 'Bavaria: Another Case of a Right to Decide?' (2017) 19 GRTP Political Theory Working Paper <https://repositori.upf.edu/bitstream/handle/10230/28277/GRTwp19.pdf?sequence=1&isAllowed=y> accessed 3 August 2022.

secessionist challenge. This issue, like in Italy, has rarely been commented on by the press, or in academic legal literature. However, it is relevant for our analysis, since it indicates that the German legal approach is similar to the Spanish and Italian approaches.[174] On 16 December 2016, the German Constitutional Court[175] unanimously deemed inadmissible a claim filed by a citizen of the Southern and rich land of Bavaria whereby he requested the option to organize a referendum on secession in the referred territory (a petition he had filed before the regional government and which had been rejected). The Court issued a short, categorical, and unappealable statement (to be precise: only three sentences) holding that:

> In the Federal Republic of Germany, which is a Nation-State based on the constituent power of the German people, *Länder* are not 'masters of the constitution'.[176] Therefore, there is no room for individual *Länder* to attempt to withdraw [from the Federation]. They would be infringing the constitutional order [author's own translation].

It can be clearly inferred that the German Basic Law does not recognize a right or a procedure for secession, which is in line with the German tradition (no right to secede can be found in the 1871 Constitution or in the 1919 Weimar Constitution). Most German legal scholars share this view.[177] This is, moreover, in accord with German constitutionalist ideas of federal loyalty. The principle of federal loyalty has been developed and understood by the German Constitutional Court as a key component of the German constitutional order: it refers to the duty of loyal, constructive, and positive behaviour of the components of the Bund (the *Länder*) towards the State.[178] It is true, however, that in the current text there is no express clause regarding the indissolubility of the German territory. Yet, the preamble clearly states that the constituent power lies in the German people as a whole. In any event, it still remains unclear if, as in the Spanish case, the German Basic Law could be amended so as to permit a secession clause. In this regard, it should be noted that the territorial integrity or the unity of the State are not included in the

[174] Ragone points out that the three legal orders can be compared in the sense that all of them have rigid constitutions that do not provide for secession. Sabrina Ragone, 'Los *Länder* no son "señores de la Constitución": el Tribunal Constitucional Federal Alemán sobre el referéndum separatista bávaro' (2018) 41 Teoría y Realidad Constitucional 407, 417.

[175] Decision only available in German <http://www.bundesverfassungsgericht.de/SharedDocs/Entscheidungen/DE/2016/12/rk20161216_2bvr034916.html> accessed 3 August 2022.

[176] The expression 'masters of the Constitution' is typical in German law, used not only with respect to *Länder* but also with regard to the EU. Thus, in a multilevel scenario, German constitutionalism places the State and its Constitution 'as a reference both bottom-up (European Union) and top-down (*Länder*)' José Antonio Montilla, 'The Independence Referendum in Germany' (*Instituto de Derecho Público*, 16 December 2016) <http://idpbarcelona.net/docs/blog/referendum_germany.pdf> accessed 3 August 2022.

[177] Ragone (n 174) 412.

[178] Francisco Sosa Wagner, 'Bávaros y Referéndum por la independencia' (2017) 202 Revista de Administración Pública 157, 164.

so-called eternity clauses of article 79.3 of the German Constitution. This provision sets forth that any amendment affecting the federal organization of the State, the protection of human dignity, and the definition of the State as democratic and social shall be inadmissible. Thus, in principle, an amendment introducing a secession clause would be permitted. However, it could also be argued that, as in the Italian case, if ever confronted, the German Constitutional Court would end up establishing an implicit material limit to the constitutional amendment procedure that would prevent the inclusion of any secession procedure.

4.5 Belgium

Flemish nationalism showed its strength in the 1960s after its formidable economic success following the Second World War. Before this, Flanders was poorer than Wallonia. When the situation was reversed, Flemish nationalists were not only concerned with cultural and linguistic matters (historical demands of the movement), but also with economic issues, or, to be precise, with the transfer of money from Flanders to Wallonia. 'The existence and persistence over time of sizable transfers between Flanders and Wallonia [particularly through the social security system] is an undisputable fact.'[179] Today, the economic argument has become the core demand of Flemish nationalists.

Given the existence of distinct and separate public spheres in Flanders and Wallonia, the absence of any significant national Belgian political parties and the robust support to pro-independence Flemish political parties in Flanders, the weakness of actual secessionist claims or the marginality of secessionism might seem surprising.[180] The reason may be found in the uniqueness of Belgian federalism and the pragmatism of some Flemish nationalists. Belgian federalism is complex: different types of constituent units (communities and regions), a high degree of decentralization (several State reforms in 1970, 1980, 1988, 1993, 2001, and 2011), and consociational rules (eg Belgian governments have to be formed by an equal number of Flemish and Francophone ministers and constitutional reforms can only be conducted with the mutual agreement of Dutch and French communities). A key characteristic of these State reforms, that have increased fiscal autonomy and decentralization towards regions, is their dynamism. 'No one reform was ever intended to be a final settlement.'[181] The Belgian State has been described as unfinished and open ended.[182] Thus, the dynamic nature of Flemish autonomy

[179] Emmanuel Dalle Mulle, *The Nationalism of the Rich: Discourses and Strategies of Separatist Parties in Catalonia, Flanders, Northern Italy and Scotland* (Routledge 2017) 79.

[180] André Lecours, *Nationalism, Secessionism and Autonomy* (OUP 2021) 97.

[181] ibid 102.

[182] As Deschouwer and Reuchamps explain, 'the Belgian federation is a compromise, a negotiated outcome between diverging views on its future. There has been no blueprint of the current Belgium and there is no blueprint of the future Belgium. It is not a federation by design but one by default. . . .

(and the subsequent expectation that future State reforms offering more autonomy are around the corner) is one of the reasons for the weak secessionist claims.[183] Besides, the most important Flemish nationalist party, N-VA (the *Nieuw-Vlaamse Alliantie* or the New Flemish Alliance) holds a gradualist policy, convinced that Belgium will eventually split off. Thus, N-VA's strategy is 'evaporation'. Through successive State reforms that slowly take more powers away from the Belgian government, the break-up of the country will be inevitable, they hope.[184] This pragmatic approach leads their members to believe that there is no reason to reject participation in federal coalition government. This willingness to take part in the governance of the country differentiates N-VA from VB (*Vlaams Blok/Vlaams Belang* or the Flemish Interest), the other Flemish nationalist party.[185]

Unlike the Catalan case, there has been no explicit reference to the launch of rupturing processes, the implementation of extraordinary actions, or the use of direct democracy in the form of referendums or popular consultation.[186] In Belgium there is no secession clause and no mechanism to hold a referendum on independence, like, arguably in the UK or Canada. Nor is there an explicit ban at constitutional level, like in Italy, according to the interpretation of their Constitutional Court. In Belgium, with one of the most rigid constitutions in Europe,[187] there has been no judicial decision on secessionist claims and among the Belgian academic literature, there has been no debate on the possibility of including a right to secede in the Constitution.[188] A unilateral secession scenario seems highly unlikely, since, as Mastromarino explains, any decision in Belgium will be the result of a long negotiation.[189] The road to a mutual divorce agreement, following the Czechoslovakian model, seems to be the only one possible if Belgians ever reach a break-up situation.[190]

The Belgian state is unfinished and open ended, but that is exactly the reason why it can exist. There will probably never be an agreement on the very nature of the federation, on its major building blocks, or on its internal boundaries.' Kris Deschouwer and Min Reuchamps, 'The Belgian Federation at the Crossroad' (2013) 23(3) Regional and Federal Studies 261, 263.

[183] Lecours (n 180)118.

[184] Glenn Duerr, *Secessionism and the European Union: The Future of Flanders, Scotland and Catalonia* (Lexington Books 2015) 70.

[185] There are other key differences. N-VA declares itself to be separatist, republican, liberal, and opposed to the ethnic nationalism of the VB. Dalle Mulle (n 169) 62.

[186] Anna Mastromarino, 'Secessionist Claims in a Federal System: The Belgian Case' in Alberto López Basaguren and Leire Escajedo (eds), *Claims for Secession and Federalism* (Springer 2019) 222. See also Anna Mastromarino, 'Modificaciones constitucionales en Bélgica. La sixième réforme de l'Etat: un proceso en marcha' (2015) 22 Revista d'Estudis Autonòmics i Federals 64, 85.

[187] Mastromarino, 'Modificaciones constitucionales en Bélgica' (n 186).

[188] Mastromarino, 'Secessionist Claims in a Federal System: The Belgian Case' (n 186) 223. On the other hand, Mancini believes that 'this right, however, is embedded implicitly in the very logic of the Belgian system'. Mancini, 'Rethinking the Boundaries of Democratic Secession' (n 18) 577.

[189] Mastromarino, 'Modificaciones constitucionales en Bélgica' (n 186) 66.

[190] Mastromarino, 'Secessionist Claims in a Federal System: The Belgian Case' (n 186) 224.

5. Conclusions

National constitutional law offers different approaches to secession, although with some common trends. Secessionist attempts are the most acute political crisis a State can endure, because they affect the integrity and continuity of the political subject that founds the State. That is why constitutional legal orders tend to be highly restrictive, as the Venice Commission noted in 2014 concerning the Crimea case: '[i]f the Constitution of Ukraine does not allow a referendum on secession, this does not in any way contradict European constitutional standards. Rather, it is typical for constitutions of Council of Europe member states not to allow secession.'[191] Spain, Italy, and Germany are good proof of that. In this sense, the Canadian and British approaches constitute outstanding exceptions to the classic paradigm inaugurated by the US. Quebec's secessionist attempts are being grasped by a legal regime largely anchored in the common-law tradition and, in that, it is much closer to Scotland than it is to Catalonia.[192] According to both the British and Canadian approaches, secession has to find accommodation in the constitutional system under the democratic ground by considering it tolerable,[193] but subject to certain requirements: (1) there is only a right to negotiate, not to secede; (2) the process will have to be subject to the law; and (3) the central authorities of the State will have to play a critical role in it. But even the flexible common-law constitutional tradition rejects a unilateral right to secede,[194] since the democratic principle has to be tempered with other principles like the rule of law, or (in the Canadian case) the supremacy of the Constitution.[195] This is in fact the common approach of liberal constitutional democracies to secession.

[191] Venice Commission, 'Opinion on Whether the decision taken by the Supreme Council of the Autonomous Republic of Crimea in Ukraine to organise a referendum on becoming a constituent territory of the Russian Federation or restoring Crimea's 1992 Constitution is compatible with constitutional principles', CDL-AD (2014) 2, 4.

[192] Gaudreault-DesBiens (n 54) 34.

[193] Alastair MacIver, 'Metaconstitutionalising Secession: The Reference and Scotland (in Europe)' in Giacomo Delledonne and Giuseppe Martinico (eds), *The Canadian Contribution to a Comparative Law of Secession* (Palgrave Macmillan 2019) 115–17.

[194] According to the unwritten constitution of the UK, there is no formal right to secede. Page (n 105) 437.

[195] 'It seems safe to affirm that unilateral secession is not permissible anywhere.' Arzoz and Suksi (n 170) 469.

5

EU Approach to Secession and Secessionist Challenges: Precedents, Statements, and Reactions

1. Introduction

Having reviewed the position of both public international law (Chapter 3) and national constitutional law regarding secession (Chapter 4), the aim of the next two chapters is to explore the position of the European Union (EU) and EU law regarding secession. This is of course a very broad subject (and also the core of this book) and it has been divided into two chapters to provide clarity for the reader. This chapter will deal with the practical argument, that is, how has the EU reacted/responded to secession? Chapter 6 goes on to deal with the normative question: how should the EU respond?

Since there has been no successful secession within the EU, this first chapter will explore the following questions: (1) how has the EU responded when there have been territorial changes affecting EU Member States, and is there any lesson that can be applied to secession within EU Member States?; (2) what has been the EU approach to secession in neighbouring countries, and again, what lessons can be drawn?; (3) what has been the content of the statements and responses of EU representatives, mainly members of the European Commission, when they have been asked about secession?; and (4) what were the reactions of EU institutions to the events in Scotland in 2014 and in Catalonia in 2017?

The aim of this chapter then is to contribute to the main question of this book with empirical data, namely to identify the policies of the EU and EU Member States with regard to secession. While the rest of the chapters are mainly theoretical, the approach of the following pages is empirical, judged in terms of political experience. Thus, this chapter is not aimed at providing reasons to justify the overall argument, but to show that the legal analysis advanced in this book is politically feasible. In effect, it will be shown that, despite the sometimes speculative approach of the book (mainly in Chapter 7), the normative hypothesis tested in these pages is in accordance with the EU's closest precedents, and it is, therefore, a workable and feasible approach.

The chapter reveals that in recent decades the EU has developed a distinctive approach to secession in its external policies (ie recognition policy provided that

Secession and European Union Law. Núria González Campañá, Oxford University Press. © Núria González Campañá 2024.
DOI: 10.1093/oso/9780198882596.003.0005

the secession process respects the rule of law), which coincides with that which it should have (normatively speaking) in internal cases, as will be shown in Chapter 6. In sum, this chapter is necessary because it demonstrates the political feasibility of the normative standard explained throughout this work.

Thus, in this chapter, first we will refer to the cases of the independence of Algeria (Section 2.1), the withdrawal of Greenland (Section 2.2), and the reunification of Germany (Section 2.3). Although they are not accurate precedents for possible secession of territories within Member States, we will identify some lessons that can be learned from those experiences in light of the current secessionist challenge. Second, we will review the case of the Turkish Republic of Northern Cyprus and the EU attitude towards it since its declaration of independence. This is an extraordinary example of how pivotal a role a Member State can play in European policy formation if its national interest is at stake. We will also examine the experiences of the countries born right after, or immediately before, the crumbling of the Soviet Union that are now part of the EU (Baltic States, dissolution of Czechoslovakia, and Yugoslavia). They are examples of national fragmentation in the post-communist world and cannot be considered genuine secessionist challenges comparable to those posed in constitutional and liberal democracies. However, some of the lessons drawn from these experiences might tell us something relevant about the EU and secession. This will be followed by an analysis of EU policies towards more recent secessionist attempts in countries such as Serbia with the key case of Montenegro, where EU involvement was paramount, and Crimea. We will then examine past statements and responses of EU representatives concerning secession. Although such statements do not constitute legally binding acts, they do offer valuable guidance as to the EU law position. Finally, the chapter will explore the reactions that the EU institutions have had when faced by secessionist challenges in EU Member States, namely, Scotland in 2014 and, particularly, Catalonia in 2017. The focus thereafter shifts to finding the legal basis for such positions, and whether such reactions were grounded on EU law. This will be the focus of Chapter 6.

2. Territorial Changes Within the European Union

There is no precedent of (successful) secession within an EU Member State. As Crawford and Boyle point out, '[t]here is no clear precedent for a metropolitan part of an EU Member State becoming independent and then either claiming automatic membership or seeking in its own right to join the EU'.[1] However, some episodes of

[1] Alan Boyle and James Crawford, *Annex A Opinion: Referendum on the Independence of Scotland—International Law Aspects* (UK Government 2013) para 143 <https://assets.publishing.service.gov.uk/government/uploads/system/uploads/attachment_data/file/79408/Annex_A.pdf> accessed 2 August 2022. On the same lines, see Alfredo Galán, 'Secesión de Estados y Pertenencia a la Unión Europea' (2013) 1 Istituzione del Federalismo 95, 111.

territorial changes affecting EU Member States (the independence of Algeria, the withdrawal from Greenland, and the reunification of Germany) deserve our attention, since they can provide 'approximate guidance',[2] or at least they can be used to test the hypothesis developed in this book.

2.1 Algeria (France)

While Algeria (technically not a French colony)[3] was under French jurisdiction, it was subject to the EC treaty provisions under article 227(2) European Economic Community (EEC) Treaty (*inter alia* on free movement of goods, agriculture, liberalization of services, competition, and institutions). The incorporation of French African territories (particularly Algeria) into the European enterprise was a central French objective during the Treaty of Rome negotiations that faced initial Dutch and German opposition.[4] It could be argued that Algeria enjoyed *de facto* membership in the Community, benefitting from all economic provisions of the Treaty except those applying to the Common Agricultural Policy.[5] During the long and bloody independence war (from 1954 to 1962), the then European Community (EC) institutions continued to approach Algeria as part of the French territory.[6]

The 'mystery', as Kalypso Nikolaidis has described the process by which Algeria came out of the EC,[7] began with Algeria's independence in 1962. In effect, Algeria's independence resulted in the continued (although limited) application of EC law in Algerian territory.[8] In December 1962 Algeria requested the provisional maintenance of the relevant articles of the EEC Treaty, pending future definition of EEC-Algeria relations.[9] Six months later the EEC agreed to the request of maintaining the *quasi* Member State status for Algeria.[10] The following year, the Algerian Minister of Foreign Affairs asked the President of the EEC Council to

[2] Boyle and Crawford (n 1) para 143.

[3] Algeria represented three French *départements* and from 1957 onwards, only two. See Dorothy Pickles, *Algeria and France* (Methuen 1963).

[4] Peo Hansen and Stefan Jonsson, 'Building Eurafrica: Reviving Colonialism through European Integration, 1920–60' in Gabrielle Maas, Kalyso Nicolaïdis, and Berny Sèbe (eds), *Echoes of Empire: Memory, Identity and Colonial Legacies* (IB Tauris 2015) 217.

[5] William Zartman, 'North Africa and the EEC Negotiations' (1986) 22(1) Middle East Journal 1, 1.

[6] See, for instance, the type of discussions within the Council of Ministers in the 1960s as for Algeria and the application of art 227(2) EEC Treaty. <http://archives.eui.eu/en/files/inventories/15312?d=inline> accessed 3 August 2022.

[7] Kalypso Nicolaïdis, 'Southern Barbarians? A Post-Colonial Critique of EUniversalism' in Kalypso Nicolaïdis, Gabrielle Maas, and Berny Sèbe (eds), *Echoes of Empire: Memory, Identity and Colonial Legacies* (IB Tauris 2015) 287.

[8] Phoebus Athanassiou and Stéphanie Laulhé Shaelou, 'EU Accession from Within?—An Introduction' (2014) 33(1) Yearbook of European Law 335, 350.

[9] Allan F Tatham, 'Don't Mention Divorce at the Wedding, Darling!': EU Accession and Withdrawal after Lisbon' in Andrea Biondi, Piet Eeckhout. and Stefanie Ripley (eds), *EU Law after Lisbon* (OUP 2012) 144.

[10] Zartman (n 5) 1.

start exploratory conversations to clarify future relations between Algeria and the EEC, since the current situation was interim.[11] At first the French delegation was hesitant to articulate a vision that would anchor the provisional situation in a legal framework. There was some reluctance to specify a binding vision of their relationship with Algeria.[12] The French were interested in protecting the comfortable interim and beneficial Algerian status and tried to postpone dealing seriously with the issue. However, they could not prevent the *de facto* erosion of some benefits given the impatience of Germany, Italy, and particularly the Netherlands.[13]

Rounds of exploratory conversations and negotiations,[14] an interim trade regime,[15] and a partial agreement on wine[16] followed until an association agreement was finally signed in 1976, which entered into force in 1978.[17] The delay in reaching an agreement was due not only to Algerian and French interests, but also to the position of some Member States, like Italy, that opposed Mediterranean associations without prior protection for its own production.[18]

From a European integration process perspective, it seems striking that Algeria remained in an interim and uncertain position for such a long period (from 1962 to 1978). The reason is that the French vision trumped the interests of other EC Member States. For our purposes, the Algerian case underlines that when an issue (in this case Algeria) is part of the national interest of a Member State (namely France) and the other Member States have no strong preferences, the EU reaction is highly vulnerable to that interest. It should be noted, though, that such early

[11] Bull EC 2-1964, point V.7.

[12] Muriam Haleh Davis, *Producing Eurafrica: Development, Agriculture and Race in Algeria, 1958–1965* (NYU PhD dissertation 2015) 245.

[13] Algeria's customs regime was slightly modified by the establishment of a triple-column tariff on 1 November 1964. In 1966, the Council decided to exclude it from further intra-community tariff cuts and various members granted it an intermediate customs position between intracommunity and Common External Tariff (CET) levels. Zartman (n 5) 2.

[14] In February 1964, a delegation of the Algerian government engaged in those exploratory conversations with a Commission delegation in order to shed light on the issue. Bull EC 4-1964, point III.3. Such exploratory conversations ended in December 1964, when both sides agreed that proper conversations could be launched. Bull EC 2-1965, point IV.63. In May 1965, the European Commission submitted to the Council its definitive report on future relations with Algeria. Bull EC 5-1965, point III.56. On 8 January 1968, the Algerian petition to engage in negotiations with the EEC was confirmed. Bull EC 3-1968, point VI.71.

[15] In February 1968, the Council asked the Commission to submit proposals to establish an interim regime of trade relations between the EEC and Algeria pending further negotiations. Bull EC 4-1968, point IV.50. The proposal was submitted on 2 May 1968. Bull EC 7-1968, point III.58.

[16] On 30 July 1968, the Council reached an agreement concerning Algerian wine, in force since 1 January 1971. Bull EC 9/10-1968, point III.79; Bull EC 12-1971, point III.91. In March 1972, the Council decide to ask Algeria to start negotiations for a global agreement. Bull EC 5-1972, point III.76. A visit from Mr Bouteflika, then Minister of Foreign Affairs, in June 1972 launched the start of the negotiations, scheduled for 10 July 1972. Bull EC 8-1972, point III.99. The global agreement was to contain, as well as a preferential trade regime, economic cooperation measures. Bull EC 9-1972, point III.100. Negotiations continued over the following years. Bull EC 9-1973, point 2304; Bull EC 12-1974, point 2323.

[17] 'Cooperation Agreement between the European Economic Community and the People's Democratic Republic of Algeria', signed on 26 April 1976.

[18] Zartman (n 5) 9.

practice predates any formal constitutionalization of the EU. Therefore, given the highly intergovernmental era, it is unsurprising that those decisions were left entirely to the national Member State level to define.

2.2 Greenland (Denmark)

When Denmark negotiated its EC membership, it decided to include Greenland as Danish territory in the EC,[19] despite Greenland's reluctance (70.3% of Greenlanders had voted against the access in a consultative referendum). Greenland's opposition to the EC grew considerably when European fishermen began to fish in Greenland waters. In 1982, the Greenland Parliament organized a referendum on EC membership, where 53 per cent of the voters were in favour of leaving the EC.[20] The Danish government (on behalf of Greenland) negotiated with the European institutions the required amendments to the treaties. All the amendments were included in an international treaty signed on 13 March 1984 and ratified unanimously by all EC Member States. On 1 January 1985, Greenland formally withdraw from the EC. In essence, the amendments provided for non-application of the treaties to Greenland and its inclusion as one of the so-called Overseas Countries and Territories (OCT) enjoying association arrangements with the EC.[21] In sum, Greenland followed the appropriate Danish legal procedures to express their opinion and Denmark, agreeing to respect that will, behaved accordingly.

It is also interesting to note the fact of acceptance by the European institutions after the Danish petition of treaties amendment. In this sense, one could mention, as an example, the 7 June 1983 European Parliament 'Resolution on the memorandum concerning the proposal by the Danish Government amending the Community Treaties with a view to Greenland's withdrawal from the Community and with a view at the same time to making the special association rules in Part Four of the EEC Treaty applicable to Greenland'.[22] In that document the European Parliament took into account not only the results of the referendum, but also the fact that two of the three political parties in Greenland were in favour of EC withdrawal (ie wide consensus) and that accordingly the Danish government (on

[19] Unlike Greenland, Denmark had expressly left Faroe Islands out of the EC. The Faroe Islands have enjoyed Home Rule since 1948 and before the Danish accession to the EC had already made clear their desire to be regarded as a third country in the context of the EC.

[20] Brit Fløistad, 'Fisheries, Greenland and the European Community. Formal Independence—Economic Dependence' (1988) 8(4) International Challenges 6.

[21] Treaty amending, with regard to Greenland, the Treaties establishing the European Communities [1985] OJ L 29/1. See also Frederik Harhoff, 'Greenland's Withdrawal from the European Communities' (1983) 20 Common Market Law Review 13.

[22] [1983] OJ C184/26. The resolution was overwhelmingly adopted with 122 votes for, 9 against, and 7 abstentions.

behalf of the Greenland inhabitants) had asked for such withdrawal. Therefore, the European Parliament:

1. Regrets yet respects the result of the referendum of 23 February 1982;
2. Recommends that the request by the Danish Government that negotiations on Greenland's withdrawal from the Community commence be granted;
3. Recommends that the request by the Danish Government that Greenland be allowed to withdraw be granted;
4. Recommends negotiation of a new status for Greenland as a non-European territory, providing for Greenland's special relations with the Community in a mutually harmonious form.

The European Parliament also endorsed the view of the European Commission, namely, the proposal of granting Greenland OCT status supplemented by a concurrent agreement between Greenland and Denmark on the one hand and the EC on the other to establish mutual rights and obligations on a lasting basis.

With regard to the concerns of this book, I should point out that a clear position of a Member State (ie Denmark on behalf of Greenland) following a procedure in accordance with the internal constitutional framework resulted in a quick adaptation of EC treaties. Despite the lack of enthusiasm, and given the consensus within the EU Member State affected, EU institutions rapidly adapted to the situation.

2.3 German Reunification

While the preceding cases became footnotes in the European integration process, German reunification was considered the catalyst for a new order in Europe.[23] After the fall of the Berlin Wall, in Germany there was an overwhelming desire for reunification.[24] But would German reunification be acceptable to the international community and, particularly, to its European neighbours? Despite initial hesitations, on 10 February 1990, President Gorbachev assured Chancellor Kohl 'that the Soviet Government would not oppose German unification'.[25] Meanwhile, the

[23] It allowed for the Maastricht Treaty, with its ambitious plans for a monetary union, EU citizenship, common foreign, and security policy. Renata Fritsch-Bournazel, *Europe and German Unification* (Berg 1992) 5.

[24] The victory of an alliance of conservative forces 'was interpreted as a plebiscite in favour of Chancellor Kohl and his offer of a "quick fix"'. Anne-Marie Le Gloannec, 'Two Germanies in One' in Wolfgang *Heisenberg* (ed), *German Unification in European Perspective* (Centre for European Policy Studies 1991) 58. See also Fritsch-Bournazel (n 23) 161.

[25] Peter Ludlov, 'The German-German Negotiations and the "Two-Plus-Four" Talks' in Wolfgang Heisenberg (ed), *German Unification in European Perspective* (Centre for European Policy Studies 1991) 24.

Bush administration had been a supporter of German reunification since the very beginning.[26]

The British government had some initial doubts about the role of an enlarged Germany, but accepted the fact that with US and Soviet support, Germany would enlarge.[27] What also became key in Europe was the French position. At first, many French citizens were not at ease with the idea of German reunification, but were finally prepared to accept it.[28] French approval was, of course, key. As former Federal Chancellor Helmut Schmidt admitted in 1990, 'Die französische Nation ist die einzige, die in den Augen all unserer anderen Nachbarn die deutsche Einheit legitimieren kann'[29] (tr: The French nation is the only one which in the eyes of all our neighbours can legitimize German unity). Mitterrand took advantage of the German reunification to strengthen European integration, his old ambition. He negotiated hard 'to ensure linkage between agreement to German unification and acceleration of the European integration process'.[30] This approach was also shared by the European Commission:

> If an enlarged Germany posed challenges for the Community and for the balance of economic power between its members, here was an opportunity for the Commission to use member states' worries to speed up progress on economic, monetary and political union. EMU and Political Union would bind Germany even more tightly into the Community system.[31]

Once the internal and external political will to ensure reunification was clear (ie wide national and international consensus), Germans themselves and Germans along with their European partners had to decide the legal route. As for the

[26] ibid 22–23. The position of the US foreign policymakers was brilliantly captured by the Washington Post columnist Richard Cohen: 'Of course, no one can ignore what happened the last time Germany was unified.... But if a unified Germany is ever to take its place among nations it has to be allowed to act much like any other nation. To treat it differently, to feed a German sense of victimization, would only repeat the mistakes of the past.' Richard Cohen, 'No double standard for Germany' *Washington Post* (Washington DC, 6 December 1989) <https://www.washingtonpost.com/archive/opinions/1989/12/06/no-double-standard-for-germany/a9954579-6a82-435a-b8fa-f02bdb50c9a9/?utm_term=.e64571c9c904> accessed 3 August 2022.

[27] Prime Minister Thatcher was particularly concerned about the lack of firm German commitment to the inviolability of the Polish border. Interview with Mrs Thatcher published by *Der Spiegel* in March 1990 <http://www.spiegel.de/spiegel/print/d-13507157.html> accessed 3 August 2022.

[28] See, for instance, the political statements of President Mitterrand on 3 November 1989 at a joint press conference with Federal Chancellor Helmut Kohl ('I am not afraid of reunification') and Mitterrand's political rival, Paris Mayor Jacques Chirac, on 8 November, admitting being in favour of German reunification 'if this is demanded by the German themselves'. Fritsch-Bournazel (n 23) 172.

[29] Helmut Schmidt, 'Nicht die Chancen verpatzen' *Die Zeit* (Hamburg, 9 March 1990) <http://www.zeit.de/1990/11/nicht-die-chance-verpatzen> accessed 3 August 2022.

[30] David Spence, 'The European Community and German Unification' (1992) 1(3) German Politics 136, 140. On the same lines, see Roger Morgan, 'Political and Institutional Implications for the European Community' in Wolfgang Heisenberg (ed), *German Unification in European Perspective* (Centre for European Policy Studies 1991) 88.

[31] Spence, 'The European Community and German Unification' (n 30) 141.

constitutional legal perspective, the Germans decided to follow the easy route established in article 23 of the *Grundgesetz*, whereby new *Länder* may opt for membership of the Federal Republic (ie simple enlargement of the territory, a short way to political unity).[32]

The internal solution adopted by Germany allowed EC institutions to adopt the moving treaty boundaries' rule,[33] which meant that the Federal Republic of Germany had no fixed territorial definition in the European treaties and thus it was free to redefine its territory without profound European treaty implications. According to the European Parliament, however, a longer process similar to an accession treaty (including the involvement of the Parliament itself) was required.[34] But the Council and the Commission could not accept that view, since it implied a much longer negotiation process and German political reality was not going to allow it.[35] German unification was then not viewed as a new accession, which would have implied the risky requirement of formal ratification of all Member States, but as an internal enlargement of a current Member State.[36] The interests of both the Federal Republic of Germany and the Member States coincided and despite the huge impact of German unification on the European Community (a less developed new population of 16.5 million was submitted to EC law), it was accepted without any treaty amendment:

> For the Federal Republic, the path of amendment would have made the extension of the area of application of the Treaties subject to completion by all Member States of national ratification procedures. This operation, naturally long in any case, could be lengthened still further by an adverse stance by a State or a national parliament.... For other Member States, non-amendment implies acceptance by Germany of all the Treaty rules, particularly those regarding the institutions, avoiding renewed questioning of weighting at the Council of Ministers and the distribution of European Parliament. It is no doubt because of agreement reached on this point that no through legal analysis was done.[37]

[32] The other path was to be found in art 146, whereby a new constitution resulting from negotiations between the two States would be necessary. This latter route would have meant the creation of a new State, which was highly problematic: uncertainty as to the international commitments of the new Germany, long negotiations to draft a new constitution, and the risk of hampering the European architecture. Le Gloannec (n 24) 58.

[33] Jochen Frowein, 'The Reunification of Germany' (1992) 86(1) American Journal of International Law 152, 159.

[34] European Parliament, 'Interim report drawn up on behalf of the Temporary Committee to consider the impact of the process of German unification on the European Community' (1990) Publications Office 24–25.

[35] Spence, 'The European Community and German Unification' (n 30) 142.

[36] David Spence, 'The European Community's Negotiations on German Unification' in Wolfgang Heisenberg (ed), *German Unification in European Perspective* (Centre for European Policy Studies 1991) 29.

[37] Jean-Paul Jacqué, 'German Unification and the European Community' (1991) 2(1) European Journal of International Law 1, 3.

The Commission submitted some preliminary work to the Dublin European Council of April 1990, where political consensus was reached:

> We are pleased that German unification is taking place under a European roof. The Community will ensure that the integration of the territory of the German Democratic Republic into the Community is accomplished in a smooth and harmonious way.... *It will be carried out without revision of the Treaties* [emphasis added].[38]

The Commission suggested (and the European Council accepted) a gradual incorporation of the German Democratic Republic into the European Community. The European Council also required the Federal Republic to keep the Community informed of developments between the two Germanies through the involvement of the Commission. In fact, the Commission was able to influence the drafting of the *Einigungsvertrag* (Unification Treaty) negotiated between the two German States.[39] On 3 October 1990 this international treaty permitted the disappearance of the German Democratic Republic as a State and the decision to merge it into the Federal Republic of Germany. Thus, the Federal Republic of Germany persisted and united Germany did not constitute a new legal subject.

In short, the European Community had welcomed (out of political interests) a major internal enlargement without the revision of any treaty, despite legal concerns. In effect, German unification was an informal form of enlargement. German unification illustrates 'the speed and effectiveness with which Community institutions can act under pressure',[40] and, it should be added, as long as there is a broad consensus. It also shows EC flexibility: '[e]verybody, from Community officials to senior politicians in the member states, was prepared to make exceptions in order to facilitate the process'.[41] Needless to say, neither Algeria nor Greenland or Germany, as has been explained, can be used as precedents in the case of secession within Member States since none of these is technically 'secession'. German reunification is widely cited as the closest precedent, but this is misleading. First, the reunification did not lead to a fragmentation of the EC but to its widening, whereas secession within an EU Member State would lead to EU fragmentation. Second, secession within an EU Member State would require immediate changes to Treaty provisions:

> In contrast with the German case, where the other Member States were glad to accept the Germany's underrepresentation following its reunification, it is clear

[38] Bull EC 4-1990, point I.4.

[39] Christian Willem Anton Timmermans, 'German Unification and Community Law' (1990) 27 Common Market Law Review 437, 446.

[40] Spence, 'The European Community and German Unification' (n 30) 157.

[41] ibid 160.

other Member States would not be willing to accept a possible overrepresentation of the remaining entity of a Member State following its breakup.[42]

However, despite no case providing clear and decisive guidance, all these situations underline a key issue: the important and decisive role of the affected Member State in the relationship between the EU and a territory under (or previously under) its jurisdiction and the prevalence of political consensus over legal objections. In effect, in all these cases, pragmatism prevailed over legal obstacles as long as there was a common political will to resolve the situation.[43] The German unification case, though, could be a particularly relevant precedent in the event of Irish reunification, as will be noted in Chapter 7.

3. Secession in Neighbouring Countries

It goes without saying that each of these conflicts is deserving of a chapter or even an entire monograph, so the next few pages will necessarily address these topics very briefly. The intention is to highlight only those aspects of the conflicts that are relevant to our analysis.

3.1 Turkish Republic of Northern Cyprus

In 1974, the Greek Military government organized a coup d'état in Cyprus and extended the Greek dictatorship to the island, which provoked the Turkish invasion through the North. In November 1983, the Turkish Cypriots declared unilaterally the Turkish Republic of Northern Cyprus (TRNC). The island has remained divided since then. The European Commission and the then 10 Member States issued statements declaring that they profoundly regretted and rejected the unilateral declaration of independence.[44] The international community as a whole also condemned the act of secession.[45] In 2002 Cyprus was invited to join the EU, but negotiations had started much earlier. The process was launched by the Greek Cypriots and the Turkish Cypriots were excluded from the process.[46] At first, the

[42] Merijn Chamon and Guillaume Van der Loo, 'The Temporal Paradox of Regions in the EU Seeking Independence: Contraction and Fragmentation versus Widening and Deepening?' (2014) 20(5) European Law Journal, 613, 620.

[43] Miquel Palomares Amat, 'Las decisiones de los Jefes de Estado y de Gobierno, en el seno del Consejo Europeo, como categoría jurídica para regular, transitoriamente, la participación en la Unión Europea de nuevos Estados surgidos de la separación de Estados Miembros' (2013) 17 Revista d'Estudis Autonòmics i Federals 146, 164.

[44] Bull EC 11-1983, point 2.2.34 and Bull EC 11-1983, points 2.4.1–2.4.2.

[45] Nathalie Tocci, *The EU and Conflict Resolution. Promoting Peace in the Backyard* (Routledge 2007) 33.

[46] ibid 41.

understanding within EU institutions was that a settlement was a precondition of accession.[47] Such conditionality gave the EU strong bargaining power in the conflict. EU accession could make both communities reconsider its opposition to reunification, which was the preferred optimistic solution.[48] Surprisingly conditionality was abandoned.[49] The main reason was Greece, the only Member State with strong and clear interests in Cyprus. It made its consent to strengthen ties with Turkey conditional on the progressive lifting of conditionality on the Greek Cypriots.[50] It also threatened to veto EU enlargement to the North and to the East.[51] When, in 2004, a divided Cyprus joined the EU, Turkish Cypriots were left outside the EU.[52] As one expert points out, '[t]he Cyprus conflict was the clearest case in which the strong national interest of one Member State played a pivotal role in determining the conduct of contractual relations with Cyprus and Turkey'.[53] The national interest of an EU Member State can play a key role in changing the whole European approach, particularly when there is no conflict with the interests of the other EU Member States. The EU's continued refusal to recognize the existence of the TRNC is yet another example of the rejection that unilateral secession arouses.

47 European Commission, 'Opinion on the Application by the Republics of Cyprus for Membership' doc/93/5, 30 June 1993.

48 George Christou, 'Cyprus and the EU: Two Years Later: The European Union: What Role in the Cyprus Conflict?' (2006) 41(2) The International Spectator 19, 19.

49 ibid 23. Brewin criticized the European refusal to get involved in the resolution of the conflict and described it as 'avoidance of responsibility'. Christopher Brewin, 'European Union Perspectives on Cyprus Accession' (2000) 36(1) Middle Eastern Studies 21, 24.

50 Etain Tannam, 'The European Union and Conflict Resolution: Northern Ireland, Cyprus and Bilateral Cooperation' (2012) 47(1) Government and Opposition 49, 52. It is worth mentioning that the Greek position towards Turkey had the tacit consent (if not encouragement) of other EU Member States also reluctant to strengthen ties with Turkey. Thus, Greek interests were not at odds with the position of other EU Member States. However, other European States, particularly the large ones, promoted the Customs Unions with Turkey as necessary to keeping Turkey pro-European while denying membership. Brewin (n 49) 26.

51 Tocci (n 45) 52.

52 George Kyris, 'Europeanization and the Turkish-Cypriot Political Parties: How Europe Matters' (2012) 13(3) Turkish Studies 471, 478. Does this mean that the EU has no contact at all with TRNC? The EU has been very cautious in dealing with Turkish-Cypriot authorities, since it could constitute, or be interpreted as, an act of recognition. Tocci (n 45) 49. Despite the absence of diplomatic recognition, the EU is trying to help the Turkish Cypriots out of their isolation. Christou (n 48) 23. This EU approach was partly triggered by the results of the Annan Plan referendum, which altered the Commission's perceptions of 'fault' and 'blame' for the situation in Cyprus, giving Turkey and the Turkish Cypriots the 'moral' high ground in efforts to find a solution. ibid 24. In effect, the European perception is that the government of Cyprus was not serious in attempting to reach a settlement with the Turkish Cypriots. Brewin (49) 30. The European Commission has two main instruments to interact with the TRNC: (1) the aid programme 'to help the Turkish Cypriots prepare for reunification' (in place since 2006); and (2) the Green Line Regulation (in place since 2004), aimed at regulating and facilitating trade between the divided island. In order to avoid direct contact with the TRNC authorities, the European Commission works closely with the TRNC Chamber of Commerce. Kyris (n 52) 479.

53 Tocci (n 45) 171.

3.2 Baltic States

At the end of the 1980s, the case for the independence of the Baltic States was clear.[54] Their forced incorporation in the Soviet Union in 1940 was a violation of international law.[55] However, the EC and its Member States did not support enthusiastically the 1990 Baltic Spring. They were particularly reluctant to accept any movement that could endanger the cordial German-Soviet relations.[56] The disintegration of the Soviet Empire in the summer of 1991 and the consolidation of President Yeltsin, who did not oppose Baltic secessions, enabled the EC and its Member States to welcome the 'restoration of the sovereignty' of the Baltic States.[57] Democratic legitimacy and historical reasons were not enough to support Baltic independence given the threat that the Soviet Union represented—a typical case of realpolitik.

3.3 Yugoslavia

In Yugoslavia, after Milosevic's ascension to power in 1987, ethnic tensions turned the country into a minefield.[58] At first, and given the risk of instability, the EC and its Member States reacted asking for a democratic and united Yugoslavia.[59] But shortly after the first declarations of independence, the EC seemed more inclined to accept Yugoslav disintegration due to the following reasons: excessive use of force by Serbia;[60] lack of Soviet reaction due to its own collapse;[61] the Opinions of the Badinter Commission admitting the irreversible breakup of the country;[62]

[54] Jan Arveds Trapans, 'The West and the Recognition of the Baltic States: 1919 and 1991. A Study of the Politics of the Major Powers' (1994) 25(2) Journal of Baltic Studies 153, 163.

[55] Maria Malksoo, 'The Memory Politics of Becoming European: The East European Subalterns and the Collective Memory of Europe' (2009) 15(4) European Journal of International Relations 653, 669.

[56] Andreas M Klein and Gesine Herrmann, 'Die Beziehungen Deutschlands zu den Baltischen Ländern seit der Wiedervereinigung' (*KAS Auslandsinformationen* October 2010) <https://www.kas.de/c/document_library/get_file?uuid=8c069c7c-a836-aaed-73ac-e2c199640514&groupId=252038> accessed 16 July 2022.

[57] Bull EC 7/8-1991, point 1.4.23. See also 6 September Declaration EC 9-1991, point 1.4.3. It is interesting to note the use of the expression 'restoration of sovereignty'. EU officials came up with an expression that could not be confused with support for secession.

[58] Robert M Hayden, 'Yugoslavia's Collapse: National Suicide with Foreign Assistance' (1992) 27 Economic and Political Weekly 1377, 1380. Croats and Slovenes feared that the Serbs wanted to dominate the country. Richard F Iglar, 'The Constitutional Crisis in Yugoslavia and the International Law of Self-determination: Slovenia's and Croatia's Right to Secede' (1992) 15 Boston College International and Comparative Law Review 213, 217.

[59] EPC Joint Statement dated 8 May. Bull EC 5-1991, point 1.4.3.

[60] Richard Caplan, *Europe and the Recognition of New States in Yugoslavia* (CUP 2005) 22.

[61] ibid 23.

[62] In its Opinion 1, dated 29 November 1991, the Badinter Commission noted 'that the Socialist Federal Republic of Yugoslavia [FRY] is in the process of dissolution'. Alain Pellet, 'The Opinions of the Badinter Arbitration Committee. A Second Breath for the Self-Determination of Peoples' (1993) 3 European Journal of International Law 178, 183. The several Opinions of the Badinter Commission set the boundaries of the successor States of Yugoslavia, and they have been considered 'as the peace treaty that ended the Cold War in Europe'. Cornelia Navari, 'Territoriality, Self-determination and Crimea

Germany's insistence on the recognition of Slovenia and Croatia;[63] and French interest in keeping a unified European policy.[64] Finally, France and Germany reached an agreement to recognize the new Republics under certain conditions.[65] Thus, the EC institutional framework had facilitated an agreement among its members despite their initial divergent positions.

The Yugoslav case had many particularities. As in the case of Czechoslovakia (and unlike the Baltic independence movements), there was no Soviet threat. But whereas the Czechs and the Slovaks were able to reach an agreement, the different Yugoslav nations engaged in wars. The lack of a peaceful settlement did not enable a quick EC recognition. However, the irreversible dissolution of the Mother State, that is, Yugoslavia (as the Badinter Commission acknowledged), together with the German impulse, allowed for a conditional EC recognition policy once it was evident that the pre-war situation could not be restored.

3.4 Czechoslovakia

Slovak disappointment within Czechoslovakia was a constant throughout the twentieth century,[66] but Czechs and Slovaks united in protest after the East German regime collapsed in November 1989. Nobody at that time expected the dissolution of the country.[67] But diverging policy views in the two enclaves exacerbated the debate over the breakup of the country. The 1992 elections accentuated the political division among the two Republics. The huge economic disparity did not help to mitigate the tense situation.[68] The political paralysis, some degree of

after Badinter' (2014) 90(6) International Affairs 1299, 1299. In any event, and despite their importance, it should also be noted that European States did not entirely follow the Badinter Commission Opinions. For instance, despite the Opinions, the EC Member States did not immediately recognize Macedonia (because of Greek objections) and opted for Croatian recognition (despite the Badinter objections), given the vigorous German support. Roland Bieber, 'European Community Recognition of Eastern European States: A New Perspective for International Law?' (1992) 86 American Society of International Law Proceedings 374, 376.

63 Caplan (n 60) 18.

64 ibid 43–46: 'Germany was among the first to realize that Serbian policies made the demise of the former Yugoslavia inevitable, and that this development had to be accepted in order to direct the process of dissolution into orderly channels and to limit its destructive effects.' Michael Libal, *Limits of Persuasion: Germany and the Yugoslav Crisis, 1991–1992* (Praeger 1997) 161.

65 Sonia Lucarelli, *Europe and the Breakup of Yugoslavia: A Political Failure in Search of a Scholarly Explanation* (Kluwer Law International 2000) 154–57.

66 Holly A Osterland, 'National Self-determination and Secession: The Slovak Model' (1993) 25 Case Western Reserve Journal of International Law 655, 685.

67 Judy Batt, 'Making a success of Montenegrin independence—lessons from Slovakia' (*ISS*, 1 June 2006) <https://www.iss.europa.eu/content/making-success-montenegrin-independence-%E2%80%93-lessons-slovakia> accessed 16 July 2022.

68 Salvatore Massa, 'Secession by Mutual Assent: A Comparative Analysis of the Dissolution of Czechoslovakia and the Separatist Movement in Canada' (1995) 14 Wisconsin International Law Review 183, 190.

indifference on the Czech side, and resentment on the Slovak side led the leaders of both Republics, Vaclav Klaus and Vladimir Meciar, to negotiate the end of the federation through the 1968 constitutional amendment process.[69] However, the process was full of legal and democratic flaws, public opinion polls showed that a majority of Czechoslovaks favoured unity,[70] and no referendum was held to ratify the decision, despite demands for it. The breakup occurred against friendly (and unofficial) advice from members of the EC.[71] However, given the peaceful and negotiated path to dissolution, the EC did not oppose it.

These three cases show that for the EC the 'agreement' factor has been key in determining its policy. As for the Baltic States, it was only after the Soviet Union opposition vanished that the EC Member States accepted their independence. In Czechoslovakia, despite a contested procedure (no popular referendum), EC Member States did not oppose the dissolution of the country since there was a peaceful agreement. And in the Yugoslav case, it was precisely the lack of such agreement (namely Serbia's opposition) that prevented a quick EC common policy. EC Member States accepted the emergence of new States in the former Yugoslavia only after violence made clear that its dissolution was an irreversible fact.

3.5 Montenegro

In 1992 Montenegro joined together with Serbia in the Federal Republic of Yugoslavia. Despite Montenegro having no history of conflict with Serbia, political trends began to turn within Montenegro.[72] In 2000 Montenegro's President Djukanovic[73] favoured independence, despite the division among the population.[74] The EU repeatedly argued against further secessionism in the Western Balkans region.[75] In the 2001 elections, pro-independence parties took the lead. Given the EU Member States' opposition to a new split in the Balkans, Javier

[69] Stephen Engelberg, 'Czechoslovakia Breaks in Two, to Wide Regret' *New York Times* (New York, 1 January 1993) <https://www.nytimes.com/1993/01/01/world/czechoslovakia-breaks-in-two-to-wide-regret.html> accessed 16 July 2022.

[70] Osterland (n 66) 692. See also Massa (n 68) 192 and Emanuela Macek-Macková, 'Challenges in Conflict Management in Multi-ethnic States—The Dissolution of Czechoslovakia and Serbia and Montenegro' (2011) 39(4) Nationalist Papers: The Journal of Nationalism and Ethnicity 615, 619.

[71] On 22 June 1992, the then EC spokesman said that dissolution was an 'internal decision'. He also revealed his disappointment 'because the aim should be integration rather than disintegration'. Jacques Rupnik, 'The International Context' in Jirí Musil (ed), *The End of Czechoslovakia* (Central European University Press 1995) 276.

[72] As Tocci says, 'Serbia's legacy of war in the Balkans and its policies towards Kosovo sparked Montenegro's desire to secede'. Tocci (n 45) 156.

[73] Macek-Macková (n 70) 619.

[74] 'Support for independence dropped after the ouster of Milosevic, and stayed below 50 per cent in most opinion polls thereafter.' Batt (n 67) 28.

[75] Stockholm European Council, 23–24 March 2001. Presidency Conclusions <http://europa.eu/rapid/press-release_DOC-01-6_en.htm> accessed 16 July 2022.

Solana stepped in and mediated the Belgrade Agreement, which gave birth to the State Union of Serbia and Montenegro. The text established a loose federal level of government and allowed for a referendum on secession in either one or in both Republics after three years of their establishment. For Serbia and Montenegro, the motivation behind it was not the State Union itself (no one wanted it), but the prospect of EU integration, since the EU had made the State Union a condition of Serbia and Montenegro's admission.[76] Despite international efforts, the regime was highly dysfunctional[77] and failed to gain domestic support and legitimacy.[78] By 2005, trends inexorably pointed towards a referendum in Montenegro. The Serbs had resigned themselves to this when faced with the political stalemate.[79] Since the situation seemed irreversible, the EU decided to cooperate and make sure that the process went as smoothly as possible, despite having invested significant effort and many hours 'trying to persuade Montenegrin Prime Minister Djukanovic to abandon his independence bid'.[80] The Constitutional Charter was revised in 2005 to ensure that an eventual referendum would comply with the guidelines of the Council of Europe's Venice Commission.[81] The EU stepped in[82] and imposed the requirement for a turnout of 50 per cent + 1 voter and a 55 per cent majority in favour of independence. The EU also supervised the formation of the Montenegrin Referendum Commission.[83] The referendum took place on 21 May 2006 with an 86.5 per cent voter turnout and a sufficient (albeit extremely narrow) 55.5 per cent majority in favour of independence. It was considered a major success for EU's soft power.[84] The EU quickly recognized its outcome and stressed both the legal conformity of the process and the agreement and consent of Serbia.[85]

3.6 Kosovo

Although the EU was committed to the maintenance of the territorial integrity of Serbia, dramatic events in the following years made part of the international community (including most EU Member States) change its mind. Serbia virtually

76 Macek-Macková (n 70) 627.
77 Tocci (n 45) 86.
78 ibid 87.
79 Macek-Macková (n 70) 628.
80 Tihomir Loza and Ky Krauthamer, 'Montenegro: The Gray Zone' (2006) 5(16) Transitions Online 1, 3.
81 Venice Commission, 'Opinion on the compatibility of the existing legislation in Montenegro concerning the organization of referendums with applicable international standards' CDL-AD(2005)041.
82 Macek-Macková (n 70) 625.
83 Tocci (n 45) 88.
84 Judy Batt, 'Montenegro and Serbia after the referendum' (*ISS*, 1 May 2006) <https://www.iss.europa.eu/content/montenegro-and-serbia-after-referendum> accessed 16 July 2022.
85 Council Meeting General Affairs and External Relations Affairs, Luxembourg, 12 June 2006 <https://ec.europa.eu/commission/presscorner/detail/en/PRES_06_161> accessed 16 July 2022.

abolished Kosovo's autonomy and a period of repression and (at least) an attempt at ethnic cleansing followed. After the NATO intervention in 1999, and the establishment of the United Nations Interim Administration Mission in Kosovo (UNMIK),[86] various rounds of negotiations between Kosovo and Serbia were held to discuss a settlement proposal. One of the guiding principles of the negotiations was that unilaterality was unacceptable.[87] But the parties were unable to make any progress[88] and in 2007 the UN Special Envoy concluded that 'the only viable option for Kosovo is independence'.[89] In February 2008 the new elected Assembly of Kosovo adopted the declaration of independence. The International Court of Justice (ICJ) assessed the compatibility of the declaration with international law and concluded that the declaration of independence did not violate any applicable rule of international law.[90]

As explained in Chapter 3, West European States hoped to present the case of Kosovo as a unique one. In its Conclusions on Kosovo, adopted immediately after the declaration of independence, the Council of the European Union noted that 'Member States will decide, in accordance with national practice and international law, on their relations with Kosovo'.[91] This pragmatic approach avoided a split within the EU, which would not have been able to agree a common stance on this issue.[92] After reaffirming the EU commitment to the stabilization of the area, the Council added that Kosovo constitutes a *sui generis* case.[93] Almost all EU Member States did recognize Kosovo's independence immediately. Only five EU Member

[86] UN doc S/RES/1244 (1999) 10 June <http://daccess-dds-ny.un.org/doc/UNDOC/GEN/N99/172/89/PDF/N9917289.pdf?OpenElement> accessed 16 July 2022.

[87] 'Guiding principles of the Contact Group for a settlement of the status of Kosovo' UN doc S/2005/709 10 November <http://www.securitycouncilreport.org/atf/cf/%7B65BFCF9B-6D27-4E9C-8CD3-CF6E4FF96FF9%7D/Kos%20S2005%20709.pdf> accessed 16 July 2022.

[88] As Weller explains, during those negotiations Serbia did not play her cards properly. At first, she was convinced (1) that traditional international law was on her side and (2) that Russia would never allow the secession of Kosovo in the United Nations Security Council. Marc Weller, 'Negotiating the Final Status for Kosovo' (2008) 114 Chaillot Paper 29. As if international law was sufficient when dealing with high politics. Serbia should not have ignored the fact that the 1999 NATO-led bombing campaign was a flagrant violation of the legal international regime of the use of force as commonly understood until then. A good account of that regime and an excellent debate on the convenience of still arguing in legal terms when it comes to the use of force to be found in Michael J Glennon, *Limits of Law, Prerogatives of Power. Interventionism after Kosovo* (Palgrave 2001).

[89] 'Report of the Special Envoy of the Secretary-General on Kosovo's future status' UN doc. S/2007/168 26 March, para 5 <http://www.unosek.org/docref/report-english.pdf> accessed 16 July 2022.

[90] *Accordance with International Law of the Unilateral Declaration of Independence in Respect of Kosovo, Advisory Opinion*, ICJ Reports (2010) 403, para 122.

[91] General Affairs and External Relations Council of the European Union, 18 February 2008 <http://www.consilium.europa.eu/uedocs/cms_data/docs/pressdata/en/gena/98818.pdf> accessed 16 July 2022.

[92] Weller (n 88) 5.

[93] Kosovo is still considered a *sui generis* case today. Andrew Forde, 'Setting Cat amongst Pigeons: Kosovo's application for Membership of the Council of Europe' (*Blog of the European Journal of International Law*, 17 May 2022) <https://www.ejiltalk.org/setting-the-cat-amongst-pigeons-kosovos-application-for-membership-of-the-council-of-europe/> accessed 17 July 2022.

States (Spain, Greece, Slovakia, Romania, and Cyprus) did not do so, out of domestic concerns.[94]

3.7 Crimea

Crimea has a long history of independence, but it belonged to the Russian Empire since the eighteenth century. It remained part of Russia until 1954, when it was ceded to Ukraine.[95] After the fall of the Soviet Empire, it remained under Ukrainian jurisdiction, with episodes of growing separatism.[96] During the 2014 Ukrainian crisis, Russian troops emerged in Crimea and the city of Sebastopol. Immediately, the Crimean regional parliament voted to hold a referendum 10 days later on the region's secession from Ukraine and possible reunification with Russia (inconsistent with the Ukrainian Constitution).[97] According to the data released, the turnout was high (around 82%) and almost 96 per cent voted in favour of reuniting with Russia. On 17 March, Russia recognized Crimea as an independent State, despite strong opposition from Ukraine. On 18 March, Russia and the Republic of Crimea signed an accession agreement. Crimea is now *de facto* part of Russia. This process received immediate condemnation from the EU (and the US). In March 2014, the EU released a Joint statement on Crimea declaring that the referendum was illegal and illegitimate and its outcome will not be recognized.[98] The EU position has not changed since then.[99]

[94] In order to honour the different positions of EU Member States concerning Kosovo, when referring to her, many EU documents include an asterisk clarifying that '[t]his designation is without prejudice to position on status, and is in line with UN Security Council Resolution 1244/99 and the International Court of Justice Opinion on the Kosovo declaration of independence'.

[95] Antonio Remiro Brotons, 'Derecho y poder en el destino de Crimea' (2018) 34 Anuario Español de Derecho Internacional 231, 232.

[96] Susan Stewart, 'Autonomy as a Mechanism for Conflict Regulation? The Case of Crimea' (2011) 7(4) Nationalism and Ethnic Politics 113, 118

[97] Detailed information about the procedure adopted in the organization of the referendum to be found at Venice Commission, 'Opinion on whether the decision taken by the Supreme Council of the Autonomous Republic of Crimea in Ukraine to organize a referendum on becoming a constituent territory of the Russian Federation or restoring Crimea's 1992 constitution is compatible with constitutional principles', CDL-AD(2014)002.

[98] European Council, 'Joint statement on Crimea by President of the European Council Herman Van Rompuy and President of the European Commission José Manuel Durao Barroso' EUCO 58/14 <https://www.consilium.europa.eu/uedocs/cms_Data/docs/pressdata/en/ec/141566.pdf> accessed 5 August 2022.

[99] Council of the EU, 'Declaration by the High Representative on behalf of the EU on Crimea' 119/15 <https://www.consilium.europa.eu/en/press/press-releases/2015/03/16/declaration-high-representative-crimea/> accessed 5 August 2022.

4. Statements and Responses from EU Officials

There is no treaty provision dealing with the secessionist challenge of a sub-national entity belonging to an EU Member State, as representatives of the Commission have repeatedly stated. For example, in June 2012 Ms Catherine Day, the former Secretary General of the Commission, stated the following: 'There is no legal base in the EU Treaties which would allow for secondary legislation to deal with the consequences of a secession of part of Member State.'[100] In effect, there are no explicit provisions regarding secession within an EU Member State in the EU treaties. Article 50 has been labelled an internal secession provision, but it only affects Member States wishing to withdraw from the EU.[101] As noted, there is no precedent of (successful) secession within an EU Member State and no case law either.

The fact that there is no EU legislation explicitly assessing the secession of a region within an EU Member State, nor any direct precedent, as has been shown in the preceding sections, has not prevented EU representatives from expressing their opinion about secession within an EU Member State. It is essential to highlight some of them in order to assess the position of the EU institutions, basically, the European Commission. For the sake of clarity, the different responses are organized chronologically:

In February 2004, Eluned Morgan, then a member of the European Parliament, asked the European Commission whether, in the event of the division of a Member State as a result of a region democratically gaining independence, the newly independent region would have to leave the EU and then apply for accession afresh. Romano Prodi, then President of the European Commission, responded in the following terms:

> When a part of the territory of a Member State ceases to be a part of that state, e.g. because that territory becomes an independent state, the treaties will no longer apply to that territory. In other words, a newly independent region would, by the fact of its independence, become a third country with respect to the Union and the treaties would, from the day of its independence, not apply anymore on its territory.[102]

This approach could be labelled the automatic expulsion theory. This was, as we shall see, the approach taken by Barroso when addressing the Scottish case. This

[100] Commission, 'Your request for registration of a proposed citizens' initiative' COM (2012) 701396.

[101] Josu de Miguel, 'La cuestión de la secesión en la Unión Europea: una visión constitucional' (2014) 165 Revista de Estudios Políticos 211, 214.

[102] Written Question by Eluned Morgan (PSE) to the Commission, 12 February 2004, P-0524/04 <http://www.europarl.europa.eu/sides/getAllAnswers.do?reference=P-2004-0524&language=EN> accessed 9 August 2017.

was also the approach adopted by the European Commission on 2 October 2017 after the outlawed Catalan referendum on independence:

> We also reiterate the legal position held by this Commission as well as by its predecessors. If a referendum were to be organised in line with the Spanish Constitution it would mean that the territory leaving would find itself outside of the European Union.[103]

However, between 2004 and the end of 2012 the Commission changed its responses and introduced more ambiguity. In a series of questions posed in 2007, 2010, 2011, and 2012 the Commission responded that 'these questions raise a number of issues concerning international law. It is not the Commission practice to give an opinion on purely hypothetical cases';[104] or that '[t]he issues referred to by the Honourable Members come entirely under the responsibility of the Member State concerned. The Commission cannot take the initiative in this respect.'[105] The Commission also stated that:

> Article 49 of the Treaty on the European Union sets out the conditions and procedure for the accession of States to the EU. The same conditions and procedure apply to any State that applies to become a member of the EU. There are no provisions in the Treaties that refer to the secession from a Member State.[106]

In the first months of 2012 the Commission continued with its cautionary approach, stating that:

> At the present time, the Commission is not able to express any view on the specific issue raised by the Honourable Member given that the terms and result of any future referendum are unknown, as is the nature of the possible future relationships

[103] European Commission, 'Statement on the events in Catalonia' (2 October 2017) <http://europa.eu/rapid/press-release_STATEMENT-17-3626_en.htm> accessed 3 August 2022.

[104] Oral question by Frank Vanhecke (ITS) to the Commission, 10 January 2007, H-0011/07 <http://www.europarl.europa.eu/sides/getDoc.do?type=QT&reference=H-2007-0011&language=EN> accessed 3 August 2022; Written question by Roger Helmer (NI) to the Commission, 1 February 2007, E-0314/07 <http://www.europarl.europa.eu/sides/getAllAnswers.do?reference=E-2007-0314&language=LT> accessed 3 August 2022; Written question by Eluned Morgan (PSE) to the Commission, 22 March 2007, P-1625/07 <http://www.europarl.europa.eu/sides/getAllAnswers.do?reference=P-2007-1625&language=EN> accessed 3 August 2022; Written question by Robert Kilroy-Silk (NI) to the Commission, 16 April 2007, E-2021/07 <http://www.europarl.europa.eu/sides/getAllAnswers.do?reference=E-2007-2021&language=LT> accessed 3 August 2022.

[105] Question for written answer by Raul Romeva (Verts/ALE), Oriol Junqueras (Verts/ALE) and Ramon Tremosa (ALDE) to the Commission, 26 July 2010, E-6073/2010 <https://www.europarl.europa.eu/doceo/document/E-7-2010-6073-ASW_EN.html?redirect> accessed 3 August 2022.

[106] Question for written answer by George Lyon (ALDE) to the Commission, 20 October 2011, P-009664/2011 <http://www.europarl.europa.eu/sides/getAllAnswers.do?reference=P-2011-009664&language=ES> accessed 3 August 2022.

> between the parties concerned and between those parties and European Union partners.[107]

In April 2012, following a European Citizens' Initiative, the Commission affirmed that '[i]n the event of secession of part of a Member State, the solution would have to be found and negotiated within the international legal order'.[108] In July 2012, in light of the response given by the Commission to the European Citizens' Initiative, the Commission was asked whether, in case of secession, citizens would immediately lose their status as EU citizens and the resultant rights and obligations. The Commission stated that 'in accordance with Article 20 of the Treaty on the Functioning of the European Union (TFEU), EU citizenship is additional to and does not replace national citizenship (that is, the citizenship of an EU Member State).' Yet, again, the Commission refused to provide further guidance: 'in the hypothetical event of a secession of a part of an EU Member State, the solution would have to be found and negotiated within the international legal order. Any other consideration related to the consequences of such event would be of a conjectural nature.'[109] Also in September 2012 the Commission refused several times to offer an opinion over the issue:

> The Commission would express its opinion on the legal consequences under EC law, on request from a Member State detailing a precise scenario;[110] It is not the role of the Commission to express a position on questions of internal organisation related to the constitutional arrangements in the Member States.[111]

[107] Question for written answer by Ramon Tremosa (ALDE) to the Commission, 23 January 2012, E-000395/2012 <http://www.europarl.europa.eu/sides/getAllAnswers.do?reference=E-2012-000395&language=EN> accessed 3 August 2022.

[108] Commission, 'Your request for registration of a proposed citizens' initiative' COM Ares(2012)701396.

[109] Question for written answer by Mara Bizzotto (EFD) to the Commission, 25 July 2012, E-007453/2012 <http://www.europarl.europa.eu/sides/getAllAnswers.do?reference=E-2012-007453&language=EN> accessed 3 August 2022.

[110] Question for written answer by Izaskun Bilbao (ALDE), Ramon Tremosa (ALDE), Salvador Sedo (PPE) and Raul Romeva (Verts/ALE) to the Commission, 12 September 2012, E-008133/2012 <http://www.europarl.europa.eu/sides/getAllAnswers.do?reference=E-2012-008133&language=EN> accessed 3 August 2022.

[111] Question for written answer by Ana Miranda (Verts/ALE), Ramon Tremosa (ALDE) and Raul Romeva (Verts/ALE) to the Commission, 21 September 2012, E-008324/2012 <http://www.europarl.europa.eu/sides/getAllAnswers.do?reference=E-2012-008324&language=EN> accessed 3 August 2022; Question for written answer by Francisco Sosa Wagner (NI) to the Commission, 28 September 2012, E-008752/2012 <http://www.europarl.europa.eu/sides/getAllAnswers.do?reference=E-2012-008752&language=EN> accessed 3 August 2022; Question for written answer by Auke Zijlstra (NI) to the Commission, 8 October 2012, E-009009/2012 <http://www.europarl.europa.eu/sides/getAllAnswers.do?reference=E-2012-009009&language=EN> accessed 3 August 2022.

However, the cautionary tone changed at the end of 2012 and the defiant view against secession within Member States expressed in 2004 by Romano Prodi re-emerged:

> The legal context has not changed since 2004 as the Lisbon Treaty has not introduced any change in this respect. Therefore, the Commission can confirm its position as expressed in 2004 in the reply to the written Question P-0524/04.[112]

The timing for such a change cannot be a coincidence: in October 2012, the UK government and Scotland had reached an agreement on holding an independence referendum in Scotland in the following years. Furthermore, September 2012 also saw the real start of the pro-independence movement in Catalonia.[113] Secession within an EU Member State no longer looked unlikely: it had become a real possibility. The Commission has maintained this approach since late 2012.[114] Moreover in 2013, the Committee of the Regions, the EU institutional chamber of subnational entities, was very clear:

> [I]f a region [where independence movements have recently been gaining strength], having achieved independence, wanted to join the EU, it would be required to make a formal application to the Council and to follow the accession

[112] Question for written answer by Gerard Batten (EFD) to the Commission, 29 October 2012, P-009862/2012 http://www.europarl.europa.eu/sides/getAllAnswers.do?reference=P-2012-009862&language=EN> accessed 3 August 2022.

[113] Xavier Pons Ràfols, *Cataluña: Derecho a decidir y Derecho Internacional* (Reus 2015) 24.

[114] Among others, Question for written answer by Ramon Tremosa (ALDE) to the Commission, 27 September 2013, E-011023/2013 <http://www.europarl.europa.eu/sides/getAllAnswers.do?reference=E-2013-011023&language=EN> accessed 3 August 2022; Question for written answer by Francisco Sosa Wagner (NI) to the Commission, 27 January 2014, E-000796/2014 <http://www.europarl.europa.eu/sides/getAllAnswers.do?reference=E-2014-000796&language=EN> accessed 3 August 2022; Question for written answer by George Lyon (ALDE), 14 February 2014, P-001676/2014 <http://www.europarl.europa.eu/sides/getAllAnswers.do?reference=P-2014-001676&language=DE> accessed 3 August 2022; Question for written answer by Mara Bizzotto (EFD) to the Commission, 21 February 2014, E-002111/2014 <http://www.europarl.europa.eu/sides/getAllAnswers.do?reference=E-2014-002111&language=EN> accessed 3 August 2022; Question for written answer by Izaskun Bilbao (ALDE) to the Commission, 24 September 2014, E-007129/2014 <http://www.europarl.europa.eu/sides/getAllAnswers.do?reference=E-2014-007129&language=EN> accessed 3 August 2022; Question for written answer by José Blanco (S&D) to the Commission, 11 November 2014, E-009058/2014 <http://www.europarl.europa.eu/sides/getAllAnswers.do?reference=E-2014-009058&language=EN> accessed 3 August 2022; Question for written answer by Santiago Fisas (PPE) to the Commission, 21 July 2015, E-011776/2015 <http://www.europarl.europa.eu/sides/getAllAnswers.do?reference=E-2015-011776&language=EN> accessed 3 August 2022; and Question for written answer by Gerolf Annemans (ENF) to the Commission, 9 February 2016, P-001148/2016 <http://www.europarl.europa.eu/sides/getAllAnswers.do?reference=P-2016-001148&language=EN> accessed 3 August 2022; Question for written answer by Beatriz Becerra (ALDE) to the Commission, 23 May 2017, E-003486-17 <http://www.europarl.europa.eu/sides/getAllAnswers.do?reference=E-2017-003486&language=EN> accessed 3 August 2022.

procedure under Article 49 TEU in the same way as any other country that wished to become an EU Member State.[115]

However, it is difficult to argue that this position (ie automatic expulsion theory)[116] constitutes a fully articulated policy.[117] Until now, as we shall see in the next section, it has proved to be correct in both the Scottish and Catalan scenarios, in the sense that this has been the approach adopted by the EU institutions. But both scenarios are very limited; in no case has the EU seen the creation of a new territorial entity.

In this regard, let us imagine a 'Yes' vote in the Scottish referendum. It is then difficult to legally justify the automatic expulsion theory especially after the incorporation of article 50 of the Treaty on European Union (TEU), that provides for negotiations before the withdrawal from a Member State in order to avoid a major disruption. Does it make any sense that automatically all the relationships between the secessionist part and the rest of the EU come to an end when, in the case of withdrawal, the Treaty provides for an extended period of negotiations? This is more particularly so, when the territorial entity wishes to keep its ties with the EU. It would be odd, in the light of article 50 TEU, if there were automatic expulsion in the event of lawful secession, while there is negotiation in the context of withdrawal. Some temporary or transitional period should be established and this requires, necessarily, some type of negotiations. This is also the position of former European Court of Justice (ECJ) judge David Edward.[118] In Chapter 6 I will offer further arguments against the automatic expulsion approach. Some have even argued that these European Commission declarations (ie the automatic expulsion approach) look more like political warnings against pro-secession movements rather than statements that necessarily anticipate the policy that European institutions would follow.[119]

[115] Committee of the Regions, 'Devolution in the European Union and the place for local and regional self-government in EU policy making and delivery' 2013/C 139/08.

[116] Other members of the Commission have expressed this same view while talking to the press. For instance, in 2013 the then vice-president of the European Commission, Joaquín Almunia affirmed that 'a part that segregates itself is not a member' and later his spokesperson confirmed that 'an independent state will be, by its very independence, regarded as a tertiary by the EU and European treaties will not apply to its territory from the moment it declares independence'. Stephen Burgen, 'Catalan EU claim may impact on Scots independence' *Scotsman* (Edinburgh, 17 September 2013) <https://www.scotsman.com/news/world/catalan-eu-claim-may-impact-scots-independence-1561073 accessed 3 August 2022. The same approach was followed by the then Commissioner on Internal Market, Michel Barnier. Pablo Allendesalazar, 'Brusselles insisteix que una Catalunya independent quedarà for a de la UE' *El Periódico* (Barcelona, 20 September 2013) <http://www.elperiodico.cat/ca/politica/20130920/brusselles-insisteix-catalunya-fora-ue-si-independent-2675309> accessed 3 August 2022.

[117] On the same lines, Carlos Closa, 'Secession from a Member State and EU Membership: The View from the Union' (2016) 12(2) European Constitutional Law Review 240, 241.

[118] David Edward, 'EU Law and the Separation of Member States' (2013) 36(5) Fordham International Law Journal 1151, 1167.

[119] This also seems to be the hope of some pro-independence scholars, who expect the answers of the Commission to be only political disincentives for secession but do not anticipate this policy being

5. EU Reactions to Secessionist Attempts Within EU Member States

5.1 Scotland (UK)

In December 2012, in response to a question posed by Lord Tugendhat, Member of the House of Lords and former Member of the European Commission and the European Parliament, the then President of the European Commission, Jose Manuel Barroso, argued that 'scenarios such as the separation of one part of a Member State or the creation of a new state would not be neutral as regards the EU Treaties'. And he reminded us of the 2004 Prodi position:

> If part of the territory of a Member State would cease to be part of that state because it were to become a new independent state, the Treaties would no longer apply to that territory. In other words, a new independent state would, by the fact of its independence, become a third country with respect to the EU and the Treaties would no longer apply on its territory.[120]

In February 2014, in an interview with the BBC, Barroso insisted that 'it will be extremely difficult to get the approval of all other member states to have a new member coming from one member state'.[121] According to Barroso, EU Member States seeking to prevent their own sub-national entities from seceding would almost certainly block Scotland's membership. Barroso also added that Scotland would have to apply for EU membership in the usual way.[122] In the next chapter we will argue that the statements of Barroso were legally correct, in the sense that he rejected the 'automatic enlargement' theory, and simply iterated the obvious political difficulties of achieving unanimity within the Council whenever the accession of a new EU Member State is discussed (art 49 TEU).

implemented afterwards. Pau Bossacoma, *Secessió i integració a la Unió Europea. Catalunya nou Estat de la Unió?* (Institut d'Estudis de l'Autogovern 2016) 57.

[120] Ref Ares(2012)1469619 - 10/12/2012 <http://www.parliament.uk/documents/lords-committees/economic-affairs/ScottishIndependence/EA68_Scotland_and_the_EU_Barroso's_reply_to_Lord_Tugendhat_101212.pdf> accessed 3 August 2022.

[121] '"Extremely difficult" for Scotland to join EU—Barroso' (*BBC*, 16 February 2014) <http://www.bbc.com/news/av/uk-politics-26215579/extremely-difficult-for-scotland-to-join-eu-barroso> accessed 3 August 2022.

[122] ibid.

5.2 Catalonia (Spain)

The events in Catalonia in September and October 2017, briefly reviewed in the previous chapter, led to a much more prominent position for the EU institutions than the 2014 Scottish referendum. As Ignacio Molina explains, although during the first stage of the pro-independence process (from 2012 to 2014) the European Commission resisted all attempts to draw it into the conflict, since 2014 (when it became clear that the Catalan government contemplated unilateralism) the new President Jean Claude Juncker responded, firmly supporting the constitutional order of Spain. During those years, the Catalan government representatives were not even allowed to meet high-ranked EU civil servants at the European Commission.[123]

On 15 September 2017, two weeks before the so-called referendum on independence of Catalonia (to be held on 1 October 2017), outlawed by the Spanish Constitutional Court, Franz Timmermans, Vice-President of the European Commission, declared at a press conference, having been asked the question by Spanish journalists, that 'within the rule of law, we ask for the respect of the Constitution of each Member State. If within these Constitutions new realities are created, they will be taken into account by the EU.' And he insisted: 'the main principle is the respect to the constitutional legal order of each EU Member State. That is what we expect both from citizens and Member States.' In the aftermath of 1 October, the European Commission issued a statement stating that under the Spanish Constitution, Catalonia's vote was not legal and that this was an issue that had to be dealt with in accordance with the Spanish constitutional legal order.[124] On 4 October, the European Parliament organized a debate to discuss the events. Franz Timmermans, again on behalf of the European Commission, delivered a speech in which he argued the following:

> In Europe … we have shaped our democratic societies based on three principles: democracy, respect for the Rule of Law and human rights. The three need each other. They cannot exclude each other.... Respect for the Rule of Law is not optional, it is fundamental. If the law does not give you what you want, you can oppose the law, you can work to change the law, but you cannot ignore the law. So, it is fundamental that the Constitutions of every one of our Member States are upheld and respected. This is the basis for the debate today.[125]

[123] A detailed analysis of the position of the different EU institutions and their leaders on the Catalan secession crisis is to be found at Ignacio Molina, 'La crisis catalana y la influencia de España en Bruselas' (*Real Instituto Elcano*, 25 April 2019) <https://www.realinstitutoelcano.org/analisis/la-crisis-catalana-y-la-influencia-de-espana-en-bruselas/> accessed 3 August 2022.

[124] European Commission, 'Statement on the events in Catalonia' (n 103).

[125] European Parliament, 'Catalonia: Political group leaders discuss situation with Frans Timmermans' (4 October 2017) <http://www.europarl.europa.eu/news/en/press-room/20171003IPR85246/catalonia-political-group-leaders-discuss-situation-with-frans-timmermans> accessed 3 August 2022.

Not surprisingly, EU institutions disregarded the unilateral declaration of independence of Catalonia of 27 October and did not recognize the existence of a new polity.[126] The next chapter will argue that the EU institutions acted in accordance with EU law, since they showed a deferential attitude towards the Spanish constitutional legal order. Despite some criticism,[127] because of the manner in which the Spanish police enforced court rulings when trying to prevent the 1 October referendum from happening, the European Commission did not consider that Spain was violating values contained in article 2 TEU. Nor has the European Commission questioned the criminal procedures and prison sentences against the political leaders responsible for the organization of the unlawful referendum and the unilateral declaration of independence of Catalonia. In short, the EU has 'in no uncertain terms, sided with the Spanish government to the detriment of the Catalan independence cause'.[128]

6. Conclusion

Some general lessons can be drawn from the territorial changes affecting Member States, the emergence of new countries out of secession in neighbouring countries, and the statements and reactions of EU institutions when confronted with pro-secession crisis within the EU. First, with the exception of the unique case of Kosovo (that included gross human rights violations), the EU opposes unilateral independence (the crises in Crimea and Catalonia are good examples). Second, the EU's main criteria for recognizing a secessionist entity has been the approval of the nation State from which an entity is seceding. The cases of the Baltic States and Montenegro are paradigmatic. Czechoslovakia, although not a secessionist process, also confirms this approach to the extent that EC Member States did not oppose the split, given that there was an agreement between the two Republics. Approval and consent have also proven essential in the partnership

[126] A tweet from the President of the European Council, Donald Tusk, was very clear in this regard: 'For EU nothing changes. Spain remains our only interlocutor.' <https://twitter.com/eucopresident/status/923914819631271936?lang=es> accessed 3 August 2022. Thus, when the Catalan crisis was effectively triggered, and despite the initial low profile, European institutions backed the Spanish government. Mattia Guidi and Mattia Casula, 'The Europeanization of the Catalan Debate. A War of Attrition?' in Carlos Closa, Costanza Margiotta, and Giuseppe Martinico (eds), *Between Democracy and Law. The Amorality of Secession* (Routledge 2020) 186.

[127] Note the second part of the abovementioned Donald Tusk tweet (n 126): 'I hope the Spanish government favours force of argument, not argument of force.' Note also the following comment included in the 2 October 2017 European Commission Statement: 'Violence can never be an instrument in politics'.

[128] Andrea Wagner, Jianna Marin, and Dorian Kroqi, 'The Catalan Struggle for Independence and the Role of the European Union' (2019) 11 Regional Science Policy and Practice 787, 801. It remains to be seen whether EU institutions will impose certain limits to the Amnesty Law (mentioned in the previous chapter) that the Spanish government aims to pass to secure the parliamentary support of Catalan pro-independence parties.

with Greenland. Third, another important lesson of the cases reviewed is that the EU position has proved to be highly vulnerable to the national interests or priorities of EU Member States when dealing with secessionist issues and territorial changes (Algeria and German reunification, for instance). Note also the case of Greece and Cyprus, where the EU accepted a radical change in its policy towards the conflict. Or the pressure exerted by Germany when the declarations of independence were made by Croatia and Slovenia. Fourth, the relevance of the secession of Montenegro should be underlined: this was the first time the EU became so deeply involved in a secessionist conflict. What should be highlighted (apart from what has been said about Serbia's acquiescence) is that the EU required respect for the rule of law and for the democratic principle (imposing certain rules for the implementation of a referendum on independence). Fifth, as a final note, it should be underlined that EU officials were prudent and cautious towards secession within EU Member States only when secessionism did not seem a likely event (before 2012). As explained earlier in Section 3, the cautionary tone changed in 2012 and the defiant view against secession within Member States expressed in 2004 by Romano Prodi re-emerged. Thus, if any general lesson could be applied to cases of secession within EU Member States, it would be the following: one can assume a fierce opposition towards pro-independence movements that breach the legal constitutional order of EU Member States and that are conducted without the agreement of the EU Member State affected. However, the position of the EU in a consensual and lawful pro-independence movement would not be so clear-cut.

Now we can proceed with a more comprehensive analysis of EU law with regard to secession and assess to what extent the conclusions drawn from practice are in accordance with EU law.

6
EU Law Approach to a Secessionist Challenge: Implicit Responses Within EU Provisions?

1. Introduction

The intention of this chapter, closely linked to the previous one, which could be described as the practical argument chapter, is to provide a general normative interpretation and identify the European Union (EU) law position towards secession that could be of relevance to any EU Member State. The position of EU law once the former sub-national unit becomes a recognized independent State, recognition policy, succession of States, and legal routes to membership, will be analysed in Chapter 7.

The chapter will review the work of those scholars who have found implicit responses to a secessionist challenge within EU provisions and values. There is a range of views in this regard, from those who consider that any secessionist movement is against the ethos of the European integration (and, therefore, EU law should oppose it), to those who believe that welcoming new States that have emerged from democratic secessionist processes is the duty of EU institutions. The view proffered in this book is a neutral one, or to be more precise, a deferential one. There should be a distinction between lawful secessions and unlawful secessions. Lawfulness is based on the legal criteria established by each EU Member State's constitutional legal order, as explained in Chapter 4.[1] In my view, the key provision that justifies the EU law response to secession is to be found in the principle of respect for fundamental constitutional structures (art 4(2) of the Treaty on European Union (TEU)). Drawing on this provision, it will be explained that EU law should respect domestic constitutional orders, with the consequence that if domestic law considers that secession is unlawful, EU law should respect that position by not recognizing the statehood of the secessionist entity. If, on the contrary, the domestic legal order regards the secessionist attempt as lawful, EU law should respect that outcome by recognizing the new entity as a sovereign State and by entering negotiations in good faith. Thus, the EU does not, and should not, take an autonomous

[1] The issues to which this national constitutional reference might give rise (eg where a certain EU Member State does not respect its own constitutional legal order) will be addressed later on.

Secession and European Union Law. Núria González Campañá, Oxford University Press. © Núria González Campañá 2024.
DOI: 10.1093/oso/9780198882596.003.0006

approach to secession, but one that is dependent on national constitutional legal orders.

The analysis goes beyond real cases or a case-specific approach, and at the end of the chapter it will address imagined scenarios that will test the thesis advanced in this book. I will then analyse other somewhat unlikely cases that might cast doubts on the preceding approach. For example, what happens if it is the EU Member State that contravenes its own constitutional order? Does this amount to constitutional mutation, the evolution or amendment of a certain constitution? What if the values of article 2 TEU are not respected while enforcing the national constitutional legal order, or when amending the constitutional legal order? What is the position of the EU then? Article 2 TEU appears as the limit to the deferential attitude proposed in the book. As long as the content of article 2 TEU is respected, the EU should respect the enforcement of national constitutional law and any amendment, evolution, or mutation in the constitutional legal order of the EU Member States. Otherwise, the EU institutions should consider whether article 7 TEU has been triggered.

The fact that there is no express provision, nor any precedent or fully articulated EU institutional policy, as seen in Chapter 5, does not mean that we cannot infer reasonable EU law responses through the interpretation of certain legal provisions and EU values. As Closa suggests, '[w]hile it is true that the EU treaties do not contain explicit rules on how to deal with a seceding territory seeking membership, EU provisions do contain sufficient contents from which to deduce a clear policy on secession'.[2] This is what some scholars have been seeking to explicate in the last few years, especially when addressing the cases of Scotland before the Brexit referendum, and Catalonia. Scholars have underscored the need to take a look at EU law itself, despite the lack of express provisions, given the autonomy of EU law:[3]

[2] Carlos Closa, 'Secession from a Member State and EU Membership: The View from the Union' (2016) 12(2) European Constitutional Law Review 240, 246. In the same vein, Kenealy and MacLennan state, 'the solution to the problem posed to the EU by an independent Scotland must first be sought in the Treaties, spirit and general principles of the EU as well as the jurisprudence of the ECJ'. Daniel Kenealy and Stuart MacLennan, 'Sincere Cooperation, Respect for Democracy and EU Citizenship: Sufficient to Guarantee Scotland's Future in the European Union?' (2014) 20(5) European Law Journal 591, 598. Thus, they disagree with Kochenov's position: 'there are no legal grounds for the Union to take sides in the internal processes of the Member States potentially leading to their territorial reconfiguration and even eventual secessions of their parts, resulting in the articulation of new statehood on the European continent'. Dimitry Kochenov and Martijn Van den Brink, 'Secession from EU Member States: The Imperative of Union's Neutrality' (2016) 6 University of Edinburgh School of Law Research Paper Series 1. This initial statement offered by Kochenov is, nonetheless, misleading, since he immediately admits that this is the case 'assuming that the process of the territorial reframing of statehood is taking place in a non-violent fashion and in full conformity with the law'. The present book (and in particular this chapter) aims at covering any type of secession, either unilateral and unlawful or consensual and lawful. And, as will be shown, EU policy differs depending on the type of secessionist challenge. Therefore, claiming neutrality is inaccurate. That is why I prefer to describe the EU approach as 'deferential'. At best, one could argue for neutrality in the event of lawful and consensual secession.

[3] The autonomy of EU law has been constantly affirmed by the European Court of Justice (ECJ) since the very beginning with the notorious *Van Gend & Loos* decision. More recently, Joined Cases C-402/05 P and C-415/05 P *Kadi v Council* [2008] ECR I-06351, para 281: 'an international agreement cannot affect the allocation of powers fixed by the Treaties or, consequently, the autonomy of the Community legal system, observance of which is ensured by the Court by virtue of the exclusive jurisdiction

> The solution to any problem for which the Treaties do not expressly provide must be sought first within the system of the Treaties, including their spirit and general scheme.[4]

After reviewing different scholars' positions, one can distinguish between: (1) dissuasive or restrictive views on secessionism; (2) legal approaches encouraging or defending secessionism within the EU; and (3) those neutral and deferential views that make a distinction between different types of secession and therefore adjust the legal response to the circumstances. As stated in the introduction and Chapter 1 above, our view is in accord with scholars who make a distinction between those pro-independence movements conducted lawfully in accordance with the national constitutional order, and those secessionist attempts that violate their own constitutional order. This position is grounded in article 4(2) TEU, which requires the EU to show a deferential attitude towards national constitutional law. The 'grey zone' scenarios where it is the parent State that is violating the law, or where there is a political agreement that trumps the legal order, that is, unlawful but consensual secession, will also be considered.

2. Restrictive Approach to Secessionism

As we will see, Weiler is the leading scholar within this intellectual camp. His thesis has been enthusiastically welcomed by many Spanish scholars, whereas he has been criticized by other colleagues. In 2012, in a famous editorial at the Blog of the European Journal of International Law, Weiler linked Catalan secessionist attempts with social and economic egoism. He argued that such pro-independence movements in Europe run diametrically contrary to the historical ethos of European integration:

> The commanding moral authority of the Founding Fathers of European integration—Schumann, Adenauer, de Gasperi and Jean Monnet himself—was a result of their rootedness in the Christian ethic of forgiveness coupled with an enlightened political wisdom which understood that it is better to look forward to a future of reconciliation and integration rather than wallow in the past.[5]

conferred on it by Article 220 EC, jurisdiction that the Court has, moreover, already held to form part of the very foundations of the Community'.

[4] David Edward, 'EU Law and the Separation of Member States' (2013) 36(5) Fordham International Law Journal 1151, 1162.

[5] Joseph HH Weiler, 'Catalonian Independence and the European Union' (*Blog of the European Journal of International Law*, 20 December 2012) <https://www.ejiltalk.org/catalonian-independence-and-the-european-union/> accessed 4 August 2022.

He went on to say that the EU struggles with a highly complex decision-making procedure that involves many members and players, but more importantly with a deep political and cultural division between rich Northern countries and poorer Southern countries[6] 'which makes it difficult to persuade a Dutch or a Finn or a German that they have a human and economic stake in the welfare of a Greek or a Portuguese, or, yes, a Spaniard'.[7] According to Weiler, the EU should not be interested in taking into the Union a polity predicated on a nationalist ethos 'which apparently cannot stomach the discipline of loyalty and solidarity that one would expect it owed to its fellow citizens in Spain'.[8] Thus, Weiler regards as particularly relevant the values of loyalty and solidarity within the EU:

> The very demand for independence from Spain, an independence from the need to work out political, social, cultural and economic differences within the Spanish polity, independence from the need to work through and transcend history, disqualifies morally and politically Catalonia and the likes as future Member States of the European Union.[9]

More recently, Marlene Wind has expressed a similar view when analysing EU reluctance to comment on any of the ongoing secessionist disputes. According to her, separatism is antithetical to European ideals.[10]

[6] Other scholars have also emphasized the deep economic culture divisions among Member States. For instance, Fabrizio Tassinari refers to the 'widening gap between the fiscally pious nations above of the Alps and the profligate countries in the South'. Fabrizio Tassinari, 'What Really Divides Northern and Southern Europe?' (2014) 31(3) New Perspectives Quarterly 18, 18.

[7] Weiler, 'Catalonian Independence and the European Union' (n 5).

[8] ibid. Piris shares this view: 'The European ideal tends towards more solidarity between European peoples, while the key objective of Catalan and Scottish independentists is less solidarity with the rest of the State to which they belong.' Jean-Claude Piris, 'Political and Legal Aspects of Recent Regional Secessionist Trends in some EU Member States (I)' in Carlos Closa (ed), *Secession from a Member State and Withdrawal from the European Union* (CUP 2017) 78.

[9] Weiler, 'Catalonian Independence and the European Union' (n 5). For some authors the principle of solidarity has even become 'a constitutional element within European Union's cooperative architecture'. Markus Kotzur, 'Solidarity as a Legal Concept' in Andreas Grimmel and Susanne My Giang (eds), *Solidarity in the European Union: A Fundamental Value in Crisis* (Springer 2017) 41.

[10] '[T]he EU is by definition a multi-state entity and a universalistic project striving both for unity and for the protection of diversity, as the motto has it in various official EU documents. In this sense, separatism is, and always will be, antithetical to European ideals. It will never become EU policy to encourage identity politics as exercised by the independence movement in Catalonia.' Marlene Wind, *The Tribalization of Europe. A Defense of our Liberal Values* (Polity 2020) 24. The populist elements of the Catalan process that are underlined by Wind in her book have also been addressed by other scholars: Juan Alberto Ruiz Casado, 'Articulations of Populism and Nationalism: The Case of the Catalan Independence Movement' (2020) 21(5) European Politics and Society 554; Argelia Queralt, 'The Populist Drift of the Catalan Pro-Independence Movement' in Jörn Axel Kämmerer, Markus Kotzur, and Jacques Ziller (eds), *Integration and Disintegration in Europe* (Nomos 2019); Astrid Barrio and others, '"Spain Steals from Us!" The "Populist Drift" of Catalan Regionalism' (2018) 16 Comparative European Politics 993. In order to summarize their contributions, one could highlight the following elements: (1) how, in the context of a harsh economic and political crisis (austerity policies and corruption scandals), the pro-independence bid became a way of distracting people from those problems; (2) how the long-used slogan 'Spain steals from us' became the battle cry of the pro-independence campaigns with the 2008 economic downturn (the idea that the subsidized Spain lives off

For Weiler, it would be hugely ironic if the prospect of an easy or qualified membership access to the EU ended up providing an incentive for disintegration. So, he concludes the 2012 blog as follows:

> There really is a fundamental difference in the welcoming into the Union of a Spain or a Portugal or a Greece emerging from ugly and repressive dictatorships and a Catalonia, part of a functioning democracy which at this very moment is in need of the deepest expression of internal and external solidarity. In seeking separation, Catalonia would be betraying the very ideals of solidarity and human integration for which Europe stands.

As it has been shown, Weiler's arguments are not addressed to EU legal doctrine, but rather the compatibility of the ontological assumption behind secession with the ontological assumptions on the nature of the EU. For him, the issue is not legal, but political. He believes that 'there should be no legal impediment for Scotland to become a Member State if she satisfies the condition for Membership, political and legal, one of which is a unanimous decision of all Member States', but at the same time he argues that '[i]t is simply ethically demoralizing to see the likes of Scotland and Catalonia reverting to an early 20th Century post World War I mentality, when the notion that a single state could encompass more than one nationality seemed impossible'.[11]

His position has found support among some scholars, notably Spanish ones,[12] who have drawn legal conclusions from his normative approach. For instance, his

the productive Catalonia was a common motto in those years); and (3) how the classical and Manichean populist opposition between the people and the elite has been adapted to pit the good and naïve Catalan people against the oppressive and corrupt Spanish State (which is nonetheless odd, for Catalan independence is a project designed by Catalan elites and supported by the Catalan middle and upper-middle class, a revolt of the rich, one could argue). Núria González Campañá, 'Constitutional Erosion in Spain: From the Catalan Pro-Independence Crisis to the (Intended) Judiciary Reforms' in Josep Maria Castellà Andreu and Marco Antonio Simonelli (eds), *Populism and Contemporary Democracy in Europe* (Palgrave MacMillan 2022) 159. Early on, Castellà Andreu had already warned about the populist trait of the movement because of the misleading approach (eg making people believe that a referendum on secession is 'normal', when in fact it is extraordinary and outlawed by other constitutional legal orders beyond Spain) to a complex and emotional issue. Josep Maria Castellà Andreu, 'La secesión catalana, entre la política y el derecho' (2014) 7 Anuario de la Facultad de Derecho Universidad de Alcalá 229, 235.

[11] Joseph HH Weiler, 'Scotland and the EU' (*Verfassungsblog*, 8 September 2014) <https://verfassungsblog.de/scotland-eu-comment-joseph-h-h-weiler-2/> accessed 4 August 2022.

[12] It must be noted, however, that apart from scholars who defend a restrictive approach of the EU to pro-independence movements, that will be analysed in this section, and those who favour a sympathetic EU attitude, whose arguments will be addressed in the next section, in Spain there are also voices advancing a more nuanced position. For instance, López Basaguren argues that the destiny of an entity seceding from a Member State will depend, essentially, on whether the independence process has been a consensual one or not. Alberto López Basaguren, 'La independencia de Escocia en la Unión Europea. Los efectos de la secesión de territorios en la UE entre política y derecho' (2014) 33 Teoría y Realidad Constitucional 69, 96.

conviction that secessionist demands stem not from a remedial situation or lack of self-government, but rather from the aspiration to avoid sharing the economic burden of less developed regions in their own States is explicitly shared by Josu de Miguel.[13] De Miguel even recommends that since the secession of a territory within an EU Member State has a clear EU effect and impact, it would be highly advisable to regulate the issue within the EU treaties.[14] In his view, EU Member States should amend the treaties to include a new provision that establishes by analogy with article 50(5) TEU that in the event of a new independent State emerging by way of secession, that State would be out of the EU, irrespective of the mode of secession.[15] In the same vein, Francesc de Carreras agrees with Weiler. De Carreras says that 'there are a lot of reasons to believe that secession within an EU Member State is contrary to Europeanism'.[16] So too Linde Paniagua, who argues that a secessionist project like the one currently in vogue in Catalonia is contrary to the values enshrined in article 2 TEU.[17] Javier Tajadura emphasizes that 'any secessionist project within an EU Member State is at odds with EU law', since it has the effects of reducing the internal market.[18] José María de Areilza affirms that EU law and the institutional functioning of the European Union contain an anti-secession regime, both from a political and a legal point of view, since leaving or withdrawing from an EU Member State, either through consensus or unilaterally, contradicts the principles, values, and basic norms upon which the EU is based.[19] For him, the evolution of the European integration process opposes the idea of secession. The

[13] Josu de Miguel, 'La cuestión de la secesión en la Unión Europea: una visión constitucional' (2014) 165 Revista de Estudios Políticos 211, 221.

[14] ibid 244. Although Fasone's starting point is different, because she holds a deferential approach to secessionism (as will be made clear in the following pages), she also advocated introducing a secession clause in the treaties: 'in the future the EU could set out in a new ad hoc provision in the Treaty the minimum requirements an aspiring seceding territory should have to meet in order to apply for EU accession afterwards'. Cristina Fasone, 'Secession and the Ambiguous Place of Regions Under EU Law' in Carlos Closa (ed), *Secession from a Member State and Withdrawal from the European Union* (CUP 2017) 65. She believes such a clause would permit the transition from secession to new EU membership to be made smoothly, if certain circumstances are met (ie compliance with national constitutional law and the constitutional traditions common to the Member States). This proposal will be further discussed in Chapter 7.

[15] ibid 245. See also Javier Tajadura, 'Más allá de un asunto interno: secesionismo e integración europea' (*Real Instituto Elcano*, 22 December 2014) <https://www.realinstitutoelcano.org/analisis/mas-alla-de-un-asunto-interno-secesionismo-e-integracion-europea/> accessed 4 August 2022.

[16] Francesc de Carreras, 'Unión Europea y secesión de Estados Miembros. ¿Deben intervenir las instituciones europeas? (2014) 33 Teoría y Realidad Constitucional 271, 278. In a similiar vein, and more recently, see Maria Isabel González Pascual, 'Unión Europea y secesionismo, ¿silencio de los tratados? La identidad regional como parte de la identidad constitucional nacional' (2018) 10 Fundamentos 377, 394.

[17] Enrique Linde, 'Contestación al trabajo de Ridao-González: la secesión de territorios de Estados Miembros de la Unión Europea, que se fundan en ideologías nacionalistas, son contrarias a los principios democráticos que rigen en los Estados occidentales y en la Unión Europea' (2015) 28 Revista de Derecho de la Unión Europea 391, 403.

[18] Javier Tajadura, 'Los Procesos Secesionistas y el Derecho Europeo' (2016) 37 Teoría y Realidad Constitucional 347, 369.

[19] José María de Areilza, *Poder y Derecho en la Unión Europea* (Civitas 2014) 193.

entire EU checks and balances system is aimed at facilitating plural loyalties: at EU, national, and regional levels.[20] Areilza argues that a sub-national political community could only ask for secession within the EU in the event of clear violations of article 2 TEU, firmly established by the EU following the article 7 TEU procedure.[21]

At the same time, Weiler's view has been subject to considerable criticism. Since Weiler accused the Catalan pro-independence movement of being linked to a 'regressive and outmoded nationalist ethos', Krisch pointed out that Weiler's intervention was 'heavily misguided in substance, in part because of a misunderstanding of the reasons behind the Catalan drive, in part because of a misreading of the nature of independence claims in general'.[22] This is not the place to analyse Krisch's defence of the Catalan pro-independence movement ('it is not some form of tribalism', but 'a form of democratic self-government, born out of frustration with the processes of a larger entity that often enough ignore the wishes and concerns of minorities').[23] Suffice it to say that from a legal point of view (and in this particular regard I agree with Krisch) there is no inconsistency with the following statements: (1) a certain sub-national community within a State wishes to leave that State and become an independent, sovereign State; and (2) at the same time that community wishes to become a member of a *sui generis* international organization predicated on political integration and solidarity, like the EU. As Krisch notes, many Catalans 'have no doubt that they owe solidarity to Europe as a whole, but they don't see why they should owe that much more to people in Andalucía than to those in Southern France (who, geographically and probably also culturally, are closer)'.[24] Although there are many historical, cultural, and political reasons to contradict this argument, it is difficult to give opposing legal reasons.

[20] ibid 197.

[21] ibid 194.

[22] Nico Krisch, 'Catalonia's Independence: A Reply to Joseph Weiler' (*Blog of the European Journal of International Law*, 18 January 2013) <https://www.ejiltalk.org/catalonias-indepence-a-reply-to-joseph-weiler/> accessed 4 August 2022. In the same vein, Kochenov: 'They seek to create a democratic society, defined and united by a common language and sense of history. I think this is what most Québécois nationalists seek, as well as most Catalan, Scottish, and Flemish nationalists. They are not trying to avoid modernity; they are precisely trying to create a modern democratic society.' Kochenov and Van den Brink (n 2) 17. Michael Keating was also very critical of Weiler and accused him of poisoning the debate because of Weiler's references to the ethnic cleansing mentality of nationalism. Michael Keating, 'The European Question' in Michael Keating (ed), *Debating Scotland. Issues of Independence and Union in the 2014 Referendum* (OUP 2017) 108.Neil Walker, 'Internal Enlargement in the European Union: Beyond Legalism and Political Expediency' in Carlos Closa (ed), *Secession from a Member State and Withdrawal from the European Union* (CUP 2017) 40.

[23] Krisch (n 22). In n 10, I have already noted some populist traits of the Catalan pro-independence movement, but notwithstanding that, I am not convinced that the normative contradiction outlined by Weiler should anticipate the EU law position towards any type of secession, as some Spanish scholars have expressed. In other words, there are two different levels here: a normative or rather a moral one, addressed by Weiler, and a legal one, addressed by some other scholars. I do not see the causal link between both levels, because a moral rejection to secessionism does not necessarily lead to a legal rejection.

[24] Krisch (n 22).

In any event, Weiler had already made clear that his concerns were not legal, but political or moral.

Pau Bossacoma also replied to Weiler. He argues that European integration and secession are compatible for various reasons.[25] First, according to Bossacoma, EU law does not contain rules that prohibit or limit secession within EU Member States. However, one could argue that this is obvious, since territorial integrity is an exclusive competence of EU Member States, as stated in article 4(2) TEU.[26] Bossacoma also argues that the demand for division from the parent State, and the demand for integration within the EU have different territorial scope and, therefore, can be compatible. However, the incompatibility pointed out by Weiler remains, since he refers to the fact that a political community aimed at independence, due to the lack of solidarity and willingness to resolve political controversies within the current legal order, is not legitimized to ask for membership within an organization aimed at, precisely, these two objectives: solidarity and legal resolution of conflicts. Thirdly, Bossacoma also indicates that the EU itself has promoted the relevance of the nation State by undermining the aspirations of European regions to take part in the EU governance system. There is strong evidence in this regard.[27] It is unclear, however, how this argument about the unintended side effects of EU integration can be used to justify a certain approach towards secession where no EU law provision points in that direction.

Also, Kochenov has called into question ('principled disagreement') Weiler's approach:

> Taking sides in the national secession/territorial rearrangement debates by preventing and/or fostering—either directly or indirectly—particular outcomes in the context of the national constitutional arrangements—is simply not among the EU's constitutional prerogatives: intervening in the resolution of these issues—thus shaping the Member States with no regard to their internal constitutional process, is not merely an *ultra vires* action: it amounts to tyranny.[28]

[25] Pau Bossacoma, '*Secessió i integració a la Unió Europea. Catalunya nou Estat de la Unió?*' (Institut d'Estudis de l'Autogovern 2016) 25 ff.

[26] As Mangas notes, 'the increase or decrease of the territory of a Member State affects primarily and exclusively to the referred State. It is not an EU issue; that is why secession from a Member State is not covered by EU law.' Araceli Mangas, 'La secesión de territorios en un Estado Miembro: efectos en el derecho de la Unión Europea' (2013) 25 Revista de Derecho de la Unión Europea 47, 57.

[27] In Chapter 1 we referred to the paradox that the EU integration has promoted, unintentionally, pro-independence movements throughout EU Member States. The EU provides a unique framework for the feasibility of new States in Europe in the sense that it has created a safety net that makes it easier for those with statehood aspirations to contemplate independence. See Christopher K Connolly, 'Independence in Europe: Secession, Sovereignty and the European Union' (2013) 24 Duke Journal of Comparative & International Law 51, 54.

[28] Kochenov and Van den Brink (n 2) 2.

Neil Walker, David Edward, and Carlos Closa, are more modest in their criticism. And although I understand and value the teleological interpretative effort made by Weiler, I share some of the concerns raised by them. Walker admits that there are other rival views of the purposes and missions of the EU. Given these competing narratives, he considers that there is insufficient consensus on this issue and, therefore, EU policy should remain more agnostic.[29] Edward follows the same approach: 'the moral arguments are ambivalent and it seems to me to be more fruitful to focus on the legal issues'.[30] And as Closa rightly points out, 'the crucial point is to establish whether EU norms reflect such a moral stance'.[31]

The principal difficulty with Weiler's approach, and related approaches (particularly those scholars who draw legal consequences from Weiler's moral reasoning), is that they do not make a clear distinction between different types of secession, and they deprive EU Member States of a fundamental margin of political decision, which is the possibility to decide who joins the EU. Why should EU Member States tie their hands with such a radical position against secession when in the future, in the event of a lawful and consensual secession within the EU, or even in the event of an illegal but consensual secession, they might wish to maintain the EU membership of the seceding entity when it becomes an independent State? In this sense, I find that the 'conservative neutrality' (in Neil Walker's words[32]) the EU has shown so far when it comes to secession is a wise option. I concur here with Beltrán De Felipe when he says that 'I believe that the EU not wanting to get involved in the secessionist processes is both constitutionally correct, and probably preferable'.[33] As legal scholars, it is difficult to disregard as illegitimate a political option that is considered lawful in certain constitutional legal orders. Bearing in mind now the Scottish case, where everything was agreed between Scotland and the UK and subject to the law (Chapter 4), how could EU law oppose a political option that had been blessed by a national constitutional legal order when the EU is obliged by virtue of article 4(2) TEU to respect the constitutional identity of Member States? This issue will be discussed again in Section 4.3.

[29] Walker, 'Internal Enlargement in the European Union' (n 22) 40.

[30] Edward (n 4) 1154.

[31] Closa, 'Secession from a Member State and EU Membership' (n 2) 246.

[32] Neil Walker, 'Beyond Secession? Law in the Framing of the National Polity' in Stephen Tierney (ed), *Nationalism and Globalisation* (Hart Publishing 2015) 168.

[33] Beltrán De Felipe considers that such non-involvement is based on: (1) EU treaties; (2) moral and historical reasons, for Europe is built on integration; (3) the principle of democracy, since it respects the domestic constitutional identity of Member States; and (4) on practical and pragmatic considerations. Miguel Beltrán de Felipe, *Myths and Realities of Secessionisms* (Palgrave 2019) 70–71.

3. Generous Approach to Secession

A group of Catalan scholars have argued that, in the event of a democratic secession, regardless of the position of the EU Member State affected, the EU should welcome the new entity. By 'welcome' they refer to the acceptance of continued EU membership of the new independent polity. I do not share this view because, as will be clear at the end of this section, I think we need to make a distinction between different types of secessionist process. Under EU law it is not enough to be 'democratic': the process has to respect the constitutional legal order of the EU Member State affected. We should, in any event, begin by reviewing the argument. The starting point is the unique nature of the EU, 'which shares elements and characteristics of international organisations and federal structures'.[34] They are particularly interested in highlighting the federal elements of the EU ('many of the characteristics of European Union's organisational structure and legal system are closer to federal models than those of international organisations'[35]). Then, they point out the importance of the democratic principle within the EU:

> [T]he European Union is an international organisation devoted to the integration of its member states and the defence of democratic principles and values.... This entire ideological foundation for the European Union has meant an effort in defending democracy not only within the member states but also throughout the world. The furtherance of democracy is therefore one of the chief objectives of European Union's foreign policy.[36]

For them, since democracy is a founding value of the EU, the EU should be obliged to respect secessionism: 'there is a possibility of expressing collective will in sub-state spheres, as well as the obligation to take into account this legitimately expressed will'.[37]

> Indeed, as stated before, the European Union is based on respect for democratic values and principles, and adopts a democratic internal functioning that is intended to disseminate and promote democracy throughout the world. It is clear that this ideological basis for the nature of the European Union included

[34] Jordi Matas and others, 'The Internal Enlargement of the European Union' (Centre Maurits Coppieters 2011) 9 <https://ideasforeurope.eu/activity/publication/the-internal-enlargement-of-the-european-union/> accessed 4 August 2022. A related argument that supports the idea of an EU accommodating approach to secession is to be found in Aidan O'Neill, 'A Quarrel in a Faraway Country?: Scotland, Independence and the EU' (*Eutopialaw*, 14 November 2011), where the author puts forward the idea that the doctrine of EU citizenship can by itself engender automatic membership of the EU for an independent Scotland. We will review (and reject) this approach in Chapter 7, when dealing with nationality issues and EU law after successful secession.

[35] ibid 15–19.

[36] ibid 22.

[37] ibid 42.

> respect for all democratic processed developed inside the member states, even though these processes are not specifically regulated in the TEU or generally in Union law.[38]

That is why a 'European Union founded on such bases cannot show political, institutional and legal contempt for scrupulously democratic processes for the dissolution of a member state or the secession of territories'.[39] This is so, even if these processes are against the law:

> We must accept the possibility that the declaration of a democratic option linked to the constitution of a new political entity breaks the status quo, renouncing constitutional rules to be mechanically applied to thwart democratic aspirations.[40]

Although they accept that the right to self-determination as recognized in international law cannot be applied to territories within the EU (as explained in Chapter 3), for them this does not imply that secession is not legitimate if this is the will of a group of citizens in a certain territory inside a State, even though they are not subject to colonial rule or a situation of oppression. For them, there is a need to respect this democratic will.[41] They conclude as follows:

> The European Union is obliged to give a positive reply to a request for internal enlargement by a state appearing through a process of secession or dissolution of the European Union's member state, and should always guarantee the continuity of effective application to the Union's legal system in the new state and particularly the effectiveness of the rights and obligations given to its citizens.[42]

Very similar reasoning was followed later on by other Catalan scholars.[43] For them, respecting the democratic principle means facilitating EU membership of the new entity.[44] They believe that there is a conflict between the democratic principle enshrined in article 2 TEU and the respect for territorial integrity of Member States established in article 4(2) TEU. They argue that the credibility of the EU would be undermined if territorial integrity prevails and the EU does not support

[38] ibid.
[39] ibid.
[40] ibid.
[41] ibid 43.
[42] ibid 45.
[43] They also consider that the democratic principle is one of the core values of the EU and is the cornerstone principle that should guide the EU approach towards secession within Member States: 'The EU's response should respect the democratic principle, that has to characterize both its behaviour and that of its Member States.' Joan Ridao and Alfonso González, 'La Unión Europea ante la eventual creación de nuevos Estados surgidos de la secesión de Estados Miembros' (2015) 28 Revista de Derecho de la Unión Europea 363, 381.
[44] ibid 382.

the new entity in its attempt to become a new Member State.[45] Linde replied directly to this approach in the very same journal where their piece was published. He offered a sociological or political argument: Linde argued that according to the polls, Catalan society is a divided one, where there is no clear majority in favour of secession. For him, under these circumstances a referendum on secession would only threaten the breakup of the Catalan society.[46]

While it may be reasonable to conclude that it is politically imprudent to hold referendums on decisive and national issues when according to polls, surveys, and electoral results there is no clear majority, the main legal concern is as to the meaning of constitutional democracy. These scholars, Matas, Jaria, González, Román, and Ridao, detach the rule of law from democracy, as if democracy could stand alone, by itself, or even prevail, forgetting that article 2 TEU refers to different but interrelated principles:

> The Union is founded on the values or respect for human dignity, freedom, democracy, equality, the rule of law and respect for human rights, including the rights of persons belonging to minorities.

In effect, the EU is founded on a set of common principles of democracy, rule of law, and fundamental rights. It does not make any sense to describe democracy as opposed to the rule of law. In a constitutional State, democracy is not only about voting, but doing so according to rules that can only be changed following the amendment procedure foreseen in the very same rules. In 2014, in the Communication about the new EU Framework to Strengthen the Rule of Law, the European Commission described the rule of law as the 'backbone of any modern constitutional democracy'.[47] The rule of law 'makes sure that all public powers act within the constraints set out by law, in accordance with the values of democracy and fundamental rights, and under the control of independent and impartial courts'.[48] Based on the ECJ case law,[49] as well as documents drawn up by the Council

[45] ibid 381.
[46] Linde (n 17) 403.
[47] European Commission, Communication, A New EU Framework to Strengthen the Rule of Law, COM(2014) 158, 2.
[48] ibid 4.
[49] The following cases were some of the first to underline the importance of rule of law for the EU: Case C-50/00 P *Unión de Pequeños Agricultores* [2002] ECR I-06677, paras 38 and 39; Joined Cases C-402/05 P and C-415/05 P *Kadi v Council* [2008] ECR I-06351, para 316; Recently, in the context of populism, constitutional erosion, and the decline of the rule of law in some Member States, the ECJ has strengthened the rule of law as a binding value within the EU starting with the landmark ruling Case C-64/16 *Associação Sindical dos Juízes Portugueses* [2018] ECLI 117. Many other rulings followed. Kochenov and Pech have recently published a report analysing these specific responses of the ECJ. Laurent Pech and Dimitry Kochenov, 'Respect for the Rule of Law in the Case Law of the European Court of Justice' (2021) 3 Swedish Institute for European Policy Studies <https://www.sieps.se/en/publications/2021/respect-for-the-rule-of-law-in-the-case-law-of-the-european-court-of-justice/> accessed 4 August 2022.

of Europe, notably the Venice Commission[50] and the European Court of Human Rights (ECtHR), and national constitutional traditions of EU Member States,[51] the Commission provided a non-exhaustive list of important elements of the notion of rule of law in the EU legal system: the principle of legality, which implies a transparent, accountable, democratic, and pluralistic process for enacting laws; legal certainty; prohibition of arbitrariness of the executive powers; independent and impartial courts; effective judicial review, including respect for human rights; and equality before the law.[52] These principles are 'the vehicle for ensuring compliance with and respect for democracy and human rights'.[53] The Commission concludes categorically:

> This means that respect for the rule of law is intrinsically linked to respect for democracy and for fundamental rights: there can be no democracy and respect for fundamental rights without respect for the rule of law and vice versa.[54]

In effect, in a constitutional democracy, like the type of democracy in EU Member States, there is no such thing as democracy outside the law, or democracy without respecting the rule of law. As the Canadian Supreme Court established in 1998:

> Constitutionalism facilitates—indeed, makes possible—a democratic political system by creating an orderly framework within which people may make political decisions. Viewed correctly, constitutionalism and the rule of law are not in conflict with democracy; rather, they are essential to it.[55]

[50] See Venice Commission, 'Report on the Rule of Law', CDL-AD (2011)003rev-e. See also Venice Commission, 'Rule of Law Checklist', CDL-AD (2016)007. The Venice Commission has built up a solid reputation on the issues of the rule of law both in EU countries and elsewhere in Europe. See Joakim Nergelius, 'The Role of the Venice Commission in Maintaining the Rule of Law in Hungary and in Romania' in Armin von Bogdandy and Pál Sonnevend (eds), *Constitutional Crisis in the European Constitutional Area: Theory, Law and Politics in Hungary and Romania* (Hart Publishing 2015) 300.

[51] 'When one examines what the rule of law entails in what are arguably the most influential national legal traditions in Europe—the British, German and French traditions—it is possible to outline some divergences between these national understandings. Yet, the importance of these divergences should not be overstated. Firstly, some degree of disagreement in reality persists within any legal system as regards the precise meaning, scope of application and normative impact of the rule of law. Secondly, these disagreements are for the most part theoretical in nature and quite remarkably, national scholarly debates are actually conducted on largely identical terms. Last but not least, national understandings have now largely converged.' Laurent Pech, 'The Rule of Law as a Constitutional Principle of the European Union' (2009) 04 Jean Monnet Working Paper 22. Therefore, one could affirm that in EU countries there is 'an identifiable consensus with regard to the core meaning, scope and impact of the rule of law as a constitutional principle'. ibid.

[52] European Commission, Communication, A New EU Framework to Strengthen the Rule of Law (n 47) 4.

[53] ibid.

[54] ibid.

[55] *Reference re Secession of Quebec* [1998] 2 SCC 217, 78.

In similar terms, Carlos Closa argues that this approach to democracy by certain scholars 'advances a shallow conception of democracy, whereby democracy becomes simply a majoritarian principle prevailing over any other consideration', democracy 'amounts to much more than mere aggregation of the preferences of the majority', and that 'respect for the rule of law is part of EU policy towards outside secessionism, since the EU made the question of constitutional validity the key factor in the EU's response to newly-gained statehood',[56] as has been shown in Chapter 5. Besides, majority is an artificial rather than a neutral concept that is constructed through political decisions by including or excluding people from the right to vote. Democratic theorists always find it necessary to refer to the pre-democratic definition of who belongs to the group (ie the nation) entitled to vote. In effect, the alleged democratic character of a referendum on secession is, at least, misleading. Such a referendum cannot be justified solely on the basis of democracy, if there is no agreement to hold it, because it is organized and designed by other pre-democratic elements: language, history, culture, etc. The elements according to which a certain political community apparently form a distinct nation separated from the rest of a bigger one. The delimitation of the demos entitled to decide is a pre-democratic choice. Margiotta explains clearly that the triggering motivation behind a referendum on secession is not democracy, but nationalism: territory and voters must, in some way, be determined before deciding anything. In practice, the right to secede is granted on the basis of nationality. That is why she argues that 'it seems impossible to justify secession entirely in terms of democracy, as it is always necessary to refer to the pre-democratic determination of criteria for belonging to the secessionist group'.[57] Or as Closa puts it, '[i]n purely democratic terms (ie majority of a group), there is not prima facie criterium to assert that the democratic right to secede of a group must prevail over the equally democratic rejection of this right expressed by a majority of the wider demos which comprises the seceding one'.[58] In effect, why is it more 'democratic' that only Catalans decide the destiny of Catalonia and Spain instead of all Spaniards? The democratic principle comes into the equation only after the demos entitled to secede has been decided. It is only then that the democratic (procedural) question enters the equation: how is the chosen demos going to decide? Therefore, the so-called democratic approach is necessarily in debt to a previous nationalist paradigm.

[56] Closa, 'Secession from a Member State and EU Membership' (n 2) 249–50.

[57] Costanza Margiotta, 'An Update on Secession as the "Ultimate Right"' in Carlos Closa, Costanza Margiotta, and Giuseppe Martinico (eds), *Between Democracy and Law. The Amorality of Secession* (Routledge 2020) 23.

[58] Carlos Closa, 'A Critique of the Theory of Democratic Secession' in Carlos Closa, Costanza Margiotta, and Giuseppe Martinico (eds), *Between Democracy and Law. The Amorality of Secession* (Routledge 2020) 55. On the same lines, Martinico considers that this approach is typical from populist movements when 'presenting democracy (understood as the rule of majority) as a kind of "trump card" which should prevail over other constitutional values, such as the rule of law'. Giuseppe Martinico, 'Constitutionalists' Guide to the Populist Challenge' in Carlos Closa, Costanza Margiotta, and Giuseppe Martinico (eds), *Between Democracy and Law. The Amorality of Secession* (Routledge 2020) 89.

Another important legal problem of the so-called 'internal enlargement' theory is that, like the restrictive approach, it prevents Member States deciding who joins the EU. The rule of unanimity (art 49 TEU) is clear in this regard.[59] EU Treaty provisions express legitimate Member States aspirations, including the decision about who they want to share the EU political community with.[60] That is why this decision, necessarily, requires unanimous agreement.[61] Indeed, this decision is so relevant for EU Member States that, for example, France has included a constitutional provision to ensure that a new enlargement will have to be accepted by the national constituency. Thus, article 88(5) of the French Constitution, amended in 2005, establishes that '[a]ny Government Bill authorizing the ratification of a treaty pertaining to the accession of a state to the European Union shall be submitted to referendum by the President of the Republic'.[62] Additionally, the new aspirant State is expected to fulfil the so-called Copenhagen criteria. It cannot be denied that a new independent State, which emerges from an existing EU Member State, will be in an advantageous position in relation to EU law compliance. But a presumption of compliance is not enough. The new State will have to pass tests on its economic viability, rule of law, protection of minorities, and the capability of its administration.[63] Furthermore, these tests are also about the political will to share a common destiny. This is a discretionary prerogative of current EU Member States. This same logic is applied in article 50(5) TEU, when it is established that '[i]f a State which has withdrawn from the Union asks to rejoin, its request shall be subject to the procedure referred to in Article 49'.

4. Neutral and Deferential Approaches to Secession

It is becoming widely accepted among scholars that the key issue is to distinguish between different types of secession. 'The compatibility of secessions with EU law depends decisively on whether they are unilateral (ie non-consensual) or consensual/agreed processes, since different EU legal provisions may be invoked in either

59 Mangas (n 26) 62. See also Linde (n 17) 407 and Alfredo Galán, 'Secesión de Estados y Pertenencia a la Unión Europea' (2013) 1 Istituzione del Federalismo 95, 114.

60 De Miguel (n 13) 238.

61 That is why I disagree with Kochenov's approach: 'Should the people of the newly emerged state express the will to remain part of the EU, moreover, the EU should aspire to employ all the available political and legal tools to ensure the continuation of EU membership and protect those citizens and companies that benefit from the internal market and important EU rights in other spheres from a temporary disapplication of the acquis.' Kochenov and Van den Brink (n 2) 11.

62 <http://www2.assemblee-nationale.fr/langues/welcome-to-the-english-website-of-the-french-national-assembly#Title15> accessed 4 August 2022.

63 Christophe Hillion, 'Scotland and the EU: Comment by Christophe Hillion' (*Verfassungsblog*, 15 September 2014) <http://verfassungsblog.de/scotland-eu-comment-christophe-hillion-2/> accessed 4 August 2022: 'the fact that its devolved administrative and judicial institutions have been involved in the application of EU law for more than 40 years would not in itself guarantee that its structures, as a state, would be in a position to implement the whole *acquis* from the day of independence'.

case, and with different effects.'[64] Scholars tend to identify or relate lawfulness with consensus and unlawfulness with unilaterality.[65] This might be the paradigm, and the only cases witnessed thus far,[66] but there are other possible instances, such as unlawful but subsequently consensual secession. For now, we will assume the common distinction that tends to relate lawfulness with consensus. The criteria of lawfulness depend on the internal legal order concerned, as shown in Chapter 4.

In this section, I will distinguish between legal arguments raised to justify a certain EU law position towards (1) lawful and consensual scenarios; (2) unlawful and non-consensual scenarios; and (3) both scenarios.

4.1 Lawful and Consensual Scenarios: Obligation to Enter into Good Faith Negotiations

Former ECJ judge David Edward has claimed that in the event of consensual secession within an EU Member State, EU institutions and Member States have an obligation to negotiate in good faith with the segregated territory before separation takes effect to determine the future relationship with the EU.[67] It should not be surprising that he uses the term 'consensual', since, in British constitutional terms, when referring to Scotland, there is an identification of consensus and lawfulness, given that the legality of a referendum on independence and, therefore, the subsequent process, depends mainly on the political will of Westminster. His view is that looking at the wording of article 50 TEU, that foresees negotiations in case

[64] Closa, 'Secession from a Member State and EU Membership' (n 2) 247. Fasone also argues that not all secessions are alike from the EU perspective and, in the event of secession, the EU's response 'should depend on how secession is achieved, in particular if it is pursued in compliance with the fundamental values of the EU, such as democracy and the Rule of Law (Article 2 TEU) and, as a consequence, if it complies with the constitutional procedures of the Member State concerned and with the constitutional traditions common to the Member States (Article 6(3) TEU)'. Fasone (n 14) 61. I think that the reference to the 'constitutional traditions common to the Member States' is accurate, since, as explained in Chapter 4, there are some common elements among the approach of liberal constitutional democracies when it comes to secession: first and foremost, the requirement to subject the democratic principle to other principles like the rule of law and the supremacy of the constitution. According to Fasone, such common approach could be summarized as follows: the procedure (1) cannot be unilateral; (2) it must comply with democratic principles and with the rule of law; and (3) it must comply with the relevant national constitutional law. ibid 64. Fasone even anticipates that if Catalonia was going to secede unilaterally, 'by no means could this be considered a new legitimate state by the EU and the other Member States'. ibid 63. The reason to refuse legitimacy to the new Catalan Republic would be, precisely, that the 2017 pro-independence process (as shown in Chapter 4) did not meet any of the standards Fasone requires.

[65] For instance, Jean-Claude Piris, when reminding us of the differences between the Scottish and the Catalan case, notes that there is a difference between Scotland, where everything was settled as between the central government and the Scottish government and Catalonia, where the Spanish Constitutional Court and the Spanish Parliament set themselves against secession. Piris (n 8) 72–73.

[66] The Scottish case would have been an example of lawful and consensual secession, while the Catalan scenario has been an example of unlawful and unilateral/non-consensual attempt to secede.

[67] Edward (n 4) 1167.

of withdrawal,[68] it is unreasonable to expect secession without negotiation, taking into account that such a scenario would put at risk budgetary, legal, political, financial, commercial, and personal relationships, liabilities, and obligations.[69]

> Looking to the presumed intention of the Treaty-makers, they cannot reasonably be supposed to have intended that there must be prior negotiation in the case of withdrawal but none in the case of separation.... In order to avoid the disruption that would otherwise ensue, negotiation would be necessary before separation took place—precisely as the Treaty requires in the case of withdrawal.[70]

Beyond the analogy with article 50 TEU and the need to avoid 'absurd and unacceptable results', Edward also bases the obligation to negotiate in article 2 TEU, that refers to democracy and the protection of minorities, non-discrimination, and solidarity as foundational values of the EU. He also invokes article 4 TEU when referring to the principle of sincere cooperation, the obligation of Member State to ensure fulfilment of EU obligations, and the duty to facilitate the achievement of EU tasks. Furthermore, Edward contends that the outcome of such negotiations cannot be predicted, which precludes an automatic right to remain within the EU for seceding entities, leaving their future relationship in the hands of an uncertain negotiation process. This is especially uncertain given that the new entity will have to come to terms with powerful players like EU institutions and large States. Edward also acknowledges that, disregarding the legal form of the agreement, ratification by all Member States would be required.[71] He also admits that '[t]he results of such negotiation are hardly, if at all, a matter of law'.[72]

This idea of an obligation to negotiate without a predicted outcome is also shared by other authors. It represents a major departure from the thesis of 'automatic internal enlargement'. For instance, Kenealy and MacLennan note that although it is not possible to become a Member State automatically after a secession process,[73] on the basis of the principle of sincere cooperation (art 4 (3) TEU), a new independent entity could claim a right to negotiate with the EU. According to both scholars, failure to enter into such negotiations would not only be against sincere cooperation, but it would also cause dislocation to the single market.[74] By

68 Although 'secession' is not the same as 'withdrawal', it is admitted that both are 'germane' concepts. Phoebus Athanassiou and Stéphanie Laulhé Shaelou, 'EU Accession from Within? An Introduction' (2014) 33(1) Yearbook of European Law 335, 336.

69 Edward (n 4) 1164 ff.

70 ibid 1167.

71 ibid.

72 David Edward, 'Scotland and the European Union' (*Scottish Constitutional Futures Forum*, 17 December 2012) <http://www.scottishconstitutionalfutures.org/OpinionandAnalysis/ViewBlogPost/tabid/1767/articleType/articleView/articleId/852/David-Edward-Scotland-and-the-European-Union.aspx> accessed 4 August 2022.

73 By 'automatic' they mean a process whereby no negotiation or treaty amendment is required. Kenealy and MacLennan (n 2) 599.

74 ibid.

refusing to address the situation, by declining to enter into negotiations, EU institutions and Member States would contravene the concluding sentence of article 4: 'Member States shall facilitate the achievement of the Union's tasks and refrain from any measure which could jeopardise the attainment of the Union's objectives.' Edward, Kenealy, and MacLennan also base the obligation to negotiate on analogy with article 50: '[i]t is inherent in the nature of the integration project that rights acquired through EU membership are complex and reciprocal, and that sudden dislocations threaten to damage the fabric of the project'.[75] The reference to article 50 is particularly welcomed by Chamon and Van der Loo:

> Article 50 does not simply regulate the exit of a Member State from the EU but provides a general framework catering for a shrinkage in the scope of application *ratione loci* of the Union *acquis*. In the absence of such a framework, the scope of application of EU law might change from one day to the next, disrupting existing relations within the integrated internal market, without anything to follow up on this rupture.[76]

According to these authors, article 50 should be read as having bigger implications beyond the withdrawal of an EU Member State. The logic of article 50 should be applied to any scenario of contraction. For them, the reason why it does not explicitly refer to secessions within EU Member States is twofold: first, only Member States are constituent entities of the EU. Second, acknowledging such a possibility would have undermined the territorial integrity of EU Member States.[77] In effect, in symbolic and political terms, admitting the feasibility of such an option could be read as undermining national cohesion. Unlike Edward, Kenealy and MacLennan also base their position on the right to self-determination,[78] yet do not offer any further explanation. This is, however, problematic for the reason given in Chapter 3, which is that outside the colonial context and the emergent theory of remedial secession,[79] 'there is no recognition of a unilateral right to secede based merely on a majority vote of the population of a given sub-division or territory'.[80] Therefore, invoking a right to external self-determination within an EU Member

[75] ibid 600.

[76] Merijn Chamon and Guillaume Van der Loo, 'The Temporal Paradox of Regions in the EU Seeking Independence: Contraction and Fragmentation versus Widening and Deepening?' (2014) 20(5) European Law Journal 613, 621.

[77] ibid.

[78] Kenealy and MacLennan (n 2) 600.

[79] 'For a people that has not been colonised, secession is then only possible when that group is being collectively denied civil and political rights and when it is subject to egregious abuses by the mother state, ie when internal self-determination has proven to be an unviable option. In such cases the group has a "remedial" right to secession. Given the political and human rights requirements which states have to meet to be eligible for EU membership, it is not likely for a subnational group in an EU Member State to be in such a position.' Chamon and Van der Loo (n 76) 616.

[80] James Crawford, *The Creation of States in International Law* (2nd edn, OUP 2006) 417.

State is not legally sound. What is also common to Edward[81] is that Kenealy and MacLennan apply their reasoning only to consensual secession. They admit that in the absence of an agreement with the parent State, in case of unilateral secession, 'the continuance, or otherwise, of the territory's EU membership would be subject to altogether different considerations which fall outside the scope of this article'.[82]

The argument in favour of an obligation to negotiate, which echoes the 1998 Canadian Supreme Court approach to the Quebec attempt to secede based on the principle of sincere cooperation, seems politically reasonable and legally founded. The principle of sincere cooperation in EU law (art 4(3) TEU) or 'EU loyalty', 'good faith', 'loyal cooperation', or 'fidelity', as it has been referred to in the past, obliges EU Member States to take all appropriate measures to ensure fulfilment of their obligations under the treaties. Such obligations arise mutually between Member States and the Union (vertical loyalty and reverse vertical loyalty) and between Member States (horizontal loyalty).[83] Thus, Member States and the EU are obliged to ensure the effectiveness of EU law. However, the scope of the loyalty obligations within the EU are 'commensurate to its complexity and level of integration as an international organization'.[84] In effect, loyalty at EU level would be more far-reaching than in any international organization, but with lesser strictures than at a truly federal level.[85] In the event of a lawful and consensual secession, the rump Member State affected has an obligation to inform the rest of the Member States and EU institutions, and to refrain from any measure that could imperil the rights and expectations of the other Member States. Thus, 'once Union interests are affected, loyalty applies irrespective of whether the matter belongs to the reserved powers of the Member States'.[86] Accordingly, it will have to negotiate the future status of the seceding entity towards the EU in good faith, avoiding a legal vacuum and major disruptions.

[81] '[The negotiation obligation] does not resolve the case of Catalonia, since, as noted above, it is to be assumed that Spain would regard the separation of Catalonia as constitutionally impossible.' Edward (n 4) 1167.

[82] Kenealy and MacLennan (n 2) 593.

[83] The terminology is owed to Marcus Klamert, *The Principle of Loyalty in EU Law* (OUP 2014) 22–25.

[84] Geert de Baere and Timothy Roes, 'EU Loyalty as Good Faith' (2015) 64 International and Comparative Law Quarterly 829, 838. In the same vein, Klamert: 'Thus, loyalty indeed could be seen as an enhanced principle of *pacta sunt servanda*, as it has been put by AG Mazák. Loyalty thus is stronger even where it is similar, such as in the obligation not to frustrate binding commitments entered into by states (a treaty before ratification in the case of international law, a directive before the expiry of the deadline for transposition in the case of EU law). Moreover, in the Union, loyalty not only ties the Member States to each other but also creates obligations towards the EU institutions, more than would be apposite in the intergovernmental setting that is the WTO.' Klamert (n 83) 46. De Baere and Roes explain that the difference between *pacta sunt servada* and EU loyalty probably lies in the will of the drafters to emphasize that Member States 'were to make the newly established Community work in practice and, to that effect, they would have to do more than the new Treaty could mention explicitly'. de Baere and Roes (n 84) 833.

[85] 'It also evidenced that the structures imposed on the German *Lander* by *Bundestreue* are more far-reaching than those imposed on the EU Member States by loyalty, which in turn are habitually more detailed and far-reaching than the duties imposed by good faith in international law more generally.' de Baere and Roes (n 84) 874.

[86] Klamert (n 83) 29.

But this does not imply the acceptance of the seceding entity membership. The EU loyalty principle obliges the rump State to take into account the interests of both the EU and the other Member States, to act in good faith by informing, consulting, and negotiating. However, this does not preclude the rump State from exercising their discretionary decisional power at the Council of accepting or refusing a future enlargement. The same could be said about the other EU Member States. The cooperation duties cannot be so far-reaching that they deny the discretionary margin EU Member States have when it comes to enlargement. As Edward rightly pointed out, the outcome of the negotiations cannot be predicted. Or as Klamert says, '[w]hile loyalty is legally enforceable in contrast to solidarity, and may even apply to areas of reserved competence of the Member States, it does not apply to the political decision-making in the Council'.[87]

In sum, as shown, both the analogy with article 50 TEU and the reference to the sincere cooperation principle (art 4(3) TEU) are strong arguments to legally justify the position of EU law towards legal and consensual secessionist attempts. The only concern with these arguments is that they are only useful for lawful and consensual secession. They are not useful to ground an EU response to other type of secession.

4.2 Unlawful and Non-Consensual Scenarios

Whenever there is a legal consensus between the seceding entity and the Member State affected, the EU should not oppose *per se* the membership application of the new independent sovereign State. This leaves for consideration a secessionist bid that is unlawful and unilateral.

4.2.1 Territorial integrity argument

Some scholars have pointed out that a unilateral declaration of independence, which is unlawful in all EU national constitutional legal orders, is against EU law, for the territorial integrity of EU Member States is particularly protected by article 4(2) TEU.[88] The problem with the argument about the territorial integrity of the

[87] ibid 84.

[88] Diego López Garrido (coord), 'Cataluña ante la Unión Europea. Las consecuencias jurídicas de la independencia' (*Fundación Alternativas*, September 2015) 6 <https://www.fundacionalternativas.org/noticias/la-fundacion/cataluna-ante-la-union-europea-las-consecuencias-juridicas-de-la-independencia> accessed 4 August 2022. See also Tajadura (n 18) 367. Tierney and Boyle admit explicitly the reasoning when they argue that 'in a case of contested secession this would indeed be a very strong objection. However, ... if the UK accepts Scottish Independence, and it is willing to cooperate with Scotland's application to join the EU, the duty on the EU to respect the territorial integrity of the UK is no longer at issue.' Stephen Tierney and Katie Boyle, 'An Independent Scotland: The Road to Membership of the European Union' (2014) ESCR Scottish Centre on Constitutional Change Briefing Paper 15–16 <https://www.centreonconstitutionalchange.ac.uk/publications/independent-scotland-road-membership-european-union> accessed 4 August 2022. In similar although not exact terms, Pérez de Nanclares explains that on the basis of the respect of the essential functions of the State like ensuring

State is the following: unless it can be proved that EU law has developed a distinct meaning of this principle, the territorial integrity principle is inherited from public international law. As explained in Chapter 3, since the end of the Second World War, this has been a cornerstone of the international legal regime, particularly in Europe. However, it does not prohibit unilateral secessions without foreign intervention. In 2010, the International Court of Justice (ICJ) had the opportunity to address this issue when deciding the Kosovo Advisory Opinion:

> Several participants in the proceedings before the Court have contended that a prohibition of unilateral declarations of independence is implicit in the principle of territorial integrity. The Court recalls that the principle of territorial integrity is an important part of the international legal order and is enshrined in the Charter of the United Nations.... [But] the scope of the principle of territorial integrity is confined to the sphere of relations between States.[89]

Thus, this principle does not operate *ad intra*, against pro-secessionist movements, but *ad extra*, and therefore the provision established in article 4(2) TEU would refer to the obligation of the EU to respect the autonomy of Member States when protecting themselves against external threats.[90] Having said that, however, it has to be remembered that the reference to 'territorial integrity' was introduced by the European Convention in 2003 out of a petition of the Spanish government, interested in having 'an EU-level response to the challenge posed by the so-called Ibarretxe Plan, which envisaged a new status for the Basque Country close to full statehood'.[91] Moreover, European leaders like former Chancellor Angela Merkel have referred to this principle[92] implying that 'all parties must respect and guarantee the national sovereignty and territorial integrity of member states'.[93] However, the legal value of this declaration is, at most, dubious. And even if EU Member States now accept that in Europe respect for territorial integrity included in article 4(2) TEU has to be understood as a prohibition of unilateral secession

the territorial integrity, the EU shall accept those legal decisions aimed at precisely guaranteeing the territorial integrity of EU Member States. José Martín y Pérez de Nanclares, 'Reflexiones jurídicas a propósito de una eventual declaración unilateral de independencia de Cataluña: un escenario político jurídicamente inviable' (*Real Instituto Elcano*, 24 September 2015) 28 <http://129.35.96.157:10040/wps/wcm/connect/bb469e0049f77f9298de9e207baccc4c/MartinPerezDeNanclares_reflexiones_juridicas_independencia_Catalunya.pdf?MOD=AJPERES&CACHEID=bb469e0049f77f9298de9e207baccc4c> accessed 4 August 2022.

[89] *Accordance with International Law of the Unilateral Declaration of Independence in Respect of Kosovo*, Advisory Opinion, ICJ Reports 2010 403, para 80.

[90] Bossacoma (n 25) 70.

[91] Closa, 'Secession from a Member State and EU Membership' (n 2) 248.

[92] Miguel González and Luis Doncel, 'Merkel reclama a Cataluña respeto al principio de integridad' territorial' *El País* (Madrid, 1 September 2015) <https://politica.elpais.com/politica/2015/09/01/actualidad/1441095737_896484.html> accessed 4 August 2022.

[93] Closa, 'Secession from a Member State and EU Membership' (n 2) 249.

(something that still has to be proven), that would be a very novel usage of the principle and given the lack of explicit and clear provisions, there would be a risk of legal uncertainty.[94]

4.2.2 Breach of rule of law principles

Some authors have also emphasized that a unilateral secessionist process which does not respect the existing framework of the rule of law in a given Member State can be perceived as violating article 2 TEU.[95] The truth is that if one takes into account the precedents in neighbouring countries (outlined in Chapter 5), 're- spect for the rule of law is part of EU policy towards outside secessionism, since the EU made the question of constitutional validity the key factor in the EU's re- sponse to newly-gained statehood'.[96] In the same vein, Graham Avery argues that 'the implicit policy of the EU in relation to independentism in Europe consists of initial reluctance followed by pragmatic acceptance, provided that the process can be considered as constitutional'.[97] This ground is legally sound, it has an explicit, clear, and legal basis and is therefore useful for building an EU legal response to unilateral and unlawful secessionism.[98] However, the reference to the breach of

[94] Case C-325/91 *France v Commission* [1993] ECR I-03283, para 26: 'Community legislation must be clear and its application foreseeable for all interested parties. As a result of that requirement for legal certainty, the binding nature of any act intended to have legal effects must be derived from a provision of Community law which prescribes the legal form to be taken by that act and which must be expressly indicated therein as its legal basis.'

[95] Jean-Claude Piris, 'Political and Legal Aspects of Recent Regional Secessionist Trends in some EU Member States (II)' in Carlos Closa (ed), *Secession from a Member State and Withdrawal from the European Union* (CUP 2017) 90–91. Freixes Sanjuán shares a very similar view. Teresa Freixes Sanjuán, 'Secesión de Estados e integración en la Unión Europea. A propósito del debate sobre la permanencia en la Unión de Escocia y Cataluña como Estados segregados del Reino Unido y España' (2014) 2 Revista Jurídica de Catalunya 298, 327.

[96] Closa, 'Secession from a Member State and EU Membership' (n 2) 250.

[97] Graham Avery, 'Independentism and European Union' (*European Policy Centre*, 7 May 2014) <https://www.epc.eu/en/Publications/Independentism-and-the-Europea~24df74> accessed 28 July 2022.

[98] Other authors have also supported this view. See, among others, Closa, 'Secession from a Member State and EU Membership' (n 2) 250. Kochenov too accepts this argument, although with some nu- ances: 'With respect to secession, adherence to the rule of law requires that secessions happen in ac- cordance with national constitutional requirements (presuming the latter are *reasonable*, of course, as opposed to the arrangements that ban any secession talk outright without giving the constitutional re- arrangement any possibility whatsoever)' (emphasis added). Kochenov and Van den Brink (n 2) 14. The reference to 'reasonable' is a tricky one. What does 'reasonable' mean? As has been explained in Chapter 4, it is not uncommon for Western constitutional tradition to require a constitutional amend- ment in order to admit secession. And constitutional amendments tend to be quite rigid. Is such rigidity reasonable? In my view, yes, indeed. As the Venice Commission admits (Venice Commission, 'Report on Constitutional Amendment', CDL-AD(2010)001), the question of constitutional amendment lies at the heart of constitutionalism and implies that 'the fundamental rules for the effective exercise of state power and the protection of individual human rights should be stable and predictable, and not subject to easy change' (para 5). That is why the general requirements for amending the constitution in most countries are quite strict (para 51). What's the purpose of such rigidity? Or as the Venice Commission puts it, 'Why should a democratic society precommit itself in the sense that it lays down constitutional rules that cannot be changed by the majority when need arises, even following perfectly democratic procedures?' (para 72). The issue here is that 'constitutions are "devices for precommitment or self- binding, created by the body politic in order to protect itself against its own predictable tendency to make unwise decisions" (Elster)' (para 73). 'A quite widely used metaphor is that of Ulysses, ordering in

principles contained in article 2 TEU is unhelpful in justifying the EU legal approach to consensual and lawful secession.

4.3 Unlawful (Non-Consensual) and Lawful (Consensual) Secession

Article 4(2) TEU establishes that:

> The Union shall respect the equality of Member States before the Treaties, as well as their national identities, inherent in their fundamental structures, political and constitutional, inclusive of regional and local self-government.

The term 'inherent in' may be used interchangeably with 'expressed in' or 'contained in'.[99] This provision has usually been understood as respect of the 'constitutional identity' of Member States.[100] Later on I will identify the nuances between the national identity and constitutional identity. In my view, article 4(2) TEU is the most appropriate legal ground to sustain the EU response to secession,[101] and can address any type of secessionist challenge within EU Member States. I am aware that this is a highly controversial clause meriting an in-depth analysis. Thus, I will address the origins of the clause before going on to review its pluralist nature. Next, I will analyse the content of the provision based on doctrine and ECJ case law. Then

advance his crew to tie him to the mast in order not to be tempted by the song of sirens. In the same way, society by adopting a rigid constitution "ties itself to the mast", in order not to be tempted or distorted by short-term political gains and passions' (para 74).

[99] Elke Cloots, *National Identity in EU Law* (OUP 2015) 136.

[100] Leonard FM Besselink, 'National and Constitutional Identity before and after Lisbon' (2010) 6 Utrecht Law Review 36, 37, and 43–44. As for the link between national and constitutional identity, see Parekh: 'National identity finds its partial but clearest expression in the Constitution of the country, a self-consciously formulated and authoritative public statement in which it tells itself and the world what kind of a community it is and what it stands for.' Bhikhu Parekh, *A New Politics of Identity: Political Principles for an Independent World* (Palgrave Macmillan 2008) 60. See also Jackson: 'Constitutions ... express national values and self-understandings; and they embody historically specific compromises and agreements. They also establish the identity and status of the nation in a community of nations.' Vicky C Jackson, 'Constitutional Comparisons: Convergence, Resistance, Engagement' (2005) 119 Harvard Law Review 109, 124. Mark Tushnet agrees with the approach, but warns that national and constitutional identities tend to coincide in well-functioning democracies, but not in dictatorships. Mark Tushnet, 'The Possibilities of Comparative Constitutional Law' (1999) 108 Yale Law Journal 1225, 1270–73.

[101] Without further elaboration, Ferreres Comella seems to align himself with this thesis when he states that 'because of this provision [art 4(2) TEU], the European Union cannot be indifferent to the constitutional identity of Member States.... In this context, it is important to stress that Member States have designed different institutional arrangements when it comes to the issue of secession. Whether or not secession is constitutionally legal, and under what conditions it can be legal, are questions that the various Member States have answered differently.' Víctor Ferreres Comella, 'Does Brexit Normalize Secession?' (2018) 53 Texas International Law Journal 139, 144.

I will address the risk of a unilateral and abusive use of article 4(2) and finally I will specifically refer to the limits of this clause.

4.3.1 Origins of article 4(2) TEU

Before exploring the origins of the concept, it is important at the outset to consider whether article 4(2) TEU refers to only Member States, or also 'national units', such as certain regions within Member States. First, '*their* national identities' (emphasis added) refers directly and solely to Member States. Second, it makes a clear distinction between 'Member States' and 'regional and local self-government', where these other 'national units' could be encapsulated. Third, in EU law terminology it is common to equate 'national' to the nation State or the central government.[102] Thus, the focus of article 4(2) TEU is on Member States rather than national groups. In fact, 'the clause excludes from its scope certain national groups which have a moral claim to respect, most notably stateless nations'.[103]

The idea of respecting national identity has been in the very origins of the EU integration process. A reference to the national identities of the Member States was first codified in the Maastricht Treaty, but it was not until the Lisbon Treaty (mainly following the wording of the 2004 Constitutional Treaty) that the TEU made explicit reference to the constitution of the States. Whereas in the Maastricht Treaty, article 6(3) TEU established that '[t]he Union shall respect the national identities of its Member States', the current article 4(2) TEU enhances the political and constitutional aspects. Thus, to the extent that the Lisbon Treaty here focuses on State structures, there is a shift in emphasis from national identity as such to constitutional identity.[104] Some scholars believe that the link between the national identity clause and the 'fundamental political and constitutional structures ... distances the notion of national identity in article 4 (2) TEU from cultural, historical or linguistic criteria and turns to the content of national constitutional orders'.[105]

Some authors have argued that such a move could be a response to the case law of national constitutional courts sending repeated signals to the EU that they were

[102] It is noteworthy here to invoke the 2001 Opinion of the Committee of the Regions concerning a European Charter of Regional Self-Government, where it is established that '[t]he definition of regional self-government recognises the existence of an intermediate tier between central government and local authorities. The task of determining the division of decision-making powers between national, regional and local authorities is a matter for national authorities.' Thus, the Committee of the Regions, probably the EU body most interested in reinforcing the position of sub-national entities within the EU, assumes naturally that 'national' refers to central government. Committee of the Regions, 'Recommendation of the Congress of Local and Regional Authorities of Europe on a European Charter of Regional Self-Government' 2001/C 144/02.

[103] Timea Drinóczi, 'Constitutional Identity in Europe: The Identity of the Constitution. A Regional Approach' (2020) 21 German Law Journal 105, 152. Similarly, Pablo Cruz, *La Identidad Nacional de los Estados Miembros en el Derecho de la Unión Europea* (Aranzadi 2021) 60.

[104] Besselink (n 100) 44.

[105] Armin von Bogdandy and Stephan Schill, 'Overcoming Absolute Primacy: Respect for National Identity under the Lisbon Treaty' (2011) 48(5) Common Market Law Review 1417, 1427.

ready to protect their national constitutional identity from EU law intrusions.[106] Needless to say, those signals were putting EU primacy at risk.[107] Komarek has explained how constitutional courts might be seen as the losers or the main victims of the EU law primacy principle, because it renders them unable to fulfil their duties to the fullest.[108] The highest national courts[109] began to use the concept of 'constitutional identity', despite this being a contested concept,[110] to denote the hard core of their constitution that could not be touched by EU law.[111] The link between that constitutional core with complex political and cultural associations, with deep historical roots, is an implicit (yet essential) assumption made by some of the highest national courts and some scholars who share this historic and cultural approach, rather than a purely legal-constitutional interpretation.[112] For them, the constitutional system does not operate in a normative vacuum:

> Outside and around the constitution are values and principles that the constitution must actualise. These are not a judge's personal values but rather the national values of the country.[113]

[106] 'Its continuous insistence that EU law takes precedence even over national constitution has been put into an entirely new light with the adoption of the Treaty of Lisbon, which explicitly shields the national constitutional identity. The latter is a response to the Member States (judicial) determination that certain formal and substantive dimensions of their constitutional structure, the so-called irreductible epistemic core, are ring fenced and are to remain untouchable shall the State retain its constitutional autonomy and political independence.' Matej Avbelj, 'Theory of European Union' (2011) 36 European Law Review 818, 833. See also Leczykiewicz: 'Article 4(2) TEU could be seen as codification of the case law of national constitutional courts, who often claim that EU law supremacy is only conditional. Whether it is the protection of human rights or the preservation of the essential structures of national constitutionalism, they cannot, the argument goes, be overridden by EU law.' Dorota Leczykiewicz, 'The 'national identity clause' in the EU Treaty: a blow to supremacy of Union law?' (*UK Constitutional Law Association Blog*, 21 June 2012) <https://ukconstitutionallaw.org/2012/06/21/dorota-leczykiewicz-the-national-identity-clause-in-the-eu-treaty-a-blow-to-supremacy-of-union-law/> accessed 4 August 2022.

[107] For an in-depth review of the tension between art 4(2) TEU and primacy, see Mary Dobbs, 'Sovereignty, Article 4(2) TEU and the Respect of National Identities: Swinging the Balance of Power in Favour of the Member States?' (2014) 33(1) Yearbook of European Law 298.

[108] Jan Komarek, 'The Place of Constitutional Courts in the EU' (2013) 9(3) European Constitutional Law Review 420, 421.

[109] Particularly: the Italian Constitutional Court (decisions of 18 December 1973 and of 8 June 1984); the German Constitutional Court (decisions of 29 May 1974, of 30 June 2009, and of 5 May 2020); the Spanish Constitutional Court (Declaracion 1/2004), the Constitutional French Council (decision of 27 July 2006). These decisions reflect the tension between a commitment to European integration and the caution against the dilution of national's core statehood by European integration. Jo Eric Khushal Murkens, 'Bundesverfassungsgericht (2BvE 2/08): "We Want Our Identity Back"—The Revival of National Sovereignty in the German Federal Constitutional Court's Decision on the Lisbon Treaty' (2010) 3 Public Law 530, 536–37. Even the Belgian Constitutional Court, usually adopting a Europhile stance, has also warned the ECJ that it cannot undermine Belgian national identity or the basic values of constitutional rights protection. Philippe Gérard and Willem Verrijdt, 'Belgian Constitutional Court Adopts National Identity Discourse' (2017) 13 European Constitutional Law Review 182, 189.

[110] Michel Rosenfeld, 'Constitutional Identity' in Michael Rosenfeld and András Sajó (eds), *The Oxford Handbook of Comparative Constitutional Law* (OUP 2012) 756.

[111] Cloots (n 99) 5.

[112] Pablo Cruz, 'Identidad Nacional y Valores de la Unión Europea: Límites a una interpretación extensiva del artículo 4.2 TUE' (2022) 114 Revista Derecho Político 247, 253.

[113] Aharon Barak, *Purposive Interpretation in Law* (Princeton UP 2007) 237.

This approach, as will be shown later in Section 4.3.4, is a risky one and it can be easily abused by an illiberal government.

4.3.2 The pluralist nature of article 4(2) TEU

The controversy between the highest national courts and EU law is a good example of the legal tension between the different legal orders in the EU. It has been argued in Chapter 2 that the relationship between EU law and national legal orders is best conceived as a pluralistic legal system, or a multilevel constitutional system, where hierarchical relationships of validity do not accord properly to the current legal reality. As noted, MacCormick introduced the concept of 'constitutional pluralism' in 1995 affirming that:

> [T]he most appropriate analysis of the relations of legal systems is pluralistic rather than monistic, and interactive rather than hierarchical. The legal system of Member States and their common legal system of EC law are distinct but interacting systems of law and hierarchical relationships of validity within criteria of validity proper to distinct systems do not add up to any sort of all-purpose superiority of one system over another.[114]

EU law and domestic legal orders have been defined 'as two interdependent, interwoven and reciprocally influential parts of one unit'.[115] Maduro has argued that one aim of Europe's constitutional pluralism is to prevent constitutional conflicts, by ensuring that the two legal systems adjust to each other.[116] Thus, Member States and the EU both claim sovereignty, but try to avoid direct conflicts through making concessions to each other. In a related vein of argument, Barber has pointed out that the European pluralist legal system arms national and EU law with weapons that may help to ensure mutual respect and restraint.[117]

Article 4(2) TEU and the concept of national identity can be seen as an expression of this pluralistic approach:[118] protecting aspects fundamental to the Member States, but on the basis of EU law.[119] In effect, the clause is 'a form of public recognition of the multinational composition of the EU and, thus, a way of showing

[114] Neil MacCormick, 'The Maastricht Urteil: Sovereignty Now' (1995) 1 European Law Journal 259, 265.

[115] Ingolf Pernice, 'The Treaty of Lisbon: Multi-level Constitutionalism in Action' (2009) 2 Walter Hallstein Institute 26. See also Neil Walker, 'Multi-level Constitutionalism: Looking Beyond the German Debate' (2009) 8 LSE 'Europe in Question' Discussion Paper Series.

[116] Miguel Maduro, 'Contrapunctual Law: Europe's Constitutional Pluralism in Action' in Neil Walker (ed), *Sovereignty in Transition* (Hart Publishing 2003) 531.

[117] Nick Barber, *The Constitutional State* (OUP 2010) 171.

[118] Armin von Bogdandy and Stephan Schill, 'Overcoming Absolute Primacy: Respect for National Identity under the Lisbon Treaty' (2011) 48 Common Market Law Review 1417, 1452.

[119] Oreste Pollicino, 'The New Relationship between National and the European Courts after the Enlargement of Europe: Towards a Unitary Theory of Jurisprudential Supranational Law?' (2010) 29(1) Yearbook of European Law 65, 96.

respect for the Member States' national identities'.[120] The EU shows its sensitive approach to the various national identities, probably aware that 'the success of any institutional structure and, indeed, of any model of government at large, depends on its capacity to reflect and give expression to the social pedigree of its constituent entities'.[121] In this sense, article 4(2) TEU is 'a core provision to understand the 'federal' nature of the European Union. It protects diversities in the EU composite legal order.[122] Article 4(2) TEU does not stand mainly to protect the principles which are common to the Member States, but to respect those values/principles and provisions which differentiate the Member States from one another. And this national identity is legally determined by the identity of the national constitution.[123]

There is of course a risk of a national unilateral reading of article 4(2) TEU and this is why there is also a need for a systematic approach and some limits to the deferential approach (in Sections 4.3.4 and 4.3.5 I will address the risks and the limits of art 4(2)). Thus, as Martinico points out 'this clause should not be read in splendid isolation, but in context'[124] and in this regard the principle of sincere co-operation of article 4(3) TEU is key. Advocates General Cruz Vilallón and Wathelet have been very clear about this:

> The obligation to respect that identity, which is set out in Article 4(2) TEU, cannot be construed independently of the obligation of sincere cooperation set out in Article 4(3) TEU. In accordance with that obligation, the Member States are required to ensure fulfilment of the obligations arising out of the Treaties or resulting from the acts of the institutions of the Union.[125]

This balanced and respectful constitutional legal approach is probably the only way a polity like the EU can survive in the long term. A pluralistic spirit like the one of this clause is aimed to ensure a satisfactory accommodation of its main constituencies.

4.3.3 Content of article 4(2) and ECJ case law

This still leaves open the issue as to how national and constitutional identities can be defined.

National identity is difficult to capture. But the Lisbon Treaty drafters provided some clarification. As Cloots explained, they circumscribed the concept

[120] Cloots (n 99) 179.
[121] Avbelj (n 106) 824.
[122] Barbara Guastaferro, Sincere Cooperation and Respect for National Identities' in Robert Schütze and Takis Tridimas (eds), *Oxford Principles of European Union Law* (vol I, OUP 2018) 350–51.
[123] Besselink (n 100) 47.
[124] Giuseppe Martinico, 'Taming National Identity: A Systematic Understanding of Article 4.2 TEU' (2021) 27 European Public Law 1, 16.
[125] Case C-673/16 *Coman* [2018] ECLI 2, Opinion of AG Wathelet, para 40. See also Advocate General Cruz Vilallón, Opinion in Case C-62/14 *Gauweiler* [2015] ECLI 7, paras 59–62.

of 'national identity' or 'constitutional identity' in two ways: 'by designating the Member States as the only legally relevant national groups, and by restricting the pertinent individuating features of a given national group (ie of a given Member State) to those that find expression in the State's fundamental structures'.[126] Constitutional identity has been defined as those elements so fundamental that they should be preserved and protected from change and/or that express some sort of meta-constitution or pre-constitutional principles.[127] Pérez Tremps, former judge at the Spanish Constitutional Court, has written that 'constitutional identity includes a safeguard for the State itself, which encompasses two formally different contents: the essential elements of the State and the essential elements of the Constitution'.[128] The identity of the Constitution is usually found among provisions of constitutional texts (particularly in the preamble and in the amendment formulas)[129] and related jurisprudence. 'The identity of a constitution may differ from jurisdiction to jurisdiction, and the applicability of constitutional provisions may be subject to the jurisdiction of the respective constitutional or high courts.'[130]

Since the Lisbon Treaty the ECJ has overcome its hesitancy about deciding whether or not a certain law or policy qualifies as an aspect of national identity.[131] While there are not many cases dealing with the topic,[132] since the ECJ has not developed the full potential of the clause (probably aware of the risks), the existing case law does provide some guidance. In some cases, the Court has recognized that the preservation of national language is a legitimate aim, but the restrictive national measures were disproportionate:[133]

> While the preservation of the national identities of the Member States is a legitimate aim respected by the legal order of the European Union, as is indeed acknowledged by Article 4(2) TEU, the interest pleaded by the Grand Duchy can,

[126] Cloots (n 100) 145.

[127] Anita Blagovjevic, 'Procedures regarding National Identity Clause in National Constitutional Court's and the CJEU's Case-Law' (2017) 1 EU and Comparative Law Issues and Challenges 210, 212.

[128] Pablo Pérez Tremps, 'National Identity in Spanish Constitutional Court Case-law' in Alejandro Saiz Arnaiz and Carina Alcoberro Llivina (eds), *National Constitutional Identity and European Integration* (Intersentia 2013) 270.

[129] Cruz, *La Identidad Nacional de los Estados Miembros en el Derecho de la Unión Europea* (n 103) 83–89.

[130] Timea Drinóczi, 'Constitutional Identity in Europe: The Identity of the Constitution. A Regional Approach' (2020) 21 German Law Journal 105, 122.

[131] The 2004 *Omega* case was a good opportunity to introduce the discourse about the protection of national identity, but the Court decided to resolve it through the reference to human rights as a general principle of law. One wonders if, after the Lisbon Treaty and the clear expression of constitutional national identity, the Court would have referred explicitly to constitutional identity. It might have done so, albeit implicitly. Case C-36/02 *Omega* [2004] ECR I-09609, paras 32–34.

[132] In his monograph, Pablo Cruz analyses in detail the few ECJ decisions involving art 4(2). Cruz, *La Identidad Nacional de los Estados Miembros en el Derecho de la Unión Europea* (n 103) 124–70. He also explains in depth a different use of the clause in an even smaller number of decisions, ie identity clause as a constraint on EU legislation or as basis for review of EU measures. See ibid 171–86. This second use is, however, not relevant for our purposes.

[133] Guastaferro (n 122) 368.

however, be effectively safeguarded otherwise than by a general exclusion of nationals of the other Member States.[134]

In *Runevic-Vardyn and Wardyn*, Lithuania argued that its national language 'constitutes a constitutional asset which preserves the nation's identity, contributes to the integration of citizens, and ensures the expression of national sovereignty, the indivisibility of the State, and the proper functioning of the services of the State and the local authorities'.[135] Other Member States also accepted that the protection of the official national language was legitimate in order to safeguard national unity and preserve social cohesion. The Court admitted the link between ensuring protection of the national language and article 4(2) TEU[136] and permitted the national Court to decide:

> If it is established that the refusal to amend the joint surname of the couple in the main proceedings, who are citizens of the Union, causes serious inconvenience to them and/or their family, at administrative, professional and private levels, it will be for the national court to decide whether such refusal reflects a fair balance between the interests in issue, that is to say, on the one hand, the right of the applicants in the main proceedings to respect for their private and family life and, on the other hand, the legitimate protection by the Member State concerned of its official national language and its traditions.[137]

[134] Case C-51/08 *Commission v Luxembourg* [2011] ECR I-04231, para 72. In this case, the Grand Duchy of Luxembourg asserted that, since the use of the Luxembourgish language is necessary in the performance of notarial activities, the nationality condition was intended to ensure respect for Luxembourgish cultural heritage. A similar approach to be found in Case C-202/11 *Anton Las v PSA Antwerp* [2013] ECLI 239, paras 26–27: 'in accordance with Article 4(2) TEU, the Union must also respect the national identity of its Member States, which includes protection of the official language or languages of those States' and 'the objective of promoting and encouraging the use of Dutch, which is one of the official languages of the Kingdom of Belgium, constitutes a legitimate interest which, in principle, justifies a restriction on the obligations imposed by Article 45 TFEU'. But in the end the Court concluded that Belgium could have found a solution less restrictive of the free movement of workers.

[135] Case C-391/09 *Runevic-Vardyn* [2011] ECR I-03787, para 84.

[136] ibid paras 86–87: 'According to the fourth subparagraph of Article 3(3) EU and Article 22 of the Charter of Fundamental Rights of the European Union, the Union must respect its rich cultural and linguistic diversity. Article 4(2) EU provides that the Union must also respect the national identity of its Member States, which includes protection of a State's official national language. 87. It follows that the objective pursued by national rules such as those at issue in the main proceedings, designed to protect the official national language by imposing the rules which govern the spelling of that language, constitutes, in principle, a legitimate objective capable of justifying restrictions on the rights of freedom of movement and residence provided for in Article 21 TFEU and may be taken into account when legitimate interests are weighed against the rights conferred by European Union law.' Note the different approach of the Court in the *Groener* case: 'The EEC Treaty does not prohibit the adoption of a policy for the protection and promotion of a language of a Member State which is both the national language and the first official language. However, the implementation of such a policy must not encroach upon a fundamental freedom such as that of the free movement of workers. Therefore, the requirements deriving from measures intended to implement such a policy must not in any circumstances be disproportionate in relation to the aim pursued and the manner in which they are applied must not bring about discrimination against nationals of other Member States.' Case C-379/87 *Groener* [1989] ECR 03967, para 19.

[137] Case C-391/09 *Runevic-Vardyn* (n 135) para 91.

Guastaferro explains how in another group of judgments, national identity has not been regarded as an autonomous ground of derogation, like in the case just mentioned, but has been used by Member States to interpret other treaty-based justifications such as public policy.[138] Thus, in either group of cases, the concept of national identity does not bring anything particularly new into the architecture of EU law.

In *Sayn-Wittgenstein*, Austria argued that the provisions at issue, which were implementing measures of the Law on the abolition of nobility, were intended to protect the constitutional identity of the Republic of Austria and that they constituted a fundamental decision for the country. Other Member States (Czech Republic, Italy, Slovakia, and Lithuania) supported the Austrian view and the Commission also considered that the case related to national identity. The Court admitted that:

> [I]n the context of Austrian constitutional history, the Law on the abolition of the nobility, as an element of national identity may be taken into consideration when a balance is struck between legitimate interests and the right of free movement of persons recognized under EU law.[139]

And the Court concluded that:

> It does not appear disproportionate for a Member State to seek to attain the objective of protecting the principle of equal treatment by prohibiting any acquisition, possession or use, by its nationals, of titles of nobility or noble elements which may create the impression that the bearer of the name is holder of such rank.[140]

There is another case more interesting for the purposes of the current discussion, that is, could the secession clause be considered part of the national identity of a country? In *Digibet and Albers*, a German court referred a preliminary question asking whether in a Member State organized as a federal State, a more liberal regime in one *Land* concerning public games of chance on the internet, called into question the effectiveness of the restrictions in force in the rest of Germany. The Court seemed to be very respectful of the internal organization of powers:

> In the present case, the division of competences between the *Länder* cannot be called into question, since it benefits from the protection conferred by Article 4(2) TEU, according to which the Union must respect national identities, inherent in

[138] Guastaferro (n 122) 370.
[139] Case C-208/09 *Sayn-Wittgenstein* [2010] ECR I-13693, para 83.
[140] ibid para 93.

their fundamental structures, political and constitutional, including regional and local self-government.[141]

There are other cases where the ECJ avoids even referring to the concept of national constitutional identity or article 4(2) TEU and resorts to less threatening concepts for EU integration like 'common constitutional traditions', but the deferential attitude remains. The ECJ thereby 'demonstrates [some] commitment to acknowledge the pluralism of the interpretations of rights and principles that are at the core of national constitutional identities'.[142] But, at the same, the cautionary approach of the Court to the clause is clear. In any event, and as noted, the provision does not provide a revolutionary interpretation. The deferential attitude was already present in EU law.

So far, the ECJ has deemed as part of the national identity, protection of the national language, the republican character of the State, and the internal organization of powers. Needless to say, there must be other elements. Cloots has drafted a set of norms that are especially regarded as mirroring the national constitutional identity of a country and, therefore, considered part of the article 4(2) TEU national identity of the Member States:[143] fundamental rights; the State's official language(s); the State's structure (unitary, federal, or something in between); the relationship among the distinct branches of government or the relationship between the State and religion tends to be bound up with the nation's particular character and self-understanding.

A legal multilevel space like the EU enables EU Member States to raise their concerns and offers the ECJ the opportunity to address those concerns based on an EU instrument. If, as mentioned, constitutional identity constitutes the core of each State, if it attempts to capture and protect the particularity and uniqueness of each State,[144] it seems reasonable that following the pluralist spirit of article 4(2) TEU Member States 'should be allowed some kind of discretion to develop the concept of constitutional identity'[145] and, in fact, as it has been said, since the 1970s national constitutional courts have been developing such notion, the German Constitutional Court being the one that has developed the most elaborate jurisprudence on constitutional identity that serves as a reference for other courts in Europe.[146]

[141] Case C-156/13 *Digibet and Albers* [2014] ECLI 1756, para 34. Needless to say, respect for local self-government cannot be used as a pretext to escape EU obligations. Case C-127/12 *European Commission v Kingdom of Spain* [2014] ECLI 2130, para 42.

[142] Giovanni Zaccaroni, 'The Good, the Bad and the Ugly: National Constitutional Judges and the EU Constitutional Identity' (2018) 10 Italian Journal of Public Law 421, 443.

[143] Cloots (n 99) 161.

[144] Drinóczi (n 103) 110.

[145] Blagovjevic (n 127) 232.

[146] ibid 224.

Article 4(2) TEU should be used mainly to protect those constitutional characteristics that are distinctive and unique to a Member State and not protected by the EU legal order.[147] In this regard, it seems the most appropriate clause to channel concerns over secession attempts, given the varied approaches within EU Member States and the lack of a unique EU approach. It is difficult to contend that a constitutional provision like the secession clause, either explicit in the constitutional text or implicit following the interpretation of the national constitutional court, does not constitute a basic element of the national identity of a country.[148] Note, for instance, that the Venice Commission has considered that secession is possibly the most important decision that a political community may take.[149] Therefore, a certain constitutional approach to secession is properly regarded as forming part of the national identity of a Member State and, therefore, merits protection according to article 4(2) TEU.[150]

Two caveats are warranted. First, since this clause might put at risk the EU legal order and is prone to abuse, it should remain the last resort and be handled with restraint by national courts.[151] Second, and more importantly, beyond the exceptionality of the use of the clause, the ECJ should always have the opportunity to assess the suitability of recourse to article 4(2) TEU. In effect, when national courts refer to constitutional identity, they are also referring to an EU law provision (ie national identity)[152] whose interpretation has to be supervised by the ECJ. The task of the Luxembourg Court is to make sure that EU law red lines are not crossed. That is why no absolute deference to national interpretations should be allowed:

> The first is that it seems to me an all but impossible task to preserve this Union, as we know it today, if it is to be made subject to an absolute reservation, ill-defined

[147] Luke Dimitrios Spieker, 'Framing and Managing Constitutional Identity Conflicts: How to Stabilize the *Modus Vivendi* between the Court of Justice and National Constitutional Courts' (2020) 57 Common Market Law Review 361, 395.

[148] Weill explains how '[c]ontrary to conventional wisdom, constitutional democracies often treat their federal structure, unitary status, and territorial integrity as unamendable'. Rivka Weill, 'Secession and the Prevalence of Both Militant Democracy and Eternity Clauses Worldwide' (2018) 40 Cardozo Law Review 905, 949.

[149] Venice Commission, 'Opinion on the Compatibility of the Existing Legislation in Montenegro concerning the Organisation of Referendums with applicable International Standards' CDL-AD(2005)041, para 24.

[150] In the case of Spain, for instance, Rosenfeld identifies as the main element of its constitutional identity precisely the balance between national unity and a meaningful measure of autonomy that precludes unilateral secession. Rosenfeld (n 110) 764.

[151] ibid 381.

[152] Guastaferro believes that there is, within academia, a misleading identification of the concept of national identity provided by article 4(2) TEU with the concept of national constitutional identities provided by national constitutional courts. Guastaferro (n 122) 352. I tend to agree with her in the sense that 'national identity' is a concept of EU law interpreted by the Court, but based on the concept of 'constitutional identity', which is a concept of national constitutional law, interpreted by national authorities. Thus, one could argue that national identity is national constitutional identity screened by the ECJ following the EU's own constitutional values (eg art 2 TEU).

> and virtually at the discretion of each of the Member States, which takes the form of a category described as 'constitutional identity.[153]

In effect, absolute deference would leave the EU legal order in an unintended subordinated position, jeopardizing primacy, coherence, and the uniform application of EU law. Thus, even if national courts determine the content of their respective identity, the ECJ should be able to apply a proportionality test and ensure that EU values or EU identity are also respected. EU values set forth in article 2 TEU are the red lines or the playing field within which article 4(2) TEU can operate. Making sure that those values are not jeopardized is the sole responsibility of the ECJ and it should be both the shield and the sword to prevent extensive recourse to constitutional identity paving the way for illiberal or populist reforms.

4.3.4 Risks of article 4(2) TEU

As mentioned earlier, there is a risk that article 4(2) TEU could be seen as a trap door to EU Member States to escape some of their EU law obligations,[154] including (and particularly) those established in article 2 TEU. Already in 2008 Advocate General Maduro warned about the risks of an abusive use of the concept of constitutional identity:

> If respect for the constitutional identity of the Member States can thus constitute a legitimate interest which, in principle, justifies a restriction of the obligations imposed by Community law, ... [i]t is, nevertheless, necessary to point out that that respect owed to the constitutional identity of the Member States cannot be understood as an absolute obligation to defer to all national constitutional rules. Were that the case, national constitutions could become instruments allowing Member States to avoid Community law in given fields. Furthermore, it could lead to discrimination between Member States based on the contents of their respective national constitutions. Just as Community law takes the national constitutional identity of the Member States into consideration, national constitutional law must be adapted to the requirements of the Community legal order.[155]

In fact, this clause has been described as a troublemaker 'due to its problematic (ab)use by some national Courts', but the fact that there have been 'abuses or misunderstandings does not exclude the possibility of a proper use of this clause'.[156] Article 4(2) TEU should not be seen as a conflict clause or a battleground, but, instead as a mutually presupposing instrument.[157] However, it is true that article 4(2)

[153] Case C-62/14 *Gauweiler and others* [2015] ECR 7, Opinion of AG Cruz Villalón, para 59.
[154] Blagovjevic (n 127) 232.
[155] Case C-213/07 *Michaniki* [2018] ECLI 544, Opinion of AG Poiares Maduro, para 33.
[156] Martinico, 'Taming National Identity' (n 124) 1 and 8.
[157] Komarek (n 108) 427.

has been exploited so as to question EU primacy and loyalty by illiberal governments.[158] As Kelemen and Pech point out, when Hungary rejected (or violated) the EU asylum *acquis* and refused to recognize the primacy of EU law in this domain, it claimed that control over migration is part of its constitutional identity. Likewise, when Poland attacked the independence of the judiciary, it claimed that such matters fall within the exclusive bounds of its authority and cited scholars of constitutional pluralism and the EU's 'national identity clause' to justify its stance.[159]

In effect, with regard to Hungary, in December 2016 the Hungarian Constitutional Court referred to the country's constitutional identity to justify the government's refusal to apply the EU's refugee relocation scheme in Hungary.[160] In fact, after that, in 2018 the concept of constitutional identity was codified in the Hungarian Constitution. Current Article R4 reads as follows: 'Each and every body of the State shall be obliged to protect the constitutional identity and the Christian culture of Hungary.'

With regard to Poland, the 2018 White Paper on the Reform of the Polish Judiciary specifically referred to article 4(2) TEU and justified its judicial reform, which was already under severe scrutiny by the European Commission and the ECJ, on the basis of this clause:

> Each country has specific constitutional solutions that are rooted in its history and legal traditions and these differences are protected by the treaty law of the European Union. Article 4 of the Treaty on European Union quoted above shows that the Union respects national identity which is inherent in the fundamental political and constitutional structures of the member states. Constitutional identity, a core value of each national community, determines not only the most fundamental values and resulting tasks for state authorities, but also sets the limit for regulatory intervention of the European Union.... The right to introduce its own sovereign institutional solutions concerning the judiciary is a pillar of each national constitutional system in Europe.[161]

More recently, on 7 October 2021 the Polish Constitutional Tribunal issued its decision in the case K 3/21, where, after an application by the Prime Minister of Poland to examine the compliance of elements of the TEU with the Polish

[158] For a detailed analysis, see Federico Fabbrini and András Sajó, 'The Dangers of Constitutional Identity' (2019) 25 European Law Journal 457.

[159] Daniel R Kelemen and Laurent Pech, 'The Uses and Abuses of Constitutional Pluralism: Undermining the Rule of Law in the Name of Constitutional Identity in Hungary and Poland' (2019) 21 Cambridge Yearbook of European Legal Studies 59, 61.

[160] Gabor Halmai, 'Abuse of Constitutional Identity. The Hungarian Constitutional Court on Interpretation of Article E(2) of the Fundamental Law' (2018) 43 Review of Central and East European Law 23.

[161] 2018 White Paper on the Reform of the Polish Judiciary, paras 169, 170, and 176.

Constitution, decided, on the basis of Polish sovereignty and national identity, that some articles of the TEU are incompatible with the Polish Constitution.[162]

From a constitutional point of view, populism or illiberal democracy represents a challenge to the main institutions of constitutional democracy. In the populist narrative advanced in Poland and Hungary, the concept of democratic legitimacy takes precedence over the principle of legality, the popular will is conceived as the main and only source of power. People's voice should have no limits, no restraints, particularly no limits coming from institutions outside the State. Checks and balances, particularly those coming from outside the State, are seen as an obstacle, instead of a guarantee of a limited government. Such claims undermine the very core idea of the rule of law. In this regard, the role of independent judges becomes one of the major issues of debate, because very often they remain the only limit on governmental desires.[163] In this sense, as it will be shown in the next section, '[a]ny recourse to Article 4(2) TEU is only permissible insofar as it respects the values enshrined in Article 2 TEU',[164] that describe the contours and the minimum content of a constitutional democracy, including the rule of law.

4.3.5 Articles 2 and 4(2) TEU: limits and boundaries

The values enshrined in article 2 TEU constitute a set of principles which are common to the EU and its Member States. By including them in a legal text, the Lisbon Treaty drafters aimed to enhance the EU's legitimacy.[165] It has been said

[162] Jakub Jaraczewski, 'Gazing into the Abyss: The K 3/21 decision of the Polish Constitutional Tribunal' (*Verfassungsblog*, 12 October 2021) <https://verfassungsblog.de/gazing-into-the-abyss/> accessed 16 June 2022. Ruling available at <https://trybunal.gov.pl/en/hearings/judgments/art/11662-ocena-zgodnosci-z-konstytucja-rp-wybranych-przepisow-traktatu-o-unii-europejskiej> accessed 16 June 2022. Note that this decision, for several reasons, cannot be compared with another recent decision of the German Constitutional Court of 5 May 2020 on the partial unconstitutionality of the ECB's PSP programme. Among other reasons, 'the Polish court establishes the unconstitutionality of central primary law norms (Art. 1 and 19 TEU) and questions in principle the established primacy of European law with regard to the Polish constitution. The Federal Constitutional Court, on the other hand, in its case law consistently accepts the primacy also over the Constitution and in its ruling only classified an individual secondary legal act of an EU institution as ultra vires by way of exception.' Alexander Thiele, 'Whoever equates Karlsruhe to Warsaw is wildly mistaken' *(Verfassungsblog, 10 October 2021)* <https://verfassungsblog.de/whoever-equals-karlsruhe-to-warsaw-is-wildly-mistaken/> accessed 16 June 2022. (See Chapter 1 for a reference to the 5 May 2020 German Constitutional Court decision, noted when analysing the relationship between EU law and national law.)

[163] Categories to describe the effects of illiberal populism on constitutional democracy are numerous, amongst them the most commonly used are: illiberal constitutionalism, constitutional coup, abusive constitutionalism, or authoritarian constitutionalism. See, among others, Timea Drinóczi and Agnieszka Bien-Kacala (eds), *Rule of Law, Common Values and Illiberal Constitutionalism: Poland and Hungary within the European Union* (Routledge 2021); Kim Lane Scheppele, 'Constitutional Coups in EU Law' in Maurice Adams, Anne Meuwese, and Ernst Hirsch Ballin (eds), *Constitutionalism and the Rule of Law* (CUP 2017) 448; David Landau, 'Abusive Constitutionalism' (2013) 47 University of California Davis Law Review 189, 195; Mark Tushnet, 'Authoritarian Constitutionalism' (2015) 100(2) Cornell Law Review 393, 449.

[164] Spieker, 'Framing and Managing Constitutional Identity Conflicts' (n 147) 396.

[165] Timothy Moorhead, 'The Values of the European Union Legal Order: Constitutional Perspectives' (2014) 16 European Journal of Law Reform 3, 7.

that 'Article 2 TEU is the landing place of an ongoing case law that from fundamental rights protection gradually evolved to include certain principles as core values of the EU legal order'.[166]

Despite some doubts as to the legal effects of article 2 TEU[167] prior to the Lisbon Treaty, the ECJ already assumed some of these values as a source of inspiration for the case law on the general principles of law. In *Les Verts*, for instance, the ECJ relied especially on the principle of democracy to legitimize the European Parliament as an institution responsible for representing the interests of the European citizens within the EU decision-making process.[168] In more recent case law, the ECJ has developed article 2 'into a judicially applicable provision justiciable before the Court'.[169]. Thus, in *ASJP*, the ECJ stated:

> According to Article 2 TEU, the European Union is founded on values, such as the rule of law, which are common to the Member States in a society in which, inter alia, justice prevails. In that regard, it should be noted that mutual trust between the Member States and, in particular, their courts and tribunals is based on the fundamental premise that Member States share a set of common values on which the European Union is founded, as stated in Article 2 TEU.[170]

And combined with article 19 TEU, it operationalized article 2 TEU.[171] Similarly, in *PPU*, the ECJ established that:

> In that regard, it must be pointed out that the requirement of judicial independence forms part of the essence of the fundamental right to a fair trial, a right which is of cardinal importance as a guarantee that all the rights which individuals derive from EU law will be protected and that the values common to the Member States set out in Article 2 TEU, in particular the value of the rule of law, will be safeguarded.[172]

As Larik says, article 2 'symbolizes a paradigm shift from a legal entity that, in the first place, exists to strive for certain goals to one which, above all, expounds what it stands for'.[173] In effect, the EU legal order has thickened by acquiring sophisticated features beyond primacy and direct effects. It now has 'normative foundations,

[166] Salvatore Fabio Nicolisi, 'The Contribution of the Court of Justice to the Codification of the Founding Vales of the European Union' (2015) 51 Revista de Derecho Comunitario Europeo 613, 622.

[167] Luke Dimitrios Spieker, 'Breathing Life into the Union's Common Values: On the Judicial Application of Article 2 TEU in the EU Value crisis' (2019) 20 German Law Journal 1182, 1200.

[168] Nicolisi (n 166) 629; Case C-294/83 *Les Verts* [1986] ECR 01339.

[169] Spieker, 'Breathing Life into the Union's Common Values' (n 167) 1202.

[170] Case C-64/16 *Associaçâo Sindical dos Juízes Portugueses* [2018] ECLI 117, para 30.

[171] ibid para 32.

[172] Case C-216/18 *PPU* [2018] ECLI 586, para 48.

[173] Joris Larik, 'From Speciality to a Constitutional Sense of Purpose: On the Changing Role of the Objectives of the European Union' (2014) 63(4) International and Comparative Law Quarterly 935, 951.

which make it more akin to a constitutional than a functional entity'.[174] Values included in article 2 would be shaping a European identity that would act as a supranational limit before national identity claims.[175] The ECJ has confirmed this view in the 16 February 2022 decision regarding the lawfulness of the so-called Conditionality Regulation:

> The values contained in Article 2 TEU have been identified and are shared by the Member States. They define the very identity of the European Union as a common legal order. Thus, the European Union must be able to defend those values, within the limits of its powers as laid down by the Treaties.... In that regard, it must be borne in mind that Article 2 TEU is not merely a statement of policy guidelines or intentions, but contains values which, as noted in paragraph 127 above, are an integral part of the very identity of the European Union as a common legal order, values which are given concrete expression in principles containing legally binding obligations for the Member States.[176]

Besides, a clear link between national identity and EU values is also to be found in the original wording of the Maastricht Treaty, whereas both principles appear in the very same article F.[177]

To be clear: the ECJ is deprived from any direct jurisdiction on article 2 TEU. Member States have preferred to include a highly political instrument (ie art 7 TEU) when it comes to addressing violations of article 2 TEU.[178] And recourse to article 2 TEU in the hands of the ECJ should not be used either to grab power or call into question the Union's federal equilibrium: it must be interpreted in a restrictive manner.[179] But this does not mean that the ECJ cannot (and will not) resort to article 2 TEU when assessing the accuracy and suitability of a national court claim regarding the constitutional identity of a Member State (art 4(2) TEU).[180] The ECJ might be called upon either via infringement proceedings initiated by the Commission or via preliminary ruling requests referred to it by national courts. At the same time, article 2 TEU can hardly impose detailed or positive obligations

[174] ibid 957.

[175] Cruz, 'Identidad Nacional y Valores de la Unión Europea' (n 112) 269.

[176] Case C-156/21 *Hungary v Parliament and Council* [2022] ECLI 97, paras 127 and 232. The Court had already expressed this view, although with less conviction, in *Kadi*. Joined Cases C-402/05 P and C-415/05 *Kadi v Council* [2008] ECR I-06351, para 304.

[177] Pietro Faraguna, 'On the Identity Clause and Its Abuses: "Back to the Treaty"' (2021) 27(3) European Public Law 427, 444.

[178] Nicolisi (n 166) 643.

[179] Spieker, 'Breathing Life into the Union's Common Values' (n 167) 1210.

[180] Needless to say, a Member State judge has a duty to interpret any national law in conformity with art 2 TEU values. In fact, in what has been called 'Reverse Solange' doctrine, any court in the European legal space, including the Court of Justice, can scrutinize any national measure by relying on the standards of art 2 TEU. Armin von Bogdandy and Luke Dimitrios Spieker, 'Countering the Judicial Silencing of Critics: Article 2 TEU Values, Reverse Solange, and the Responsibilities of National Judges' (2019) 15(3) European Constitutional Law Review 391, 407.

upon the Member States on how to organize its fundamental political structures. This would ignore the existing constitutional pluralism in the Union.[181] But article 2 TEU can determine negatively what is not allowed, that is to say, it can draw red lines.[182]

4.4 Other Scenarios

The following scenarios have not been reviewed by scholars. This may be because Scotland and Catalonia are, respectively, cases of (1) consensual and lawful attempt of secession and (2) unilateral and unlawful attempt of secession. Furthermore, the secessionist examples in neighbourhood territories such as Montenegro[183] and Crimea[184] also followed the same pattern. Montenegro was an example of consensual (or agreed) and lawful secession, while Crimea was a case of unilateral (or non-consensual) and unlawful secession. Thus, in the recent experience of these real cases there is a strong relationship between, on the one hand, consensus and lawfulness, and, on the other hand, lack of consensus and unlawfulness. This might explain why scholars have not paid attention to those imagined scenarios where there is no alignment between consensus and lawfulness. In any event, the analysis of these imagined scenarios deserves some attention, because it will reinforce the argument of the need to invoke article 4(2) TEU when exploring the legal basis of the EU reaction towards any type of secession.

4.4.1 Consensual but unlawful secession

The paradigm of a consensual but unlawful secession is one where, for example, there is a legal framework that requires a certain procedure or plainly outlaws secession, but the central government nonetheless reaches a political deal with the secessionist entity. In such a scenario there would be a constitutional transformation

[181] Spieker, 'Breathing Life into the Union's Common Values' (n 167) 1210. See also von Bogdandy and Spieker (n 180) 422.

[182] Maciej Taborowski and others, 'Guest Editorial: A Potential Constitutional Moment for the European Rule of Law—The Importance of Red Lines' (2018) 55 Common Market Law Review 983, 989.

[183] In the 2737th General Affairs and External Relations Council meeting, dated 12 June 2006, EU Member State representatives acknowledged that Serbia had recognized the new territorial reality and that Montenegro had acted in accordance with constitutional provisions and that 'therefore' the EU and its Member States had decided to develop further relations with the Republic of Montenegro as a sovereign, independent State. <https://www.consilium.europa.eu/uedocs/cms_data/docs/pressdata/en/gena/90014.pdf> accessed 16 July 2022.

[184] On 16 March 2014, the EU released a Joint statement on the unilateral referendum on Crimea by President of the European Council Herman Van Rompuy and President of the European Commission José Manuel Durao Barroso declaring that 'The European Union considers the holding of the referendum on the future status of the territory of Ukraine as contrary to the Ukrainian Constitution and international law. The referendum is illegal and illegitimate and its outcome will not be recognised.' <http://www.consilium.europa.eu/uedocs/cms_Data/docs/pressdata/en/ec/141566.pdf> accessed 16 July 2022.

in that Member State, where, by definition, the constitutional identity of the country is in the making, since there would be a profound mismatch between the legal order and the political legitimacy that underpins it. There would therefore be a transitional constitutional moment. As explained in Chapter 2, once the deal (ie new constitutional pact) is consolidated (either ultimately through a formal amendment or without it), the constitutional identity of the country has changed or evolved. In such a scenario—a transitional constitutional moment—EU institutions should remain neutral, but vigilant that the values and principles included in article 2 TEU are not violated. Once the political situation and the new, evolved national constitutional legal order is consolidated and the constitutional crisis is over, the EU should, according to article 4(2) TEU, recognize the new and evolved national constitutional identity and, therefore, recognize the new territorial polity.

4.4.2 Non-consensual but lawful secession

This scenario is exemplified by the situation where the central government refuses to accept the result of a lawful secessionist attempt. There might, therefore, be a violation of the constitutional order by the Member State. We should distinguish the type and extent of the unlawfulness. If the violation grossly affects values and principles enshrined in article 2 TEU, EU institutions will have to resort to article 7 TEU.[185] The debate about the violation of article 2 TEU and the recourse to article 7 TEU, however interesting, falls outside the scope of this book. But if the unlawfulness is not systematic and grave, and does not require recourse to article 7 TEU, it might also entail evolution of the political consensus that is the basis of the constitutional pact. In such a case, there would be a constitutional crisis. EU institutions should, once again, remain neutral and vigilant, making sure that article 2 TEU is respected and reacting only when the constitutional order is consolidated.

4.4.3 Non-consensual, unlawful secession but widely supported secession move

In the event of a non-consensual, unlawful secession, but widely supported secession move, the EU obligation enshrined in article 4(2) TEU and the deferential approach still holds valid, provided that the values of article 2 TEU are not violated. In this regard, I share the view of Campins Eritja, who believes that if an EU Member State does not facilitate a political solution, and engages in obstruction through silence and persistent refusal that might be considered a grave political

[185] I am not implying that this is a quick or satisfactory mechanism, since I am aware of the Union's vulnerabilities and deficiencies in the domain of upholding the rule of law, both in the EU's design and its day-to-day functioning. Recent accounts can be found in Dimitry Kochenov, 'The EU and the Rule of Law—Naiveté or a Grand Design?' in Maurice Adams and others (eds), *Constitutionalism and the Rule of Law: Bridging Idealism and Realism* (CUP 2017) and Laurent Pech, 'Article 7 TEU: From "Nuclear Option" to "Sisyphean Procedure"?' in Uladzislau Belavusau and Aleksandra Gliszczyńska-Grabias (eds), *Constitutionalism under Stress* (OUP 2020).

error, but 'it falls short of being a systematic threat to democracy, the rule of law and human rights that are required for the application of article 7 of the TEU'.[186]

Undoubtedly, if the constitutional crisis provokes political instability or jeopardizes the functioning of the internal market, political interests might convince EU institutions of the need to mediate with the Member State concerned in order to find a solution for the crisis. This consideration also holds for any of the situations described above and goes beyond any legal analysis of the situation. If the internal constitutional disorder triggers instability across the EU, EU institutions might be tempted to intervene and engage in diplomatic negotiations.

5. Conclusion

Having reviewed the relevant scholarly literature, it has been argued that the principal criterion to shape the EU law position is the distinction between lawful and consensual secession, and unlawful and unilateral secession. Since the legality criteria are, as seen in Chapter 4, established by the national constitutional legal orders, and given that the EU is obliged to respect the constitutional identity of the Member States (art 4(2) TEU), EU law should show a deferential attitude, as long as article 2 TEU is respected, in an exercise of constitutional tolerance, 'one of Europe's most important constitutional innovations'. As Weiler has explained: '[n]o matter how close the Union, it is to remain a union among distinct peoples, distinct political identities, and distinct political communities'.[187] In effect, when referring to the rationale behind article 4(2) TEU and the legal pluralism within this multilevel system, 'European integration is necessarily based on a minimum level of tolerance, acceptance and trust of the Member States.... Historically and originally, European integration is a response to intolerance between states.'[188]

The national constitutional identity clause resolves the different scenarios of a secessionist challenge: (1) in the event of lawful and consensual secession, it provides a legal reason as to why the EU has to respect and therefore take into consideration the membership application, although this only entails negotiations, the outcome of which is unknown and subject to unanimity. Here the analogy to article 50 and the reference to the principle of sincere cooperation becomes relevant

[186] Mar Campins Eritja, 'The European Union and the Secession of a Territory from a EU Member State' (2015) 2(XVII) Diritto Pubblico Comparato ed Europeo 479, 480. The same reasoning can be found at Matt Qvortrup, 'Independence Referendums. History, Legal Status and Voting Behaviour' in Carlos Closa, Costanza Margiotta, and Giuseppe Martinico (eds), *Between Democracy and Law. The Amorality of Secession* (Routledge 2020) 138: 'While the Spanish government, arguably acted in a way that appeared grossly disproportionate (to wit police violence and arrest of democratically elected politicians which appears disproportional notwithstanding the letter of the law), the legal argument remains the same. Catalonia is not currently part of a non-democratic state.'

[187] Joseph HH Weiler, 'On the Power of the Word: Europe's Constitutional Iconography' (2005) 3(2–3) International Journal of Constitutional Law 173, 186–87.

[188] Besselink (n 100) 47.

again. Thus, in the case of a 'Yes' vote in Scotland in 2014, the appropriate EU reaction would have been to enter into good faith negotiations with the Scottish authorities; (2) in the event of non-consensual and unlawful secession, it offers a legal ground as to why the EU cannot accept such process. Therefore, a hypothetical unilateral declaration of independence within an EU Member State would not trigger the expulsion of that territory from the EU, but it would be seen as the refusal to admit a new legal reality, as happened with the secessionist attempt of Catalonia in October 2017. Thus, the reactions of the EU institutions outlined in the previous chapter were in accordance with EU law, since they did respect the constitutional legal order of Spain by not recognizing the Catalan unilateral declaration of independence.

However, there might be other scenarios where lawfulness and consensus do not coincide. Even in these cases of constitutional identity in transition, the rule of article 4(2) TEU together with article 2 still holds valid, because while the new constitutional order is in the making, the EU should remain vigilant that article 2 TEU is not violated. When the new legal order is consolidated, and provided it does not oppose article 2 TEU, the EU, again, will have to show a tolerant attitude towards the national constitutional identity.

In sum, the EU constrains the behaviour of the Member States: EU Member States are allowed to have different national constitutional responses to secession, but only provided such responses and their subsequent application and enforcement respect the values included in article 2 TEU. This provides a good example of the dialogical non-hierarchical relationship between legal orders that has been advanced throughout this work.[189]

[189] Kelemen and Pech, given the abusive use of constitutional identity by some Member States, advocate for the dismantling of constitutional pluralism: 'In an age when liberal, constitutional democracy is facing a clear and present danger, the time has come to dismantle constitutional pluralism.' Kelemen and Pech (n 159) 74. It is true that the ambiguity of the clause has been exploited by some Member States to question supranational loyalty. However, it is my view that such abuse is not a strong enough argument to defy the normative construction of constitutional pluralism that has defined the relationship between the EU legal order and national legal orders in the last 70 years. Article 4(2) certainly does not give a blank cheque to national constitutional courts to adopt measures blatantly violating fundamental EU values such as the rule of law, particularly judicial independence. However, EU institutions might be more deferential in other areas (such as abortion, religious freedom, gay marriage, or same sex parenting) that lie at the core of a values battle that is taking place in many Western democracies where there is no common constitutional European tradition. In this regard, it is interesting to note that, aware of such concerns, in the *Pancharevo* case (same sex parenting) Advocate General Kokott recommended a nuanced solution: on the one hand, a Member State must recognize the parenthood of a child for the purpose of the exercise of the freedom of movements rights conferred by EU law on EU citizens, but, on the other hand, she also recommended relying on national identity (and the Bulgarian concept of a traditional family) in order to refuse to recognize the parental relationship of two married women. Case C-490/20 *Pancharevo* [2021] ECLI 296, Opinion of AG Kokott. The Court, in the end, refused any reference to national identity and opted for a more assertive decision in favour of recognizing (at least functionally) same sex parenting, in line with the *Coman* jurisprudence (same sex marriage, Case C-673/16 *Coman* [2018] ECLI 385). Case C-490/20 *Pancharevo* [2021] ECLI 1008. It is my view that the Kokott approach is the most appropriate to accommodate Member State values concerns and, at the same, to guarantee EU law uniform application.

7
EU Law in Relation to States Emerging out of Secession

1. Introduction

This chapter will explore the legal situation that arises when a new State has emerged and has been recognized by the European Union (EU) and EU Member States following the recognition policy explained in previous chapters. Needless to say, if the entity is not recognized, as happened with the so-called 'Catalan Republic' in 2017, nothing changes and there is no need for further analysis. But, in the event of the creation of a new, sovereign and independent European State out of secession from a current EU Member State, what happens in relation to its EU membership? Will it retain it? Will it have to ask for it? In that event, what is the most appropriate legal path? And what will happen as regards EU citizenship rights of the new State's nationals? It should be said at the outset that some sections of this chapter are highly speculative and conjectural, but no book on secession and EU law would be complete without, at least, taking into consideration all these questions.

The chapter will initially address the debate about State continuity and succession. We will define the terms and then explore the different alternatives: will the rump Member State be the continuing State maintaining its EU membership, while the seceding territory becomes a new, successor State that would have to ask for membership? Or, following an internal enlargement theory, will both States maintain EU membership? Alternatively, and given the profound change of circumstances, another option would be to consider that both States should have to ask for EU membership. It will be argued that the rump State will continue with its EU membership, while the new State that seceded will have to ask for EU membership, notwithstanding the quick access that could be designed if a political agreement between the candidate and the rest of EU Member States were reached.

A further important issue, in the event that the new State is interested in EU accession, concerns the route towards EU membership, thereby requiring discussion of article 49 of the Treaty on European Union (TEU) and article 48 TEU. Thus, should the new independent State follow the ordinary path of article 49 TEU, or is there any possibility to treat this accession as an amendment to the treaties and, therefore, invoke article 48 TEU? And, is this difference relevant at all? In my view, the discussion about the accession routes is relevant only to a certain extent, since regardless of the legal route chosen, both require a high degree of political

Secession and European Union Law. Núria González Campañá, Oxford University Press. © Núria González Campañá 2024.
DOI: 10.1093/oso/9780198882596.003.0007

consensus, unanimity, and a ratification process throughout all EU Member States. Therefore, the practical consequences are minor. In any event, it will be argued that from a legal standpoint the most suitable approach is recourse to article 49 TEU.

The chapter will also consider the debate about EU citizenship, nationality, and secession. The discussion here is highly speculative, since this regime will depend on the negotiations between the rump State and the new seceded territory. However, what deserves analysis it the extent to which nationality law (that, in principle, is governed mainly by internal law) is constrained by international, and, above all, EU law. In other words, and specifically, would the withdrawal of national citizenship rights and consequently EU citizenship rights as a possible result of the negotiations violate EU law? Could EU citizenship have any effect at all in the EU approach towards secession? It is my assumption that, despite some European Court of Justice (ECJ) case law (ie *Rottmann* and *Ruiz Zambrano*), EU Member States still have an important degree of autonomy when it comes to defining nationality and, therefore, the impact of EU citizenship can only be limited. This assumption has only been reinforced by recent ECJ case law on EU citizenship following Brexit, that will be addressed in Section 4.2.2.

Finally, the chapter will briefly address the hypothetical situation of an independent Scotland or the reunification of Ireland after Brexit. As is widely speculated, the British withdrawal from the EU might become the catalyst both for the secession of Scotland and the reunification of Ireland. In that event, will an independent Scotland, provided it is recognized by EU Member States and the new independent country is interested in EU membership, present a different scenario that alters the legal reasoning developed in the chapter? And what would happen in the case of an enlarged Ireland?

2. State Continuity and Succession of States

2.1 State Continuity and Succession of States under Public International Law

State continuity refers to cases where the same State continues to exist despite changes in the territory and population, whereas State succession makes reference to the legal issues when there is a change of sovereignty over a territory. Undoubtedly, secession, as defined in Chapter 2, (1) implies State succession, the seceded entity, and (2) it might also refer to State continuity provided that the parent State continues to exist, that is, the rump State. As Piris recalls, 'were a secession to be conducted in conformity with the law (national, European and international), the new entity would become a legal entity distinct from its State of origin, as from the date of its independence'.[1] Each EU Member State, as any

[1] Jean Claude Piris, 'Political and Legal Aspects of Recent Regional Secessionist Trends in Some EU Member States (II)' in Carlos Closa (ed), *Secession from a Member State and Withdrawal from the European Union* (CUP 2017) 91.

other State around the world, would be free to decide unilaterally to recognize the seceded entity as an independent and sovereign State. Before exploring the issues that the new entity will have to deal with after recognition, such as legal routes to EU accession, and the position of its own nationals vis a vis EU law, we will focus on the international legal status of the territorial entities concerned, that is, the rump State and the seceded entity. This has, as will be seen, been the object of a heated discussion among scholars examining secession and EU law, since international law is far from offering a straightforward answer to this question. As Athanassiou and Shaelou note, 'state continuity' and 'state succession' are areas of great uncertainty and controversy and 'the relevant state practice is far from uniform or unambiguous'.[2]

In Chapter 5, we reviewed some of the answers provided by the European Commission to questions posed by Members of the European Parliament focused on future membership of seceding entities, such as State succession. In some answers the European Commission referred to negotiations within public international law.[3] In effect, the truth is that although internally the relations of the Member States and their peoples in matters covered by the European treaties are governed by European law, the question of the territorial extent of a State has been treated by the EU as a matter of international law.[4] Indeed, this legal corpus has been part of the scholarly discussion when examining secession within the EU, as made clear in Chapters 2 and 3.[5] It is noteworthy here to address the international law approach, although, as we will see, it does not provide conclusive answers and is of limited help. Thus, we will only refer to the main lines of argument summarizing the key conclusions.

[2] Phoebus Athanassiou and Stéphanie Laulhé Shaelou, 'EU Accession from Within? An Introduction' (2014) 33(1) Yearbook of European Law 335, 359–60.

[3] For instance, Question for written answer by Mara Bizzotto (EFD) to the Commission, 25 Juy 2012, E-007453/2012 <http://www.europarl.europa.eu/sides/getAllAnswers.do?reference=E-2012-007453&language=EN> accessed 5 August 2022.

[4] Case 148/77 *Hansen v Hauptzollamt Flensburg* [1978] ECR 1787, para 10: 'It follows from Article 227 (1) that the status of the French overseas departments within the Community is primarily defined by reference to the French constitution under which, as the French Government has stated, the overseas departments are an integral part of the Republic.' As Boyle and Crawford established, the ECJ made clear that 'a Member State's territory depends on that Member State's own constitution, not on the EU treaties. No treaty amendment is therefore required simply as a result of a change to the borders of a state's territory.' Alan Boyle and James Crawford, *Annex A Opinion: Referendum on the Independence of Scotland—International Law Aspects* (UK Government, 2013) para 159 <https://assets.publishing.service.gov.uk/government/uploads/system/uploads/attachment_data/file/79408/Annex_A.pdf> accessed 5 August 2022. That is why, even if a Member State suffers loss of its territory, EU treaties would continue to apply to its reduced territory, provided that the country is not on the verge of dissolution.

[5] Some authors have challenged the resort to public international law: 'given the complex relationship between EU law and international law, the question of successor and continuator status is perhaps not as relevant to the issue at hand as the Commission seems to think'. Daniel Kenealy and Stuart MacLennan, 'Sincere Cooperation, Respect for Democracy and EU Citizenship: Sufficient to Guarantee Scotland's Future in the European Union?' (2014) 20(5) European Law Journal 591, 597.

The Vienna Convention on Succession of States in Respect of Treaties of 1978 is the legal document usually referred to when addressing secession, the formation of new States, and the status of legal relationships between the parent State, the new entity, and the rest of the international community. Succession of States is defined in its article 2(1)(b) as the 'replacement of one State by another in the responsibility for the international relations of territory'. Article 34 of the treaty provides for a general rule of continuation (or automatic accession) in cases of separation of parts of a State:

> 1. When a part or parts of a territory of a State separate to form one or more States, whether or not the predecessor State continues to exist:
>
> Any treaty in force at the date of the succession of States in respect of the entire territory of the predecessor State continues in force in respect of each successor State so formed;

However, article 4 of the same document expressly states that 'the effect of state succession on membership of an international organisation depends on the relevant rules of that organisation'. This means that the very same treaty admits that despite the existence of a general automatic succession rule, what matters ultimately is the opinion of the international organization concerned, which, in the end, means the opinion of the States that belong to that organization, in the case at hand, the EU Member States. In its commentary on article 4, the International Law Commission (ILC) confirmed this view:

> In many [international] organizations membership, other than original membership, is subject to a formal process of admission. Where this is so, practice appears now to have established the principle that a new State is not entitled automatically to become a party to the constituent treaty and a member of the organization as a successor State, simply by reason of the fact that at the date of the succession its territory was subject to the treaty and within the ambit of the organization.[6]

Thus, the wording of the treaty (arts 4 and 34 read together) and the interpretation offered by the ILC both reject the theory of automatic succession. In fact, what public international law is signalling is that what matters in the events at hand—secession and membership of an international organization—is the position of the international organization affected. In any event, although the Vienna Convention is in force, it has only been ratified by a few EU Member States, namely,

[6] International Law Commission, 'Draft Articles on Succession of States in respect of Treaties with commentaries' text adopted by the International Law Commission at its twenty-sixth session in 1974. <http://legal.un.org/ilc/texts/instruments/english/commentaries/3_2_1974.pdf> accessed 5 August 2022.

Croatia, the Czech Republic, Estonia, Slovakia, Slovenia, and Cyprus,[7] and its status as customary international law is doubtful.[8] Thus, the applicability of the treaty remains unclear, which would leave us with no applicable international law. However, many authors accept as a well-established customary rule the norm that in the event of succession of States, the rules for international organization membership status for new independent entities have to be found within the organization at stake.[9] In the event that the organization at stake, such as the EU, does not have specific provisions governing succession of States, what becomes particularly relevant is the extent to which there is some consistency in the practice of international organizations, and the extent to which that practice has been understood by the international community as legally binding, that might have led to the emergence of some sort of substantive customary law, beyond the procedural norm that what matters is the law of the organization affected.

In this sense, Scharf has argued that, despite some controversy among scholars, it is possible to map with some precision the contours of a customary law of succession to membership for rump States. He maintains that automatic succession is possible only if the successor can establish sufficient legal identity with the former member, then becoming the continuing State.[10] He suggests that in determining whether a potential successor is the continuation of a member or whether the member's international personality has been extinguished, the State has to retain: (1) a substantial majority of the former member's territory; (2) a majority of its population; (3) a majority of its resources; (4) a majority of its armed forces, and (5) the seat of government and control of most central government institutions. Boyle and Crawford advance the same thesis:

[7] Check ratification status at <https://treaties.un.org/pages/ViewDetails.aspx?src=TREATY&mtdsg_no=XXIII-2&chapter=23&clang=_en#EndDec> accessed 5 August 2022.

[8] Boyle and Crawford (n 4) para 124; on the same lines, Jo E Murkens, 'Scotland's Place in Europe' (2001) The Constitution Unit UCL 10 <http://cadmus.eui.eu/bitstream/handle/1814/46232/Murkens_2001.pdf?sequence=1&isAllowed=y> accessed 5 August 2022. Also, the Catalan Council for National Transitional, a consultative body set up by the Catalan government to advise on the path towards independence, has expressed its doubts as to the effectiveness of this treaty. Consell Assessor per la Transició Nacional, *La integració a la comunitat internacional* (Catalan Government 2014) 17.

[9] 'The 1978 Vienna Convention on succession of states in respect of Treaties defines the international law position. Article 4 establishes that the effects of state succession on membership of an international organisation depend on the relevant rules of that organisation. *Even though only seven EU states are party to the Convention, it provides a solid reference point in this regard*' (emphasis added). Carlos Closa, 'Secession from a Member State and EU Membership: The View from the Union' (2016) 12(2) European Constitutional Law Review 240, 251; see also Alfredo Galán, 'Secesión de Estados y Pertenencia a la Unión Europea' (2013) 1 Istituzione del Federalismo 95, 106; and Miquel Palomares, 'Las decisiones de los Jefes de Estado y de Gobierno, en el seno del Consejo Europeo, como categoría jurídica para regular, transitoriamente, la participación en la Unión Europea de nuevos Estados surgidos de la separación de Estados Miembros' (2013) 17 Revista d'Estudis Autonòmics i Federals 146, 151.

[10] Michael P Scharf, 'Musical Chairs: The Dissolution of States and Membership in the United Nations' (1995) 29(1) Cornell International Law Journal 29, 67. On the same lines, Athanassiou and Shaelou: 'It nevertheless stands to reason that there should be at least a presumption of state continuity where the rump state involves what may be regarded as fundamentally the same territorial and governmental unit'. Athanassiou and Shaelou (n 2) 360; see also Boyle and Crawford (n 4) paras 77–78.

> In general, state practice shows that continuity depends on the criteria for statehood: a state is the same if it involves what may be regarded as the same independent territorial and governmental unit at the relevant times, despite changes in its population, territory or system of government.[11]

For instance, when referring to past international practice, when it came to the partition of India and Pakistan, India was considered the continuing State of pre-split India, since it retained most of British India's territory and population. It maintained its founding United Nations (UN) membership, whereas Pakistan had to apply in its own right, as it was considered a new State, not a continuing one.[12] A similar scenario is to be found in the separation of Singapore from Malaysia in 1965. While Malaysia retained its international identity and UN membership because it was considered the continuing State, Singapore was treated as a new State and had to ask for UN membership.[13] After the separation from Pakistan, Bangladesh was considered a new State and had to ask for international recognition,[14] while Pakistan (former West Pakistan) was considered the continuing State. The dissolution of the USSR posed a major challenge for international practice. After initial uncertainty, the Russian Federation was considered the continuing State of the USSR, retaining its legal personality, UN membership, and, particularly relevant, the permanent seat and veto power at the UN Security Council.[15] The former Soviet Socialist Republics had to ask for UN membership, since they were treated as new States. In 1993 Ethiopia was considered the continuing State of Ethiopia after the secession of Eritrea and continued its UN membership, while Eritrea had to be admitted in its own right.[16] A more recent example can be found in the case of Sudan. The new State of South Sudan, which had seceded from the North, was admitted to the UN in 2011, while Sudan (the Northern part) continued with its membership as the continuing State.[17] In sum, the successor continuing State remains bound by treaties concluded by the preceding State, and remains a member of the same international organizations with the same rights and duties.[18]

If, on the contrary, there is no State retaining the majority of the population, resources, and territory, then what has occurred can be better described as

[11] Boyle and Crawford (n 4) para 52.
[12] UN doc S/RES/29 (1947) 22 May.
[13] UN doc S/RES/213 (1965) 20 September.
[14] UN doc S/RES/351 (1974) 10 June.
[15] Yehuda Z Blum, 'Russia Takes over the Soviet Union's Seat at the United Nations' (1992) 3 European Journal of International Law 354, 360. Blum considers that, legally speaking, the arguments of the Russian Federation were flawed, but major political interests prevailed and thus the international community accepted the Russian claim to consider it the continuing State of the USSR and, therefore, maintain the former privileged status of the USSR within the UN Security Council.
[16] UN doc S/RES/828 (1993) 26 May.
[17] UN doc S/RES/1996 (2011) 8 July.
[18] Piris, 'Political and Legal Aspects of Recent Regional Secessionist Trends in Some EU Member States (II)' (n 1) 92.

dissolution or division of the State rather than secession of one of its territories. In this latter case, the former legal international identity is extinct. As a result, no entity can be considered a continuing State. Thus, the newborn States established by secession, successors but not continuing States, have to apply for new membership of international organizations. Thus, after the dissolution of Czechoslovakia, both the Czech Republic and Slovakia had to apply for UN membership. Both were considered successor States, not continuing States. This implicit rule, to the effect that if a State is a continuing State then its international organizations memberships will continue, whereas a new State must be formally admitted,[19] has been the practice of the UN[20] and also of European regional organizations.[21] This practice has been traditionally linked to the so-called 'clean slate' rule: 'a new state that was not party to a treaty cannot be bound by it, nor can other parties to a treaty be bound to accept a new party in their midst'.[22] In the past this approach had very obvious justifications. When a new State emerges, it should commence international life free from the treaty rights and obligations applicable to its former sovereign, it should not be bound by the treaties of the predecessor. However, although this justification of the 'clean slate' rule made sense in a decolonization context, it is unclear whether it is suitable in the current scenario of the EU.

2.2 State Continuity and Succession of States under European Union Law

In the case of the EU: (1) there is no EU law provision governing the issue and, therefore, we have to have recourse to public international law; (2) there is no international treaty on the issue ratified by EU Member States; (3) scholars tend to admit as a customary rule a treaty provision that establishes that, in the event of succession of States, the rules for international organization membership status have to be found within the organization itself, which is of little help in the case at hand; (4) scholars have also identified as a customary rule out of State and international organizations practice in recent decades that automatic succession and maintenance of membership are possible only if the successor can establish sufficient legal identity with the former member State. Otherwise, the 'clean slate' rule applies.

This leads us to the fundamental question: in a scenario of secession within the EU, which State will be considered a successor and continuing State, and therefore

19 Boyle and Crawford (n 4) para 128. See also Athanassiou and Shaelou (n 2) 359–61.

20 Boyle and Crawford (n 4) para 129.

21 Matthew Happold, 'Independence: In or out of Europe? An Independent Scotland and the European Union' (2000) 49(1) International and Comparative Law Quarterly 15, 22–25, 27. See also Murkens, 'Scotland's Place in Europe' (n 8) 11.

22 Athanassiou and Shaelou (n 2) 361.

entitled to remain automatically an EU Member State? And which State will be considered a successor but not a continuing State and, consequently, will have to apply for new EU membership?

In the first event, in the case of a continuing State, we would be referring to a situation where the 'new' State retains the majority of the population, territory, and resources. As explained in the previous section, customary international law states that only under these circumstances can a 'new' State be considered a continuing State. Accordingly, we would be referring to a rump State like Spain after the secession of Catalonia, Italy after the secession of Veneto, France after the secession of Corsica, or Germany after the secession of Bavaria. It is difficult to deny that only the rump Spain, Italy, France, or Germany would be considered continuing States, since they would retain the majority of the former population, resources, territory, seat of government, and control of most central government institutions.[23] For Boyle and Crawford (referring to the UK after the loss of Scotland before Brexit) this 'will be evident, without further elucidation'.[24] Take into account, for instance, the case of the UK after the independence of Ireland:

> There is no indication in the Articles of Agreement for a Treaty between the Great Britain and Ireland of 6 December 1921 that either party questioned the UK's continuity; on the contrary, it appears to have been premised on the personality of the UK continuing uninterrupted.[25]

Thus, the rump State's rights and obligations remain unaffected, since 'the coming into being of one or more seceding state entities does not normally affect the existence of the rump state in the international stage, nor does it raise issues of state continuity and succession'.[26] Under these circumstances then, according to customary international law, the rump State would not need to ask for EU membership:

> It seems unlikely that anyone would suggest that its EU membership could somehow lapse as a consequence of the loss of population and territory occasioned by Scottish independence.[27]

[23] Only a few scholars or pro-independence politicians claimed that after Scottish independence there would be two States (ie the remaining UK and Scotland) that could be considered continuing States and maintain their status within the EU, although subject to negotiations. Paul S Henderson, 'Review: Scottish Independence' (2003) 45 Scottish Affairs 97, 100: 'Certainly, the two new states would have to negotiate with the European Union over such matters as the number of votes in the Council of Ministers and number of seats in the European Parliament, but neither would be expelled.'

[24] Boyle and Crawford (n 4) para 50.

[25] ibid para 65.

[26] Athanassiou and Shaelou (n 2) 360.

[27] Boyle and Crawford (n 4) para 145.

Athanassiou and Shaelou share the same view:

> In light of the above, the EU law position of the rump Member State in a genuine secession scenario is, in the authors' opinion, clear: the rump Member State would carry forward its legal personality and continue to enjoy its EU membership rights and obligations notwithstanding secession.[28]

In effect, since the EU treaties do not define the territory of EU Member States, they can continue to apply to the reduced or to the extended territory of an EU Member State. Indeed, 'the territorial scope of application of EU law can be changed unilaterally by a member state giving independence (decolonisation) to a territory or incorporating a territory'.[29] Needless to say, retaining EU membership will not prevent the rump State from minor adjustments related to its terms of membership, such as, for example, the number of Members of the European Parliament elected on its territory, or the weight of its vote in the Council.[30] However, 'there is nothing in the Treaties to suggest the existence of any obligation for the rump Member State to withdraw from the EU, or to otherwise re-negotiate its relationship with its partners merely because of incidents of secession affecting its territory and population'[31] beyond the referred adjustments, if any at all.

In the second event, in the case of a successor but not a continuing State, we would be referring to a situation where the 'new' State does not retain the majority of the population, territory, and resources of a current EU Member State: for example, an independent Catalonia, Veneto, Corsica, or Bavaria.[32] Since there are,

[28] Athanassiou and Shaelou (n 2) 342.

[29] Ziller explains that the size of EU 'territory' relies on Member States' unilateral decisions, which shows that the EU lacks at least one of the major components of a State: territory. Jacques Ziller, 'The European Union and the Territorial Scope of European Territories' (2007) 38(1) Victoria University of Wellington Law Review 51, 52–53. In this regard, the lessons drawn from the territorial changes affecting France after Algerian independence, Denmark after Greenland's withdrawal, or Germany after reunification are revealing.

[30] Piris also refers to other adjustments like 'the modalities of participation in the budget of the EU (Article 310 TFEU), the number of members of the Committee of the Regions (Article 301 TFEU) and of the Economic and Social Committee (Article 305 TFEU), subscription to the capital of the European Investment Bank (Article 5 of Protocol 5 to the EU Treaties), participation in various European funds, etc.'. Piris, 'Political and Legal Aspects of Recent Regional Secessionist Trends in some EU Member States (II)' (n 1) 93.

[31] Athanassiou and Shaelou (n 2) 340.

[32] The case of Belgium (see discussion in Chapter 4), where Flanders could be pushing for independence in the future, is much more difficult, since it could lead to the dissolution of Belgium, as in the case of Czechoslovakia or the former Yugoslavia. Unlike in the abovementioned scenarios of Spain, Italy, or France, where the identification of the rump States (successor and continuing States) on the one hand, and the newborn States on the other, seems evident, the case of Belgium is much more complex. Previous practice does not provide much guidance and the decision on whether the newborn States should be considered successor and continuing States of Belgium or not will be adopted following international negotiations. Thus, any opinion would be purely conjectural. Besides, although this is highly speculative, one should not rule out the possibility that the borders of the two new States would be an important source of dispute. Negotiations would be required, even if the Badinter Borders Principle is invoked, which states that the former internal borders become international borders following a dissolution. Since it is not clear whether this principle applies only in cases of dissolution, or also in cases of

as seen above, no legal rules within the EU that specifically govern the situation, we must have recourse to public international law. In this scenario, provided the new States were interested in EU membership, and in accord with customary international law, they would have to ask for EU membership. The reason for this is, as Happold explains, that membership of an international organization gives rise to rights and obligations, it offers their members the possibility to share and decide a common destiny, at least in certain areas. It is, therefore, necessary to give States the possibility to negotiate and decide with whom they want to work and collaborate.[33] In the same vein, Jenkt states that:

> The membership of an international organization has a personal quality and it is both reasonable and psychologically sound and wise that a new member of the international community should be required to apply for membership.[34]

As Chamon and Van der Loo state, '[t]his is very relevant to the EU, which probably has the most stringent procedure for admission of all international organizations'.[35] Thus, when translating and applying public international law to the EU situation, one could infer that, following international law, any new independent State like Catalonia, Veneto, Corsica, or any other such territory 'would not automatically join on independence unless the EU's rules had that result'.[36] Boyle and Crawford add that 'on the face of the EU treaties and other indications, it seems likely that Scotland would be required to join the EU as a new Member State'.[37] This view is shared by Araceli Mangas:

> The region that starts a *de iure* process (Scotland) or a *de facto* process (Catalonia) towards independence will be separated from the parent State and will become a third State vis a vis the EU. This is the consequences of its deeds. It decides on a voluntary basis its withdrawal from the EU[38] [own translation].

secession, negotiations would be needed to determine the new borders. Peter Radan, 'Post-Secession International Borders: A Critical Analysis of the Opinions of the Badinter Arbitration Commission' (2000) 24(1) Melbourne University Law Review 50, 54–57.

33 Happold (n 21) 27.
34 Wilfred Jenk, 'State Succession in Respect of Law-Making Treaties' (1952) 29 British Yearbook of International Law 105, 134.
35 Merijn Chamon and Guillaume Van der Loo, 'The Temporal Paradox of Regions in the EU Seeking Independence: Contraction and Fragmentation versus Widening and Deepening?' 2014 (20)5 European Law Journal 613, 618.
36 Boyle and Crawford (n 4) para 142. Needless to say, the references made to Scotland can be easily applied to any European region.
37 ibid para 153.
38 Araceli Mangas, 'La secesión de territorios en un Estado Miembro: efectos en el derecho de la Unión Europea' (2013) 25 Revista de Derecho de la Unión Europea 47, 64.

From an EU perspective, although there are no express EU provisions that cover this issue, the argument invoked in the previous chapter concerning the rights of current Member States to decide who can join the EU should also be taken into account. We should bear in mind that EU treaty provisions express legitimate Member States' aspirations, one of which is the decision about with whom they wish to share the EU political community. That is why this decision, necessarily, requires a unanimous agreement, as stated in article 49 TEU. That is also why the entrance of a new State, regardless of its origins, should respect the right conferred by the treaties on current Member States to exercise the veto, or possibility to deny the accession of any new State. Furthermore, as explained in Chapter 6, the new aspirant State is expected to fulfil the so-called Copenhagen criteria. It cannot be denied that a new, independent State that emerges from an already existing EU Member State will be in an advantageous position in relation to EU law compliance. But a presumption of compliance is not enough. As will be in Section 3.2.2, the new State will be tested on its economic viability, rule of law, protection of minorities, and the capability of its administration. Finally, the conclusion that any new State emerging by way of secession would have to accede to the EU as a new Member State is fully consistent with statements on the subject by EU officials, as has been seen in Chapter 5.[39] Having said that, as Boyle and Crawford state:

> All this is not to suggest that it is inconceivable for Scotland automatically to be an EU member. The relevant EU organs or Member States might be willing to adjust the usual requirements for membership in the circumstances of Scotland's case. But that would be a decision for them, probably made on the basis of negotiations; it is not required as a matter of international law, nor, at least on its face, by the EU legal order.[40]

In effect, in the event of a successful secession, at some point negotiations among Member States would start and political interests rather than legal provisions would determine the outcome of the challenge. This prompts the following question: what does the European Commission mean when it says that the debate about membership after secession will have to be resolved in accordance with public international law, if it is only of limited help? It would seem that the European Commission is not only underlining the lack of EU rules in the area, but it is also stressing the intergovernmental logic of the issue and the relevant position of EU Member States in addressing the situation. It would seem that the European

[39] In 2014, during an interview with the BBC, the then President of the European Commission explained that an independent Scotland would have to apply for EU membership in the usual way. '"Extremely difficult" for Scotland to join EU—Barroso' (*BBC*, 16 February 2014) <http://www.bbc.com/news/av/uk-politics-26215579/extremely-difficult-for-scotland-to-join-eu-barroso> accessed 5 August 2002.

[40] Boyle and Crawford (n 4) para 164.

Commission was advancing the idea that in the event of secession, recognition of independence and subsequently expressed will of EU membership, negotiation, and the national interest of the Member States will be key. This is also why Boyle and Crawford assumed that 'the consequences of Scottish independence within the EU will depend on the attitude of other EU Member States and organs, and on negotiations'.[41] There is no doubt that the same reasoning could be applied to other European sub-national entities.

3. Route towards Accession: Article 48 TEU or Article 49 TEU

Let us turn our attention to the specific legal path that the new State born out of secession must follow in order to acquire EU membership. In the previous section, we indicated that, according to public international law and EU law, newborn States will have to ask for EU membership. There are, however, no EU law provisions specifically governing how a new State born out of secession, that used to be subjected to EU law, should apply for accession. Scholars have taken different approaches to this issue. Some believe that the classic legal path for ordinary accession, article 49 TEU, is the appropriate route in the case at hand. Others contend that given the special circumstances, article 48 TEU is the most suitable path. Article 48 TEU deals with amendments to the treaties by existing members, while article 49 TEU deals with the applications of third non-EU countries. Together with the conditions known as the Copenhagen criteria, it defines the political, legal, economic, and procedural requirements. Clearly, neither article specifically governs the situation of a territory of an existing Member State becoming independent and wishing to become a new EU Member State. And that is why, at least partially, Cristina Fasone advocated for the introduction of a new ad hoc provision that would: (1) establish the requirements an aspiring seceding territory should meet in order to apply for EU membership; and (2) make the transition to new EU Member State smooth.[42]

[41] ibid para 144.

[42] Cristina Fasone, 'Secession and the Ambiguous Place of Regions Under EU Law' in Carlos Closa (ed), *Secession from a Member State and Withdrawal from the European Union* (CUP 2017) 65. Although Fasone does not specify the wording of the clause, she considers that such a hypothetical provision would have three beneficial effects: (1) to allow the EU to monitor if the EU's fundamental values are respected throughout the secession process; (2) to limit the problem of leaving a seceding region and its citizens in a sort of limbo; and (3) to lead the parties to take a more faithful and cooperative approach and even to create a disincentive against the most groundless attempts to secede. ibid 66. The tendency to want to regulate everything is common among jurists. Law hates a vacuum, so it should not be surprising that there have been proposals for clauses of this type, such as the one we have seen in the previous chapter defended by Josu de Miguel. However, I am not convinced of their feasibility, because Member States have never expressed their desire to regulate their behaviour in such circumstances, since they prefer to have a free hand in this matter.

In any event, and given that for the time being, there is no specific secession clause at the EU level, we must focus on studying the two current alternatives at our disposal. And, in effect, throughout the years prior to the 2014 Scottish referendum, there was in Scotland and the rest of the UK significant debate about whether to follow the article 48 TEU path or article 49 TEU route. In its 2013 Scotland's Future report, the Scottish government affirmed that:

> The alternative to an Article 49 procedure, and a legal basis that the Scottish Government considers is appropriate to the prospective circumstances, is that Scotland's transition to full membership is secured under the general provisions of Article 48. Article 48 provides for a Treaty amendment to be agreed by common accord on the part of the representatives of the governments of the member states.
>
> Article 48 is therefore a suitable legal route to facilitate the transition process, by allowing the EU Treaties to be amended through the ordinary revision procedure before Scotland becomes independent, to enable it to become a member state at the point of independence.[43]

To the contrary, the UK House of Commons Scottish Affairs Committee explained that: (1) '[e]xperts are divided on whether Article 48 can be used to increase the membership of the European Union as the Scottish Government suggests';[44] (2) EU senior officials have rejected this route and have shown their preferences for Article 49;[45] (3) the UK government has described it as 'utterly implausible';[46] and (4) even in the unlikely event that this route was the chosen approach, Scotland would be dependent on the UK team during the negotiations, and it could not reasonably expect it 'to raise issues that would be to the detriment of the citizens of England, Wales and Northern Ireland. Key objectives identified made by the Scottish Government in its White Paper would not, therefore, be realised.'[47] The following explores both procedures in depth.

3.1 Opinions in Favour of the Article 48 TEU Procedure

As indicated, during the debate concerning EU membership for an independent Scotland, the UK government took the view that the preferred route is article

[43] Scottish Government, 'Scotland's Future' (2013) 220 <https://www.gov.scot/resource/0043/00439021.pdf> accessed 5 August 2022.

[44] House of Commons Scottish Affairs Committee, 'The Referendum on Separation for Scotland: Scotland's Membership of the EU' Twelfth Report of Session 2013–14, para 18 <https://publications.parliament.uk/pa/cm201314/cmselect/cmscotaf/1241/1241.pdf> accessed 3 August 2018.

[45] ibid.

[46] ibid para 26.

[47] ibid.

49 TEU, while the Scottish government voiced its preference for article 48 TEU. As noted above, legal experts are divided. Douglas-Scott explains that the view adopted by the UK government, Barroso, and Van Rompuy 'is not inevitable, and may not even be well-reasoned'.[48] She bases her reasoning in the *sui generis* nature of the EU, its distinctive new legal order, and its pragmatism.[49] She argues that the use of article 49 TEU would entail 'the risk that a newly independent Scotland [or Catalonia, Corsica, Veneto, etc] would be cast into the wilderness, its ties with the EU cut on the date of independence'.[50] In her opinion, article 48 TEU 'would be a form of internal enlargement for the EU, and in this way, Scotland's uninterrupted membership of the EU could be preserved'.[51] Avery also suggests that 'it would be in the interest of the EU to follow an "internal" procedure under Article 48 of the Treaty'.[52] Kenealy and MacLenan share a similar viewpoint, but admit that article 48 TEU entails difficulties, since it also requires the unanimous agreement of all existing EU Member States. They do not view article 48 TEU as a smooth and straightforward 'internal enlargement', unlike Douglas-Scott. However, they still prefer article 48 TEU route for the following reasons:

> We suggest that the process of treaty amendment would better reflect the general principles of the EU and the acquired rights of EU citizens. The Article 49 route would place Scotland, only because of the result of its democratic referendum, on the same footing as all other states outside of the EU. Whilst there would be no guarantees involved in the Article 48 route, it would (1) recognise that the situation of Scottish independence was qualitatively different from accession conventionally understood, and (2) offer a greater chance of successively transitioning Scotland to Member State status in time for its date of independence.[53]

[48] Sionaidh Douglas-Scott, 'How Easily Could an Independent Scotland Join the EU?' (2014) 46 University of Oxford Legal Research Papers 1, 7.

[49] ibid 8.

[50] ibid 24.

[51] ibid.

[52] Graham Avery, 'Could an independent Scotland join the EU?' (*European Policy Centre Policy Brief*, 28 May 2014) <https://www.epc.eu/en/Publications/Could-an-independent-Scotland~24e550> accessed 5 August 2022. What is also interesting to note about Avery and Douglas-Scott is that both admit the risk that the art 48 TEU route could encounter political mistrust among certain EU Member States with pro-independence movement tensions. Thus, Douglas-Scott distinguishes the Scottish case with unilateral declarations of independence and affirms that '[i]n such cases of unilateral independence, good faith negotiations with EU institutions and other member states, and use of Article 48 procedure, is unlikely to be possible'. Douglas-Scott (n 48) 24. Avery, in turn, considers that in this respect 'the case of Scotland is different from Kosovo or Catalonia, since the Scottish referendum is not unilateral but part of a constitutional process agreed by London ... To satisfy the concerns of Spain and others, the EU would reaffirm its respect for the constitutional arrangements of member states.' Avery (n 52). Thus, both authors underline the important difference outlined in Chapter 6 between unilateral (and unlawful) and consensual (and lawful) independence processes.

[53] Kenealy and MacLennan (n 5) 601.

The main assumption behind this approach is that European leaders tend to decide first what they want to do and only then they look for the legal path to proceed.[54] In any event, as stated, even if the article 48 route was to be followed, it also requires the unanimous acceptance by the other Member States. It is unthinkable to believe that the European Council would proceed with the procedure without such unanimity.[55]

3.2 Opinions in Favour of the Article 49 TEU Procedure

Tierney and Boyle consider that, although article 48 TEU 'provides a feasible route', it is 'more likely that Scotland will be required to make an application to join the European Union by way of the Article 49 of the Treaty on the European Union'.[56] This is the opinion of many other scholars when confronted with (1) secession within an EU Member State and (2) petition for EU accession after independence. For these scholars, there are various reasons to oppose the article 48 TEU procedure. For instance, the choice of legal instruments is not to be decided only by taking into account the political convenience of those concerned. In this regard, the *lex specialis*, among other reasons, suggests that the article 49 TEU procedure is the most appropriate route. Furthermore, the article 49 TEU route ensures application of the Copenhagen criteria, while article 48 TEU does not.

3.2.1 Legal choice and *lex specialis*

Closa underlines the fact that '[t]he choice of legal basis is not the free prerogative of EU agents'.[57] In effect, as the ECJ has held, 'the choice of legal basis for a Community measure must rest on objective factors amenable to judicial review, which include, in particular, the aim and content of the measure'.[58] According to the Court, it follows from this approach that if the treaty contains different provisions that could be capable of constituting the legal basis for the measure in question,

[54] Michael Keating, 'Would an Independent Scotland Be in the European Union?' in Charlie Jeffery and Ray Perman (eds), *Scotland's Decision: 16 Questions to Think about for the Referendum on 18 September* (Birlinn 2014) 46–49. The idea that EU pragmatism and flexibility will prevail should Catalonia become independent (assuming that some sort of internal accommodation will finally be adopted) has also been stressed by the Catalan Council for National Transitional. Consell Assessor per la Transició Nacional, *Les vies d'integració de Catalunya a la Unió Europea* (Catalan Government 2014) 13.

[55] Alberto López Basaguren, 'La independencia de Escocia en la Unión Europea. Los efectos de la secesión de territorios en la UE entre política y derecho' (2014) 33 Teoría y Realidad Constitucional 69, 87.

[56] Stephen Tierney and Katie Boyle, 'An Independent Scotland: The Road to Membership of the European Union' (*ESRC Scottish Centre on Constitutional Change Briefing Paper*, 20 August 2014) <https://www.centreonconstitutionalchange.ac.uk/publications/independent-scotland-road-membership-european-union> accessed 5 August 2022.

[57] Closa (n 9) 261.

[58] Case C-338/01 *Commission v Council* [2004] ECR I-4852, para 54.

one should invoke the more specific provision.[59] Basically, the ECJ is opting for the *lex specialis* criterion, a general principle of law: a provision governing a specific question like accession, article 49 TEU, should trump provisions dealing with more general issues like treaty amendments, article 48 TEU.

Piris explains that article 49, 'the only correct, necessary and sufficient basis',[60] has a threefold meaning: (1) to check if all the criteria for admission are met; (2) to negotiate the specific terms of accession; and (3) to adopt the necessary EU adjustments *ad intra*.[61] Likewise, Hillion points out that article 49 TEU is a *lex specialis*, since it sets forth the specific EU procedure for admitting a new State into the EU: 'irrespective of whether the aspirant comes from within or outside, its exclusive function in the system of the treaties is to alter the *state* composition of the EU by admitting a new member'.[62] By way of contrast, article 48 TEU has a distinct purpose, which is to allow existing Member States to modify the treaties: 'it is not purported to include new parties to the existing treaties, or to introduce the necessary legal changes to EU primary and secondary law, or transitional arrangements for making that inclusion possible'.[63] Murkens also admits that article 48, unlike article 49, 'was not designed to bring about the institutional changes needed to accommodate a new Member State'.[64] That is why relying on article 48 TEU is 'far from persuasive on technical legal grounds'.[65] As Closa affirms, '[p]lainly stated, Article 49 is the *lex specialis* regulating accession'.[66]

[59] ibid para 60.

[60] Jean Claude Piris, 'Political and Legal Aspects of Recent Regional Secessionist Trends in some EU Member States (I)' in Carlos Closa (ed), *Secession from a Member State and Withdrawal from the European Union* (CUP 2017) 86. Freixes Sanjuán shares the same view. Teresa Freixes Sanjuán, 'Secesión de Estados e integración en la Unión Europea. A propósito del debate sobre la permanencia en la Unión de Escocia y Cataluña como Estados segregados del Reino Unido y España' (2014) 2 Revista Jurídica de Catalunya 298, 305. See also Mar Campins Eritja, 'The European Union and the Secession of a Territory from a EU Member State' (2015) 2(XVII) Diritto Pubblico Comparato ed Europeo 479, 492–98.

[61] Piris, 'Political and Legal Aspects of Recent Regional Secessionist Trends in some EU Member States (I)' (n 60) 83.

[62] Christophe Hillion, 'Scotland and the EU' (*Verfassungsblog*, 15 September 2014) <https://verfassungsblog.de/scotland-eu-comment-christophe-hillion-2/> accessed 5 August 2022. The same argument is found in Nikos Skoutaris, 'On Brexit and Secession(s)' in Carlos Closa, Costanza Margiotta, and Giuseppe Martinico (eds), *Between Democracy and Law. The Amorality of Secession* (Routledge 2020) 202: 'In other words, if the Treaty on European Union is interpreted in accordance with the ordinary meaning to be given to its terms, following the well-established rule of Article 31(1) of the Vienna Convention on the Law of the Treaties, it would be difficult to justify the use of the generic provision on the amendment of the Treaties (Article 48 TEU) when there is a special provision regulation the accession of new Member States (Article 49 TEU).'

[63] Hillion (n 62).

[64] Jo E Murkens, 'Scotland and the EU: A Comment' (*UK Constitutional Law Association Blog*, 10 September 2014) https://ukconstitutionallaw.org/2014/09/10/debate-jo-murkens-scotland-and-the-eu-a-comment/ accessed 5 August 2022.

[65] ibid.

[66] Closa (n 9) 262.

3.2.2 Copenhagen criteria

Another reason to support the article 49 TEU procedure is through examination of the Copenhagen criteria. The presumption of fulfilment,[67] as explained in Chapter 6, should be ruled out. Therefore, the idea of an 'internal enlargement', or negotiations following article 48 TEU without the need to test whether the new State fulfils the accession criteria, seems unfounded and legally incorrect. Needless to say, the situation of a territory that has been applying EU law for decades cannot be completely compared with the situation of the Western Balkans countries, to name some of the current candidate countries. However, this does not mean that such territories, once in the way of acquiring statehood, will be exempted from the accession criteria.[68] For instance, the issues of the protection of minorities, or the good neighbourhood relations criterion, might be thorny issues for some new countries like Catalonia or Flanders.[69] As Piris states, '[a] new State is a new State. Nothing can establish that "by definition" a new State would be founded with the same values, have the same capabilities and be able to fulfil the necessary conditions to become a Member State of the EU in its own right.'[70]

Notwithstanding the above, it might transpire that even following article 49 TEU, the new State application could be fast-tracked, in the sense that accession negotiations could be facilitated or accelerated. In the words of Piris: '[l]egally, the fact that Catalonia and Scotland might both be able rapidly to fulfil the necessary conditions to become EU Member State could help accelerate the procedure, but could not dispense with following it'.[71] Since there is no exhaustive list of strictly defined Copenhagen criteria, 'the pragmatic approach of the European Council as regards accession conditions may result in new criteria, tailor-made for the applying newly independent states'.[72] In effect, as the ECJ recalled in *Mattheus v Doego* when referring to the accession provisions, the conditions of accession are to be drawn up by the applicant country and the EU Member States following negotiations: '[t]hus the legal conditions for such accession remain to be defined in the context of that procedure without its being possible to determine the content judicially in advance'.[73] Negotiations could start following a potential pro-independence vote within the territory and during the process of formally acquiring statehood,

[67] Given the current EU membership, the Catalan government assumes that the fulfilment of the Copenhagen criteria by the new Catalan Republic would be 'evident'. Consell Assessor per la Transició Nacional, *Les vies d'integració de Catalunya a la Unió Europea* (n 54) 51. The inaccuracy of this approach has been explained in Chapter 6, and in this chapter.

[68] Chamon and Van der Loo (n 35) 623.

[69] ibid. Although these requirements should not be overemphasized either, since if there is enough political will, the EU institutions will find the way to tone down the conditions, as the flexible approach to Cyprus illustrates.

[70] Piris, 'Political and Legal Aspects of Recent Regional Secessionist Trends in Some EU Member States (I)' (n 60) 84.

[71] ibid.

[72] Chamon and Van der Loo (n 35) 622.

[73] Case C-93/78 *Mattheus v Doego* [1978] ECR I- 2203, para 7.

so that formal independence and EU membership are achieved consecutively.[74] Furthermore, the possibility of the establishment of ad hoc and transitional measures to accommodate the secessionist entity cannot be ruled out. In this regard, a reverse Cyprus approach during the negotiations has been suggested,[75] by virtue of which EU law would still be applicable in the territory of the seceded entity, despite the fact that the new sovereign has not yet attained full membership.[76]

In sum, '[a]ccession via EU reform procedure (ie art 48 TEU) seems unfounded and legally incorrect, while the traditional procedure (ie art 49 TEU), emerges as the proper route'.[77] In any case, the key challenge of the accession process, which affects both procedures, is the fact that all Member States have to agree on the application. Needless to say, other EU Member States could have reasons to slow down the accession process, or create difficulties. Furthermore, some countries may require a nationwide referendum prior to ratification. Given the increased Euroscepticism in some EU countries, the ratification process might encounter difficulties, thus resulting in a 'No' vote in the ratification referendum, even if the rejection of the enlargement is not so much directed against the candidate country, but against the EU project as a whole.[78]

[74] There are some precedents of the EU negotiating with entities on their way to statehood like Kosovo (eg 2015 Stabilisation and Association agreement between the EU and the European Atomic Energy Community and Kosovo), or the Palestine Liberation Organization (eg 1997 Euro-Mediterranean Interim Association Agreement on trade and cooperation between the European Community, of the one part, and the Palestine Liberation Organization for the benefit of the Palestinian Authority of the West Bank and the Gaza Strip).

[75] Kai-Olaf Lang, 'Katalonien auf dem Weg in die Unabhängigkeit?' (2013) SWP-Deutsches Institut für Internationale Politik und Sicherheit Aktuell 8 <https://www.swp-berlin.org/fileadmin/contents/products/aktuell/2013A50_lng.pdf> accessed 5 August 2022. See, in the same vein, Cristina Fassone's proposal outlined earlier in this chapter. Fasone (n 42) 65.

[76] In fact, the applicability of EU law depends entirely on the political will of the seceded entity. For instance, art 10.2 of the Law 20/2017, of 8 September, on Juridical Transition, passed by the Catalan Parliament weeks before the unsuccessful Catalan unilateral declaration of independence, sets forth that EU law shall also continue to be applied in Catalonia after independence. This law was the legal framework that had to prevail over the current Spanish one should a majority of Catalans vote in favour of independence in the 1 October referendum. A completely different discussion is required as to the extent to which the institutions of the new entity and its inhabitants will benefit from the rights derived from EU law and from those EU provisions that require EU intervention or EU Member States reciprocity. English version of the Catalan law available at <http://exteriors.gencat.cat/web/.content/00_ACTUALITAT/notes_context/Law-20_2017-on-Juridical-Transition.pdf> accessed 5 August 2022.

[77] Closa (n 9) 263.

[78] Something similar to what occurred during the 2004 Constitutional Treaty ratification process: 'as the number of referenda grows, so do the chances of rejection in one or more member states. And the reason for rejection would not, it is respectfully submitted, be linked to any specific provision of the new constitution, nor even to its overall material content. I am arguing, rather, that such rejection may be linked to extraneous issues rooted in national politics, to a general "anti-Europe" sentiment, and, most intriguingly, to something other than the content of the new Treaty of Rome but rather to the very idea of a European constitution.' Joseph HH Weiler, 'On the Power of the Word: Europe's Constitutional Iconography' (2005) 3(3) International Journal of Constitutional Law 173, 178.

4. EU Citizenship After Independence Following Secession

A detailed legal analysis of the issues that emerge after successful secession (like State continuity and succession of States or the appropriate route towards accession) would not be complete without examining nationality issues that will have to be negotiated between the rump State and the new independent sovereign State. The discussion about nationality issues after independence fits necessarily into the current chapter because it is the one dealing with successful secession attempts (the appropriate temporal momentum for nationality discussions). However, some of the findings of the following pages (see Section 3.2.2) in fact, sustain the overall argument of the book, explained in detail in Chapter 6. In effect, it will be shown that the doctrine of EU citizenship cannot by itself engender automatic membership of the EU for an independent country born out of a region within a EU Member State. This supports the thesis of the book: namely, that EU law does not possess an autonomous approach to secession, but a deferential one towards the constitutional legal orders of EU Member States, provided that certain conditions posed by EU law itself (respect for values enshrined in art 2 TEU) are fulfilled.

Nationality law is not just another area of the legal order. It has traditionally been considered a domain reserved for States, as it is a highly politically sensitive matter. As D'Oliveira explains, '[t]he power to determine who belongs to a particular state, to define a state's body of citizens, is essential to the existence and the identity of the state'.[79] Indeed, '[a] member state's citizens are an integrating and essential component of the sovereign statehood of the member state'.[80] Needless to say, nationals of the rump State will maintain their nationality and, therefore, their EU citizenship. But what would occur with the nationals of the newborn State?

In the event of a quickly negotiated EU access and a short interim/transitional period the situation does not give rise to many questions. However, in the event of a long non-EU membership period, different scenarios arise: (1) the States concerned might negotiate a dual nationality regime, which would guarantee the maintenance of EU citizenship to nationals residing in a third country; but (2) the States concerned might also reach an agreement to grant a right of option, and, therefore, in the event of choosing the nationality of the newborn State, that could lead to the dispossession of the nationality, and therefore EU citizenship, of the continuing State inhabitants. As stated, the outcome of the negotiations is purely political and conjectural. But the key legal question in the case at hand is the extent to which nationality law, usually governed by internal law, is constrained by international and EU law? Specifically, would the withdrawal of national citizenship rights, and as a result the withdrawal of EU citizenship, violate international law and EU law?

[79] Ulli Jessurun d'Oliveira, 'Decoupling Nationality and Union Citizenship?' (2011) 7 European Coinstitutional Law Review 138, 148.

[80] ibid.

It is my assumption that, despite some ECJ case law (eg mainly *Rottmann* and *Ruiz Zambrano*),[81] EU Member States still hold an important degree of autonomy when it comes to define citizenship and nationality law, particularly in a situation like a secession crisis. This is, I believe, one of the conclusions one might draw from more recent ECJ case law (addressed in Section 4.2.2) following the challenges brought by British citizens residing in the UK and abroad who argued that UK's withdrawal violated their rights as EU citizens.

In any event, and although nationality law is essentially governed by internal law, States are also constrained by public international law and by EU law. These constraints and, particularly, the impact of EU citizenship when it comes to secession will be considered below.

4.1 Public International Law Constraints

In relation to public international law, four international instruments merit attention, the relevance of which has been accepted by the ECJ.[82] First, the Universal Declaration of Human Rights (UDHR, 1948): Article 15 recognizes that '[e]veryone has the right to a nationality' and '[n]o one shall be arbitrarily deprived of his nationality nor denied the right to change his nationality'. Thus, the dispossession of nationality should not be arbitrary and should not lead to statelessness. Second, the ILC's Articles on the Nationality of Natural Persons in Relation to the Succession of States:[83] Article 4 of the text encourages States to prevent persons from becoming stateless as a result of succession of States. Article 24 covers the situation that would result in the event of secession, since it deals with separation of part or parts of the territory. It sets forth that in general terms:

> When part or parts of the territory of a State separate from that State and form one or more successor States while the predecessor State [rump State] continues to exist, a successor State [seceded entity] shall, unless otherwise indicated by the exercise of a right of option, attribute its nationality to (a) persons concerned having their habitual residence in its territory.

Thus, in principle, those residing in the seceded territory, unless there is a negotiated right of option (foreseen in art 26) or an agreement over a dual nationality

[81] Case C-135/08 *Janko Rottmann v Freistaat Bayern* [2010] ECR I-01449 and Case C-34/09 *Gerardo Ruiz Zambrano v Office national de l'emploi (ONEM)* [2009] ECR I-01177.

[82] Case C-135/08 *Janko Rottmann v Freistaat Bayern* (n 81) para 14.

[83] The Articles on Nationality of Natural Persons in Relation to the Succession of States were adopted by the ILC at its fifty-first session, in 1999. By resolution 55/153 of 12 December 2000, the General Assembly took note of the Articles, the text of which was annexed to the resolution, inviting governments to take into account, as appropriate, the provision contained therein in dealing with the relevant issues <http://legal.un.org/avl/ha/annprss/annprss.html> accessed 5 August 2022.

regime, will acquire the nationality of the newborn State. Article 25 contends that rump States shall withdraw their nationality from persons qualified to acquire the nationality of the seceded State. However, rump States will have to make sure before dispossession that those persons have previously acquired a new nationality. Third, the Convention on the Reduction of Statelessness (1961),[84] which attempts to reduce statelessness: article 8 sets forth that States 'shall not deprive people of their nationality so as to render them stateless'. However, withdrawal of nationality is accepted where nationality has been acquired by misrepresentation or fraud. Fourth, the European Convention on Nationality (1997):[85] this upholds the same principle that 'statelessness shall be avoided' and it only allows for one exception: in the case of acquisition of the nationality of the State Party by means of fraudulent conduct, false information or concealment of any relevant fact attributable to the applicant.

Although, as explained in the footnotes, the legal binding force of all these international instruments is contested and dubious (except for the UDHR), it would seem that in general terms and as regards to our main issue: (1) withdrawing nationality is not prohibited by international law, provided that it does not lead to statelessness,[86] which in the context at hand would mean that a rump State will not violate international law if it decides to dispossess those citizens residing in the seceded entity from their nationality as long as the persons concerned have opted for acquiring the nationality of the new entity; (2) there might be an agreement between the rump State and the seceded entity to grant a right of option to the citizens concerned; however, there is no international duty to do so; and (3) there is no international obligation to grant dual nationality. This is as far as public international law can take us. The constraints imposed are very limited and offer a wide variety of options for the negotiations between the States concerned.

4.2 European Union Law Constraints

We have seen that public international law sets some constraints on States when it comes to nationality law. Such constraints, however, are not deemed to be stifling. EU law might, however, impose more far-reaching constraints. This was the

[84] The Convention on the Reduction of Statelessness is a UN multilateral treaty signed in 1961 and entering into force in 1975. It has been ratified by 11 EU Member States. However, Spain, Portugal, Italy, Belgium, Poland, and France have not ratified it.

[85] The European Convention on Nationality is a comprehensive convention of the Council of Europe dealing with the law of nationality. It was signed in 1997 and it entered into force in 2000. It has been ratified by 20 European States. Spain, the UK, France, Italy, Greece, and Poland are among those countries which have not ratified the Convention. In fact, Spain and the UK have not even signed the treaty.

[86] In effect, as has been explained, '[i]n international law, the most important principle concerns protection against statelessness occurring as a result of the creation of a new state'. Jo Shaw, 'Unions and Citizens: Membership Status and Political Rights in Scotland, the UK and the EU' in Carlos Closa (ed), *Secession from a Member State and Withdrawal from the European Union* (CUP 2017) 164–65.

interpretation of some scholars in the light of some early ECJ decisions. It will be shown, though, that this interpretation needs to be nuanced. In Sections 4.2.1–4.2.3, we will be dealing with the question of the extent of the discretion available to the Member States to determine who their nationals are. Or as Advocate General Maduro put it:

> In so far as citizenship of the European Union, which depends, admittedly, on enjoyment of the status of national of a Member State, is established by the Treaty, can the powers of the Member States to lay down the conditions for the acquisition and loss of nationality still be exercised without any right of supervision for Community law?[87]

4.2.1 EU treaty provisions

In effect, the point at issue here is the extent to which the EU citizenship regime, created in the 1992 Maastricht Treaty, constrains EU Member States' autonomy to govern nationality law as regards secession. Article 20(1) of the Treaty on the Functioning of the European Union (TFEU) provides that 'every person holding the nationality of a Member State shall be a citizen of the Union. Citizenship of the Union shall be additional to and not replace national citizenship'. Union citizenship is presented 'as being a dependent variable of the possession of the nationality of a member state'.[88] One cannot become an EU citizen without first being a national of one of its Member States. Declaration no 2 attached to the Maastricht Treaty established:

> The Conference declares that, wherever in the Treaty establishing the European Community reference is made to nationals of the Member States, the question whether an individual possesses the nationality of the Member State shall be settled *solely* by reference to the national law of the Member State concerned[89] [emphasis added].

With this declaration, EU Member States underlined their prominence in designing nationality law. Furthermore, the Commission has systematically adopted the view that nationality law is a matter exclusively to be governed by the Member States and, therefore, it has refused to make substantial statements on EU Member States' nationality law, because it has claimed to lack competence to do so.[90] In 1992 the European Council also recalled that:

[87] Case C-135/08 *Janko Rottmann v Freistaat Bayern* (n 81), Opinion of AG Poiares Maduro.
[88] D'Oliveira (n 79) 147.
[89] OJ 1992 C 191, p 98.
[90] D'Oliveira (n 79) 145.

> [T]he citizenship of the Union gives nationals of the Member States *additional* rights and protection ... *They do not in any way take the place of national citizenship*. The question whether an individual possesses the nationality of a Member State will be settled solely by reference to the national law of the Member State concerned [emphasis added].[91]

EU Member States were thereby trying to underline the additional character of EU citizenship: EU citizenship is dependent on the nationality of the Member States. Thus, in principle, if secession means dispossession of national citizenship, which is not necessarily the case, since the rump State and the new sovereign might accept a dual nationality regime, then it would also mean dispossession of EU citizenship. Or as Medina points out, assuming there is no dual nationality regime in place: '[i]f a part of a Member State secedes, their citizens would lose their EU citizenship', for 'EU citizenship is vicarious to national citizenship'.[92] EU officials have also been clear in this regard. As explained in Chapter 5, in July 2012, the Commission was asked whether in case of secession, citizens would immediately lose their status as EU citizens and the resultant rights and obligations. The Commission stated that 'in accordance with Article 20 of the Treaty on the Functioning of the European Union (TFEU), EU citizenship is additional to and does not replace national citizenship (that is, the citizenship of an EU Member State)'.[93] However, some authors have contended that ECJ decisions might have altered this approach. The ECJ has constantly repeated that 'Union citizenship is destined to be the fundamental status of nationals of the Member States'.[94] What exactly does this mean in the context of the effect of EU citizenship on secession?

4.2.2 ECJ case law

In *Micheletti*, a case involving a dual national Argentine-Italian dentist who wanted to practise in Spain, the Court considered the degree of latitude of the Member States to organize their laws concerning nationality. The ECJ explained that '[u]nder international law, it is for each Member State, *having due regard to Community law*, to lay down the conditions for the acquisition and loss of nationality'[95] (emphasis added). The Court wished to emphasize that prominence over a domain, in the form of Member States' internal legislation governing nationality

[91] OJ 1992 C 348, p 1.

[92] Manuel Medina Ortega, 'The Political Rights of EU Citizens' in Carlos Closa (ed), *Secession from a Member State and Withdrawal from the European Union* (CUP 2017) 147.

[93] Question for written answer by Mara Bizzotto (EFD) to the Commission, 25 July 2012, E-007453/2012 <http://www.europarl.europa.eu/sides/getAllAnswers.do?reference=E-2012-007453&language=EN> accessed 5 August 2022.

[94] Case C-184/99 *Grzelczyk v Centre public d'aide sociale d'Ottignies-Louvain-la-Neuve* [2002] ECR I-6193, para 31.

[95] Case C-369/90 *Mario Vicente Micheletti and others/Delegación del Gobierno en Cantabria* [1992] ECR I-4258, para 10.

law, does not preclude influence of EU law. Although *Micheletti* was a landmark case, the decisions that are particularly relevant in our context are *Rottmann* and *Ruiz Zambrano*.

In *Rottmann*, a case involving an Austrian national who had been dispossessed of Austrian nationality after acquiring German citizenship, which was later withdrawn, it was 'clear that the ECJ [wa]s willing to challenge member states' autonomy in nationality matters'.[96] The ECJ decided to discuss openly the indirect influence of EU law on the nationality laws of the EU Member States. Although the ECJ had already sent signals about the limits placed by EU citizenship on the EU Member States' autonomy in previous decisions,[97] in *Rottmann* the Court expressly clarified the following:

> [T]he situation of a citizen of the Union who, like the applicant in the main proceedings, is faced with a decision withdrawing his naturalisation, adopted by the authorities of one Member State, and placing him, after he has lost the nationality of another Member State that he originally possessed, in a position capable of causing him to lose the status conferred by Article 17 EC and the rights attaching thereto falls, by reason of its nature and its consequences, within the ambit of European Union law.[98]

In other words, the 'loss of the newly acquired member state nationality consequently means loss of Union citizenship'.[99] And the Court found that such a situation involving loss of Union citizenship falls within the scope of EU law. It has, therefore, become clear that revocation of EU citizenship, as opposed to its initial granting, is a matter of interest to EU law.[100] The ECJ concluded that while EU Member States have the power to lay down the conditions for the acquisition and loss of nationality, they must take into account the following:

> [I]n respect of citizens of the Union, the exercise of that power, in so far as it affects the rights conferred and protected by the legal order of the Union, as is in

[96] Gerard René de Groot and Anja Seling, 'The Consequences of the Rottmann Judgment on Member State Autonomy—The European Court of Justice's Avant-Gardism in Nationality Matters' (2011) 7 European Constitutional Law Review 150, 150.

[97] Although the decision was labelled as a 'milestone' in the area of nationality law, René de Groot also argues that 'the judgement cannot be considered as very surprising, or as coming "out of the blue" and based solely on the ECJ's creativity ... the active stance of the Court with regard to shaping the concept of Union citizenship was already clear in cases such as Baumbast (C-413/99), Martínez-Sala (C-85/96), Grzelczyk (C-184/99), Garcia Avello (C-148/02)'. De Groot and Seling (n 96) 151.

[98] Case C-135/08 *Janko Rottmann v Freistaat Bayern* (n 80) para 42.

[99] De Groot and Seling (n 96) 153.

[100] Athanassiou and Shaelou remind us that in *Rottmann* the ECJ 'distinguished the situation of the applicant to that of the applicant in *Kaur* ... where a third country national did not meet the definition of a national of a given Member State and could not therefore as such be deprived of the rights deriving from the status of Union citizen, which he had never enjoyed in the first place'. Athanassiou and Shaelou (n 2) 355.

> particular the case of a decision withdrawing naturalisation such as that at issue in the main proceedings, is amenable to judicial review carried out in the light of European Union law.[101]

In exercising this judicial review, the Court found that a decision withdrawing naturalization because of deception[102] is a legitimate reason of public interest:

> In this regard, it is legitimate for a Member State to wish to protect the special relationship of solidarity and good faith between it and its nationals and also the reciprocity of rights and duties, which form the bedrock of the bond of nationality.[103]

The Court noted that this was in line with public international law. However, it also held that it is 'for the national court to ascertain whether the withdrawal decision at issue in the main proceedings observes the principle of proportionality'.[104] Thus, the question that EU law asks is the extent to which the withdrawing or dispossession of nationality can be considered proportionate. This is one of the relevant questions that we should be asking ourselves when considering secession, EU law, and dispossession of nationality: is it proportionate to dispossess nationality from millions of current citizens who have opted for a new nationality in the event of secession?

However, before answering the question about the proportionality of nationality dispossession in case of secession, it is important to consider *Ruiz Zambrano*, since this case further limited the autonomy of Member States by prohibiting the application of national immigration laws to a significant group of third-country nationals. In effect, the ECJ claimed that the treaty 'precludes national measures which have the effect of depriving citizens of the Union of the genuine enjoyment of the substance of the rights conferred by virtue of their status as citizens of the Union'.[105] In the case at hand, the Court held that article 20 TFEU

> precludes a Member State from refusing a third country national upon whom his minor children, who are European Union citizens, are dependent, a right of residence in the Member State of residence and nationality of those children, and from refusing to grant a work permit to that third country national, in so far as such decisions deprive those children of the genuine enjoyment of the substance of the rights attaching to the status of European Union citizen.[106]

[101] Case C-135/08 *Janko Rottmann v Freistaat Bayern* (n 81) para 48.

[102] Janko Rottmann had obtained German nationality without revealing that he was wanted in Austria as a suspect for a professional offence. When the German authorities heard of it, his naturalization was revoked.

[103] Case C-135/08 *Janko Rottmann v Freistaat Bayern* (n 81) para 51.

[104] ibid para 55.

[105] Case C-34/09 *Gerardo Ruiz Zambrano v Office national de l'emploi* (n 81) paras 42–44.

[106] ibid para 45.

It could be argued that, as in *Rottmann*, the Court considered that 'European citizenship provisions by their very nature fall outwith the "purely internal" situation'.[107] And, as it had previously done in *Rottmann*, 'the Court [took] the determinative step of recognising the unique "nature" of European citizenship rights as giving rise to the requisite link with Union law'.[108] *Ruiz Zambrano* has been read as a decision that 'constitutes a highly significant encroachment into an area previously outwith the scope of Union regulation'.[109] Clearly, 'national citizenship law is not entirely independent of EU law, and should respect its principles to the extent that it can have an impact on the enjoyment by individuals of their EU law-derived rights'.[110] More importantly, the ECJ has moved beyond its classic cross-border thinking. There is no need to establish a cross-border situation for EU citizenship to protect the substance of the rights of the Member States' nationals.[111]

The salient issue here is the extent to which these cases impact the discussion on EU law and secession.[112] For some, the effect is profound. Given the position of the ECJ in *Rottmann* and *Ruiz Zambrano*, and bearing in mind the importance placed by the EU Charter of Fundamental Rights to individuals, who lie at the heart of EU activities, O'Neill argues the following:

> [R]ather than analyse the matter from the classic viewpoint of public international law—which recognizes only States and international organisations are the subject and object of international rights and obligations—EU law requires to look at the issue [secession within the EU] from the viewpoint of the individual citizen.[113]

107 Anja Lansbergen and Nina Miller, 'Court of Justice of the European Union. European Citizenship Rights in Internal Situations: An Ambiguous Revolution? Decision of 8 March 2011, Case C-34/09 Gerardo Ruiz Zambrano v Office national de l'emploi (ONEM)' (2011) 7(2) European Constitutional Law Review 287, 292.

108 ibid 293.

109 ibid 301.

110 Athanassiou and Shaelou (n 2) 354.

111 Dimitry Kochenov, 'The Right to Have What Rights? EU Citizenship in Need of Clarification' (2013) 19(4) European Law Journal 502, 508.

112 The discussion about the concrete influence of these rulings goes beyond the scope of this chapter, and indeed this book. Suffice it to say that the Court was also criticized for engaging in a cherry-picking exercise and lack of predictability since, in subsequent decisions, like *McCarthy*, and despite a similar set of circumstances, the Court denied the applicant the benefits granted to Ruiz Zambrano. Kenealy and MacLennan (n 5) 609. See also Kochenov (n 111).

113 Aidan O'Neill, 'A Quarrel in a Faraway Country?: Scotland, Independence and the EU' (*Eutopialaw*, 14 November 2011) <https://eutopialaw.wordpress.com/2011/11/14/685/> accessed 5 August 2022. O'Neill's argumentation, without further elucidation, continues by affirming that, if faced with the question of secession within the EU, based on the previous arguments about EU citizenship being the fundamental status of nationals of EU Member States, the ECJ's most likely position would be to accept the automatic accession of the seceded entity. This is, however, very unlikely. Douglas Scott also rejects the argument: 'To be sure, the doctrine of EU citizenship cannot by itself engender automatic membership of the EU for an independent Scotland. It would be necessary for the treaties to be amended, at the least according to the procedures in Art 48.' See Douglas-Scott (n 48) 19. So do Kenealy and McLennan: '[w]e conclude that no matter how it is examined, the notion that EU citizenship could be in some way generative of EU membership for Scotland is far-fetched'. See Kenealy and MacLennan (n 5) 602. Closa is also critical of the argument: 'Most perspicuous scholars have rightly indicated that

Douglas Scott shares this same view:

> [T]he critical question here is whether the Court of Justice would consider that Scottish independence deprived Scottish citizens of their acquired rights as EU citizens. Given the importance accorded by the Court to the primacy of EU law, and EU citizenship as being 'the fundamental status of nationals of the Member States', it is unlikely that the Court would hold this to be the case.[114]

In sum, these authors consider that a national measure from the rump State that rejected a dual nationality regime, or directly dispossessed those residing in the newborn State of their previous nationality (provided they acquired the nationality of the new seceded entity), would violate EU law, for such a measure would lead to the dispossession of EU citizenship.

This reasoning can, however, be questioned. We should refrain from providing EU citizenship with a constitutional significance far beyond that which has been admitted by the ECJ. In *Rottmann* the Court dealt specifically with the lawfulness of the withdrawal of citizenship, and the ECJ admitted its lawfulness provided that the dispossession satisfies a proportionality test. Is it reasonable to assume as proportionate a national measure that consists of the dispossession of nationality to those who have opted for the nationality of the newborn State out of secession? I contend that such a measure should be considered proportionate and, therefore, lawful under EU law. One must recall that citizenship laws 'generally set the prima facie boundaries of political demos, in the sense of providing—in most cases—the preliminary determination of who can vote and who can stand for election, especially in national elections'.[115] As Kenealy and MacLennan stress, we should not forget the following:

EU citizenship is not sufficient to guarantee or generate EU membership for a particular territory.' Closa (n 9) 257. Also, Athanassiou and Shaelou, when referring to the extent of the legitimate expectations of the nationals of a newly created state entity, admit 'the absence of any right of automatic accession of the seceding entity to the EU'. See Athanassiou and Shaelou (n 2) 357. The reasoning is also dismissed by Crawford and Boyle (n 4) paras 178–80. Lastly, it should be pointed out that 'a breakaway from the mother state also means a breakaway from the EU, since any subnational entity that forms part of the EU does so by virtue of being an integral part of the national Member State. From the perspective of EU law, it is only this national Member State that exists. The fact that the regional entities making up this state, no matter how autonomous they may be under national public law, do not have special status under EU law is a recurring feature in the case-law of the Court of Justice.' Chamon and Van der Loo (n 35) 619. The ECJ has, moreover, held that '[i]t is not possible for the European Communities to comprise a greater number of Member States than the number of States between which they were established'. Case C-95/97 *Région wallonne v Commission of the European Communities* [1997] ECR I-1787, para 6.

[114] Douglas-Scott (n 48) 19.
[115] Shaw (n 86) 160.

> The objective of citizenship is to create a determinate class of persons who owe a duty of loyalty to the state.... It is submitted that, where a class of individuals vote to secede from a state, withdrawing citizenship from that class is a proportionate course of action on the part of that state. It is therefore submitted that, notwithstanding the question as to whether or not the Scottish case constitutes a purely internal situation, the withdrawal of citizenship from Scots nationals would nonetheless satisfy the proportionality standard required by the Court in *Rottmann*.[116]

This view is echoed by Closa, who states that 'any proposed obligation to grant citizenship to several million people now facing life as citizens of an independent state could well be considered disproportionate'.[117] Furthermore, as Piris notes, consistent practice in international relations has been that where citizens of the newborn State have new nationality, this leads to removal of nationality by the rump State.[118] Nothing precludes rump EU Member States from offering a dual nationality regime to those residing in the seceded entity. However, no law can force them to do so. In fact, article 9 of the Law 20/2017, of 8 September, on Juridical Transition, passed by the Catalan Parliament weeks before the unsuccessful Catalan unilateral declaration of independence, admitted the need to negotiate with Spain the dual nationality of the new Catalan Republic:

> 1. The attribution of Catalan nationality does not require the renunciation of Spanish or any other nationality.
> 2. In the briefest time frame possible, the Catalan Government will seek negotiations with the Spanish government in order to draw up a treaty on nationality.[119]

[116] Kenealy and MacLennan (n 5) 610.

[117] Closa (n 9) 257.

[118] Piris, 'Political and Legal Aspects of Recent Regional Secessionist Trends in Some EU Member States (II)' (n 1) 94.

[119] English version of the Catalan law available at <http://exteriors.gencat.cat/web/.content/00_ACTUALITAT/notes_context/Law-20_2017-on-Juridical-Transition.pdf> accessed 5 August 2022. Another line of reasoning that has been echoed by some Catalan scholars is to invoke current Spanish legislation (mainly the Spanish Constitution, section 11.2), which provides that '[n]o person of Spanish birth may be deprived of his or her nationality'. Based on this constitutional provision, some authors have argued that in the event of secession, Catalans (who are Spanish citizens by birth), even if they opt for Catalan nationality, cannot be deprived of Spanish nationality. Mariona Illamola, 'Nacionalitat catalana i/o nacionalitat espanyola. I l'europea?' 2017 (25) Revista d'Estudis Autonòmics i Federals 93, 104. See also Eduard Segarra, 'Nacionalidad catalana' in Eduard Segarra (ed), *¿Existe el Derecho a Decidir?* (Tibidabo Ediciones 2014) 37. Therefore, they will continue to enjoy all the rights attached to EU citizenship. However, this argument seems to ignore an important point. It is difficult to imagine that in the event of Catalan secession, a major constitutional disruption, Spain would not amend its Constitution to accommodate the new situation. In this scenario, nothing prevents Spanish constitutional lawmakers from amending that specific provision. Therefore, relying on the current legal state of affairs seems a risky enterprise.

Moreover, I believe that the ECJ itself has nuanced the interpretation offered at *Rottmann* and *Ruiz Zambrano* in the more recent cases of *Wightman*, *Préfet du Gers*, and *Silver*.[120] These cases have been brought by British nationals deprived of their EU citizenship following Brexit. Some of the arguments advanced by the applicants were that such a loss infringes the principles of legal certainty and proportionality, arguments that could also be used by nationals of a new seceded entity. However, the ECJ has been very clear. For instance, in *Préfet du Gers*, a case involving a British national living in France and removed from the electoral roll of her city and therefore unable to take part in the French municipal elections, the ECJ Grand Chamber stated that, since the citizenship of the EU requires possession of the nationality of a Member State, 'the authors of the Treaties thus established an inseparable and exclusive link between possession of the nationality of a Member State and not only the acquisition, but also the retention, of the status of a citizen of the Union' (para 48). Second, since the UK made a sovereign choice to leave the EU, the UK is no longer a Member State and 'UK nationals no longer hold the nationality of a Member State, but that of a third State' (para 56). And 'possession of the nationality of a Member State is an essential condition for a person to be able to acquire and retain the status of citizen of the Union and to benefit fully from the rights attaching to that status. The loss of nationality of a Member State therefore entails, for the person concerned, the automatic loss of his or her status as a citizen of the Union' (para 57). Very importantly, the Court established that '[i]t is irrelevant, in that regard, that United Kingdom nationals have previously exercised their right to reside in a Member State' (para 58).

Is this outcome disproportionate? The Court simply argued that the loss of EU citizenship 'is the automatic result of a sovereign decision made by a former Member State' (para 59). And, immediately, the Court distinguished Brexit from the earlier case law previously outlined (eg *Rottmann*): '[t]he cases in which the Court set out the obligation to carry out an individual examination of the proportionality of the consequences of the loss of Union citizenship concerned specific situations falling within the scope of EU law, where a Member State had withdrawn its nationality from individual persons, pursuant to a legislative measure of that Member State' (para 62). Therefore, concludes the ECJ, '[t]he case-law arising from those various judgments cannot therefore be applied to a situation such as that in the main proceedings' (para 62).

The latest decision, *Silver*, handed down on 15 June 2023, confirms the line of reasoning already outlined both in *Wightman* and *Préfet du Gers*. What does this case law tell us? As Steve Peers pointed out, the ECJ has made clear that EU citizenship is not a status conferred upon individuals, but a status linked to a State's

[120] Case C-621/18 *Wightman* [2018] ECLI 999; Case C-673/20 *Préfet du Gers* [2022] ECLI 449; Case 499/21 P *Silver* [2023] ECLI 479.

membership of the EU.[121] The Court follows a very simple linguistic interpretation of the treaties: EU citizenship is conferred upon nationals of Member States, the UK is no longer a Member State and therefore UK nationals are no longer EU citizens. The ECJ leaves out of its reasoning the influence of any other principles. It is my understanding that in case of secession, the ECJ would follow this same interpretation (unless there is an agreement to establish an interim period or/and a fast-track accession process): becoming an independent State, or a third State, results from a sovereign choice and the loss of EU citizenship is an automatic consequence of that decision.

Again, the absence of an automatic right to EU citizenship does not preclude the establishment of a transitional period that mitigates the effects of the dispossession:

> The absence of an automatic right to EU citizenship (the existence of which would imply the continuing enjoyment of the rights deriving therefrom), does not necessarily mean that, in the interim period between secession and accession to the EU, the nationals of a newly created state entity would not have a legitimate expectation to the survival of certain aspects of their former EU Citizenship rights. What it does, however, mean is that these expectations can only be given effect through negotiations, involving the rump Member State and other EU Member States, on the one hand, and the seceding state entity, on the other, informed by the need to avert some of the adverse consequences, for individuals, of the act of secession.[122]

In effect, any agreement as regards the interim period will depend on the goodwill of the different parties involved, since we would, otherwise be faced with 'secession a la carte'.[123]

In conclusion, it appears that in a secession scenario the inhabitants of the new State born out of secession cannot oppose the possible withdrawal of the rump State nationality and, consequently, the dispossession of EU citizenship. Or to put it differently: 'the enjoyment by the inhabitants of the newly created state entity of EU citizenship cannot be automatic'.[124] It will depend on the negotiations between

[121] Steve Peers, 'It's the end—but the moment has been prepared for: the CJEU confirms that UK citizens have lost EU citizenship' (*EU Law Analysis*, 9 June 2022) <http://eulawanalysis.blogspot.com/2022/06/its-end-but-moment-has-been-prepared.html> accessed 8 August 2023.

[122] Athanassiou and Shaelou (n 2) 359.

[123] Medina also shares this approach when he admits that a transitional status for residents of the seceding territory could be considered: 'This could have been the case for the citizens of Scotland, as the referendum for secession was negotiated in a friendly manner between the governments of Scotland and the UK. In the spirit of friendly relations between a rump UK State and a seceding Scotland, the UK could have been expected to facilitate the entry of an independent Scotland in the EU. If the citizens of Scotland had been left outside the EU for a short period pending the formal admission of Scotland as a new Member, it would have made sense to establish transitional arrangements to maintain their rights as EU citizens in the interim.' Medina Ortega (n 92) 151.

[124] Athanassiou and Shaelou (n 2) 358–59.

the States concerned. It is for this reason that the constraints on EU Member States imposed by public international law and EU law are only of limited effect.

5. The Hypothetical Scenario of an Independent Scotland or a Reunified Ireland After Brexit

On 23 June 2016, a slight majority of British voters (52%) decided to leave the EU. However, in Scotland and Northern Ireland the results differed. In Scotland 62 per cent voted to remain in the EU, while in Northern Ireland 56 per cent did so. Whether Brexit might trigger further territorial changes in the UK (namely, Scottish independence and the reunification of Ireland respectively) remains under a question mark and, therefore, the following pages contain material that is necessarily highly speculative and conjectural.

In Scotland, although there was no initial post-Brexit bounce in support for independence, it now seems that the situation has evolved and there is a strong case for a second independence referendum, as discussed more in depth in Chapter 4. In the event of Scottish independence, the new independent country will face a unique situation: it will become an independent State, a third country vis a vis the EU, but with a long history within it. Should an independent Scotland follow the same type of accession procedure (ie art 49 TEU) as any other third country? Are there reasons to believe that Scotland could receive special treatment? The legal arguments developed in this chapter that favour the route of article 49 TEU instead of the arguably easier option of article 48 TEU hold valid in the case of a future independent Scotland. If today there is certain consensus among scholars that, for instance, an independent Catalonia should follow the requirements established in article 49 TEU in the event of EU accession, there are no reasons to maintain that an independent new State (ie Scotland) out of a third country (ie the UK) should not be subject to those requirements. Needless to say, as Skoutaris notes, the Member States, as Masters of the treaties, could always amend the treaties in order to provide for an easier accession procedure,[125] but such amendment, again, requires a unanimous consensus.[126]

[125] Skoutaris, 'On Brexit and Secession(s)' (n 62) 203.

[126] When referring to Scottish accession to the EU, there has always been uncertainty surrounding the requirement of unanimity: 'with Scotland being a small country that had already been inside the EU, meeting its rules, a veto is unlikely—unless, as has often been suggested, Spain might do so, in order not to give any encouragement to Catalan independence'. However, as the same author concedes, 'if Scotland achieved independence through a legal and constitutional process agreed with the UK, there is unlikely to be an EU veto for that reason (as some Spanish politicians have also said)'. Kirsty Hughes, 'Brexit, Scottish Independence and Leaving a Union' (2019) 7 Policy Paper Scottish Centre on European Relations, 11 <https://fedtrust.co.uk/brexit-scottish-independence-and-leaving-a-union-lessons-to-learn/> accessed 5 August 2022.

Debates around Scottish independence have to deal with many difficult questions,[127] including legal ones concerning the organization of a second referendum on independence, but from an EU law perspective the uncertainties around membership have been diminished. It seems evident that an independent Scotland would join the EU through article 49 TEU. At the same time, it also seems clear that even if EU institutions will not publicly encourage Scottish independence, once (and if) it occurs lawfully, it will be in the political interest of the EU institutions and EU Member States to speed up the process of Scottish EU membership as much as possible. I am not implying here that Scottish EU membership would be an easy and smooth process, for the Scottish–English border, that is, another external EU border,[128] would be a source of many concerns and negotiations. But the initial position of EU law, at least, stands clear: Scotland will have to be treated as a third country asking for membership.[129]

As for Northern Ireland, British withdrawal effects (particularly the re-imposition of a hard land-border) could trigger the territorial enlargement of an EU Member State, the Republic of Ireland. It has been argued that:

> [T]he UK withdrawal creates a set of conditions for Northern Ireland that will weaken the capacity of the political system to maintain peace and build economic development. The result of the referendum vote alone indicated that the internal political divisions in Northern Ireland are being reinforced by the changed relationship of the UK to the EU.[130]

[127] Keating notes, interestingly, that if Scotland were independent in the EU but the rest of the UK remained outside, there would be a hard border between them, which is not the type of independence offered in 2014. 'Scotland does around four times as much trade with the rest of the UK as it does with the EU. This meant that the harder the new border between the EU and the UK created by Brexit, the greater the grievance in Scotland, but the more difficult independence became.' Michael Keating, 'Taking Back Control? Brexit and the Territorial Constitution of the United Kingdom' (2022) 29(4) Journal of European Public Policy 491, 498. Another example is the 2014 Scottish National Party (SNP) suggestion of a currency union with England (ie 'the sterling zone') after Scottish independence. Would that be still possible with a UK outside the EU?

[128] Nicola McEwen and Mary C Murphy, 'Brexit and the Union: Territorial Voice, Exit and Re-entry Strategies in Scotland and Northern Ireland After EU Exit' (2022) 43(3) International Political Science Review 374, 384.

[129] In a similar vein, Nikos Skoutaris, 'Territorial Differentiation in EU Law: Can Scotland and Northern Ireland Remain in the EU and/or the Single Market?' (2017) 19 Cambridge Yearbook of European Legal Studies 287, 296.

[130] John Doyle and Eileen Connolly, 'Brexit and the Future of Northern Ireland' (2017) Working Paper 1 DCU Brexit Institute 2. Phinnemore and Hayward share these concerns of the disruptive effects that Brexit could have: 'Remove one of these states from the EU and immediately there are problems, not just economically and legally but also in terms of heightened political sensitivities as to the diverging trajectories of the two guarantors of the Good Friday Agreement. Divergence between the UK and Ireland automatically has a polarizing effect on the two main political communities in Northern Ireland. Furthermore, that the UK and the Irish governments find themselves on opposite sides of the negotiating table in Brussels makes it almost impossible for them to facilitate agreement between the political parties, as has been essential for all major steps of progression in the peace process to date.' David Phinnemore and Katy Hayward, 'UK withdrawal ("Brexit") and the good Friday agreement' (2017) Study for the AFCO Committee. <https://www.europarl.europa.eu/RegData/etudes/STUD/2017/596826/IPOL_STU%282017%29596826_EN.pdf> accessed 5 August 2022. One has

Political divisions, already deep and enduring in Northern Ireland, might be reinforced after Brexit, but this does not mean, necessarily, the emergence of a united Ireland in the near future. Precisely such divisions might be the ones impeding a united Northern Ireland voice able to conduct a reunification process.[131] It is my belief that unless there is a clear majority, sustained over a certain period of time, in favour of a constitutional change, any discussion of a reunification referendum is premature and destabilizing. Any major constitutional redesign requires a broad popular support. Additionally, the credibility of the exit threat has also been hampered by the Irish government's support for existing territorial arrangements enshrined in the Belfast Agreement and lukewarm support for the Irish unity agenda.[132]

But, if the political momentum arrives, as explained in Chapter 4, there is a constitutionally foreseeable path to reunification with Ireland, although extremely difficult and to certain extent ambiguous.[133] In any event, such a situation (ie the territorial enlargement of an EU Member State, reshaping the borders of a Member State) would not be a novelty for the EU, since it would resemble German reunification (as has been explained in Chapter 5), where the application of the *acquis communitaire* was extended to East Germany without any formal amendment of the treaties. In the Northern Ireland case, the situation will be technically much easier, since EU law is already being applied (and has been for many years). In fact, this possibility of a reunification with the Republic of Ireland after a border poll was already envisaged by the European Council after persistent Irish government diplomatic efforts with other EU Member States:

> The European Council acknowledges that the Good Friday Agreement expressly provides for an agreed mechanism whereby a united Ireland may be brought about through peaceful and democratic means; and, in this regard, the European Council acknowledges that, in accordance with international law, the entire territory of such a united Ireland would thus be part of the European Union.[134]

to bear in mind that the Belfast Agreement and EU membership had diminished the importance of the border, not only politically speaking, but also from an economic point of view. Colin RG Murray and Aoife O'Donoghue, 'Life after Brexit: Operationalising the Belfast/Good Friday Agreement's Principle of Consent' (2018) 42(1) Dublin University Law Journal 147, 153.

[131] No poll within Northern Ireland suggests a clear majority in favour of Irish reunification. McEwen and Murphy (n 128) 380. Besides, as some unionists believe, Brexit might potentially make it more difficult to integrate Northern Ireland into Ireland, for the latter will continue to be an EU Member State while the former will diverge from the EU. Murray and O'Donoghue (n 130) 175.

[132] McEwen and Murphy (n 128) 378.

[133] For instance, what would happen should the UK fail to fulfil the Belfast Agreements terms (eg by refusing to allow the border poll)? The truth is that there is no dispute settlement clause and the ICJ jurisdiction is excluded. Murray and O'Donoghue (n 130) 165 ff.

[134] European Council, 'Minutes of Special Meeting of the European Council (Art. 50) Held on 29 April 2017' EUCO XT 20010/17. <https://data.consilium.europa.eu/doc/document/XT-20010-2017-INIT/en/pdf> accessed 5 August 2022.

Thus, the European Council, albeit without mentioning it, relied heavily on the German precedent in the event Northern Ireland opts for a territorial status quo change.[135] The fact is that for the EU, Northern Ireland is not a purely internal British question, like the Scottish independence debate. The EU has declared an interest, given the importance of the European framework to the peace settlement and the Irish border.[136]

6. Conclusions

There is no clear EU law guidance when it comes to govern the life of a new State born out of secession within the EU. Because of the absence of a clear EU legal regime, we have considered public international law, the few EU law provisions that could provide some help, ECJ case law, and theories developed by EU law scholars to address the main questions that might arise in the event the new entity is interested in EU membership. These questions include the following. Will the new entity be considered a successor but not a continuing State of the rump State? Should it ask for EU membership, or could we assume an internal enlargement procedure? Will it have to follow article 49 TEU, or is there any way to avoid the procedural difficulties? Can the EU citizenship regime influence the negotiations between the rump State and the seceded entity by limiting the autonomy of the former and forcing it to offer dual nationality?

Given the hypothetical character of these questions (there is no precedent of successful secession within the EU), this chapter has not been able to offer unqualified conclusions. Nor can we rule out completely ad hoc solutions, should the EU face a successful independence process in the future. However, this chapter has shed light on the legal debate around these issues. It has been shown that seceded territories cannot be considered continuing States of the rump State. Therefore, such entities will have to ask for EU membership. EU law can be very pragmatic and history has proven that law is not a hurdle when there is enough political will (see Chapter 5). However, as has also been pointed out throughout this book, the EU is a community based on the rule of law, and cannot avoid the legal discipline of certain procedures. Thus, given the *lex specialis* argument, an accession procedure requires compliance with article 49 TEU, which demands, *inter alia*, unanimous agreement of all EU Member States. All the more reason the same rule applies to a hypothetical independent Scotland. Having said that, and given the political pragmatism of the EU, even this procedure and the negotiations themselves can be accelerated in order to avoid any major disruption to the internal market. If, as a

[135] Keating (n 127) 499.

[136] European Commission, 'Guiding Principles for the dialogue on Ireland/Northern Ireland' TF50 (2017) 15. <https://ec.europa.eu/info/sites/default/files/dialogue_ie-ni.pdf> accessed 5 August 2022.

result of secession, the rump State dispossesses from its nationality all those residents who opt for the nationality of the new State, there is no right to maintain EU citizenship. Nor does EU law force the rump State to offer a dual nationality regime to the inhabitants of the seceded entity. Many of the final results will, perforce, depend on negotiations. Thus, the attitude of those involved in the negotiations—the rump State, seceded entity, and the other EU Member States—will be key to determine the solutions adopted.

8
Conclusions

This book has dealt with the European Union (EU) legal response to pro-independence movements throughout EU Member States. Statehood is an issue that transcends the current Catalan crisis in Spain and affects many other movements aimed at redrawing the map of Europe. The book has offered normative support for the position of EU institutions towards secession. The intention has been to offer a legal reflection that goes beyond a case-specific approach that can, therefore, be of relevance to any EU Member State.

The first conclusion is that with regard to secession within EU Member States, there is no conflict between international law and EU law and, therefore, that international law does not constrain the EU's position. The customary right to self-determination, that might lead to the creation of an independent and sovereign State, cannot be applied to regions within EU Member States, as long as they remain well-functioning democracies, although international law does not prohibit secession either. Therefore, there is no obligation to reject, *prima facie*, all types of secession. In sum, the impact of international law is limited.

The second conclusion is that the criteria of consent and lawfulness when it comes to secession are to be found mainly in constitutional legal orders. While international law does not contain any guidance for secession within democracies, constitutional law does. As has been explained throughout the book, secessionist attempts are the most acute political crisis a State can endure, because they affect the integrity and continuity of the political subject that founds the State. That is why constitutional legal orders tend to be highly restrictive. It is in fact typical for the constitutions of the Council of Europe Member States not to allow secession or even the organization of self-determination referendums, following the classic paradigm initiated by the US (eg Spain, Italy, Germany). The British and the Canadian positions constitute outstanding exceptions, as they do admit a right to negotiate. In any event, the common approach of all liberal constitutional democracies rejects a unilateral right to secede, since the democratic principle has to be tempered with other principles like the rule of law. In this sense, from a constitutional law standpoint unilateralism tends to be equated with unlawfulness.

The third conclusion is that there is no clear and explicit EU law provision regarding secession within EU Member States, no precedent either, and the statements delivered so far by the EU institutions cannot be considered a fully articulated policy. Therefore, and despite some scholars taking a different view, it has been concluded that the EU does not have its own legality criteria for secession.

Secession and European Union Law. Núria González Campañá, Oxford University Press. © Núria González Campañá 2024.
DOI: 10.1093/oso/9780198882596.003.0008

This does not mean that the EU does not have its own approach to secession. The thesis propounded in the preceding pages is that the EU is obliged to respect the national identity and fundamental constitutional structures of the Member States (according to art 4(2) of the Treaty on European Union (TEU)), which necessarily includes unity or secession clauses (in a broad sense). EU law should therefore show a deferential attitude towards the constitutional legal orders of the Member States. Drawing on a pluralist reading of the relationship between EU law and national law, I conclude that what is unique about the EU is the constitutional tolerance it has to show towards EU Member States' provisions on secession. Accordingly, if domestic law considers that secession is 'unlawful', EU law should respect that position by not recognizing the statehood of the secessionist entity. In this regard, it has been concluded that the EU reaction to the 2017 Catalan crisis was in accordance with EU law. If, on the contrary, the domestic legal order has enabled the secessionist attempt, EU law should respect that outcome by recognizing the new entity as a sovereign State and enter into good faith negotiations. However, this deferential attitude has certain limits: when enforcing secession clauses, EU Member States will have to respect the values enshrined in article 2 TEU.

The fourth conclusion refers to the fact that the EU has a distinctive approach to secession in its external policy. In effect, EU institutions' practice in past relevant territorial changes within the EU Member States and secession in neighbouring countries coincides with the main claim developed in this book, namely, that the EU rejects unilateralism and takes into account the legal order of the parent State affected. Thus, we have seen that with the exception of the unique case of Kosovo (that included gross human rights violations) the EU has always opposed unilateral independence. One of the EU's main criteria for recognizing a secessionist entity has been the approval of the nation State from which an entity is seceding, that is, consensus. Czechoslovakia, although not a secessionist process, confirms this approach to the extent that EC Member States did not oppose the split, given that there was an agreement between the two Republics. In the case of Montenegro, where the EU got deeply involved in a secessionist conflict for the first time, the EU additionally required respect for the rule of law and for the democratic principle (imposing certain rules for the implementation of a referendum on independence).

This means that ultimately the EU has not only asked for consensus and agreement (as in the case of the dissolution of Czechoslovakia), but it has also requested respect for the constitutional legal order. Thus, one could argue that EU policy has undergone an evolution. If, previously, EU institutions only demanded consensus and agreement between the sides involved in the conflict, in the cases of Montenegro and Crimea, the EU is now emphasizing the need to respect the relevant constitutional legal orders. In other words, it seems, parallel to the increasing constitutionalization of the EU, that norms constrain and shape foreign policy to a larger extent than they used to do in the past. In sum, consensus or agreement and respect for the constitutional legal order of the parent State are the criteria developed by the EU institutions to recognize a secessionist entity. Thus, the legal analysis developed throughout the book is not only legally sound, but also politically feasible.

One can assume a fierce opposition towards pro-independence movements that breach the legal constitutional order of EU Member States and that are conducted without the agreement of the EU Member State affected (as the Catalan crisis has proved). However, the position of the EU in a consensual and lawful pro-independence movement (like the Scottish case) would not be so obvious.

The fifth conclusion relates to the life of a new State emerging out of secession within the EU. Despite the hypothetical nature of the situation and the fact that there is no clear EU law guidance (ie no precedent of successful secession), it has been argued that seceded territories cannot be considered continuing States of the rump State. Therefore, such entities will have to ask for EU membership. EU law can be very pragmatic and history has proven that law is not a hurdle when there is enough political will. However, as has been also pointed out throughout this book, the EU is a community based on the rule of law, and cannot avoid the legal discipline of certain procedures. Thus, given the *lex specialis* argument, an accession procedure requires compliance with article 49 TEU, which demands, *inter alia*, unanimous agreement of all EU Member States. Having said that, and given the political pragmatism of the EU, even this procedure and the negotiations can be accelerated in order to avoid major disruption to the internal market. If, as a result of secession, the rump State dispossesses from its nationality all those residents who opt for the nationality of the new State, there is no right to maintain EU citizenship. Nor does EU law force the rump State to offer a dual nationality regime to the inhabitants of the seceded entity. Many of the final results will, perforce, depend on negotiations. Thus, the attitude of those involved in the negotiations, the rump State, the seceded entity, and the other EU Member States, will be key to determining the solutions adopted.

Finally, this book has pointed out that the EU cannot fully develop its constitutional ambitions since, when tackling issues that touch on citizens' sense of national constitutional identity, the ultimate decision lies with Member States. National identity remains much stronger than European identity. I think that Dieter Grimm's warnings about the lack of a European people are as relevant today as they were almost 30 years ago, when they were written.[1] I believe that the secession debate might be proving that scepticism about EU constitutionalism is right, for it has certain limits. This book has highlighted one of these limits. The pluralist legal order established in the European milieu establishes obligations (art 4(2) TEU) to respect the constitutional identity of EU Member States, to show a deferential and tolerant attitude. But, at the same time, it is also true that the EU constrains the

[1] Dieter Grimm, 'Does Europe Need a Constitution?' (1995) 1(2) European Law Journal 282

behaviour of the Member States: EU Member States are allowed to have different national constitutional responses to secession, but only provided such responses and their subsequent application and enforcement respect the values included in article 2 TEU. The analysis of secession and EU law carried out in this book shows that a legal pluralist reading is the most appropriate way to review legally the phenomenon of secession in a territory where three different legal orders interact.

APPENDIX

Questions of European Parliament Members to the European Commission

Question for written answer by Eluned Morgan (PSE) to the Commission, 12 February 2004, P-0524/04

Oral question by Frank Vanhecke (ITS) to the Commission, 10 January 2007, H-0011/07

Question for written answer by Roger Helmer (NI) to the Commission, 1 February 2007, E-0314/07

Question for written answer by Eluned Morgan (PSE) to the Commission, 22 March 2007, P-1625/07

Question for written answer by Robert Kilroy-Silk (NI) to the Commission, 16 April 2007, E-2021/07

Question for written answer by Raul Romeva (Verts/ALE), Oriol Junqueras (Verts/ALE) and Ramon Tremosa (ALDE) to the Commission, 26 July 2010, E-6073/2010

Question for written answer by George Lyon (ALDE) to the Commission, 20 October 2011, P-009664/2011

Question for written answer by Ramon Tremosa (ALDE) to the Commission, 23 January 2012, E-000395/2012

Question for written answer by Izaskun Bilbao (ALDE), Ramon Tremosa (ALDE), Salvador Sedo (PPE) and Raul Romeva (Verts/ALE) to the Commission, 12 September 2012, E-008133/2012

Question for written answer by Ana Miranda (Verts/ALE), Ramon Tremosa (ALDE) and Raul Romeva (Verts/ALE) to the Commission, 21 September 2012, E-008324/2012

Question for written answer by Francisco Sosa Wagner (NI) to the Commission, 28 September 2012, E-008752/2012

Question for written answer by Auke Zijlstra (NI) to the Commission, 8 October 2012, E-009009/2012

Question for written answer by Gerard Batten (EFD) to the Commission, 29 October 2012, P-009862/2012

Question for written answer by Ramon Tremosa (ALDE) to the Commission, 27 September 2013, E-011023/2013

Question for written answer by Francisco Sosa Wagner (NI) to the Commission, 27 January 2014, E-000796/2014

Question for written answer by George Lyon (ALDE) to the Commission, 14 February 2014, P-001676/2014

Question for written answer by Mara Bizzotto (EFD) to the Commission, 21 February 2014, E-002111/2014

Question for written answer by Izaskun Bilbao (ALDE) to the Commission, 24 September 2014, E-007129/2014

Question for written answer by José Blanco (S&D) to the Commission, 11 November 2014, E-009058/2014

Question for written answer by Santiago Fisas (PPE) to the Commission, 21 July 2015, E-011776/2015

Question for written answer by Gerolf Annemans (ENF) to the Commission, 9 February 2016, P-001148/2016

Question for written answer by Beatriz Becerra (ALDE) to the Commission, 23 May 2017, E-003486-17

Bibliography

'Badinter Commission Opinions' (1992) 3 European Journal of International Law 182 and (1993) 4 European Journal of International Law 74

'Guiding principles of the Contact Group for a settlement of the status of Kosovo' United Nations doc. S/2005/709 10 November

'Report of the Special Envoy of the Secretary-General on Kosovo's future status' United Nations doc. S/2007/168 26 March

'Report of the European Union/United States/Russian Federation Troika on Kosovo' United Nations doc. annexed to S/2007/723 4 December

'Scotland constitutional future' (UK Government 2012)

'Scotland's Future' (Scottish Government 2013)

'Consultation on a Draft Referendum Bill' (Scottish Government 2016)

Ackerman B, *We the People. Foundations* (Harvard UP 1991)

Aja E, *Estado Autonómico y Reforma Federal* (Alianza Editorial 2014)

Albert R, 'How Unwritten Constitutional Norms Change Written Constitutions' (2015) 38(2) Dublin University Law Journal 387

Alesina A and Spolaore E, *The Size of Nations* (MIT Press 2003)

Alonso R, 'Pathways Out of Terrorism in Northern Ireland and the Basque Country: The Misrepresentation of the Irish Model' (2004) 16(4) Terrorism and Political Violence 695

Anderson G, 'Unilateral Non-Colonial Secession and Internal Self-Determination: A Right of Newly Seceded Peoples to Democracy' (2017) 34(1) Arizona Journal of International and Comparative Law 1

Antola E, 'The Future of Small States in the EU' in Mary Farrell and others (eds), *European Integration in the 21st century* (SAGE 2002)

Arias Maldonado M, 'Sobre la legitimidad de la secesión territorial dentro del marco liberal-democrático' in Pere Almeda (ed), *Cataluña-Espanya. Del conflicto al diálogo* (Catarata 2021)

Armstrong KA, 'A Matter for Another Day? Will the Supreme Court Accept the Lord Advocate's Independence Referendum Reference?' (*UK Constitutional Law Association Blog*, 29 June 2022)

Arzoz X and Suksi M, 'Comparing Constitutional Adjudication of Self-determination Claims' (2018) 25(4) Maastricht Journal of European and Comparative Law 452

Athanassiou P and Shaelou SL, 'EU Accession from Within? An Introduction' (2014) 33(1) Yearbook of European Law 335

Aughey A, 'Northern Ireland Narratives of British Democracy (2012) 33(2) Policy Studies 145

Avbelj M, 'Theory of European Union' (2011) 36 European Law Review 818

Avery G, 'Independentism and European Union' (*European Policy Centre*, 7 May 2014)

Avery G, 'Could an independent Scotland join the EU?' (*European Policy Centre*, 28 May 2014)

Bassani M, 'John C. Calhoun: Nullification, Secession, Constitution' (*Abbevilleinstitute*, 8 August 2014)

Baquero Cruz J, 'The Legacy of the Maastricht—Urteil and the Pluralist Movement' (2007) 13 EUI Working Papers

Barak A, *Purposive Interpretation in Law* (Princeton UP 2007)

Barber N, *The Constitutional State* (OUP 2010)

Barber N, 'Scottish Independence and the Role of the United Kingdom' (*UK Constitutional Law Association Blog*, 11 January 2012)

Barber N, 'The Constitutional Regulation of Scottish Secession' (2015) 38 Oxford Legal Studies Research Paper 1

Barrio A and others, '"Spain Steals from Us!" The "Populist Drift" of Catalan Regionalism' (2018) 16 Comparative European Politics 993

Basler RP and others (eds), *Collected Works of Abraham Lincoln* (vol 4, Rutgers UP 1954)

Basta K, 'The State between Minority and Majority Nationalism: Decentralization, Symbolic Recognition, and Secessionist Crises in Spain and Canada' (2017) 48(1) Publius: The Journal of Federalism 51

Batt J, 'The Question of Serbia' (2005) 81 ISS Chaillot Paper

Batt J, 'Montenegro and Serbia after the referendum' (*Institute for Security Studies*, 1 May 2006)

Batt J, 'Making a success of Montenegrin independence—lessons from Slovakia' (*Institute for Security Studies*, 1 June 2006)

Bel G, *Anatomia d'un desengany* (Destino 2013)

Beltrán de Felipe M, *Myths and Realities of Secessionisms* (Palgrave 2019)

Bengoetxea J, 'Secession v Forceful Union. A Provisional Enquiry into the Right to Decide to Secede and the Obligation to Belong' in Carlos Closa, Costanza Margiotta, and Giuseppe Martinico (eds), *Between Democracy and Law. The Amorality of Secession* (Routledge 2020)

Benjamin JP, 'The Right of Secession (December 31, 1860)' in Jon L Wakelyn (ed), *Southern Pamphlets on Secession. November 1860–April 1861* (University of North Carolina Press 1996)

Besselink LFM, 'National and Constitutional Identity before and after Lisbon' (2010) 6 Utrecht Law Review 36

Bieber R, 'European Community Recognition of Eastern European States: A New Perspective for International Law?' (1992) 86 American Society of International Law Proceedings 374

Blagovjevic A, 'Procedures regarding National Identity Clause in National Constitutional Court's and the CJEU's Case-Law' (2017) 1 EU and Comparative Law Issues and Challenges 210

Blais A and Nadeau R, 'To Be or Not to Be Sovereignist: Quebeckers' Perennial Dilemma' (1992) XVIII(1) Canadian Public Policy/Analyse de politiques 89

Blum YZ, 'Russia Takes over the Soviet Union's Seat at the United Nations' (1992) 3 European Journal of International Law 354

Bossacoma P, *Secessió i integració a la Unió Europea. Catalunya nou Estat de la Unió?* (Institut d'Estudis de l'Autogovern 2016)

Bossacoma P, *Morality and Legality of Secession. A Theory of National Self-Determination* (Palgrave 2020)

Boyle A and Crawford J, *Annex A Opinion: Referendum on the Independence of Scotland—International Law Aspects* (UK Government 2013)

Brandon ME, 'Secession, Constitutionalism and American Experience' in Stephen Macedo and Allen Buchanan (eds), *Secession and Self-Determination* (NYU Press 2003)

Brewin C, 'European Union Perspectives on Cyprus Accession' (2000) 36(1) Middle Eastern Studies 21

Buchanan A, *Secession: The Morality of Political Divorce from Fort Sumter to Lithuania and Quebec* (Westview 1991)

Buchanan A, 'Democracy and Secession' in Margaret Moore (ed), *National Self-Determination and Secession* (OUP 1998)

Buchheit LC, *Secession: The Legitimacy of Self-determination* (Yale UP 1978)

Burrows N, 'Scotland's European Strategy' in Roger Scully and Richard Wyn Jones (eds), *Europe, Regions and Regionalism* (Palgrave MacMillan 2010)

Cairns AC, 'The Charlottetown Accord: Multinational Canada vs. Federalism' in Douglas E Williams (ed), *Reconfigurations: Canadian Citizenship and Constitutional Change—Selected Essays by Alan C. Cairns* (McClelland and Stewart 1995)

Campins Eritja M, 'The European Union and the Secession of a Territory from a EU Member State' (2015) 2(XVII) Diritto Pubblico Comparato ed Europeo 479

Caplan R, *Europe and the Recognition of New States in Yugoslavia* (CUP 2005)

Cartabia M, 'The Italian Constitutional Court and the Relationship Between the Italian Legal System and the European Community' (1990) 12(1) Michigan Journal of International Law 173

Cassese A, *Self-Determination of Peoples. A Legal Reappraisal* (CUP 1995)

Cassese A, *International Law* (OUP 2003)

Castellà Andreu JM, 'La secesión catalana, entre la política y el derecho' (2014) 7 Anuario de la Facultad de Derecho Universidad de Alcalá 229

Castellà Andreu JM, 'Tribunal Constitucional y proceso secesionista catalán: respuestas jurídico-constitucionales a un conflicto político-constitucional' (2016) 37 Teoría y Realidad Constitucional 561

Castellà Andreu JM, 'Sobre el encaje constitucional del pretendido referéndum de secesión en Cataluña' in Eva Sáenz and Carlos Garrido (eds), *La Funcionalidad del Referéndum en la Democracia Representativa* (Tirant Lo Blanch 2017)

Castellà Andreu JM, 'Constitution and Referendum on Secession in Catalonia' in Alberto López Basaguren and Leire Escajedo (eds), *Claims for Secession and Federalism* (Springer 2019)

Chamon M and Van der Loo G, 'The Temporal Paradox of Regions in the EU Seeking Independence: Contraction and Fragmentation versus Widening and Deepening?' (2014) 20(5) European Law Journal 613

Chernichenko SV and Kotliar VS, 'Ongoing Global Legal Debate on Self-determination And Secession: Main Trends' in Julie Dahlitz (ed), *Secession and International Law* (T.M.C. Asser Press 2003)

Choudhry S, 'Globalization in Search of Justification: Toward a Theory of Comparative Constitutional Interpretation' (1999) 74(3) Indiana Law Journal 819

Choudhry S (ed), *The Migration of Constitutional Ideas* (CUP 2007)

Christou G, 'Cyprus and the EU: Two Years Later: The European Union: What Role in the Cyprus Conflict?' (2006) 41(2) The International Spectator 19

Cloots E, *National Identity in EU Law* (OUP 2015)

Closa C (ed), 'Troubled Membership: Dealing with Secession from a Member State and Withdrawal from the EU' (2014) 91 EUI Working Papers

Closa C, 'Secession from a Member State and EU Membership: The View from the Union' (2016) 12(2) European Constitutional Law Review 240

Closa C (ed), *Secession from a Member State and Withdrawal from the European Union* (CUP 2017)

Commission, 'Communication: A New EU Framework to Strengthen the Rule of Law' COM (2014) 158

Committee of the Regions, 'Recommendation of the Congress of Local and Regional Authorities of Europe on a European Charter of Regional Self-Government' 2001/C 144/02

Committee of the Regions, 'Devolution in the European Union and the place for local and regional self-government in EU policy making and delivery' 2013/C 139/08

Connolly CK, 'Independence in Europe: Secession, Sovereignty and the European Union' (2013) 24 Duke Journal of Comparative & International Law 51

Consell Assessor per la Transició Nacional, *La integració a la comunitat internacional* (Catalan Government 2014)

Consell Assessor per la Transició Nacional, *Les vies d'integració de Catalunya a la Unió Europea* (Catalan Government 2014)

Cotterrell R, 'Why Must Legal Ideas Be Interpreted Sociologically? (1998) 25(2) Journal of Law and Society 171

Craig P, 'Constitutions, Constitutionalism and the European Union' (2001) 7(2) European Law Journal 125

Craig P, 'Transnational Constitution-Making: The Contribution of the Venice Commission on Law and Democracy' (2017) 2 UC Irvine Journal of International, Transnational, and Comparative Law 57

Crameri K, 'Do Catalans have the right to decide? Secession, legitimacy and democracy in the twenty-first century Europe' (2016) 6(3) Global Discourse: An Interdisciplinary Journal of Current Affairs and Applied Contemporary Thought 423

Crawford J, *The Creation of States in International Law* (2nd edn, OUP 2006)

Cruz P, *La Identidad Nacional de los Estados Miembros en el Derecho de la Unión Europea* (Aranzadi 2021)

Cruz P, 'Identidad Nacional y Valores de la Unión Europea: Límites a una interpretación extensiva del artículo 4.2 TUE' (2022) 114 Revista Derecho Político 247

Culver K and Giudice M, 'Not a System but an Order' in Julie Dickson and Pavlos Eleftheriadis (eds), *Philosophical Foundation of European Union Law* (OUP 2012)

D'Aspremont J and Dopagne F, 'Kadi: The ECJ's Reminder of the Elementary Divide between Legal Orders' (2008) 5 International Organizations Law Review 371

D'Oliveira UJ, 'Decoupling Nationality and Union Citizenship?' (2011) 7 European Constitutional Law Review 138

Dalle Mulle E, *The Nationalism of the Rich: Discourses and Strategies of Separatist Parties in Catalonia, Flanders, Northern Italy and Scotland* (Routledge 2017)

Dann P, 'Thoughts on a Methodology of European Constitutional Law' (2005) 6(11) German Law Journal 1453

Davis MH, *Producing Eurafrica: Development, Agriculture and Race in Algeria, 1958–1965* (NYU PhD dissertation 2015)

De Areilza JM, *Poder y Derecho en la Unión Europea* (Civitas 2014)

De Baere G and Roes T, 'EU Loyalty as Good Faith' (2015) 64 International and Comparative Law Quarterly 829

De Burca G, 'The EU, the European Court of Justice and the International Legal Order after Kadi' (2009) 1(51) Harvard International Law Journal 1

De Carreras F, 'Unión Europea y secesión de Estados Miembros. ¿Deben intervenir las instituciones europeas?' (2014) 33 Teoría y Realidad Constitucional 271

De Groot GR and Seling A, 'The Consequences of the Rottmann Judgment on Member State Autonomy—The European Court of Justice's Avant-Gardism in Nationality Matters' (2011) 7 European Constitutional Law Review 150

De Miguel J, 'La cuestión de la secesión en la Unión Europea: una visión constitucional' (2014) 165 Revista de Estudios Políticos 211

De Witte B, 'The Nature of the Legal Order' in Paul Craig and Grainne de Búrca (eds), *The Evolution of EU Law* (OUP 2011)

Della Porta D, O'Connor F, and Portos M, 'The Framing of Secessionism in the Neo-liberal Crisis' in Carlos Closa, Costanza Margiotta, and Giuseppe Martinico (eds), *Between Democracy and Law. The Amorality of Secession* (Routledge 2020)

Deschouwer K and Reuchamps M, 'The Belgian Federation at the Crossroad' (2013) 23(3) Regional and Federal Studies 261

Dimitrovova B, 'Imperial Re-bordering of Europe: The Case of the European Neighbourhood Policy' (2012) 25(2) Cambridge Review of International Affairs 249

Dion S, 'Why Is Secession Difficult in Well-established Democracies? Lessons from Quebec' (1996) 26(2) British Journal of Political Science 269

Dion S, 'Secession and Democracy: A Canadian Perspective' (*Real Instituto Elcano*, 9 April 2013)

Dobbs M, 'Sovereingty, Article 4(2) TEU and the Respect of National Identities: Swinging the Balance of Power in Favour of the Member States?' (2014) 33(1) Yearbook of European Law 298

Douglas-Scott S, 'How Easily Could an Independent Scotland Join the EU?' (2014) 46 University of Oxford Legal Research Papers 1

Douglas-Scott S, 'A Second Scottish Independence Referendum in the UK Supreme Court' (*Verfassungsblog*, 14 October 2022)

Doyle J and Connolly E, 'Brexit and the Future of Northern Ireland' (2017) Working Paper 1 DCU Brexit Institute

Drinóczi T, 'Constitutional Identity in Europe: The Identity of the Constitution. A Regional Approach' (2020) 21 German Law Journal 105

Duerr G, *Secessionism and the European Union: The Future of Flanders, Scotland and Catalonia* (Lexington Books 2015)

Dugard J, 'A Legal Basis for Secession—Relevant Principles and Rules' in Julie Dahlitz (ed), *Secession and International Law* (T.M.C. Asser Press 2003)

Eckes C, 'Judicial Review of European Anti-Terrorism Measures—The Yusuf and Kadi Judgments of the Court of First Instance' (2008) 14 European Law Journal 74

Edward D, 'Scotland and the European Union' (*Scottish Constitutional Futures Forum*, 17 December 2012)

Edward D, 'EU Law and the Separation of Member States' (2013) 36(5) Fordham International Law Journal 1151

Eeckhout P, 'Community Terrorism Listings, Fundamental Rights, and UN Security Council Resolutions. In Search of the Right Fit' (2007) 3 European Constitutional Law Review 183

Elliot JH, *The Revolt of the Catalans. A Study in the Decline of Spain (1598–1640)* (CUP 1963)

Elliot JH, *History in the Making* (Yale UP 2012)

Fabbrini F and Sajó A, 'The Dangers of Constitutional Identity' (2019) 25 European Law Journal 457

Fabry M, *Recognizing States. International Society and the Establishment of New States Since 1776* (OUP 2010)

Pietro Faraguna, 'On the Identity Clause and Its Abuses: "Back to the Treaty"' (2021) 27(3) European Public Law 427

Farber D, *Lincoln's Constitution* (University of Chicago Press 2003)
Fasone C, '"Italian-style" secession and the semi-indifference of national politics' (*Verfassungsblog*, 21 April 2015)
Fasone C, 'Secession and the Ambiguous Place of Regions Under EU Law' in Carlos Closa (ed), *Secession from a Member State and Withdrawal from the European Union* (CUP 2017)
Ferreres Comella V, *The Constitution of Spain. A Contextual Analysis* (Hart Publishing 2013)
Ferreres Comella V, 'The Spanish Constitutional Court Confronts Catalonia's "Right to Decide" (Comment on the Judgment 42/2014)' (2014) 10(3) European Constitutional Law Review 571
Ferreres Comella V, 'Does Brexit Normalize Secession?' (2018) 53 Texas International Law Journal 139
Fløistad B, 'Fisheries, Greenland and the European Community. Formal Independence–Economic Dependence' (1988) 8(4) International Challenges 6
Forde A, 'Setting the Cat amongst Pigeons: Kosovo's Application for Membership of the Council of Europe' (*Blog of the European Journal of International Law*, 17 May 2022)
Freixes Sanjuán T, 'Secesión de Estados e integración en la Unión Europea. A propósito del debate sobre la permanencia en la Unión de Escocia y Cataluña como Estados segregados del Reino Unido y España' (2014) 2 Revista Jurídica de Catalunya 298
Fritsch-Bournazel R, *Europe and German Unification* (Berg 1992)
Frowein J, 'The Reunification of Germany' (1992) 86(1) American Journal of International Law 152
Galán A, 'Secesión de Estados y Pertenencia a la Unión Europea' (2013) 1 Istituzione del Federalismo 95
Gale WG and West DM, 'How seriously should we take talk of US state secession?' (*Brookings*, 13 December 2021)
Gaudreault-DesBiens JF, 'The Law and Politics of Secession: From the Political Contingency of Secession to a "Right to Decide"? Can Lessons Be Learned from the Quebec Case?' in Giacomo Delledonne and Giuseppe Martinico (eds), *The Canadian Contribution to a Comparative Law of Secession* (Palgrave 2019)
Gérard P and Verrijdt W, 'Belgian Constitutional Court Adopts National Identity Discourse' (2017) 13 European Constitutional Law Review 182
Ginsburg T and Versteeg M, 'From Catalonia to California: Secession in Constitutional Law' (2019) 70 Alabama Law Review 923
Glennon MJ, *Limits of Law, Prerogatives of Power. Interventionism after Kosovo* (Palgrave 2001)
González Campañá N, 'Small States and the EU: Does the EU Promote Secession Within EU Member States?' (2020) 190 Revista de Estudios Políticos 43
González Campañá N, 'Constitutional erosion in Spain: From the Catalan Pro-Independence Crisis to the (Intended) Judiciary Reforms' in Josep Maria Castellà Andreu and Marco Antonio Simonelli (eds), *Populism and Contemporary Democracy in Europe* (Palgrave MacMillan 2022)
González Pascual MI, 'Unión Europea y secesionismo, ¿silencio de los tratados? La identidad regional como parte de la identidad constitucional nacional' (2018) 10 Fundamentos 377
Grimm D, 'Does Europe Need a Constitution?' (1995) 1(2) European Law Journal 282
Grimm D, 'The Constitution in the Process of Denationalization' (2005) 12 Constellations 447
Guastaferro B, Sincere Cooperation and Respect for National Identities' in Robert Schütze and Takis Tridimas (eds), *Oxford Principles of European Union Law* (vol I, OUP 2018)
Habermas J, *The Postnational Constellation* (MIT Press 2001)

Haljan D, *Constitutionalizing Secession* (Hart Publishing 2014)
Halmai G, 'Abuse of Constitutional Identity. The Hungarian Constitutional Court on Interpretation of Article E(2) of the Fundamental Law' (2018) 43 Review of Central and East European Law 23
Hannum H, 'Rethinking Self-determination' (1993) 34(1) Vienna Journal of International Law 1
Hannum H, *Autonomy, Sovereignty, and Self-Determination. The Accommodation of Conflicting Rights* (revisited edn, University of Pennsylvania Press 1996)
Hannum H, 'The Advisory Opinion on Kosovo: An Opportunity Lost, or a Poisoned Chalice Refused?' (2011) 24(1) Leiden Journal of International Law 155
Hansen P and Jonsson S, 'Building Eurafrica: Reviving Colonialism through European Integration, 1920–60' in Gabrielle Maas, Kalypso Nicolaïdis, and Berny Sèbe (eds), *Echoes of Empire: Memory, Identity and Colonial Legacies* (IBTauris 2015)
Happold M, 'Independence: In or out of Europe? An Independent Scotland and the European Union' (2000) 49(1) International and Comparative Law Quarterly 15
Harhoff F, 'Greenland's Withdrawal from the European Communities' (1983) 20 Common Market Law Review 13
Hayden RM, 'Yugoslavia's Collapse: National Suicide with Foreign Assistance' (1992) 27(27) Economic and Political Weekly 1377
Henderson PS, 'Review: Scottish Independence' (2003) 45 Scottish Affairs 97
Herrero de Miñón M, 'La Constitución como pacto' (1998) 44 Revista de Derecho Político 17
Herzog D, *Sovereignty, RIP* (Yale UP 2020)
Higgins R, 'Self-determination and Secession' in Julie Dahlitz (ed), *Secession and International Law* (T.M.C. Asser Press 2003)
Hillion C, 'Scotland and the EU: Comment by Christophe Hillion' (*Verfassungsblog*, 15 September 2014)
Hinojosa Martínez LM, 'Bad Law for Good Reasons: The Contradictions of the Kadi Judgment' (2008) 5 International Organizations Law Review 339
Hogg PW, *Meech Lake Constitutional Accord Annotated* (Carswell 1988)
Hogg PW, *Constitutional Law of Canada* (6th edn, Carswell 2015)
Horowitz DL, *Ethnic Groups in Conflict* (2nd edn, University of California Press 2000)
Horowitz DL, 'Explaining the Northern Ireland Agreement: The Sources of an Unlikely Constitutional Consensus' (2002) 32 British Journal of Political Science 193
Horowitz DL, 'The Cracked Foundations of the Right to Secede' (2003) 14(2) Journal of Democracy 5
House of Commons Scottish Affairs Committee, 'The Referendum on Separation for Scotland: Scotland's Membership of the EU' (2013) 14
Hughes K, 'Brexit, Scottish Independence and Leaving a Union' (2019) 7 Policy Paper Scottish Centre on European Relations
Humphrey JP, 'Political and Related Rights' in Theodor Meron (ed), *Human Rights in International Law: Legal and Policy Issues* (vol 1, OUP 1984)
Iglar RF, 'The Constitutional Crisis in Yugoslavia and the International Law of Self-Determination: Slovenia's and Croatia's Right to Secede' (1992) 15 Boston College International and Comparative Law Review 213
Illamola M, 'Nacionalitat catalana i/o nacionalitat espanyola. I l'europea?' (2017) (25) Revista d'Estudis Autonòmics i Federals 93
Jackson VC, 'Constitutional Comparisons: Convergence, Resistance, Engagement' (2005) 119 Harvard Law Review 109

Jackson VC, 'Comparative Constitutional Law: Methodologies' in Michael Rosenfeld and András Sajó (eds), *The Oxford Handbook of Comparative Constitutional Law* (OUP 2013)

Jacqué JP, 'German Unification and the European Community' (1991) 2(1) European Journal of International Law 1

Jaraczewski J, 'Gazing into the Abyss: The K 3/21 decision of the Polish Constitutional Tribunal' (*Verfassungsblog*, 12 October 2021)

Jeffery C, 'Regions and the European Union: Letting Them in, and Leaving Them Alone' in Stephen Weatherill and Ulf Bernitz (eds), *The Role of Regions and Sub-national Entities in Europe* (Hart Publishing 2005)

Jenk CW, 'State Succession in Respect of Law-Making Treaties' (1952) 29 British Yearbook of International Law 105

Johnston AM, 'Self-determination in Comparative Perspective: Northern Ireland and South Africa' (1990) 17(2) Politikon: South African Journal of Political Studies 5

Keating M, 'European Integration and the Nationalities Question' (2004) 32(3) Politics & Society 367

Keating M, *The Independence of Scotland. Self-government and the Shifting Politics of Union* (OUP 2009)

Keating M, 'Would an Independent Scotland Be in the European Union?' in C Jeffery and R Perman (eds), *Scotland's Decision: 16 Questions to Think about for the Referendum on 18 September* (Birlinn 2014)

Keating M and Harvey M, 'The Political Economy of Small European States: And Lessons for Scotland' (2014) 227(1) National Institute Economic Review 54

Keating M, 'The European Question' in Michael Keating (ed), *Debating Scotland. Issues of Independence and Union in the 2014 Referendum* (OUP 2017)

Keating M, 'Taking Back Control? Brexit and the Territorial Constitution of the United Kingdom' (2022) 29(4) Journal of European Public Policy 491

Kelemen DR and Pech L, 'The Uses and Abuses of Constitutional Pluralism: Undermining the Rule of Law in the Name of Constitutional Identity in Hungary and Poland' (2019) 21 Cambridge Yearbook of European Legal Studies 59

Kenealy D and MacLennan S, 'Sincere Cooperation, Respect for Democracy and EU Citizenship: Sufficient to Guarantee Scotland's Future in the European Union?' (2014) 20(5) European Law Journal 591

Kennedy D, 'One, Two, Three, Many Legal Orders: Legal Pluralism and the Cosmopolitan View' (2007) 31 New York University Review of Law and Social Change 641

Keukeleire S and Delreux T, *The Foreign Policy of the European Union* (2nd edn, Palgrave 2014)

Kissane B, *New Beginnings: Constitutionalism and Democracy in Modern Ireland* (University College Dublin Press 2011)

Klabbers J, 'Straddling the Fence: The EU and International Law' in Anthony Arnull and Damian Chalmers (eds), *The Oxford Handbook of European Union Law* (OUP 2015)

Klamert M, *The Principle of Loyalty in EU Law* (OUP 2014)

Klein AM and Herrmann G, 'Die Beziehungen Deutschlands zu den Baltischen Ländern seit der Wiedervereinigung' (2010) 9 KAS Auslandsinformationen

Kochenov D, 'The Right to Have What Rights? EU Citizenship in Need of Clarification' (2013) 19(4) European Law Journal 502

Kochenov D and Van den Brink M, 'Secessions from EU Member States: The Imperative of Union's Neutrality' (2016) 6 University of Edinburgh School of Law Research Paper Series

Kochenov D, 'The EU and the Rule of Law—Naiveté or a Grand Design?' in Maurice Adams and others (eds), *Constitutionalism and the Rule of Law: Bridging Idealism and Realism* (CUP 2017)

Kochenov D and Pech L, 'Respect for the Rule of Law in the Case Law of the European Court of Justice' (2021) 3 Swedish Institute for European Policy Studies

Kohen MG, 'Introduction' in Marcelo G Kohen (ed), *Secession: International Law Perspectives* (CUP 2012)

Komarek J, 'The Place of Constitutional Courts in the EU' (2013) 9(3) European Constitutional Law Review 420

Kommers DP, 'The Value of Comparative Constitutional Law' (1976) 9(3) John Marshall Journal of Practice and Procedure 685

Koskenniemi M, 'National Self-Determination Today: Problems of Legal Theory and Practice' (1994) 43 International and Comparative Law Quarterly 241

Kotzur M, 'Solidarity as a Legal Concept' in Andreas Grimmel and Susanne My Giang (eds), *Solidarity in the European Union: A Fundamental Value in Crisis* (Springer 2017)

Krisch N, 'Catalonia's Independence: A Reply to Joseph Weiler' (*Blog of the European Journal of International Law*, 18 January 2013)

Kumm M, 'Who Is the Final Arbiter of Constitutionality in Europe?: Three Conceptions of the Relationship between the German Federal Constitutional Court and the European Court of Justice' (1999) 36 Common Market Law Review 351

Kumm M, 'The Jurisprudence of Constitutional Conflict: Constitutional Supremacy in Europe before and after the Constitutional Treaty' (2005) 11 European Law Journal 262

Kyris G, 'Europeanization and the Turkish-Cypriot Political Parties: How Europe Matters' (2012) 13(3) Turkish Studies 471

Laible J, *Separatism and Sovereignty in the New Europe* (Palgrave MacMillan 2008)

Laitin DD, 'Linguistic Revival: Politics and Culture in Catalonia' (1989) 31(2) Comparative Studies in Society and History 297

Landau D, 'Abusive Constitutionalism' (2013) 47 University of California Davis Law Review 189

Lang KO, 'Katalonien auf dem Weg in die Unabhängigkeit?' (2013) August SWP-Deutsches Institut für Internationale Politik und Sicherheit Aktuell

Lansbergen A and Miller N, 'Court of Justice of the European Union. European Citizenship Rights in Internal Situations: An Ambiguous Revolution? Decision of 8 March 2011, Case C-34/09 Gerardo Ruiz Zambrano v Office national de l'emploi (ONEM)' (2011) 7(2) European Constitutional Law Review 287

Lansing R, *The Peace Negotiations. A Personal Narrative* (Constable and Company Ltd 1921)

Larik J, 'From Speciality to a Constitutional Sense of Purpose: On the Changing Role of the Objectives of the European Union' (2014) 63(4) International and Comparative Law Quarterly 935

Lauterpacht H, *Recognition in International Law* (CUP 1947)

Le Gloannec AM, 'Two Germanies in One' in Wolfgang *Heisenberg* (ed), *German Unification in European Perspective* (Centre for European Policy Studies 1991)

Lecours A, *Nationalism, Secessionism and Autonomy* (OUP 2021)

Leczykiewicz D, 'The "national identity clause" in the EU Treaty: a blow to supremacy of Union law?' (*UK Constitutional Law Association Blog*, 21 June 2012)

Lerner CS, 'Saving the Constitution: Lincoln, Secession, and the Price of Union' (2004) 102(6) Michigan Law Review 1263

Levinson S, 'Is Secession the Achilles Heel of "Strong" Federalism?' in Jörg Fedtke and Basil S Markesinis (eds), *Patterns of Regionalism and Federalism* (Hart Publishing 2006)

Levrat N and others, *Catalonia's Legitimate Right to Decide. Paths to Self-Determination* (Catalan Government 2017)
Libal M, *Limits of Persuasion: Germany and the Yugoslav Crisis, 1991–1992* (Praeger 1997)
Linde E, 'Contestación al trabajo de Ridao-González: la secesión de territorios de Estados Miembros de la Unión Europea, que se fundan en ideologías nacionalistas, son contrarias a los principios democráticos que rigen en los Estados occidentales y en la Unión Europea' (2015) 28 Revista de Derecho de la Unión Europea 391
Loewenstein K, *Political Power and the Governmental Process* (University of Chicago Press 1957)
López Basaguren A, 'Estado democrático y secesión de territorios. Un análisis comparado sobre el tratamiento democrático de las reclamaciones secesionistas' in Joseba Arregi Aranburu (ed), *La Secesión de España* (Tecnos 2014)
López Basaguren A, 'La independencia de Escocia en la Unión Europea. Los efectos de la secesión de territorios en la UE entre política y derecho' (2014) 33 Teoría y Realidad Constitucional 69
López Garrido D (ed), *Cataluña ante la Unión Europea. Las consecuencias jurídicas de la independencia* (Fundación Alternativas 2015)
López Bofill H, 'Hubris, Constitutionalism and the "Indissoluble Unity of the Spanish Nation"' (2019) 17(3) International Journal of Constitutional Law 943
López Martín AG and Perea Unceta JA, *Secession and Statehood* (Routledge 2022)
Loughlin M, 'Constitutional Pluralism: An Oxymoron?' (2014) 3(1) Global Constitutionalism 9
Loza T and Krauthamer K, 'Montenegro: The Gray Zone' (2006) 5(16) Transitions Online
Lucarelli S, *Europe and the Breakup of Yugoslavia: A Political Failure in Search of a Scholarly Explanation* (Kluwer Law International 2000)
Ludlov P, 'The German-German Negotiations and the "Two-Plus-Four" Talks' in Wolfgang Heisenberg (ed), *German Unification in European Perspective* (Centre for European Policy Studies 1991)
MacCormick N, 'The Maastricht Urteil: Sovereignty Now' (1995) 1 European Law Journal 259
MacCormick N, *Questioning Sovereignty* (OUP 1999)
MacCormick N, 'Is There a Constitutional Path to Scottish Independence?' (2000) 53 Parliamentary Affairs 721
Macek-Macková E, 'Challenges in Conflict Management in Multi-Ethnic States—The Dissolution of Czechoslovakia and Serbia and Montenegro' (2011) 39(4) Nationalist Papers: The Journal of Nationalism and Ethnicity 615
MacIver A, 'Metaconstitutionalising Secession: The Reference and Scotland (in Europe)' in Giacomo Delledonne and Giuseppe Martinico (eds), *The Canadian Contribution to a Comparative Law of Secession* (Palgrave Macmillan 2019)
Maduro Poiares M, 'Contrapunctual law: Europe's Constitutional Pluralism in Action' in Neil Walker (ed), *Sovereignty in Transition* (Hart Publishing 2003)
Maduro Poiares M, 'The Three Claims of Constitutional Pluralism' in Matej Avbelj and Jan Komarek (eds), *Constitutional Pluralism in the European Union and Beyond* (Hart Publishing 2012)
Maduro Poiares M, 'Some Preliminary Remarks on the PSPP Decision of the German Constitutional Court' (*Verfassungsblog*, 6 May 2020)
Malksoo M, 'The Memory Politics of Becoming European: The East European Subalterns and the Collective Memory of Europe' (2009) 15(4) European Journal of International Relations 653

Mancini S, 'Rethinking the Boundaries of Democratic Secession: Liberalism, Nationalism, and the Right of Minorities to Self-determination' (2008) 6(3–4) International Journal of Constitutional Law 553

Mancini S, 'Secession and Self-determination' in Michael Rosenfeld and András Sajó (eds), *The Oxford Handbook of Comparative Constitutional Law* (OUP 2012)

Mangas A, 'La secesión de territorios en un Estado Miembro: efectos en el derecho de la Unión Europea' (2013) 25 Revista de Derecho de la Unión Europea 47

Margiotta C, *L'ultimo diritto. Profili storici e teorici della secession* (Il Mulino 2005)

Margiotta C, 'An Update on Secession as the "Ultimate Right"' in Carlos Closa, Costanza Margiotta, and Giuseppe Martinico (eds), *Between Democracy and Law. The Amorality of Secession* (Routledge 2020)

Martín y Pérez de Nanclares J, 'Reflexiones jurídicas a propósito de una eventual declaración unilateral de independencia de Cataluña: un escenario político jurídicamente inviable' (*Real Instituto Elcano*, 24 September 2015)

Martinico G, 'Identity Conflicts and Secession before Courts: Three Case Studies' (2017) 21 Revista de Derecho Público Comparado 1

Martinico G, '"A Message of Hope": A Legal Perspective on the Reference' in Giacomo Delledonne and Giuseppe Martinico (eds), *The Canadian Contribution to a Comparative Law of Secession* (Palgrave 2019)

Martinico G, *Il diritto costituzionale come speranza. Secessione, democrazia e populismo alla luce della Reference Re Secession of Quebec* (G. Giappichelli Editore 2019)

Martinico G, 'Constitutionalists' Guide to the Populist Challenge' in Margiotta C, 'An Update on Secession as the "Ultimate Right"' in Carlos Closa, Costanza Margiotta, and Giuseppe Martinico (eds), *Between Democracy and Law. The Amorality of Secession* (Routledge 2020)

Martinico G, 'Taming National Identity: A Systematic Understanding of Article 4.2 TEU' (2021) 27 European Public Law 1

Massa S, 'Secession by Mutual Assent: A Comparative Analysis of the Dissolution of Czechoslovakia and the Separatist Movement in Canada' (1995) 14 Wisconsin International Law Review 183

Mastromarino A, 'Modificaciones constitucionales en Bélgica. La sixième réforme de l'Etat: un proceso en marcha' (2015) 22 Revista d'Estudis Autonòmics i Federals 64

Mastromarino A, 'Secessionist Claims in a Federal System: The Belgian Case' in Alberto López Basaguren and Leire Escajedo (eds), *Claims for Secession and Federalism* (Springer 2019)

Matas J and others, *The Internal Enlargement of the European Union* (Centre Maurits Coppieters 2011)

McEvoy K and Morison J, 'Beyond the "Constitutional Moment?: Law, Transition, and Peace-making in Northern Ireland' (2002) 26(4) Fordham International Law Journal 961

McEwen N and Murphy MC, 'Brexit and the Union: Territorial Voice, Exit and Re-entry Strategies in Scotland and Northern Ireland after EU Exit' (2022) 43(3) International Political Science Review 374

Medina Ortega M, *El Derecho de Secesión en la Unión Europea* (Marcial Pons 2014)

Medina Ortega M, 'The Political Rights of EU Citizens' in Carlos Closa (ed), *Secession from a Member State and Withdrawal from the European Union* (CUP 2017)

Menéndez AJ, 'Editorial: A European Union in Constitutional Mutation?' (2014) 20(2) European Law Journal 127

Molina I, 'La crisis catalana y la influencia de España en Bruselas' (*Real Instituto Elcano*, 25 April 2019)

Montilla JA, 'The independence referendum in Germany' (*Instituto de Derecho Público*, 16 December 2016)

Moore M, 'Introduction' in Margaret Moore (ed), *National Self-determination and Secession* (OUP 1998)

Moore M, 'The Ethics of Secession and a Normative Theory of Nationalism' (2000) 13 Canadian Journal of Law & Jurisprudence 225

Moorhead T, 'The Values of the European Union Legal Order: Constitutional Perspectives' (2014) 16 European Journal of Law Reform 3

Morgan R, 'Political and Institutional Implications for the European Community' in Wolfgang Heisenberg (ed), *German Unification in European Perspective* (Centre for European Policy Studies 1991)

Morgan A, *The Belfast Agreement: A Practical Legal Analysis* (The Belfast Press 2000)

Morici P, 'A Sovereign Quebec and US National Interests' (1997) 27(1) The American Review of Canadian Studies 143

Mullen T, 'The Scottish Independence Referendum 2014' (2014) 41(4) Journal of Law and Society 627

Müllerson R, 'Sovereignty and Secession: Then and Now, Here and There' in Julie Dahlitz (ed), *Secession and International Law* (T.M.C. Asser Press 2003)

Munro CR, 'Scottish Devolution: Accommodating a Restless Nation' in Stephen Tierney (ed), *Accommodating National Identity. New Approaches in International and Domestic Law* (Kluwer Law International 2000)

Murkens J, 'Bundesverfassungsgericht (2BvE 2/08): "We Want Our Identity Back"—The Revival of National Sovereignty in the German Federal Constitutional Court's Decision on the Lisbon Treaty' (2010) 3 Public Law 530

Murkens J, 'Scotland and the EU: A Comment' (*UK Constitutional Law Association Blog*, 10 September 2014)

Murphy WT and Roberts S, 'Introduction' (1987) 50(6) Modern Law Review 677

Murray CRG and O'Donoghue A, 'Life after Brexit: Operationalising the Belfast/Good Friday Agreement's Principle of Consent' (2018) 42(1) Dublin University Law Journal 147

Musgrave TD, *Self-Determination and National Minorities* (OUP 1997)

Nagel KJ, 'Bavaria: Another Case of a Right to Decide?' (2017) 19 GRTP Political Theory Working Paper

Navari C, 'Territoriality, Self-determination and Crimea after Badinter' (2014) 90(6) International Affairs 1299

Neff SC, 'Secession and Breach of a Compact: The Law of Nature Meets the United States Constitution' (2012) 45(2) Akron Law Review 405

Nergelius J, 'The Role of the Venice Commission in Maintaining the Rule of Law in Hungary and in Romania' in Armin von Bogdandy and Pál Sonnevend (eds), *Constitutional Crisis in the European Constitutional Area: Theory, Law and Politics in Hungary and Romania* (Hart Publishing 2015)

Nicolaides P, 'The ECB Is Responding to the Federal Constitutional Court of Germany: A Comparison of Monetary Policy Accounts' (EULawLive, 29 June 2020)

Nicolaïdis K, 'Southern Barbarians? A Post-Colonial Critique of EUniversalism' in Kalypso Nicolaïdis, Gabrielle Maas, and Berny Sèbe (eds), *Echoes of Empire: Memory, Identity and Colonial Legacies* (IB Tauris 2015)

Nicolisi SF, 'The Contribution of the Court of Justice to the Codification of the Founding Vales of the European Union' (2015) 51 Revista de Derecho Comunitario Europeo 613

Nielsen K, 'Secession: The Case of Quebec' (1993) 10 Journal of Applied Philosophy 29

Norman W, 'The Ethics of Secession as the Regulation of Secessionist Politics' in Margaret Moore (ed), *National Self-determination and Secession* (OUP 1998)

O'Neill A, 'A Quarrel in a Faraway Country?: Scotland, Independence and the EU' (*Eutopialaw*, 14 November 2011)

Oeter S, 'The Role of Recognition and Non-Recognition with Regard to Secession' in Christian Walter, Antje von Ungern-Sternberg, and Kavus Abushov (eds), *Self-determination and Secession in International Law* (OUP 2014)

Oklopcic Z, 'Independence Referendums and Democratic Theory in Quebec and Montenegro' in Matt Qvortrup (ed), *Nationalism, Referendums and Democracy. Voting on Ethic Issues and Independence* (Routledge 2014)

Oliver P, 'Canada's Two Solitudes' in Stephen Tierney (ed), *Accommodating National Identity. New Approaches in International and Domestic Law* (Kluwer Law International 2000)

Osterland HA, 'National Self-determination and Secession: The Slovak Model' (1993) 25 Case Western Reserve Journal of International Law 655

Pabón J, *Cambó. 1876–1947* (Alpha 1999)

Page A, 'El referéndum de independencia escocés' (2016) 37 Teoría y Realidad Constitucional 437

Palermo F, 'Towards a Comparative Constitutional Law of Secession?' in Giacomo Delledonne and Giuseppe Martinico (eds), *The Canadian Contribution to a Comparative Law of Secession* (Palgrave 2019)

Palermo F and Kössler K, *Comparative Federalism. Constitutional Arrangements and Case Law* (Hart Publishing 2017)

Palomares M, 'Las decisiones de los Jefes de Estado y de Gobierno, en el seno del Consejo Europeo, como categoría jurídica para regular, transitoriamente, la participación en la Unión Europea de nuevos Estados surgidos de la separación de Estados Miembros' (2013) 17 Revista d'Estudis Autonòmics i Federals 146

Parekh B, *A New Politics of Identity: Political Principles for an Independent World* (Palgrave Macmillan 2008)

Paulsen MS, 'The Civil War as Constitutional Interpretation' (2004) 71 University of Chicago Law Review 691

Pavkovic A and Radan P, *Creating New States* (Ashgate 2007)

Payne S, 'Catalan and Basque Nationalism' (1971) 6(1) Journal of Contemporary History 15

Payne S, 'Nationalism, Regionalism and Micronationalism in Spain' (1991) 26(3/4) Journal of Contemporary History 479

Pazartzis P, 'Secession and International Law: The European Dimension' in Marcelo G Kohen (ed), *Secession: International Law Perspectives* (CUP 2012)

Pech L, 'The Rule of Law as a Constitutional Principle of the European Union' (2009) 04 NYU Jean Monnet Working Paper

Pech L, 'Article 7 TEU: From "Nuclear Option" to "Sisyphean Procedure"?' in Uladzislau Belavusau and Aleksandra Gliszczyńska-Grabias (eds), *Constitutionalism under Stress* (OUP 2020)

Peers S, 'It's the end—but the moment has been prepared for: the CJEU confirms that UK citizens have lost EU citizenship' (*EU Law Analysis*, 9 June 2022)

Pellet A, 'The Opinions of the Badinter Arbitration Committee: A Second Breath for the Self-determination of Peoples' (1992) 3(1) European Journal of International Law 178

Pegoraro L and Rinella A (eds), *Derecho Constitucional Comparado 2. Sistemas constitucionales* (vol A, Giappichelli Editore 2018)

Penney JW, 'Deciding in the Heat of the Constitutional Moment' (2005) 28 Dalhousie Law Journal 217

Pérez Tremps P, 'National Identity in Spanish Constitutional Court Case-law' in Alejandro Saiz Arnaiz and Carina Alcoberro Llivina (eds), *National Constitutional Identity and European Integration* (Intersentia 2013)

Pernice I, 'The Treaty of Lisbon: Multi-level Constitutionalism in Action' (2009) 2 WHI 26

Peters A, 'The Position of International Law Within the European Legal Order' (1997) 40 German Yearbook of International Law 9

Peters A, 'Crimea: Does "The West" Now Pay the Price for Kosovo?' (*Blog of the European Journal of International Law*, 22 April 2014)

Petkar P, 'A Second Scottish Independence Referendum and Schrodinger's Sub-State Constituent Power' (*IACL-AIDC*, 29 November 2022)

Philpott D, 'In Defense of Self-Determination' (1995) 105(2) Ethics 352

Pickles D, *Algeria and France* (Methuen 1963)

Pierdominici L, 'The Theory of EU Constitutionalism Pluralism: A Crisis in a Crisis?' (2017) 9(2) Perspectives on Federalism 119

Piris JC, 'Political and Legal Aspects of Recent Regional Secessionist Trends in some EU Member States (I)' in Carlos Closa (ed), *Secession from a Member State and Withdrawal from the European Union* (CUP 2017)

Piris JC, 'Political and Legal Aspects of Recent Regional Secessionist Trends in Some EU Member States (II)' in Carlos Closa (ed), *Secession from a Member State and Withdrawal from the European Union* (CUP 2017)

Plaza C, 'Catalonia's Secession Process at the Constitutional Court: A Never-Ending Story' (2018) 24(3) European Public Law 373

Pollicino O, 'The New Relationship between National and the European Courts after the Enlargement of Europe: Towards a Unitary Theory of Jurisprudential Supranational Law?' (2010) 29(1) Yearbook of European Law 65

Pomerance M, *Self-determination in Law and Practice. The New Doctrine in the United Nations* (Martinus Nijhoff 1982)

Pons Ràfols X, *Cataluña: Derecho a decidir y derecho internacional* (Reus 2015)

Popescu N, *EU Foreign Policy and Post-Soviet Conflicts. Stealth Intervention* (Routledge 2011)

Priest GL, 'The Growth of Interdisciplinary Research and the Industrial Structure of the Production of Ideas: A Reply to Judge Edwards' (1993) 91(8) Michigan Law Review 1929

Queralt A, 'The Populist Drift of the Catalan Pro-Independence Movement' in Jörn Axel Kämmerer, Markus Kotzur, and Jacques Ziller (eds), *Integration and Desintegration in Europe* (Nomos 2019)

Qvortrup M, 'The Referendum Challenge to Constitutional Sovereignty: The Case of Scotland' (2013) 9 Jus Politicum

Qvortrup M, 'Independence Referendums. History, Legal Status and Voting Behaviour' in Carlos Closa, Costanza Margiotta, and Giuseppe Martinico (eds), *Between Democracy and Law. The Amorality of Secession* (Routledge 2020)

Radan P, 'Post-Secession International Borders: A Critical Analysis of the Opinions of the Badinter Arbitration Commission' (2000) 24(1) Melbourne University Law Review 50

Radan P, 'An Indestructible Union ... of Indestructible States: The Supreme Court of the United States and Secession' (2006) 10 Legal History 187

Radan P, 'Secession: A Word in Search of a Meaning' in Aleksandar Pavkovic and Peter Radan (eds), *On the Way to Statehood, Secession and Globalization* (Ashgate 2008)

Radan P, 'Secessionist Referenda in International and Domestic Law' in Matt Qvortrup (ed), *Nationalism, Referendums and Democracy. Voting on Ethical Issues and Independence* (Routledge 2014)

Ragone S, 'Los *Länder* no son "señores de la Constitución": el Tribunal Constitucional Federal Alemán sobre el referéndum separatista bávaro' (2018) 41 Teoría y Realidad Constitucional 407

Remiro Brotons A, 'Derecho y poder en el destino de Crimea' (2018) 34 Anuario Español de Derecho Internacional 231

Rich R, 'Recognition of States: The Collapse of Yugoslavia and the Soviet Union' (1993) 4(1) European Journal of International law 36

Ridao J and González A, 'La Unión Europea ante la eventual creación de nuevos Estados surgidos de la secesión de Estados Miembros' (2015) 28 Revista de Derecho de la Unión Europea 363

Rodríguez-Vergara A, 'Moving towards Independence—Breaching the Law: Self-determination and Secession in Catalonia' (2019) XVII Rassegna di diritto pubblico europeo 343

Roosvelt E, 'The Universal Validity of Man's Right to Self-determination' (1952) XXVII(702) Department of State Bulletin 891

Rosenfeld M, 'Constitutional Identity' in Michael Rosenfeld and András Sajó (eds), *The Oxford Handbook of Comparative Constitutional Law* (OUP 2012)

Rubin EL, 'Law and the Methodology of Law' (1997) 3 Wisconsin Law Review 521

Ruiz Casado JA, 'Articulations of Populism and Nationalism: The Case of the Catalan Independence Movement' (2020) 21(5) European Politics and Society 554

Rupnik J, 'The International Context' in Jiri Musil (ed), *The End of Czechoslovakia* (Central European UP 1995)

Russell PH, *Constitutional Odyssey: Can Canadians Become a Sovereign People?* (3rd edn, University of Toronto Press 2004)

Ryan E, 'Secession and Federalism in the Unites States: Tools for Managing Regional Conflict in a Pluralist Society' (2017) 96 Oregon Law Review 123

Santos Vara J, 'The Consequences of *Kadi*: Where the Divergence of Opinion between EU and International Lawyers Lies?' (2011) 17(2) European Law Journal 252

Scharf MP, 'Musical Chairs: The Dissolution of States and Membership in the United Nations' (1995) 29(1) Cornell International Law Journal 29

Scheppele KL, 'Constitutional Coups in EU Law' in Maurice Adams, Anne Meuwese, and Ernst Hirsch Ballin (eds), *Constitutionalism and the Rule of Law* (CUP 2017)

Schütze R, 'On "Middle Ground". The European Community and Public International Law' (2007) 13 EUI Law Working Paper

Segarra E, 'Nacionalidad catalana' in Eduard Segarra (ed), *¿Existe el Derecho a Decidir?* (Tibidabo Ediciones 2014)

Shaw M, *International Law* (8th edn, CUP 2017)

Shaw J, 'Unions and Citizens: Membership Status and Political Rights in Scotland, the UK and the EU' in Carlos Closa (ed), *Secession from a Member State and Withdrawal from the European Union* (CUP 2017)

Shelton D, 'Self-determination and Secession: The Jurisprudence of International Human Rights Tribunals' in Julie Dahlitz (ed), *Secession and International Law* (T.M.C. Asser Press 2003)

Shorten A, 'Constitutional Secession Rights, Exit Threats, and Multinational Democracy' (2014) 62(1) Political Studies 99

Skoutaris N, 'Territorial Differentiation in EU Law: Can Scotland and Northern Ireland Remain in the EU and/or the Single Market?' (2017) 19 Cambridge Yearbook of European Legal Studies 287

Skoutaris N, 'On Brexit and Secession(s)' in Carlos Closa, Costanza Margiotta, and Giuseppe Martinico (eds), *Between Democracy and Law. The Amorality of Secession* (Routledge 2020)
Sosa Wagner F, 'Bávaros y Referéndum por la independencia' (2017) 202 Revista de Administración Pública 157
Spence D, 'The European Community's Negotiations on German Unification' in Wolfgang Heisenberg (ed), *German Unification in European Perspective* (Centre for European Policy Studies 1991)
Spence D, 'The European Community and German Unification' (1992) 1(3) German Politics 136
Spieker LD, 'Breathing Life into the Union's Common Values: On the Judicial Application of Article 2 TEU in the EU Value Crisis' (2019) 20 German Law Journal 1182
Spieker LD, 'Framing and Managing Constitutional Identity Conflicts: How to Stabilize the *modus vivendi* between the Court of Justice and National Constitutional Courts' (2020) 57 Common Market Law Review 361
Sterio M, *The Right to Self-determination under International Law. "Selfistans", Secession, and the Rule of the Great Powers* (Routledge 2013)
Sterio M, *Secession in International Law* (Edward Elgar 2018)
Stewart S, 'Autonomy as a Mechanism for Conflict Regulation? The Case of Crimea' (2011) 7(4) Nationalism and Ethnic Politics 113
Strauss DA, 'The Irrelevance of Constitutional Amendments' (2001) 114(5) Harvard Law Review 1457
Suksi M, *Bringing in the People: A Comparison of Constitutional Forms and Practices of the Referendum* (Martinus Nijhoff 1993)
Summers J, *Peoples and International Law: How Nationalism and Self-determination Shape a Contemporary Law of Nations* (Martinus Nijhoff 2007)
Sunstein CR, 'Constitutionalism and Secession' (1991) 58 University of Chicago Law Review 633
Taborowski M and others, 'Guest Editorial: A Potential Constitutional Moment for the European Rule of Law—The Importance of Red Lines' (2018) 55 Common Market Law Review 983
Tajadura J, 'Más allá de un asunto interno: secesionismo e integración europea' (*Real Instituto Elcano*, 22 December 2014)
Tajadura J, 'Los procesos secesionistas y el derecho europeo' (2016) 37 Teoría y Realidad Constitucional 347
Tancredi A, 'A Normative "Due Process" in the Creation of States through Secession' in Marcelo G Kohen (ed), *Secession: International Law Perspectives* (CUP 2012)
Tannam E, 'The European Union and Conflict Resolution: Northern Ireland, Cyprus and Bilateral Cooperation' (2012) 47(1) Government and Opposition 49
Tarr A, 'Introducció' in John C Calhoun, *Discurs sobre la Constitució i el govern dels Estats Units i alters textos* (Institut d'Estudis Autonòmics 2009)
Tassinari F, 'What Really Divides Northern and Southern Europe?' (2014) 31(3) New perspectives quarterly 18
Tatham AF, 'Don't Mention Divorce at the Wedding, Darling!: EU Accession and Withdrawal after Lisbon' in Andrea Biondi, Piet Eeckhout, and Stefanie Ripley (eds), *EU Law after Lisbon* (OUP 2012)
Taylor Ch, *La ética de la autenticidad* (Paidós 1994)
Taylor Ch, *Acercar las soledades* (Tercera Prensa-Hirugarren Prentsa 1999)
Thatcher M, *The Downing Street Years* (HarperCollins 1995)

Thiele A, 'Whoever equates Karlsruhe to Warsaw is wildly mistaken' (*Verfassungsblog*, 10 October 2021)
Thürer D and Burri T, 'Secession' (Max Planck Encyclopedia of Public International Law 2009)
Tierney S, 'Constitutional Referendums: A Theoretical Inquiry' (2009) 72(9) The Modern Law Review 360
Tierney S, 'The Long Intervention in Kosovo: A Self-Determination Imperative?' in James Summers (ed), *Kosovo: A Precedent? The Declaration of Independence, the Advisory Opinion and Implications for Statehood, Self-Determination and Minority Rights* (Martinus Nijhoff 2011)
Tierney S, *Constitutional Referendums: The Theory and Practice of Republican Deliberation* (OUP 2012)
Tierney S, 'Legal Issues Surrounding the Referendum on Independence for Scotland' (2013) 9 European Constitutional Law Review 359
Tierney S and Boyle K, 'An Independent Scotland: The Road to Membership of the European Union' (2014) August ESCR Scottish Centre on Constitutional Change Briefing Paper
Timmermans CWA, 'German Unification and Community Law' (1990) 27 Common Market Law Review 437
Tocci N, *The EU and Conflict Resolution. Promoting Peace in the Backyard* (Routledge 2007
Todd J, 'Contested Constitutionalism? Northern Ireland and the British-Irish Relationship since 2010' (2017) 70 Parliamentary Affairs 301
Tomkins A, 'Scotland's Choice, Britain's Future' (2014) 130 Law Quarterly Review 215
Torrance D, 'Scottish Independence Referendum: Legal Issues' (2022) House of Commons Library 1
Torroja Mateu H, *La libre determinación de los pueblos, ¿un derecho a la independencia para cualquier pueblo?* (Thomson Reuters Aranzadi 2022)
Trapans JA, 'The West and the Recognition of the Baltic States: 1919 and 1991. A Study of the Politics of the Major Powers' (1994) 25(2) Journal of Baltic Studies 153
Trifunovska S, 'The Impact of the Kosovo Precedent on Self-Determination Struggles' in James Summers (ed), *Kosovo: A Precedent? The Declaration of Independence, the Advisory Opinion and Implications for Statehood, Self-Determination and Minority Rights* (Martinus Nijhoff 2011)
Tushnet M, 'The Possibilities of Comparative Constitutional Law' (1999) 108 Yale Law Journal 1225
Tushnet M, 'Authoritarian Constitutionalism' (2015) 100(2) Cornell Law Review 393
Van Driest SF, *Remedial Secession. A Right to External Self-determination as a Remedy to Serious Injustices?* (Intersentia 2013)
Venice Commission, 'A general legal reference framework to facilitate the settlement of ethno-political conflicts in Europe', CDL-INF (2000) 16-e
Venice Commission, 'Opinion on the Compatibility of the Existing Legislation in Montenegro concerning the Organisation of Referendums with applicable International Standards, CDL-AD (2005) 041
Venice Commission, 'Report on Constitutional Amendment', CDL-AD (2010) 001-e
Venice Commission, 'Report on the Rule of Law', CDL-AD (2011) 003 rev
Venice Commission, 'Opinion on whether the decision taken by the Supreme Council of the Autonomous Republic of Crimea in Ukraine to organise a referendum on becoming a constituent territory of the Russian Federation or restoring Crimea's 1992 Constitution is compatible with constitutional principles', CDL-AD (2014) 2
Venice Commission, 'Rule of Law Checklist', CDL-AD (2016) 007

Vick DW, 'Interdisciplinarity and the Discipline of Law' (2004) 31(2) Journal of Law and Society 163

Vidmar J, 'Catalonia: The Way Forward Is Comparative Constitutional Rather than International Legal Argument' (*Blog of the European Journal of International Law*, 24 October 2017)

Von Bogdandy A, 'Pluralism, Direct Effect, and the Ultimate Say: On the Relationship vetween International and Domestic Constitutional Law' (2008) 6 International Journal of Constitutional Law 397

Von Bogdandy A, 'Neither an International Organization nor a Nation State: The EU as a Supranational Federation' in Erik Jones, Anand Menon, and Stephen Weatherhill (eds), *The Oxford Handbook of the European Union* (OUP 2012)

Von Bogdandy A and Schill S, 'Overcoming Absolute Primacy: Respect for National Identity under the Lisbon Treaty' (2011) 48(5) Common Market Law Review 1417

Von Bogdandy A and Spieker LD, 'Countering the Judicial Silencing of Critics: Article 2 TEU Values, Reverse Solange, and the Responsibilities of National Judges' (2019) 15(3) European Constitutional Law Review 391

Wagner A, Marin J, and Kroqi D, 'The Catalan Struggle for Independence and the Role of the European Union' (2019) 11 Regional Science Policy and Practice 787

Wakengela M and Koko S, 'The Referendum for Self-Determination in South Sudan and its Implication for the Post-Colonial State in Africa' (2001) 3 Conflict Trends 20

Walker N, 'Late Sovereignty in the European Union' in Neil Walker (ed), *Sovereignty in Transition* (Hart Publishing 2003)

Walker N, 'Multi-level Constitutionalism: Looking Beyond the German Debate' (2009) 8 LEQS Paper

Walker N, 'The Receding Tape' (*UK Constitutional Law Association Blog*, 22 September 2013)

Walker N, 'Beyond Secession? Law in the Framing of the National Polity' in Stephen Tierney (ed), *Nationalism and Globalisation* (Hart Publishing 2015)

Walker N, 'Internal Enlargement in the European Union: Beyond Legalism and Political Expediency' in Carlos Closa (ed), *Secession from a Member State and Withdrawal from the European Union* (CUP 2017)

Walter C, 'The Kosovo Advisory Opinion. What It Says and What It Does Not Say' in Christian Walter, Antje von Ungern-Sternberg, and Kavus Abushov (eds), *Self-determination and Secession in International Law* (OUP 2014)

Weill R, 'Secession and the Prevalence of Both Militant Democracy and Eternity Clauses Worldwide' (2018) 40 Cardozo Law Review 905

Weiler JHH, 'The Transformation of Europe' (1991) 100 Yale Law Journal 2403

Weiler JHH, 'On the Power of the Word: Europe's Constitutional Iconography' (2005) 3(2–3) International Journal of Constitutional Law 173

Weiler JHH, 'Catalonian Independence and the European Union' (*Blog of the European Journal of International Law*, 20 December 2012)

Weiler JHH, 'Scotland and the EU' (*Verfassungsblog*, 8 September 2014)

Weinstock D, 'Constitutionalizing the Right to Secede' (2001) 9(2) Journal of Political Philosophy 182

Weller M, 'The International Response to the Dissolution of the Socialist Federal Republic of Yugoslavia' (1992) 86(3) The American Journal of International Law 569

Weller M, 'Negotiating the Final Status for Kosovo' (2008) 114 ISS Chaillot Paper

Weller M, 'Modesty Can Be a Virtue: Judicial Economy in the ICJ Kosovo Opinion?' (2011) 24(1) Leiden Journal of International Law 127

Weller M, 'Secession and Self-determination in Western Europe: The Case of Catalonia' (*Blog of the European Journal of International Law*, 18 October 2017)

Wendel M, 'Constructive Misunderstandings—How the PSPP Conflict Was Eventually Settled and How it Reflects Constitutional Pluralism' in Matej Avbelj (ed), *The Future of EU Constitutionalism* (Hart Publishing 2023)

Wheare KC, *Federal Government* (4th edn, OUP 1963)

Wheatley S, 'Modelling Democratic Secession in International Law' in Stephen Tierney (ed), *Nationalism and Globalization* (Hart Publishing 2015)

Williams G, 'The Case that Stopped a Coup? The Rule of Law and Constitutionalism in Fiji' [2001] Oxford University Commonwealth Law Journal 73

Williams PR and Ardalan S, 'The Northern Ireland Peace Agreement: Evolving the Principle of Self-Determination' (1999) 12 Leiden Journal of International Law 155

Wind M, *The Tribalization of Europe. A Defense of our Liberal Values* (Polity 2020)

Wittman D, 'The Wealth and Size of Nations' (2000) 44(6) The Journal of Conflict Resolution 868

Wivel A, 'The Security Challenge of Small EU Member States: Interests, Identity and the Development of the EU as a Security Actor' (2005) 43(2) Journal of Common Market Studies 393

Wivel A, 'From Small State to Smart State: Devising a Strategy for Influence in the European Union' in Robert Steinmetz and Anders Wivel (eds), *Small States in Europe* (Ashgate 2010)

Young AL, 'Will Scotland hold an independence referendum in October 2023?' (*Constitutional Law Matters*, 29 June 2022)

Zartman W, 'North Africa and the EEC Negotiations' (1986) 22(1) Middle East Journal 1

Ziller J, 'The European Union and the Territorial Scope of European Territories' (2007) 38 (1) Victoria University of Wellington Law Review 51

Zweigert K and Kötz H, An Introduction to Comparative Law (3rd edn, OUP 1998)

Index

For the benefit of digital users, indexed terms that span two pages (e.g., 52–53) may, on occasion, appear on only one of those pages.